PRACTICAL
PowerPivot
& DAX FORMULAS
FOR EXCEL® 2010

Art Tennick

New York   Chicago   San Francisco   Lisbon
London   Madrid   Mexico City   Milan
New Delhi   San Juan   Seoul   Singapore
Sydney   Toronto

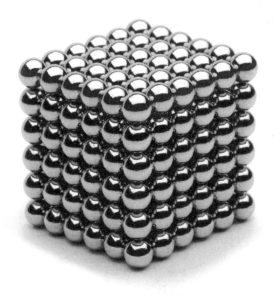

G000067404

The McGraw·Hill Companies

Cataloging-in-Publication Data is on file with the Library of Congress

McGraw-Hill books are available at special quantity discounts to use as premiums and sales promotions, or for use in corporate training programs. To contact a representative, please e-mail us at bulksales@mcgraw-hill.com.

Practical PowerPivot & DAX Formulas for Excel® 2010

1234567890   DOC DOC   109876543210

ISBN   978-0-07-174685-4
MHID   0-07-174685-4

Sponsoring Editor
Wendy Rinaldi

Editorial Supervisor
Patty Mon

Project Manager
Vasundhara Sawhney, Glyph International

Acquisitions Coordinator
Joya Anthony

Technical Editor
Olivier Matrat

Copy Editor
Margaret Berson

Proofreader
Laura Bowman

Indexer
Karin Arrigoni

Production Supervisor
Jean Bodeaux

Composition
Glyph International

Illustration
Glyph International

Art Director, Cover
Jeff Weeks

Cover Designer
Jeff Weeks

For those who helped along the way—G.T.L. Chapman,
Guy C. Routh, Brian Smart, and Wendy Rinaldi

About the Author

Art Tennick (Brighton, U.K.) has worked in relational database design, SQL queries, and spreadsheets for over 20 years. He has been involved in pivot tables, multidimensional database design, cubes, data mining, and DMX and MDX queries for 10 years. Based in the United Kingdom, he has been a software consultant, trainer, and writer for some 25 years. Recently, he has worked with several major retail and banking corporations to implement BI solutions using Microsoft SQL Server, SSAS, SSIS, SSRS, PowerPivot, DAX, and Excel 2010. This is his twentieth book and he has also written over 300 articles for computer magazines in the United States, the United Kingdom, and Ireland. His web site is www.MrCube.net.

About the Technical Editor

Olivier Matrat is a Senior Program Manager with the Microsoft SQL Server group, and one of the founding members of the engineering team behind PowerPivot. He has worked in business intelligence for 15 years, holding various technical roles in software and consulting companies, before becoming the founding CEO of a leading French Microsoft Gold Partner for BI, a position he held until joining Microsoft four years ago. Olivier lives with his wife and their daughter in Redmond, Washington, in the United States.

Contents

Part II   DAX

Part III   PowerPivot and DAX Applied

Foreword

PowerPivot: What a name! Or I should really say what's in a name? Powerful Pivoting? Pivot-table for power users?

PowerPivot is a lot more than that. When I started the PowerPivot project back in 2007, along with Amir Netz (Microsoft BI Distinguished Engineer), the incubation project was called BI Sandbox. We had been looking at a problem that had often been raised to us by IT people over years of trying to implement a BI system with both Microsoft and non-Microsoft software. How could they set up an environment to enable their business users to build their own BI applications without needing assistance from IT? They wanted to focus on building the right data store for the enterprise, secure it, and ensure its quality, but also get out of the business of building one-off applications or reports for business users. And thus the BI Sandbox project was born. We would build an environment for users to play (sandbox) and do what they needed to do without needing to rely on IT folks to build it for them. Now IT would provide and provision the infrastructure and data source access, but they wouldn't need to get involved in the building work for the application itself. This did make a lot of sense as business users understand their needs better than anyone else and often don't have the patience or simply the luxury of time to wait for IT to queue this project behind all the other ones and build it three to six months later. So we had our vision and a real problem to solve.

The next question was: how do we do that? Well let's see, IT is focused on building ERPs, SharePoint farms, Enterprise Data warehouses… Users, on the other end, are busy trying to learn and use what reporting and analytical application IT gives them, or more often ignore it and build whatever they need to do in a tool familiar to them. And what is the most often used tool by users to answer any sort of data- or BI-related questions? Excel, Excel, Excel… followed by Access, which is actually a fairly distant second. Users love Excel. IT often hates Excel. Excel is bad, Excel is uncontrolled, Excel's data is bad, unsecured, and unreliable. We've even heard some IT folks talking about "Excel Hell." But users love it and build very sophisticated and complex applications with it. Let's face it. Most companies worldwide run on Excel today. Whether you know it or not, parts of your business, and often critical parts of your business, are managed by an Excel-based application built by an analyst or power user and running on someone's desktop. So after hundreds of discussions with users and IT, we realized that there was no way users would ever drop Excel. Even if we gave them something else, they would keep using Excel behind the scene as a shadow application. All users ask is that whatever tool you give them has one and only one feature: Export to Excel. That feature is the only common denominator between every single data or BI software tools on the planet today! So that is when we had our "Ah-ha" moment: Let's not fight Excel; let's embrace it! The way to build the BI sandbox is to provide an Excel-based environment for users to do what they need, better than the way they do it with raw Excel. But—and here was the critical moment—let's make sure that when users use this environment, it is in an IT-managed workspace or infrastructure.

And here the concept of Managed Self-Service BI was born. Self-Service BI has been there forever—whether called by that name or not, it has been there. But before PowerPivot, Self-Service equated to tools enabling users to build tons of disconnected, uncontrolled, unmanaged islands of data. We wanted the BI Sandbox environment to be attractive to business users: We wanted to make it super easy to load data from enterprise and non-enterprise data sources or from structured and non-structured data sources, to build models using Excel language and formulae, and to build reports using Excel Pivottable and Pivotchart or any other BI tools (Reporting Services, PerformancePoint, or any third-party tool that knows how to talk MDX). But we also wanted to make sure that when this happened, the business users' work in this environment would be properly saved and backed up, and the data would be refreshed regularly from the data sources so that the data didn't become stale. We also wanted to make it easy for people to collaborate with this work without duplicating these workbooks all over the place in the file or email systems; and we also wanted to be able to provide usage pattern statistics. Now this would make it both valuable to business users as well as IT. What if IT were able to have knowledge of the existence of these "special workbooks," know what data sources they use, and when they are refreshed? And more importantly, what if IT knew when the refresh failed and why, who is using the data sources, how big they are, and how many people are using them, so that they can ensure that these models live on the appropriately provisioned machines, but can do all of this without necessarily even having access to the content of the workbooks themselves? Because, after all, these workbooks are the users' property and none of IT's business. Now that is "Managed Self-service BI." And because of the duality of this value proposition both to the IT and business users, we needed a new name. Twin values to the two big population categories in an enterprise: The IT folks and the business user folks. And that is how the Gemini code name was born: The Twins.

So now you know all about the history and value proposition of this project, which grew from within a few folks' minds in 2007 (including Olivier Matrat, who was the first program manager on the project and who also tech edited this book) to what it became when we released it with SQL Server 2008 R2 in 2010. This book focuses mostly on introducing the reader to the bells and whistles of the PowerPivot add-in for Excel. It does an excellent job of walking the reader through every single capability, highlighting its value and providing many different examples of how to best use it. This book will be handy at first when you are using the first few chapters to get a handle on the tool and get started, but it will remain very handy for years when new business questions arise and you need to build a specific business rule or logic and you need a specific function, as this book does an excellent job highlighting how to best use all the Excel-like functions as well as all the new PowerPivot functions, such as Time navigation functions or even table lookup type functions. This book might start on a night table but will most likely migrate and remain on the desk at work for months to come. I hope you will enjoy its reading as much as we have enjoyed building this product and all of the capabilities you will discover through this book.

Thierry D'hers
Group Program Manager
Microsoft SQL Server Business Intelligence

Acknowledgments

As always, I am indebted to Wendy Rinaldi, my editor at McGraw-Hill, who manages to keep me on track, and is a source of inspiration when I am floundering. I would like to extend my sincere thanks to Olivier Matrat for his invaluable assistance as technical reviewer of the book. Olivier is one of the main folks at Microsoft responsible for this wonderful product called PowerPivot for Excel. Many people were involved in producing this book, as well as my other books for McGraw-Hill. Thank you—Joya Anthony and Patty Mon at McGraw-Hill; Vasundhara Sawhney, Deepti Narwat Agarwal, Madhu Bhardwaj, and Smita Rajan at Glyph International; Melinda Lytle, Bart Reed, Laura Bowman, Karin Arrigoni, Jean Bodeaux, and Jeff Weeks at various places. I am also grateful for the help received from numerous patient people at Microsoft who tolerated my questions.

Introduction

PowerPivot and DAX

PowerPivot for Excel 2010 helps you to extract real, actionable Business Intelligence (BI), and increase effective decision making. It's ideal for the average Excel user—and it's a non-developer entry point into BI. This is BI for the masses. Furthermore, PowerPivot for Excel is a free download from www.powerpivot.com.

BI is wonderful. However, implementing BI solutions (before PowerPivot) is not for the faint-hearted. Traditionally, the first step is to build a relational star schema database (possibly in SQL Server), and then to construct an SSAS (SQL Server Analysis Services) cube from the star schema. Building a star schema requires an understanding of SQL Server (or Oracle, or DB2, or MySQL), the SQL language, and quite often the ability to develop SSIS (SQL Server Integration Services) packages to do all the heavy lifting. In addition, the user has to know SSAS well in order to design useful cubes. Often, knowledge of SSRS (SQL Server Reporting Services) and/or the MDX (MultiDimensional Expressions) query language is required in order to extract the data.

Implementing BI (before PowerPivot) is certainly not easy and usually requires developer experience and expertise in lots of skill sets. A traditional BI solution can take months to implement. With PowerPivot for Excel, the average Excel user or power user can have a BI solution *within minutes*. All that's needed is some familiarity with Excel.

The incredible capabilities of PowerPivot can, optionally, be extended and refined with DAX (Data Analysis Expressions). DAX is a new language for extracting business intelligence within the familiar environment of Excel, and much of it is similar to already well-known Excel functions. DAX is part of PowerPivot. It's ideally suited for Excel users and power-users, and requires no knowledge of the rest of Microsoft's BI stack. If the user is comfortable in Excel, they will be up and running with DAX functions and formulas, and impressive pivot table and pivot chart results, within a few minutes.

This book is an introduction to PowerPivot for Excel, and the DAX language. The first half concentrates on PowerPivot using the graphical interface, while the second half is mostly DAX. The book is practical and hands-on, with a minimum of concepts and theory. There are over 250 DAX formulas in the book—all downloadable from www.mhprofessional.com/computingdownload. It's aimed at Excel users, Excel professionals, non-developers and developers, report designers, Excel power users, decision makers, and all business intelligence professionals. The DAX formulas can be used immediately in a corporate business intelligence environment and/or easily customized for a specific business need.

Prerequisites

You will need Excel 2010, either 32-bit or 64-bit. You will also need PowerPivot for Excel (32-bit or 64-bit to match your version of Excel 2010). PowerPivot for Excel (either 32-bit or 64-bit) is a free download from www.powerpivot.com. You *don't* need SQL Server, or SharePoint, or PowerPivot for SharePoint to follow all the text, screenshots, examples, and practicals in this book.

DAX Formulas Download

The source DAX for all the formulas in this book is available for download. You can simply copy and paste into your DAX calculated columns or calculated measures to save you some typing (even with AutoComplete, you still have to type the occasional closing parenthesis and comma). You can download the source DAX formulas from www .mhprofessional.com/computingdownload.

Sample Excel Data Download

Over 99 percent of the PowerPivot and DAX text, screenshots, examples, and practicals in this book use the good old Northwind database. If you have SQL Server, you can use the SQL Server version of Northwind. If you don't have SQL Server, you can use the pre-Access 2007 version of Northwind. As of this writing, both of these versions of Northwind are still available for download from www.microsoft.com. Alternatively, you might want to try an Excel version of Northwind. An Excel version can be downloaded from this book's Web site at www.mhprofessional.com/computingdownload. The workbook is called Northwind.xlsx. There is, again as of this writing, a freely available data feed version of Northwind. The URL for this data feed is given in Chapter 2, when importing data from a data feed is discussed.

Full instructions of how to load SQL Server Northwind into PowerPivot are given in Chapter 1. Full instructions of how to load the Access or Excel or data feed versions of Northwind are given in Chapter 2. Chapter 2 also shows how to connect to the data feed version.

Acronyms

▶ **BI**   Business Intelligence

▶ **BIDS**   SQL Server Business Intelligence Development Studio

▶ **DAX**   Data Analysis Expressions

▶ **DMX**   Data Mining Extensions

▶ **KPI**   Key Performance Indicator

▶ **MDX**   MultiDimensional Expressions

▶ **SQL**   Structured Query Language

▶ **SSAS**   SQL Server Analysis Services

▶ **SSIS**   SQL Server Integration Services

▶ **SSMS**   SQL Server Management Studio

▶ **SSRS**   SQL Server Reporting Services

▶ **XMLA**   XML for Analysis

Chapter Content

Part I: PowerPivot

Chapter 1—PowerPivot: Quick Start   This is a short "quick start" chapter. It shows just how easy it is to create business intelligence (BI) with PowerPivot for Excel. Essentially a practical chapter, it does not contain much by way of theory or concepts—these are introduced gradually throughout the rest of the book. The chapter shows how to build quite a sophisticated pivot table in just a few minutes.

Chapter 2—PowerPivot: Overview   Chapter 1 was a very quick introduction to PowerPivot for Excel. It concentrated on importing data from SQL Server. This chapter takes a more detailed look at data import from SQL Server. It also shows how to import data from Access, Excel, and data feeds. You are shown relationships between PowerPivot tables and how to set them up, if they are missing. DAX (Data Analysis eXpressions) is used to create both calculated columns in PowerPivot tables and measures in PowerPivot pivot tables in Excel. In addition, a measure is added through the GUI, without the need for DAX. You get to construct a sophisticated pivot table and a pivot chart linked to the pivot table. Various ways of filtering data in a pivot report (pivot table or pivot chart) are introduced. This chapter consolidates and extends the example in the previous chapter. It should give you a good overview of some of the main features and capabilities of PowerPivot. Subsequent chapters build upon this chapter—in particular, the next chapter is a full in-depth look at PowerPivot.

Chapter 3—PowerPivot: In-Depth   This chapter goes a lot further than the previous two introductory chapters. It's a detailed and comprehensive guide to all of the ribbons: Excel PowerPivot ribbon, PowerPivot Home ribbon, PowerPivot Design ribbon, PowerPivot Linked Table ribbon. All of the ribbon groups and buttons are discussed, some with step-by-step examples for you to follow. In the course of this chapter, you will become familiar with most of the dialog boxes and menus that are relevant to PowerPivot. This is essentially a grand tour of the PowerPivot graphical user interface. Everything you are likely to meet in a PowerPivot window is covered. The DAX language is introduced only briefly—Chapter 4 is specifically devoted to DAX. Later in the book there are also many chapters providing a reference guide to DAX syntax. Pivot table manipulation and customization is covered in Chapter 5.

Chapter 4—DAX: Overview   DAX (Data Analysis eXpressions) is a new language that makes its debut with PowerPivot for Excel. It is a language designed to use formulas, which in turn are based on one or more DAX functions. Some of its functions will look familiar to veteran Excel users, although there are differences between DAX and Excel functions. These differences are elaborated in this chapter. You get to see where and how to write DAX functions and formulas and there are a number of examples to try. The all-important concept of filter context is discussed in detail. Other topics include data types and operator precedence. Two of the most popular functions, RELATED() and CALCULATE(), are covered in depth. The difference between DAX calculated columns and DAX measures is explained. Hopefully, there is enough DAX in this overview chapter to get you started. The second part of this book provides a comprehensive reference, with examples, of all the DAX functions.

Chapter 5—Pivot Tables and Pivot Charts: Overview   This chapter is concerned with looking at pivot reports—that is, pivot tables and pivot charts. The chapter is an overview; a whole book could easily be written about pivot tables in Excel, and another one just on pivot charts! The emphasis here is on creating pivot tables and charts. The most important focus is on how to add data to a pivot report using the PowerPivot Field List. But, once this is done, there are dozens of context menus, drop-down menus, and quite a few ribbons with dozens of buttons. Some of these are explored in this chapter, especially where they are particularly relevant to working with PowerPivot. These menu options and buttons help you organize, control, and format your pivot reports. By the end of the chapter, you should be in a position to create meaningful and attractive pivot tables and charts.

Part II: DAX

Chapter 6—Fundamental Functions: Filter, Logical, and Miscellaneous Functions   This is a wide-ranging chapter on some of the fundamental DAX functions. It includes syntax and examples for all of the Filter functions and all of the Logical functions. In addition, it discusses some uncategorized functions—these are often referred to as information or IS() functions. An example is ISBLANK(). There is also one Text function, BLANK(), which has been added here because of its close relationship to ISBLANK(). The Filter functions, in particular, are extremely powerful. Among other things, they allow you to override the filter context that a user chooses in a pivot table. They help to display classic BI values such as "percentage of parent" or "percentage of all." Some of the examples are shown as calculated columns, others as measures. With measures, in particular, your results may differ from those shown in the screenshots, as there a few different incarnations of Northwind—not always with the same data!

Chapter 7—Aggregate Functions: Statistical Functions and SUM()/SUMX() Functions   The aggregate functions include the Statistical functions and both SUM() and SUMXX() from the Math & Trig functions. Such functions often result in numeric values. The functions can be used equally well as calculated columns or as measures. If used as calculated columns, they are often added to the Values drop-zone in the PowerPivot Field List and displayed in the central data area of a pivot table. They are ideally suited for producing totals and subtotals. In this chapter, the alphabetical order of the functions has not been observed completely. For example, AVERAGEX() appears before AVERAGEA(), but after AVERAGE()—this is to highlight the difference between a base column function, such as AVERAGE() and its table function equivalent, AVERAGEX(). AVERAGEA(), another column function, then follows.

In general, the X-functions, for instance, AVERAGEX(), accept a table argument. The base functions, like AVERAGE(), accept a column argument, and operate on numeric or date values. The A-functions, for example, AVERAGEA(), also accept a column argument, but usually work on every value in a column, even text and blank values.

Chapter 8—Date & Time Functions 1/2: Date and Time Basic Functions For the purposes of clarity, the Date & Time functions in DAX have been divided into two chapters. This is the first of those two chapters and deals with the more basic date and time functions. The next chapter is devoted to a group of Date & Time functions that are often referred to as time intelligence functions. The basic functions are often simpler and more forgiving. The time intelligence functions usually require that you have put some thought into how your dates are stored in the PowerPivot model. The emphasis in this chapter is on parsing, manipulating, and returning dates. The basic functions generally return dates and times. The time intelligence functions generally return measures or values associated with dates and times.

Chapter 9—Date & Time Functions 2/2: Time Intelligence Functions This is the second chapter dealing with DAX Date & Time functions. The previous chapter discusses some of the basic Date and Time functions. In this chapter, the emphasis is on the time intelligence Date and Time functions. The time intelligence functions are primarily used to *navigate* dates. In particular, they allow you to jump ahead or back in time and retrieve relevant data. This is useful if you wish to compare your data across or between time periods. Practical applications would include year-on-year changes. They allow you to compare the present date, in your filter context, with past and future dates. In addition, these functions can help you define ranges of dates or dates up to a particular date. A practical application here might be year-to-date sales. The basic functions generally return dates and times. The time intelligence functions generally return measures or values associated with dates and times.

Chapter 10—Text Functions This chapter deals with text (or string) manipulation. Most of the text functions are the same as their Excel function equivalents; however, they accept text or column parameters rather than worksheet cells or ranges. Many of these text functions return text, and as such are usually more suitable for creating calculated columns in PowerPivot tables rather than measures—text values can't be added together to give subtotals and totals in a pivot table (unless you do a COUNT ( )). Having said that, if the text value can be converted into a number (for example the string "123"), then it may be used as an additive measure. Usually, PowerPivot will implicitly do the conversion, but you can always do it explicitly with the VALUE ( ) function. Please note, the FORMAT ( ) text function also operates against numbers as well as against text.

Chapter 11—Math & Trig Functions   This is the final chapter dealing with DAX functions and formulas. It deals with the Math & Trig functions. However, you won't find any trigonometric functions, as such—expect these to appear in a later version of PowerPivot for Excel. Some of the functions, for example, EXP() and LN(), are probably for specialized use only. However, many of the others are going to be very popular—particularly, the eight functions devoted to rounding numbers. SUM() and SUMX() are Math & Trig functions, although they have much in common with the Statistical functions as well. They were both covered in an earlier chapter on aggregate functions (that is, Statistical functions with SUM() and SUMX()), but are mentioned here again for completeness. In any case, SUMX() is worth a second look, as it's going to be very useful in many BI situations.

Part III: PowerPivot and DAX Applied

Chapter 12—A Few Ideas: PowerPivot and DAX Solutions   The real world is the real world. Software, and books about software, can only give you "out-of-the-box" solutions easily. Real-world solutions require a bit more work. This chapter presents a few ideas for moving beyond "out-of-the-box" answers. It is all about implementing PowerPivot and DAX to deal with common business problems. The three appendixes that follow this chapter have a narrower focus: how to write SQL, MDX, and DMX queries for assembling data in your PowerPivot model. In contrast, this chapter is more concerned with using DAX and the PowerPivot GUI to provide solutions, once you already have the data in place. That said, there is a little on importing data to address the problem of working effectively with dates and dealing with self-joins.

Working with dates can lead to a number of problems—some of these are addressed here. There are also a few "classic" BI solutions in this chapter—percentage of total and subtotal, running totals, changes over time, moving averages, suppressing totals for non-additive numbers, dealing with semi-additive numbers, customizing DAX formulas for individual rows or columns, predefining filters, predefining Column Labels and Row Labels with named sets, working without pivot tables, sharing your pivot reports with others through SharePoint, and a few other things.

Part IV: Appendixes: Queries for PowerPivot

Appendix A—SQL Queries for PowerPivot   This is a short appendix. It's aimed at those readers who need a brief introduction to SQL, with some basic syntax examples. We also discuss the reasons for writing your own queries to import data into PowerPivot, rather than simply importing complete tables. A few query fundamentals are covered: filtering, sorting, grouping, and denormalizing data with joins and self-joins. There are also examples of using a stored procedure and writing SQL against Excel.

Appendix B—MDX Queries for PowerPivot   MDX (MultiDimensional eXpressions) is a very powerful query language for extracting data from cubes. While PowerPivot can generate sophisticated MDX for you, you may want the total control that writing your own MDX gives you. You can use MDX to import from either an SSAS cube or a PowerPivot model that has been published to PowerPivot for SharePoint. This appendix demonstrates some of the fundamentals of MDX. It also shows how best to adapt your MDX for PowerPivot.

Appendix C—DMX Queries for PowerPivot   You may have SSAS data mining structures and data mining models. You normally query these objects using DMX (Data Mining eXtensions), perhaps from SSMS (SQL Server Management Studio) or from SSRS (SQL Server Reporting Services). Although this release of PowerPivot supports the graphical design of SQL and MDX queries, it does not support the graphical design of DMX queries. You can, however, write your own DMX. You do so by connecting to an SSAS source and entering the DMX into the MDX Statement area of the Specify a MDX Query dialog, in the Table Import Wizard. Another way is to embed your DMX query within a SQL query and import the data returned from the outer SQL query. To do that, you connect to a SQL Server source and enter the SQL/DMX into the SQL Statement area of the Specify a SQL Query dialog of the Table Import Wizard. Alternatively, you can query *some* data mining data from Excel itself—for this you will need to download the data mining add-in for Excel (the data mining results are shown in an Excel worksheet when you use the Table Tools/Analyze ribbon, rather than the Data Mining ribbon), and you can then import or link into the PowerPivot window from the Excel worksheet. Stand-alone DMX, or DMX embedded in SQL, works for DMX Cases, Content, Prediction and other queries. This appendix includes sample code for a few Cases, Content, and Prediction queries.

Part I

PowerPivot

Chapter 1

PowerPivot: Quick Start

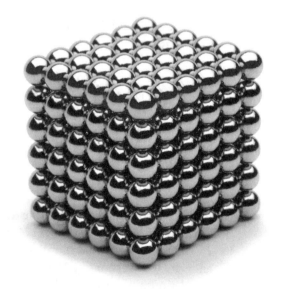

This is a short "quick start" chapter. It shows just how easy it is to create business intelligence (BI) with PowerPivot for Excel. Essentially a practical chapter, it does not contain much by way of theory or concepts—these are introduced gradually throughout the rest of the book. The chapter shows how to build quite a sophisticated pivot table in just a few minutes.

▶ **Key concepts**   Quick introduction to PowerPivot, quick introduction to Data Analysis eXpressions (DAX), importing data, creating calculated columns and measures, creating a PowerPivot pivot table in Excel

This is real business intelligence—it's a PowerPivot pivot table in an Excel 2010 worksheet, as shown in Figure 1-1—and, with a little practice, you can build this pivot table in less than five minutes!

Let's try building this business intelligence right now, and learn a little about PowerPivot for Excel and Data Analysis eXpressions (DAX) formulas.

The example here uses data from the SQL Server Northwind sample database. Of course, you may not have SQL Server—and if you do, you may not have the Northwind database! Fortunately, there are lots of alternatives and solutions to this.

▶ If you don't have SQL Server, you can download an Evaluation Edition from www.microsoft.com.

▶ If you have SQL Server, but not the Northwind sample database, instructions on how to download Northwind are in the introduction.

▶ What if you don't want to (or can't) download and install an evaluation copy of SQL Server? That's fine—you can always use the pre-Access 2007 version of Northwind (Northwind.mdb). Again, if you don't have this, download instructions are in the introduction. As another alternative, this book's Web site has an Excel version of Northwind if you want to work with that. As of this writing, there is also a data feed version of Northwind, freely available on the Internet.

This "quick start" chapter uses the SQL Server version of Northwind. If you don't have this, alternatives are presented in the next chapter—even so, hopefully, the examples in this chapter will make perfect sense without having to click along. In Chapter 2, all of the steps are explained in more detail. In addition, that chapter has detailed instructions on how to use the Access version, the Excel version, and a data feed version of Northwind. In the meantime, you may be able to adapt this chapter to work with the Access version of Northwind. If so, please use the pre-Access 2007 Northwind (Northwind.mdb), so the data and structures match those here. The Excel and data feed versions of Northwind require a couple of extra steps (specifically, setting up relationships between tables)—these extra steps are fully documented in Chapter 2.

	A	B	C	D	E	F	G	H

Year 🔻

| 1996 |
| 1997 |
| 1998 |

Category 🔻

Beverages	Condiments	Confections
Dairy Products	Grains/Cereals	Meat/Poultry
Produce	Seafood	

Column Labels 🔻

	⊞ Beverages		⊞ Condiments		⊞ Confections	
Row Labels 🔻	**Sum of Sales Amount**	**Share**	**Sum of Sales Amount**	**Share**	**Sum of Sales Amount**	**Share**
⊞ Argentina	1798	0.13%	907	0.07%	2135.1	0.16%
⊞ Austria	26452.05	1.95%	16802.4	1.24%	14653.35	1.08%
⊞ Belgium	5864.4	0.43%	2714.7	0.20%	7711.18	0.57%
⊞ Brazil	40400.5	2.98%	12139	0.90%	12164.73	0.90%
⊞ Canada	13829.7	1.02%	5010.6	0.37%	9302.4	0.69%
⊞ Denmark	12025.7	0.89%	4455.4	0.33%	2815.3	0.21%
⊞ Finland	2222	0.16%	1873	0.14%	1033.05	0.08%
⊞ France	13670	1.01%	7148.4	0.53%	13215.85	0.98%
⊞ Germany	57644.6	4.26%	17395.1	1.28%	37799.44	2.79%
⊞ Ireland	3339.4	0.25%	3898.5	0.29%	1739.2	0.13%
⊞ Italy	1155	0.09%	1448.25	0.11%	2787.7	0.21%
⊞ Mexico	8097.5	0.60%	1235.45	0.09%	2066.95	0.15%
⊞ Norway	2756	0.20%	234	0.02%	280.15	0.02%
⊞ Poland	828.5	0.06%	627	0.05%	779.1	0.06%
⊞ Portugal	1190.4	0.09%	3869.45	0.29%	1122.5	0.08%
⊞ Spain	1363.2	0.10%	1789.45	0.13%	1809.05	0.13%
⊞ Sweden	13407.05	0.99%	4970.3	0.37%	5675.65	0.42%
⊞ Switzerland	2357.5	0.17%	2054.3	0.15%	3246.16	0.24%
⊞ UK	7596.2	0.56%	4576.05	0.34%	9223.26	0.68%
⊞ USA	63361.15	4.68%	18555.85	1.37%	38804.05	2.86%
⊞ Venezuela	7168.1	0.53%	1990.55	0.15%	8734.93	0.64%
Grand Total	286526.95	21.15%	113694.75	8.39%	177099.1	13.08%

Sheet1 Sheet4 Sheet2 Sheet3

Figure 1-1   *Instant business intelligence*

To create your business intelligence:

1. Start Excel 2010.

2. Click the PowerPivot tab to see the PowerPivot ribbon (see Figure 1-2). If there's no PowerPivot tab to click, it means that PowerPivot for Excel is not installed. PowerPivot for Excel is available as a free download (if you don't have it yet, go to www.powerpivot.com or www.microsoft.com and search for *PowerPivot for Excel* to find the download page—there's also *PowerPivot for SharePoint*, which

Figure 1-2 *PowerPivot ribbon in Excel*

is beyond the scope of this book—it's PowerPivot for Excel that you need to work through this book). Make sure that you choose the relevant version for your computer; there are 32-bit and 64-bit versions.

3. Click the PowerPivot Window button in the Launch group of the ribbon. A new PowerPivot window opens with its own ribbons. You now have two windows—the original Excel workbook and the new PowerPivot window (Figure 1-3), which is linked to the original Excel workbook.

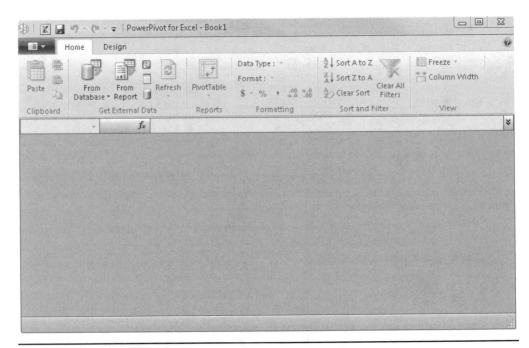

Figure 1-3 *PowerPivot window*

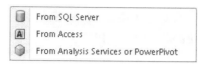

Figure 1-4   *Choosing a data source*

4. On the Home ribbon in the PowerPivot window, click From Database in the Get External Data group. Now you have a choice of source data from the drop-down menu (see Figure 1-4). The next step is for connecting to SQL Server Northwind. If you don't have SQL Server Northwind, try to connect to Access Northwind (northwind.mdb) instead—it's an almost identical process.

5. Click From SQL Server (if you have the SQL Server Northwind). This opens the Table Import Wizard. You'll need to enter a server name (or choose your SQL Server from the drop-down) and then select Northwind as the database (as shown in Figure 1-5), before clicking Next.

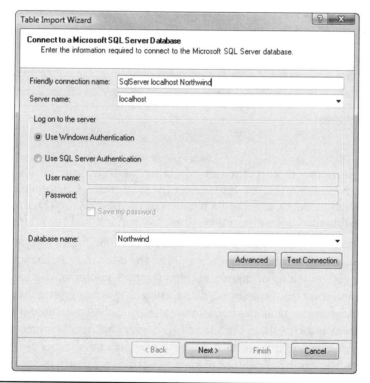

Figure 1-5   *Specifying server and database names for SQL Server*

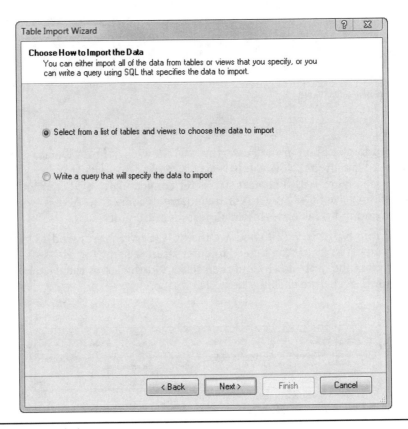

Figure 1-6 *Import method*

6. On the next screen, keep the default, which is to import tables and/or views, and click Next again (Figure 1-6). Select the Categories, Customers, Employees, Order Details, Orders, and Products tables in the next dialog (Figure 1-7). Click Finish and finally Close, after PowerPivot has imported all the tables.

Your PowerPivot window should now have six tabs, one for each table (Figure 1-8). The table names are reflected in the names of the tabs. You can change the table names by right-clicking or double-clicking the tabs. Each table includes all of the columns and rows from the source data by default—although the Picture column from the Categories table has been automatically excluded because it's a *binary large object*, known as a BLOB, in both the SQL Server and Access source databases. There is virtually no limit on the number of rows in a table; especially on 64-bit computers, you can have millions of rows in a table (computer memory permitting and subject to a 4GB memory limit on workbook size).

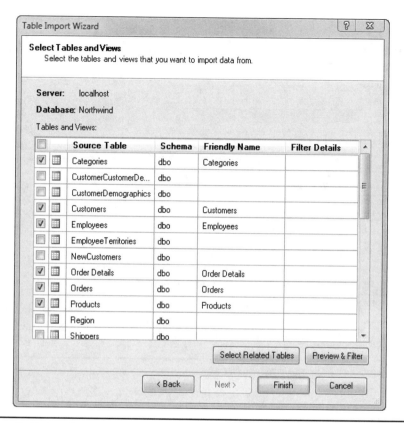

Figure 1-7   *What to import*

7. Click the Orders tab and find the first empty column with a column header of Add Column—you may have to scroll in order to see it. Click anywhere inside the column to activate the formula bar.

8. Now, for your first DAX! Type the following syntax (you can use AutoComplete to save typing and to eliminate syntax errors and typos):

    ```
    =YEAR(Orders[OrderDate])
    ```

    Because the column is in the same table, you can omit the table name. Then press ENTER to commit the formula and calculate the values. Don't worry about the syntax just yet; there are plenty of explanations of DAX syntax in the rest of this book. But take a look at the column, which now has a new column header of CalculatedColumn1—it contains the year that each order was made.

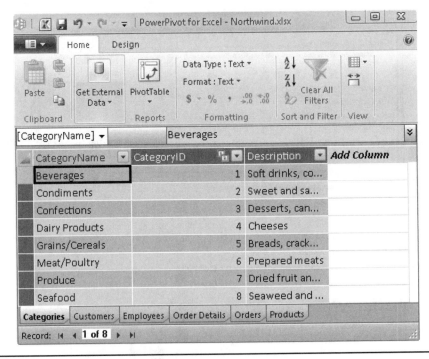

Figure 1-8 *PowerPivot window with imported tables*

Double-click the column header and type **Year**, and then press ENTER to rename the column (the result is shown in Figure 1-9). As Northwind has been around for a while, and the years have changed, your values for the Year column may be different.

9. Now click the Order Details tab to see that table. Again click in the Add Column column and enter the following DAX formula:

```
='Order Details'[Quantity] * 'Order Details'[UnitPrice]
```

Again, you can leave out the table name, as all of the columns are in the same table. This is a formula that simply multiplies the quantity sold by the price to give the value of sales for each product that appears in an order line. First press ENTER to initiate the calculation, and then double-click the column header, rename the column to Sales Amount, and press ENTER again. The result is shown in Figure 1-10.

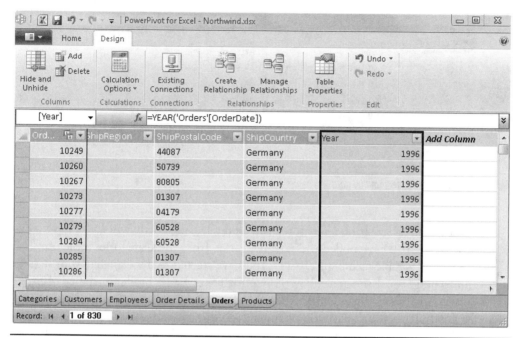

Figure 1-9   *DAX calculated column for year values*

10. Now add a calculated column to the Products table to show the category for each product. The DAX syntax is

    ```
    =RELATED(Categories[CategoryName])
    ```

    Here, the table name is obligatory, as the referenced column is in another table. Rename the column to Category. The DAX has been used to create a calculated column. This is one of two situations in which you write a DAX formula—the

Ord...	Produ...	UnitPrice	Quantity	Discount	Sales Amount	Add Column
10508	39	£18	10	0	£180	
10521	35	£18	3	0	£54	
10530	76	£18	50	0	£900	
10546	35	£18	30	0	£540	
10553	35	£18	6	0	£108	
10566	76	£18	10	0	£180	
10569	76	£18	30	0	£540	
10575	76	£18	10	0	£180	

Figure 1-10   *DAX calculated column showing sales*

nStock	UnitsOnOrder	ReorderLevel	Discontinued	Category	Add Column
39	0	10	FALSE	Beverages	
17	40	25	FALSE	Beverages	
13	70	25	FALSE	Condiments	
53	0	0	FALSE	Condiments	
0	0	0	TRUE	Condiments	
120	0	25	FALSE	Condiments	
15	0	10	FALSE	Produce	
6	0	0	FALSE	Condiments	

Figure 1-11   *DAX used to denormalize data*

other situation (creating a measure) will be described shortly when you have a pivot table. You have pulled the category name from the Categories table into the Products table (see Figure 1-11). You have started to denormalize your data and to build a star schema—PowerPivot for Excel uses a hidden instance of SQL Server Analysis Services (SSAS) behind the scenes to automatically create a cube for you (but you don't have to understand anything about star schemas or cubes—that's the beauty of PowerPivot for Excel). SSAS runs in the same process as Excel.

11. On the Home ribbon (of the PowerPivot window), click PivotTable in the Reports group and select PivotTable from the drop-down menu (Figure 1-12). In the ensuing Create PivotTable dialog, select Existing Worksheet and click OK (Figure 1-13). You should be back in the Excel workbook, looking at an empty pivot table and a PowerPivot Field List at the right (Figure 1-14). If you can't see the Field List, click inside the pivot table. If it's still not visible, click Field List in the Show/Hide group of the PowerPivot ribbon. You now have two windows open, Excel and PowerPivot. To move between them, you can use the task bar. If you close the PowerPivot window, simply click the PowerPivot Window button

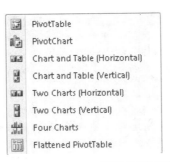

	PivotTable
	PivotChart
	Chart and Table (Horizontal)
	Chart and Table (Vertical)
	Two Charts (Horizontal)
	Two Charts (Vertical)
	Four Charts
	Flattened PivotTable

Figure 1-12   *Creating a pivot table*

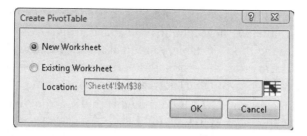

Figure 1-13 *Location of new pivot table in Excel*

on the PowerPivot ribbon in Excel (this also switches to the PowerPivot window, if it's already open). When you inserted the pivot table, you were switched automatically back into Excel. You can move manually from the PowerPivot window to the Excel window at any time—click the Switch to Workbook icon on the Quick Access toolbar in PowerPivot.

Figure 1-14 *PowerPivot Field List in Excel*

If you expand the Orders and the Order Details tables in the PowerPivot Field List, you can see the two new columns you added using DAX: Year and Sales Amount. Under the Products table, you can also see your new Category column. It looks no different from the original imported columns. You are ready to build your first PowerPivot pivot table (hosted in Excel) by adding columns.

12. Right-click Category under the Products table (not CategoryName under Categories) and choose Add to Column Labels. You can also drag and drop to the Column Labels drop-zone. Do the same for ProductName. Under the Customers table, right-click Country and choose Add to Row Labels (yes, columns can become rows!). Do the same for City. Under the Order Details table, right-click Sales Amount and choose Add to Values. Next, under the Orders table, right-click Year and choose Add to Slicers Horizontal. Repeat this for the Category column in the Products table. There should be seven entries in the bottom half of the PowerPivot Field List—by default, the lower section of the PowerPivot Field List contains drop-zones for different areas of the pivot table. Category appears twice, and Sales Amount (in the Values section) is named Sum of Sales Amount. Your PowerPivot Field List should look something like Figure 1-15.

13. Now is probably a good point at which to save your work. You save from Excel as you normally do, although you can also save from the PowerPivot window. Both the Excel workbook and the PowerPivot model, including both metadata and data, are saved as one single .xlsx file. You have just created a multidimensional cube without having to know anything about star schemas or cubes or dimensions or facts/measures or SSAS. If you copy the .xlsx file and rename with a zip extension, you can unzip the file. It contains quite a lot! In the customData subfolder of the xl folder, there's a file called item1.data, which is fairly big. This file is your PowerPivot data.

14. In the pivot table, right-click on Argentina under Row Labels and choose Expand/Collapse, followed by Collapse Entire Field. Repeat this process for Beverages under Column Labels. Your pivot table should resemble Figure 1-16. That's pretty good for a few minutes' work, isn't it? You might want to experiment with expanding and collapsing the countries and the categories. Something you may not have seen before are the two slicers at the top. Try clicking individual years or product categories to implement filters and watch the data change (it's really fast). To select more than one filter in a particular slicer, click the first tile and hold down the CTRL key as you click others—the data will not refresh until you release the CTRL key. Or you can hold down the mouse button to select contiguous slicer tiles. To show all of the data and clear any slicer filters, click the small filter funnel (which has a red cross when a filter is in operation) at the top right of a slicer.

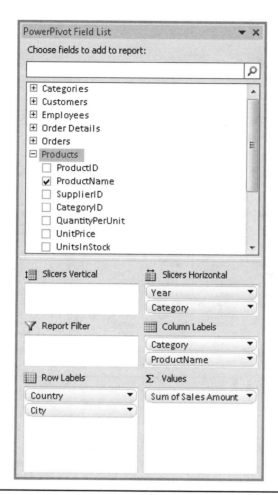

Figure 1-15 *PowerPivot Field List with entries*

This is a really cool pivot table. But we can make it even better. For example, there are some blank cells, which you might wish to change to zeros—our Norwegian customers are not keen on Grains/Cereals. Maybe the Sales Amount could be formatted a little better. And it might be nice to show market shares by country/city and category/product, as a percentage of the overall total sales (1354458.59 in the bottom-right corner). All of this, and much more, can be accomplished with your mouse from the GUI— Chapter 5 goes into detail about pivot table possibilities. For example, you can exploit the power of Excel's conditional formatting capabilities. However, we are going to add some new data to show percentage market share using DAX. When you work with cells in the

Sum of Sales Amount	Beverages	Condiments	Confections	Dairy Products	Grains/Cereals	Meat/Poultry	Produce	Seafood	Grand Total
Argentina	1798	907	2135.1	1143.5	390		1139	606.5	8119.1
Austria	26452.05	16802.4	14653.35	30342.9	14854.25	12001.48	13755.95	10634.25	139496.63
Belgium	5864.4	2714.7	7711.18	8825	3226	2258.5	3223.2	1312	35134.98
Brazil	40400.5	12139	12164.73	16894.5	6638	8008.12	5385.15	13338.48	114968.48
Canada	13829.7	5010.6	9302.4	10102	5765.1	4266	2112	4946.3	55334.1
Denmark	12025.7	4455.4	2815.3	2753.2	105	3700.7	4626	4300.95	34782.25
Finland	2222	1873	1033.05	6027.8	2800	3345.25	1161.05	1316.3	19778.45
France	13670	7148.4	13215.85	9318.9	6493.45	11142.96	8769.8	15739.4	85498.76
Germany	57644.6	17395.1	37799.44	53170.9	14603.15	22607.44	17265.9	24154.1	244640.63
Ireland	3339.4	3898.5	1739.2	11093.4	1442.4	24040.9	3821.7	7941.89	57317.39
Italy	1155	1448.25	2787.7	4376.8	1794	1167	2216.8	1759.6	16705.15
Mexico	8097.5	1235.45	2066.95	4912.4	559.5	2828.9	2517.75	1855	24073.45
Norway	2756	234	280.15	786		164	578.4	936.6	5735.15
Poland	828.5	627	779.1	810		22.35	306	159	3531.95
Portugal	1190.4	3869.45	1122.5	1008	2415.2	1355.9	763.2	744	12468.65
Spain	1363.2	1789.45	1809.05	646	1843	7919.1	2120	1942.09	19431.89
Sweden	13407.05	4970.3	5675.65	6585.2	3250	9625.95	9116	6893.55	59523.7
Switzerland	2357.5	2054.3	3246.16	7747.3	4931	7155.64	2236	3191.6	32919.5
UK	7596.2	4576.05	9223.26	14553.7	5195.2	6445.15	8142.8	4884.15	60616.51
USA	63361.15	18555.85	38804.05	41549.3	20411.3	45394.06	10465.9	25025.37	263566.98
Venezuela	7168.1	1990.55	8734.93	18683.7	4010.25	4739.4	5546	9941.96	60814.89
Grand Total	286526.95	113694.75	177099.1	251330.5	100726.8	178188.8	105296.6	141623.09	1354458.59

Figure 1-16   *PowerPivot pivot table in Excel*

Values area, you are working with measures (sometimes referred to as facts). *Measures* are usually numeric values that are used to show totals and subtotals—more on this later.

Earlier, you used DAX to add columns to tables—these are DAX calculated columns. The second situation when we use DAX is to create measures. DAX formulas are either calculated columns or measures. As you progress through the book, the difference between calculated columns and measures should become clear. If you have star schema experience, you can think of them as dimensions and facts. If you have cube experience, you might know them as dimensions and measures. However, to use PowerPivot and DAX, you don't need any knowledge of either star schemas or cubes. The whole point of PowerPivot for Excel is to shield you from such technicalities.

To create your first DAX measure:

1.   Click New Measure in the Measures group of the PowerPivot ribbon in the Excel workbook. This opens the Measure Settings dialog box (Figure 1-17). If New Measure is disabled, click inside the pivot table. An alternative is to right-click on the table in the Field List and choose Add New Measure.

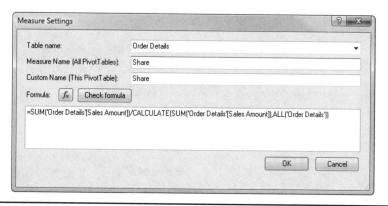

Figure 1-17 *Measure Settings dialog*

2. Enter **Share** as the name for the new measure for Measure Name (All Pivot Tables) and make sure that Order Details is selected in the Table name drop-down. Then, enter the following DAX in the Formula box (if you need a bit more room to type, expand the size of the dialog box and the Formula box will enlarge). When you finish the entry, click Check Formula to verify your syntax.

```
=SUM('Order Details'[Sales Amount])/
CALCULATE(SUM('Order Details'[Sales Amount]),
ALL('Order Details'))
```

There's quite a bit going on here. Click OK to accept the DAX formula and it should be added to the Values section. The new calculated measure, Share, also appears under Order Details and has a calculator icon next to it. If it's not in the Values section, right-click the measure and choose Add to Values.

3. As a final, cosmetic step, let's align our new Share measure and show it as a percentage. Click on one of the values for Share in the main body of the pivot table. Click PivotTable Tools, then click the Options tab to open its ribbon.

4. Check that the Active Field in the Active Field group is Share and click Field Settings. This opens the Value Field Settings dialog. In this dialog, click the Number Format button to open the Format Cells dialog. Select Percentage and click OK twice. A quicker alternative is to right-click on one of the values in the pivot table and choose Number Format. Well done, you have a really nice BI pivot table—hopefully, it looks similar to Figure 1-18.

This was a short, quick chapter—but it covered a lot of ground. Despite the chapter's brevity, you've seen many of the important features and the versatility of PowerPivot for Excel. If you tried the example, you have imported data into PowerPivot and created some DAX calculated columns (and a DAX measure) to extend the data. In addition,

Row Labels	Sum of Sales Amount	Share	Sum of Sales Amount	Share	Sum of Sales Amount	Share
	⊞Beverages		⊞Condiments		⊞Confections	
⊞Argentina	1798	0.13%	907	0.07%	2135.1	0.16%
⊞Austria	26452.05	1.95%	16802.4	1.24%	14653.35	1.08%
⊞Belgium	5864.4	0.43%	2714.7	0.20%	7711.18	0.57%
⊞Brazil	40400.5	2.98%	12139	0.90%	12164.73	0.90%
⊞Canada	13829.7	1.02%	5010.6	0.37%	9302.4	0.69%
⊞Denmark	12025.7	0.89%	4455.4	0.33%	2815.3	0.21%
⊞Finland	2222	0.16%	1873	0.14%	1033.05	0.08%
⊞France	13670	1.01%	7148.4	0.53%	13215.85	0.98%
⊞Germany	57644.6	4.26%	17395.1	1.28%	37799.44	2.79%
⊞Ireland	3339.4	0.25%	3898.5	0.29%	1739.2	0.13%
⊞Italy	1155	0.09%	1448.25	0.11%	2787.7	0.21%
⊞Mexico	8097.5	0.60%	1235.45	0.09%	2066.95	0.15%
⊞Norway	2756	0.20%	234	0.02%	280.15	0.02%
⊞Poland	828.5	0.06%	627	0.05%	779.1	0.06%
⊞Portugal	1190.4	0.09%	3869.45	0.29%	1122.5	0.08%
⊞Spain	1363.2	0.10%	1789.45	0.13%	1809.05	0.13%
⊞Sweden	13407.05	0.99%	4970.3	0.37%	5675.65	0.42%
⊞Switzerland	2357.5	0.17%	2054.3	0.15%	3246.16	0.24%
⊞UK	7596.2	0.56%	4576.05	0.34%	9223.26	0.68%
⊞USA	63361.15	4.68%	18555.85	1.37%	38804.05	2.86%
⊞Venezuela	7168.1	0.53%	1990.55	0.15%	8734.93	0.64%
Grand Total	286526.95	21.15%	113694.75	8.39%	177099.1	13.08%

Figure 1-18   *A completed business intelligence PowerPivot pivot table*

you placed much of the data into a PowerPivot pivot table in Excel and saw just how easy it is to build business intelligence. Please don't be fooled by the small tables in these examples—PowerPivot can handle millions of records in tables. This business intelligence may be self-service and takes only a few minutes, but it's truly industrial strength. The next chapter consolidates what you've learned—it has more detailed instructions. It also extends this chapter and shows how to import data from Access and Excel and data feeds, as well as SQL Server again. The next chapter also shows how to create relationships between PowerPivot tables, if they are not inherited from your source data, which is always the case with Excel and data feed imports.

Chapter 2

PowerPivot: Overview

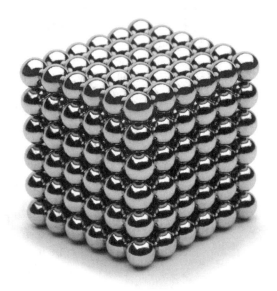

Chapter 1 was a very quick introduction to PowerPivot for Excel. It concentrated on importing data from SQL Server. This chapter takes a more detailed look at importing data from SQL Server. It also shows how to import data from Access, Excel, and data feeds. You are shown relationships between PowerPivot tables and how to set them up, if they are missing. Data Analysis eXpressions (DAX) is used to create both calculated columns in PowerPivot tables and measures in PowerPivot pivot tables in Excel. In addition, a measure is added through the GUI, without the need for DAX. You get to construct a sophisticated pivot table and a pivot chart linked to the pivot table. Various ways of filtering data in a pivot report (pivot table or pivot chart) are introduced.

This chapter consolidates and extends the example in the previous chapter. It should give you a good overview of some of the main features and capabilities of PowerPivot. Subsequent chapters build upon this chapter—in particular, the next chapter is a full in-depth look at PowerPivot.

> ▶ **Key concepts** Starting PowerPivot; importing data into PowerPivot from SQL Server, Access, Excel, and data feeds; setting up relationships; DAX calculated columns; DAX measures; pivot tables; pivot charts; filters; slicers

Starting PowerPivot

When you start Excel 2010, you are probably looking at the Excel Home ribbon as shown in Figure 2-1.

If the Home ribbon is hidden, as in Figure 2-2, double-click the Excel Home (or any) tab to re-enable ribbon display. If you single-click rather than double-click, the ribbons are going to obscure the top part of your worksheet. If that happens, try a double-click.

To display the PowerPivot ribbon, click the PowerPivot tab. The result is shown in Figure 2-3. Maybe we should call this the Excel PowerPivot ribbon, as you're still in an Excel workbook. PowerPivot itself has its own separate window and ribbons, as you'll see in a minute. The PowerPivot ribbon has a number of groups. Presently, the Measures, Report, and Show/Hide groups are disabled—these will become enabled once you have added your first pivot table or created your first PowerPivot table.

When you create a pivot table from PowerPivot data, the pivot table is hosted within an Excel worksheet. It is slightly different from a normal Excel pivot table, so it really can be called a PowerPivot pivot table, although both can be seen in an Excel worksheet. A PowerPivot pivot table (and/or a pivot chart) is where you visualize your Business Intelligence (BI)—it's your interface to your data. Perhaps I shouldn't call it data any more. Rather, it's going to be information (meaningful data), or better still, intelligence.

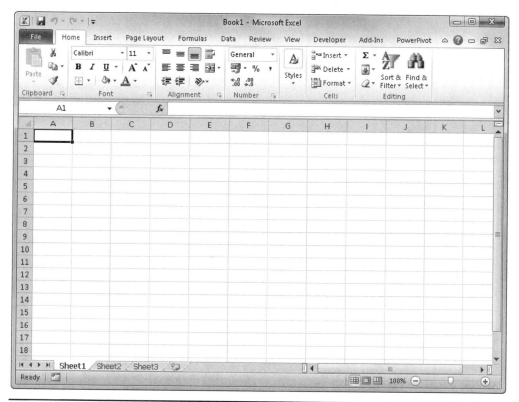

Figure 2-1   *Excel with ribbons*

Intelligence or business intelligence has many definitions. It's information that is easily found, easily visualized, and easily actionable. That means it's going to form the basis for sound and timely decision making. It gives you that competitive edge, and PowerPivot makes it so easy!

If you don't see a PowerPivot tab, and therefore you don't have the PowerPivot ribbon, it means you haven't got PowerPivot! PowerPivot is not included with a default installation of Excel 2010. Don't worry; you can easily download PowerPivot for Excel for free. You can find the download on the main PowerPivot Web site at www.PowerPivot.com, and it's also available from www.microsoft.com. Once you download and install, you should be back with us with your PowerPivot ribbon open, as shown in Figure 2-3.

On the PowerPivot ribbon, in Excel, click the PowerPivot Window button—the only one in the Launch group. This opens PowerPivot; see Figure 2-4. Veteran Excel users may find this a little unusual. You now have two windows—the original Excel workbook and the new PowerPivot window. Although they appear in two separate

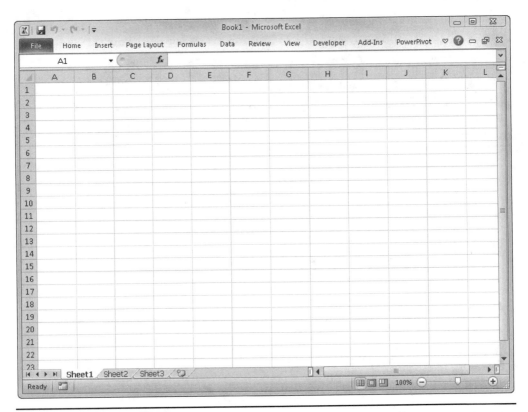

Figure 2-2   *Excel without ribbons*

windows, they are intimately related. When you save your Excel workbook in the normal way, the PowerPivot window and its contents are saved as part of the Excel workbook. Any data and settings inside the PowerPivot window are saved with the Excel workbook. If you use the Save button in the Quick Access toolbar in the PowerPivot window, it saves the outer Excel workbook and the PowerPivot window within it. The PowerPivot window is not a separate workbook file that you can open separately. If you have closed both windows, and you want to return to your PowerPivot window, you open the Excel workbook first and click the PowerPivot Window button on the Excel PowerPivot ribbon.

It's easy to switch between the two windows. From the PowerPivot window, you click the Switch to Workbook button in the Quick Access toolbar at the top. From Excel, click the PowerPivot Window button in the Launch group of the PowerPivot ribbon—this puts you back in the PowerPivot window. If this is the first time you've clicked, it opens an empty PowerPivot window. If you had closed the PowerPivot

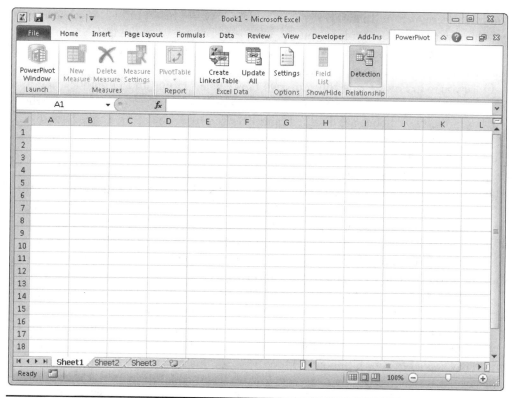

Figure 2-3   *PowerPivot ribbon in Excel*

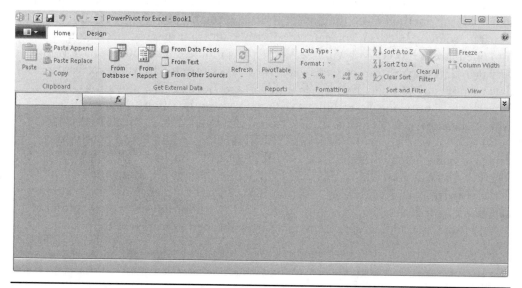

Figure 2-4   *PowerPivot window*

window, this reopens it. In addition, you could also try normal Windows methods for switching windows. For example, you can click either window on the task bar or press ALT-TAB—but be careful; you can have multiple Excel and PowerPivot windows open at the same time, so make sure you select the right one.

Once you're in PowerPivot, there are two tabs labeled Home and Design leading to two ribbons. If you've not done any work yet in your PowerPivot window, many of the buttons in the two ribbons are disabled (and later you may see a third Linked Table ribbon). The formula bar is also disabled and there are no tabs in the window. You'll see the first tabs shortly.

The PowerPivot window (from now on, I'll often simply call it PowerPivot) is where you assemble the data you wish to analyze. It's where you start turning data into intelligence. Mostly, you'll assemble the data by importing it from another source or from multiple sources, although you can also copy and paste or link to data. The beauty of PowerPivot is that you can create real business intelligence and display it in a pivot table back in Excel, even if your source data is far from perfect. The next few sections show how to assemble your data within PowerPivot.

There are three different ways to get data into PowerPivot. One, you can import data from one or more external sources. You do this from the Get External Data group in the Home ribbon of PowerPivot. Two, from the Clipboard group on the same ribbon you can paste in data (possibly from an existing Excel list or table) that you've previously copied to your Clipboard. Three, you can link back to an Excel table (a range or list gets automatically converted into an Excel table) through the Excel Data group on the PowerPivot ribbon in Excel. The first two methods are available from the PowerPivot window, and the third method is accessed from the Excel window.

It's possible to use any of these methods, or to use more than one. It's also possible to employ any method more than once, perhaps bringing in data from multiple disparate sources. In effect, you can consolidate data from heterogeneous sources into one place, a PowerPivot window. With a few mouse clicks you can have your very own data mart within minutes—a central repository for all of the relevant data without any complex Extract, Transform, and Load (ETL) operations. Before PowerPivot came along, assembling a data mart was quite often a daunting task. Now you can have data from text files, Access databases, Excel spreadsheets, data feeds, SQL Server Reporting Services (SSRS) reports, and high-end relational database management systems such as SQL Server or Oracle or DB2, all joined together. You can even add to this data from a multidimensional cube hosted in SQL Server Analysis Services (SSAS)—so you can have multidimensional and relational data working together, which is quite tricky to do without PowerPivot. And there's more! How about adding data from another established PowerPivot for SharePoint workbook, or from your big SQL Server in the sky, SQL Azure? You can even paste from a Word table.

Let's work through the steps involved in assembling some or all of this data. You won't necessarily have all of the data sources mentioned. In that case, try the ones that are relevant to you. But in order to follow the steps in this book on your computer, rather than just read about them, it would be helpful if you have the Northwind database in either its SQL Server or Access or Excel incarnation. Details of how to download Northwind for Access or SQL Server are given in the introduction. There is also, as of this writing, a Northwind data feed that you might use instead. I have also created an Excel version—again, download details are mentioned earlier. Should you not have any of these versions of Northwind, it should be relatively easy to adapt the instructions that follow to your own data sources. Please note that, because of structure and data changes, you'll need the pre-Access 2007 copy of Northwind to follow the examples here (that is, Northwind.mdb, not Northwind.accdb). You can load Northwind.mdb into Access 2010 or Access 2007 and convert it to Northwind.accdb—that will also work fine. Just be careful that you don't save and overwrite any original Northwind.accdb that you may have.

The data in the Access and SQL Server and Excel and data feed Northwinds is identical (at least for the tables and columns we'll be working with), so once you've done the import, the steps in this book should work for everyone. In essence, this means that *you don't have to have SQL Server*—even if the full official name of PowerPivot for Excel is Microsoft SQL Server PowerPivot for Excel 2010. You do need SQL Server (in order to have SSAS, or SQL Server Analysis Services) if you wish to view your PowerPivot pivot reports in SharePoint, using a Web browser, rather than in Excel. You will also need to enable Excel Services in SharePoint. This book is about PowerPivot for Excel (where you create everything in the first place) rather than PowerPivot for SharePoint, where you can deploy the results and make them available through your SharePoint Web site if you wish. So all you need is Excel 2010, with PowerPivot for Excel 2010 installed, and preferably one of the four possible Northwinds.

The next four sections demonstrate how to import Northwind data from SQL Server and Access and Excel and a data feed in turn. You only need to do one of these, whichever is appropriate to your situation, although for future reference it might be beneficial to read the other three. If you wish to try more than one, and you have the relevant Northwinds, please remove the tables from PowerPivot first. Otherwise, you will end up with tables being duplicated. To delete a table, you right-click its tab and choose Delete. You need to be in the PowerPivot window, not the Excel one (unless you are first linking to an Excel table), to import or delete data. Here goes.

Importing from SQL Server

If you're wondering why we're going to use Northwind rather than Adventure Works (the classic sample databases for SQL Server 2005 and 2008) or the newer Contoso sample database, it's so that readers who don't have SQL Server can use an Access, Excel, or Northwind data feed, and everyone can follow along with the same practicals. An Access version of Adventure Works is not readily available for download, and an Excel. version would be pretty big. Northwind contains everything we need to learn about every aspect of PowerPivot for Excel and its associated DAX language.

If you don't have SQL Server and the Northwind database, then maybe try the next section, "Importing from Access," or the subsequent sections on importing from Excel or a data feed. For future reference, I recommend that you read this section on SQL Server anyway, even if you are not in a position to try it just yet. To import some tables from SQL Server Northwind:

1. Click the From Database button in the Get External Data group of the Home ribbon in PowerPivot. This opens the menu shown in Figure 2-5.

2. In this menu choose From SQL Server to open the Table Import Wizard. You first need a Server name and a Database name. Enter the name of your SQL Server in the Server Name field, and choose Northwind from the Database Name drop-down. In Figure 2-6, you can see I've been lazy and used the dot shorthand for localhost (in a production environment, it's good practice to enter the server name explicitly). It's a good idea to click the Test Connection button before you click Next. If the connection fails, you may have to switch from Use Windows Authentication to Use SQL Server Authentication and enter your SQL Server login and password (optionally, saving your password; this is particularly important if you later deploy to PowerPivot for SharePoint). If the connection is taking too long, for example, if a server is unavailable, you can cancel the operation

Figure 2-5   *Choosing an external data source*

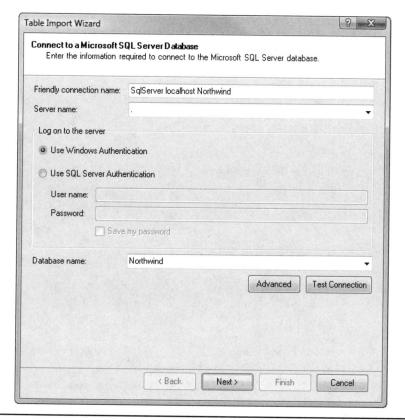

Figure 2-6   *Entering a server name and choosing a database name*

at any time. Note the Friendly Connection Name; this is the name by which the connection will be known in PowerPivot. By default, it includes your server and database names—you can change these if you wish.

3.   The next dialog is where you choose how to import your data. The default is to select tables and/or views as your data sources. If you wish to manipulate the data in any way, you can write your own SQL queries. If you're an old hand at relational databases, you may be tempted to denormalize tables by writing inner joins. With PowerPivot, this is not necessary as some very simple DAX (easier than the SQL!) will do this for you. Accept the default to choose from a list of tables and views, as shown in Figure 2-7, and click Next.

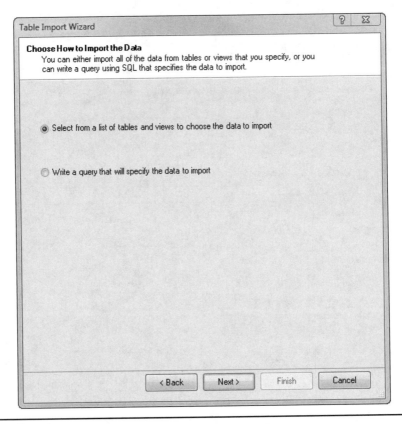

Figure 2-7   *How to import*

4.   You are now at the Select Tables and Views stage of the Table Import Wizard, as shown in Figure 2-8. There's quite a lot going on here. Before we discuss that, select the check boxes for the Categories, Customers, Employees, Order Details, Orders, and Products tables. The very top check box allows you to select or deselect all tables and views en masse. You can sort the tables by clicking the column header. You can also see the Schema name for your tables and views and a Friendly Name. If you wish, you can alter the Friendly Name—this is the name that will appear in PowerPivot and any pivot tables or pivot charts that you create back in Excel. However, it's possible to change the name later, in the PowerPivot

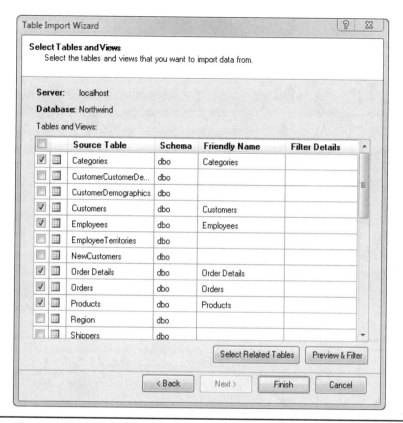

Figure 2-8   *What to import*

window by renaming tables. The Select Related Tables button will find all tables directly related to a currently selected table. This is very handy when your source database has referential integrity between tables and is complex, or if you're not sure about how the tables relate together—maybe there's a lookup table that contains essential data that you're not aware of.

5. If you click the Preview & Filter button, it opens the Preview Selected Table dialog of the Table Import Wizard (see Figure 2-9), on the currently selected table. This is so you can check that your data is arranged as you want it. Here, you can remove columns from the table by unselecting check boxes for the columns. In addition, you can set up filters and sorting. A *filter* is the equivalent

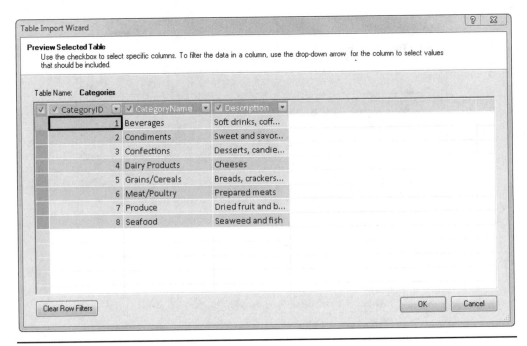

Figure 2-9   *Previewing data*

of a SQL Where clause, and a *sort* is the equivalent of a SQL Order By clause. Filtering and sorting are covered in the next chapter, so for now, cancel out of the dialog box if you opened it. Please note that if multiple tables are selected, the Preview & Filter button is disabled. To complete the import of tables, click Finish.

6. The Importing dialog box (see Figure 2-10) informs you that all six tables have been successfully imported. All you have to do now is to click Close and you are returned to the PowerPivot window, which now looks a little different. It contains a tab for each of the six tables. Before examining the PowerPivot window and its tables, let's see how to import the same data from Access, and Excel, and data feed sources—Access first.

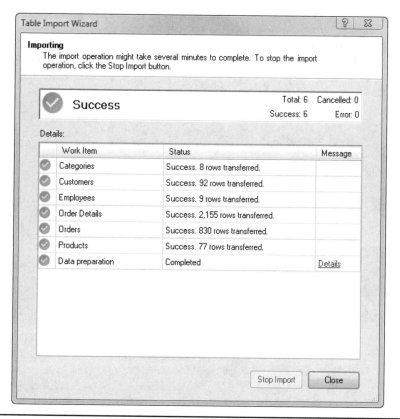

Figure 2-10   *A successful import*

Importing from Access

If you don't have the Access Northwind.mdb database (or Northwind.mdb saved as Nortwind.accdb) and you weren't able to complete the previous SQL Server import, try the next section, "Importing from Excel," instead. However, I strongly recommend that you read this short section anyway—it may prove useful in the future.

To import some tables from Access Northwind:

1. In PowerPivot, click From Database in the Get External Data group of the Home ribbon. Select From Access in the resulting menu (see Figure 2-5 in the earlier section on importing from SQL Server).

Figure 2-11 *Connecting to an Access database*

2. The dialog box that opens is different from that for SQL Server. Instead of specifying a server and a database, you browse to find the Access database file (see Figure 2-11). When you click the Browse button, by default it's only going to find Access .accdb databases. In order to locate Access .mdb databases, change the drop-down entry in the Open dialog to Microsoft Office Access 97-2003 Database (*.mdb). Once you've found your Northwind.mdb, click Open. You may want to click Test Connection before choosing Next.

3. The subsequent dialog is where you decide whether to select tables and/or views from a list or to write your own SQL queries to extract the data. This dialog is identical to the one seen during a SQL Server import, as shown in Figure 2-7 earlier. For now, accept the default and click Next.

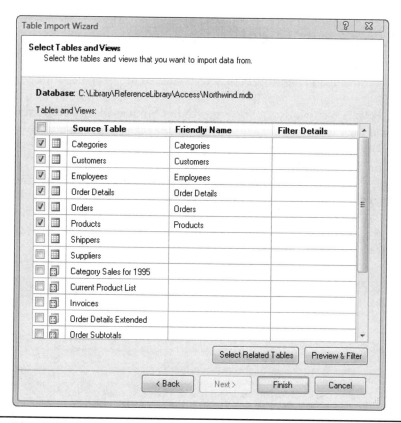

Figure 2-12 *What to import*

4. The Table Import Wizard is now at the Select Tables and Views dialog as in Figure 2-12. This is subtly different from the SQL Server equivalent. This time there is no column for Schema—Access databases do not support schemas. Turn on the check boxes for six tables: Categories, Customers, Employees, Order Details, Orders, and Products. Then click Finish.

5. The last dialog in the Table Import Wizard is called Importing. You saw this earlier for a SQL Server import in Figure 2-10. Click Close in this dialog. You are returned to the PowerPivot window, which now has six tabs, one for each table. Just before we examine the PowerPivot window, here's a quick look at importing the same data from Excel itself.

Importing from Excel

In order to follow this section as a practical, you'll need the Northwind Excel workbook, which you can download from this book's Web site. To import data from Excel:

1. In the PowerPivot window, click From Other Sources in the Get External Data group on the Home ribbon. This opens the dialog seen in Figure 2-13. From this menu, choose Excel File (towards the bottom of the list) and click Next.

2. You should be in the Connect to a Microsoft Excel File stage of the Table Import Wizard, as shown in Figure 2-14. Click Browse to find your Excel spreadsheet, and then click Open. If you want to follow the examples here exactly, locate the Excel version of Northwind that you may have downloaded. Please note the check

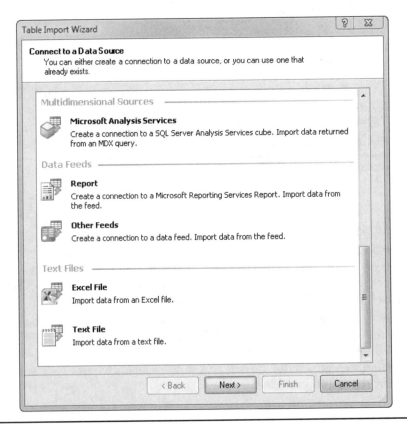

Figure 2-13 *Choosing the type of data to import*

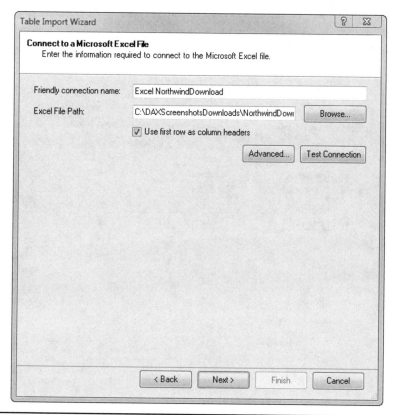

Figure 2-14   *Connecting to an Excel data source*

box indicating that the first row in a worksheet contains column headers—turn this on, as the sample you may have downloaded does include the column names. Click Test Connection to verify it's a valid Excel workbook, and click Next to move on.

3. You are at the Select Tables and Views stage. Unlike with SQL Server and Access, you have not been given the option of writing SQL, instead of simply choosing tables. The Select Tables and Views dialog is sufficiently different from the SQL Server and Access equivalents to justify another screen shot; see Figure 2-15. I have taken a few steps to simplify mine. When you do this against your own Excel sources, it may appear a little more complex. You can import from Excel lists and/ or tables (there is no such thing as a view in Excel). Excel lists were confusingly called tables before Excel 2007. By *list*, I mean a contiguous range of data on a single worksheet. A *table* (in Excel 2007 and Excel 2010) is a list that has been

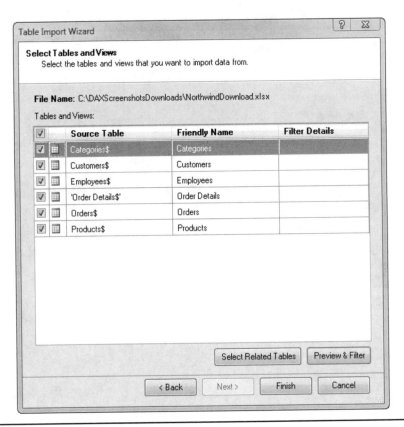

Figure 2-15   *Choosing Excel lists or tables to import*

explicitly turned into a table—one way to do that is by clicking the Format as Table button in the Styles group of the Home ribbon. Excel tables allow you to filter and sort data easily, and you possibly have a lot of experience with Excel tables already. Incidentally, your PowerPivot tables (very soon, I promise!) are similar to Excel tables. The Source Table column displays the Excel worksheet tab name followed by a dollar symbol ($), for example, Categories$—you are importing a list contained within a worksheet called Categories. If the Friendly Name column is followed by a space and a number, you probably already have those tables in PowerPivot—that's very likely if you did the SQL Server or Access steps earlier in the same PowerPivot window. You'll notice the single quotes around the Source Table name for Order Details, but this is not reflected in the Friendly Name and they are not strictly necessary. Also, the Select Related Tables button is not much help this time. This is perfectly sensible as Excel (unlike SQL Server and Access earlier) does not have the concept of related tables. But thanks to PowerPivot, we are going to create relationships on non-relational Excel lists/tables in a while!

4. Select all six tables (Categories, Customers, Employees, Order Details, Orders, and Products). Click Finish.

5. The last dialog in the wizard is called Importing. It's virtually the same as the one at the end of an Access or SQL Server import (Figure 2-10), except the final row, Data Preparation, is missing. Data Preparation is where relationships are detected and created—this does not apply to Excel imports. Click Close.

Importing from a Data Feed

You can also import from a data feed on the Internet. As of this writing, there is a data feed for the Northwind database. URLs come and go. I hope, but don't promise, that this URL is still working when you read this book. Here are the steps to import from a Northwind data feed:

1. Click From Data Feeds in the Get External Data group on the PowerPivot Home ribbon.

2. Enter **http://services.odata.org/Northwind/Northwind.svc/** as the Data Feed URL. Click Test Connection, and if successful, click Next.

3. Choose six tables: Categories, Customers, Employees, Order_Details (note the underscore), Orders, and Products. Then click Finish, followed by Close.

The data imported (assuming the URL is still valid) is the same as the SQL Server or the Access or the Excel data—there are minor differences, but they do not affect any of the examples in this book.

PowerPivot Window

Once a data import has finished, you are returned to the main PowerPivot window. Now it will include six PowerPivot tables, each with its own tab. In the previous sections you might have imported six tables from SQL Server, Access, Excel, or a data feed. Your window should look like that shown in Figure 2-16—there may be some minor differences in your tables (that is, column names, number of columns, and icons in some column headers), depending upon the source of your data.

You are not restricted only to SQL Server, Access, Excel, or data feed imports. There are many different sources you can use. All are covered in this book, some in great detail, for example, SQL Server Analysis Services (SSAS). This is a salient point at which to mention that you can combine table imports from *more* than one source.

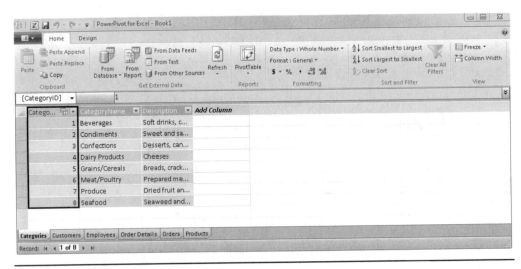

Figure 2-16   *PowerPivot tables*

In our example, you could just as easily have imported a couple of the tables from Excel, a couple from Access, *and* a couple from SQL Server. PowerPivot is an excellent way to consolidate multiple data sources into one, before you view the resulting business intelligence in a pivot table. It also allows you to define relationships between tables from differing sources. In effect, it helps you to design and build a data mart with a minimum amount of effort. In addition, it can handle very large data sets. You are *not* limited to the current Excel maximum of just over one million rows per worksheet. The limit now depends on available memory. On a 32-bit system, that means it can handle millions of rows or more in each table. On 64-bit systems, you can have even more rows. You are, however, limited by a maximum workbook size of 2GB.

Before moving on to those topics in more detail, let's see how PowerPivot handled the table imports. You will find a few differences, depending on whether you imported from SQL Server/Access or from Excel/data feed. The color scheme you see for your PowerPivot tables is determined by your settings in Excel for Table Style Medium 11. You can check this style by clicking the Format as Table button in the Styles group of the Home ribbon from the Table Styles group of the Table Tools/Design ribbon. First, we'll look at the Categories table (Figure 2-17).

In your version of the Categories table, you *may* see a small icon in the column header for the CategoryID column. The icon includes two small tables. CategoryID is a column that can be referenced by other tables. If you are from a relational database background, CategoryID is a primary key and PowerPivot recognized it as such during the import from SQL Server and Access. If you are looking at your own Excel or data

Catego...	CategoryName	Description
1	Beverages	Soft drinks, coffees, teas, beers, and ales
2	Condiments	Sweet and savory sauces, relishes, spreads, and ...
3	Confections	Desserts, candies, and sweet breads
4	Dairy Products	Cheeses
5	Grains/Cereals	Breads, crackers, pasta, and cereal
6	Meat/Poultry	Prepared meats
7	Produce	Dried fruit and bean curd
8	Seafood	Seaweed and fish

Figure 2-17   *Categories table in PowerPivot*

feed import, you won't see the symbol—Excel lists and tables do not have a concept of a primary key. Shortly, we'll discuss how to make it a primary key for the Excel/data feed import.

To qualify as a primary key in a PowerPivot table, a column must contain only unique values and no blanks. If you compare the PowerPivot version to the original in SQL Server or Access, notice that the Picture column has been automatically eliminated. In Access it has a data type of OLE Object, and in SQL Server it's an image data type. These are binary large objects, known as BLOBs (in this case a graphic), and are not supported in PowerPivot. The Excel/data feed sources did not contain this column in the first place. All versions include the Description column. This is from a *character large object* (CLOB)—it's a Memo data type in Access and ntext in SQL Server. CLOBs are supported in PowerPivot. Now take a look at the CategoryID column once more. Click anywhere inside the column to highlight it. Make sure you are on the PowerPivot Home ribbon.

In the Data Type drop-down in the Formatting group, notice the data type for the column. For SQL Server and Access versions of the import, it's Whole Number. For the Excel version, it's Decimal Number—Excel does not have explicit data types, so PowerPivot has made a guess. In fact, the CategoryID should always be an integer—so change it to Number (Whole), if necessary, and accept Yes in the warning dialog. You shouldn't lose any data in this case.

Figure 2-18 shows the Customers table. The SQL Server version may have three extra columns: ModifiedWho, ModifiedWhen, and ModifiedHow. These are not needed further, and to make all four imports similar, you may want to remove these columns. To do so, right-click the column and choose Delete Columns, then accept Yes in the warning dialog—it doesn't matter which of the PowerPivot ribbons is current. You can select and delete multiple columns at the same time, if you need to.

Custom...	CompanyName	ContactName	ContactTitle	Address	City
ALFKI	Alfred Futterkiste	Maria Anders	Sales Represe...	Obere Str. ...	Berlin
ANATR	Ana Trujillo Empa...	Ana Trujillo	Owner	Avda. de l...	Méxic...
ANTON	Antonio Moreno ...	Antonio Moreno	Owner	Matadero...	Méxic...
AROUT	Around the Horn	Thomas Hardy	Sales Represe...	120 Hanov...	London
BERGS	Berglunds snabbk...	Christina Berglu...	Order Admini...	Berguvsvä...	Luleå
BLAUS	Blauer See Delika...	Hanna Moos	Sales Represe...	Forsterstr....	Mann...
BLONP	Blondesddsl père...	Frédérique Cite...	Marketing Ma...	24, place ...	Strasb...
BOLID	Bólido Comidas p...	Martín Sommer	Owner	C/ Araquil...	Madrid
BONAP	Bon app'	Laurence Lebihan	Owner	12, rue de...	Marse...

Figure 2-18 *Customers table*

In Figure 2-19, you can see the Employees table. The SQL Server import version may have a PhotoPath column, which you can delete to bring it into line with the other versions.

The next figure, Figure 2-20, shows the Order Details table. The Excel/data feed import has no primary key icon in a column header—we are going to fix this soon. The Access and SQL Server versions have no primary key, but two distinct foreign keys on OrderID and ProductID, pointing to the Orders and Products reference tables, respectively. You should see a small magnifying glass in the headers for those two columns, which indicates a foreign key. You can navigate to the related table by right-clicking. This release of PowerPivot does not support composite primary keys—if you want a composite primary key, you can use DAX to combine multiple columns into a single column. The data type for the UnitPrice column in the Excel import is

EmployeeID	LastName	FirstName	Title	TitleOfCourtesy	BirthDate	HireDate
1	Davolio	Nancy	Sales ...	Ms.	08/12/1948	01/05/1992
2	Fuller	Andrew	Vice P...	Dr.	19/02/1952	14/08/1992
3	Leverling	Janet	Sales ...	Ms.	30/08/1963	01/04/1992
4	Peacock	Margaret	Sales ...	Mrs.	19/09/1937	03/05/1993
5	Buchanan	Steven	Sales ...	Mr.	04/03/1955	17/10/1993
6	Suyama	Michael	Sales ...	Mr.	02/07/1963	17/10/1993
7	King	Robert	Sales ...	Mr.	29/05/1960	02/01/1994
8	Callahan	Laura	Inside ...	Ms.	09/01/1958	05/03/1994
9	Dodsworth	Anne	Sales ...	Ms.	27/01/1966	15/11/1994

Figure 2-19 *Employees table*

OrderID	ProductID	UnitPrice	Quantity	Discount	Add Column
10508	39	£18	10	0	
10521	35	£18	3	0	
10530	76	£18	50	0	
10546	35	£18	30	0	
10553	35	£18	6	0	
10566	76	£18	10	0	
10569	76	£18	30	0	
10575	76	£18	10	0	
10576	1	£18	10	0	
10577	39	£18	10	0	

Figure 2-20   *Order Details table*

Decimal Number. If you are working on an Excel copy, change it to Currency. To do so, click in the column, click the Home tab to view the Home ribbon, and use the Data Type drop-down.

The next table (the tabs are in the order in which they were imported) is the Orders table (Figure 2-21). Note that you can change the order of the tables by dragging a table or by right-clicking and choosing Move. If you are following along with the Excel import, let's bring it into conformity with the Access, SQL Server, and data feed ones. You'll need to change the data type of the OrderID, EmployeeID, and ShipVia columns to Whole Number from Decimal Number. In addition, change the Freight data type to Currency.

OrderID	CustomerID	EmployeeID	OrderDate	RequiredDate
10249	TOMSP	6	05/07/1996	16/08/1996
10260	OTTIK	4	19/07/1996	16/08/1996
10267	FRANK	4	29/07/1996	26/08/1996
10273	QUICK	3	05/08/1996	02/09/1996
10277	MORGK	2	09/08/1996	06/09/1996
10279	LEHMS	8	13/08/1996	10/09/1996
10284	LEHMS	4	19/08/1996	16/09/1996
10285	QUICK	1	20/08/1996	17/09/1996
10286	QUICK	8	21/08/1996	18/09/1996

Figure 2-21   *Orders table*

Finally, there is the Products table (see Figure 2-22). Again, let's make some changes for those of you who imported this from Excel. Change the following to Whole Number: ProductID, SupplierID, CategoryID, UnitsInStock, UnitsOnOrder, and ReorderLevel. The UnitPrice column should be Currency. For all versions of the import, note that the Discontinued column is TRUE/FALSE. Why all the changes for tables imported from Excel? In both Access and SQL Server, the data types are part of the table design and PowerPivot honors these. Excel does not have data types for numbers, so PowerPivot plays safe by assigning Number (Decimal). It is just possible that a ReorderLevel in a source Excel list or table could be 10.5 in the future. However, Excel dates are correctly set as Date—the OrderDate column in the Orders table is an example. The data types of columns imported from a data feed are defined in the data feed and may or may not be what you want. It's always best to check.

Notice the small icon on the CategoryID column (in the Products table, this time, *not* the Categories table) if you are working with a SQL Server or Access import. The two small tables indicate it's a related column—if you hover the mouse, you can see the other table and column involved in the relationship. In addition, there is a small magnifying glass—this is used to show that the column is on the many side of a relationship (in relational speak, it's a foreign key). Primary keys (on the one side of a relationship) have the two small tables but not the magnifying glass—you can check this by looking, once more, at the CategoryID column in the Categories table. If you are working with an Excel or data feed import, you'll be able to see the column icons after the next section, where you will see how to establish relationships.

ProductID	ProductName	SupplierID	CategoryID	QuantityPerUnit	UnitPrice
1	Chai	1	1	10 boxes x 20 bags	£18
2	Chang	1	1	24 - 12 oz bottles	£19
3	Aniseed Syrup	1	2	12 - 550 ml bottles	£10
4	Chef Anton's Ca...	2	2	48 - 6 oz jars	£22
5	Chef Anton's Gu...	2	2	36 boxes	£21.35
6	Grandma's Boys...	3	2	12 - 8 oz jars	£25
7	Uncle Bob's Org...	3	7	12 - 1 lb pkgs.	£30
8	Northwoods Cr...	3	2	12 - 12 oz jars	£40
9	Mishi Kobe Niku	4	6	18 - 500 g pkgs.	£97

Figure 2-22 *Products table*

Checking Relationships

In order for pivot tables (and charts) and DAX formulas to work with multiple tables, it's important for PowerPivot to understand any relationships that may exist between the tables. For example, customers place orders, so the Customers and the Orders tables have some kind of connection or relationship. In order to understand relationships, it helps if you have a background in relational databases. PowerPivot honors any relationships defined in a relational source (for example, SQL Server or Access or Oracle) and imports them for you. In Excel, SSAS, data feeds, and other non-relational sources (such as tables imported from text files), you can help PowerPivot establish the necessary relationships. Without relationships, it is likely that your pivot tables and charts may not display the correct data. When you create a pivot table, PowerPivot will suggest that relationships are required (if it can't find them) and optionally offer to create them for you. If that happens, you will see a "relationship needed" message at the top of the pivot table's field list along with a Create button. It is recommended that you create the relationships yourself, if you can—after all, PowerPivot may not find and create all the correct relationships.

Let's see if PowerPivot has inherited any relationships from our source data. To view relationships, go to the Design ribbon (Figure 2-23) and click Manage Relationships in the Relationships group. You should be looking at something similar to either Figure 2-24 (Access and SQL Server sources) or Figure 2-25 (Excel/data feed source).

You either have relationships or you don't! Let's deal with the first situation that applies when you import from a relational database like Access or SQL Server. In our example, there are five relationships established. These are as follows (although the order may be different):

1. Order Details to Orders (using the OrderID column)
2. Order Details to Products (using the ProductID column)
3. Orders to Customers (using the CustomerID column)
4. Orders to Employees (using the EmployeeID column)
5. Products to Categories (using the CategoryID column)

Figure 2-23 *Design ribbon*

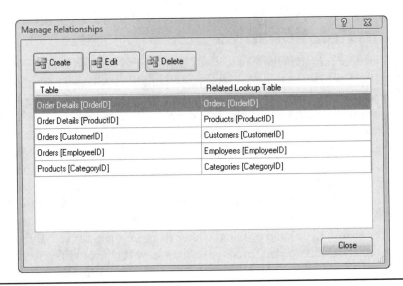

Figure 2-24 *Manage Relationships dialog showing relationships*

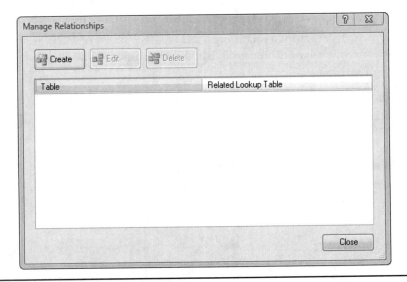

Figure 2-25 *Manage Relationships dialog without relationships*

If you are already conversant with relational databases, notice that each relationship must go from the many side (the child table) to the one side (the parent or lookup table). In a one-to-one relationship (not shown here), the order is not important. Each pair of tables in a relationship is linked by a column. That column has to appear in both tables. On the left or many side, it's known as the *foreign key*. On the right or one side, it's known as a *primary key* or the lookup key.

If you followed along with the Excel/data feed import, there are no relationships—Excel/data feeds don't support relationships, so there's nothing for PowerPivot to inherit as you import the data. This situation will also arise if you mix even relational imports. For example, if you import a SQL Server table and an Access one, or two Access tables from separate databases, the source databases do not include cross-database or cross-software relationships. You can create relationships in two places from the Relationships group on the Design ribbon. One, you can click Manage Relationships, and then click the Create button in the Manage Relationships dialog. Two, you can click the Create Relationship button directly. Both methods open the Create Relationship dialog (Figure 2-26), where you have to create relationships one at a time. You can also create relationships by right-clicking on a column header—this has the advantage of entering the table and column name for you on the many side of the relationship.

If you want to follow along with your Excel/data feed example (if you have one), you have to choose a Table and a Column at the top of the dialog. This should be a table at the many side of a relationship (or any side, in a one-to-one relationship), and the column must be the foreign key. Underneath, you choose the Related Lookup Table

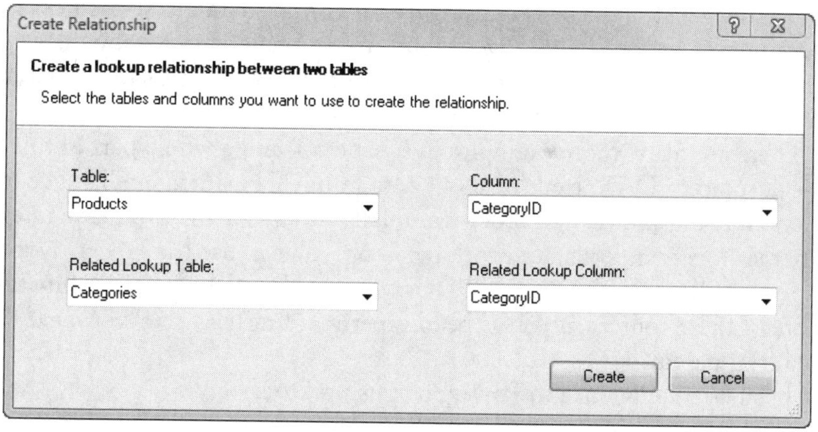

Figure 2-26 *Create Relationship dialog*

and the Related Lookup Column. The table is on the one side of a relationship and the column is its primary (lookup) key. If you get the tables in the wrong order, PowerPivot will automatically reverse them for you. For the Excel/data feed import only:

1. Click the Design tab and choose Create Relationship.
2. Implement all of the five necessary relationships from the preceding list.

Adding Columns

It's quite possible that your source data does not include everything you want in a subsequent pivot report (table or chart). For example, you may wish to analyze and compare sales amounts by year. Neither the sales amount nor the year exists in our source data. It's also likely that it does not include the necessary degree of denormalization. Denormalization is a process of reassembling data from a segmented and normalized transactional database to help in your BI analysis. Here, you might want to analyze by both category name (that is, product categories) and product name at the same time. Currently, the product name and the category name are in two separate tables (Products and Categories). If you were to have them both in one table, your pivot reports will display the correct data—for example, the product Chai will appear under the Beverages category and not under the Seafood category. If you are able to implement these and similar changes, you are creating business intelligence from often-unfriendly source data that may originate from many different sources. PowerPivot makes this (and more) easy. Not only does it centralize and assemble data, it helps you to transform that data into intelligence.

One powerful, yet straightforward, way to change your data into intelligence is to create new columns in your PowerPivot tables. You are helped in this by the versatility of DAX formulas. In the upcoming example, we are going to use DAX three times. In this chapter, the DAX examples are to give you a taste and get you started (and possibly excited!). There are many more examples in Chapter 3, and a whole part of this book (Part II) is devoted to DAX. Let's turn our data into real business intelligence by adding the sales amount, and the year an order was made, and by having product names and category names together. If you are working along, you can use the PowerPivot tables imported from either Excel, Access, SQL Server, or a data feed (or a combination of two or more of these sources, if you've been experimenting). PowerPivot makes the source data transparent.

To add business intelligence to PowerPivot using DAX:

1. Click on the tab for the Order Details table to make it current.
2. You'll see an empty column at the right of the table with the heading Add Column. Click anywhere in this column and type the following DAX formula

(instead of typing the table and column names, it's much easier to type the letter "o" after the equal sign (=), and use the arrow keys to highlight, then press TAB):

```
='Order Details'[Quantity] * 'Order Details'[UnitPrice]
```

The formula appears in the formula bar as you start to type. When you are finished, press ENTER and you have a new column of data—the column is probably now entitled CalculatedColumn1. The table name is not absolutely necessary, provided you are using columns from the same table. The following syntax is a shorter alternative—in this case, type the letter "q" after the equal sign (=):

```
=[Quantity] * [UnitPrice]
```

3. Rename the column to Sales Amount by double-clicking the column header, typing the new name, and finally pressing ENTER. Your result should look like Figure 2-27.

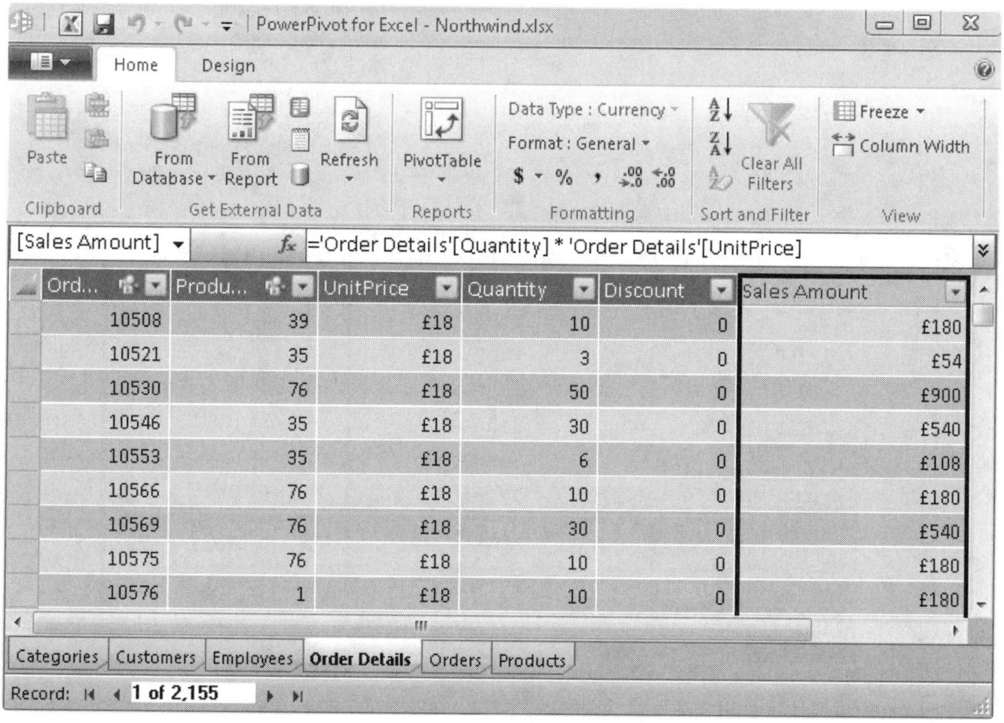

Figure 2-27   *DAX calculated column for Sales Amount*

That's the Sales Amount done. Now, to work out the year for each order:

1. Click the Orders tab to make the Orders table current. If you can't click the tab, you might still be in the formula bar—pressing ENTER will exit from the formula bar. Scroll, if necessary, to find the first empty column with a heading of Add Column (or click the Add button on the Design menu). Click in the column and type the following DAX (the single quotes are optional if there is no space in the table name), and then press ENTER:

    ```
    =YEAR('Orders'[OrderDate])
    ```

2. Again, rather than type the table and column name, type the letter "o" and then select 'Orders'[OrderDate] and press TAB. This is known as AutoComplete—it's pretty useful. Rename the column to **Year** and press ENTER. The result is shown in Figure 2-28. The following shorter syntax also works:

    ```
    =YEAR([OrderDate])
    ```

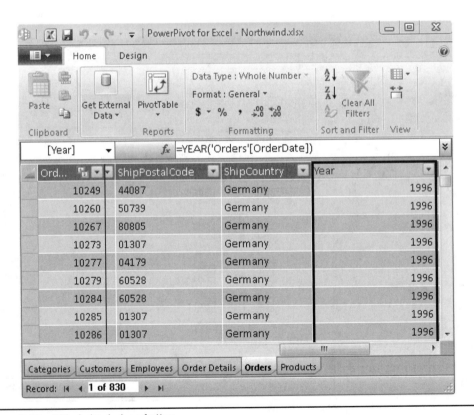

Figure 2-28 *DAX calculated column for Year*

Finally, to put the category name and product name together:

1. Click the Products tab to view the Products table. Click in the Add Column column, and type the following DAX (you can type the letter "c" and use AutoComplete to save typing the table name and the column name). If you type the letter "r" after the equal sign (=), you can save typing the function name in full:

    ```
    =RELATED('Categories'[CategoryName])
    ```

2. Press ENTER to accept the DAX formula (to back out at any time as you enter DAX, press ESC). The single quotes are optional. Rename the column to Category by double-clicking, typing the new name, and pressing ENTER. Hopefully, you are looking at something like Figure 2-29. All of the three DAX formulas here are known as calculated columns.

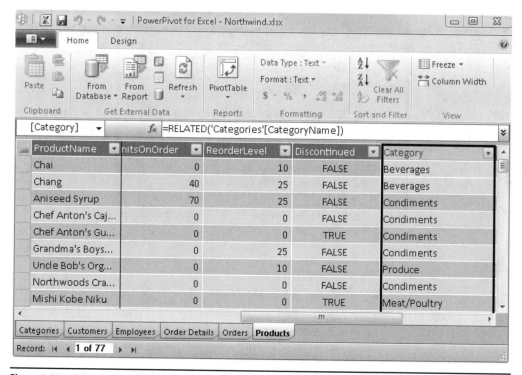

Figure 2-29 *DAX calculated column for Category*

If you are from a business intelligence background and are familiar with SSAS, be aware that you have created a star schema and a cube in a few minutes! In fact, this *is* an SSAS cube—although SSAS is nowhere to be seen. There is a hidden copy of SSAS running behind PowerPivot—even without you having to install SSAS (the hidden copy is installed automatically when you install PowerPivot for Excel). If you are completely new to business intelligence, you have just accomplished something that normally (before PowerPivot) might take days. Cool.

A Quick Pivot Table

It would be nice to see your new "cube" as a cube—we are still looking at our data as separate tables; PowerPivot enables us to do much better. One of the best ways to visualize business intelligence is through a *pivot report*, which can be a pivot table or a pivot chart (or multiple pivot tables and pivot charts). The pivot table uses MultiDimensional eXpressions (MDX) and the Excel CUBE() functions to extract the data from the "hidden," in-memory PowerPivot SSAS cube. Pivot reports incorporate a vast range of functionality. There is a separate chapter later (Chapter 5) just on pivot tables and charts. In this overview chapter we are going to create a simple (yet quite powerful) pivot table just as a starter.

To create a pivot table from PowerPivot tables:

1. Click the Home tab to display the Home ribbon in PowerPivot. In the Reports group of the Home ribbon, click PivotTable followed by PivotTable in the drop-down menu—the menu is shown in Figure 2-30.

2. In the Create PivotTable dialog (Figure 2-31), either accept New Worksheet (the default) or choose Existing Worksheet. You are switched out of the PowerPivot window back into the original Excel workbook, and an empty pivot table is displayed in an Excel worksheet. You can view the underlying connection by

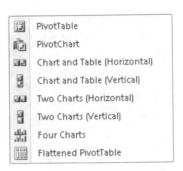

Figure 2-30   *PivotTable menu*

Figure 2-31 *Create PivotTable dialog*

going to the Data ribbon and clicking the Connections button in the Connections group. This opens the Workbook Connections dialog. If you click the Properties button, the Connection Properties dialog opens. In this dialog, the Definition tab shows a data source of $Embedded$ in the Connection string text box. Under no circumstances should you attempt to make any changes—you may lose the connection altogether.

At the right of the worksheet, there is the PowerPivot Field List (this is often simply called the *Field list*). This lists tables and columns from PowerPivot, as well as drop-zones labeled Slicers Vertical, Slicers Horizontal, Report Filter, Column Labels, Row Labels, and Values. If you can't see the PowerPivot Field List, click inside the pivot table itself. If you still can't see it, with the focus inside the pivot table, click Field List in the Show/Hide group of the Excel PowerPivot ribbon.

Before we begin to add table columns to the pivot table, try just one more DAX formula. The reason for doing so is to give you a quick glimpse of the second main use for DAX. This is to create measures—the previous three DAX formulas were used for calculated columns. Chapter 3 examines the difference between calculated columns and measures in some depth. For now, it's sufficient to know that a *measure* is often a numeric value that appears in the main body of the pivot table (Values drop-zone in the PowerPivot Field List) and allows you to create totals, subtotals, and other context-sensitive calculations. Measures are often called *facts* or *metrics*—we are going to create one that shows sales of individual product and category as percentages of total sales. Calculated columns allow you to expand upon your source data and are often attributes that describe the measures. Calculated columns are often added to the slicers, columns, or rows of a pivot table; they give your measures context.

You have just created a calculated column called Year, if you are following the practicals. As a result, you can analyze sales by year. The Sales Amount calculated column created earlier can be used as a measure. When you explicitly create a measure (using the following steps), it's done from the Excel workbook. These explicit measures *generally* appear as numeric values in the center of the pivot table. When you create a calculated column, you do so in the PowerPivot window. Calculated columns can be used as attributes that describe, and are used to slice and dice, the values in a pivot table (Year is an example—for SSAS and MDX veterans, such attributes are the equivalent of non-measure dimension attributes in SSAS cubes) *or* they can be used as measures (Sales Amount is an example). To add a calculated DAX measure:

1. In Excel, click New Measure in the Measures group of the PowerPivot ribbon to open the Measure Settings dialog (Figure 2-32).

    The Measure Settings dialog is where you specify the name and the DAX formula for the new measure. In addition, you also select a PowerPivot table to act as a host for the measure. It's a good idea to assign new measures to a table that already contains measures (or facts or metrics). In this case, Order Details is perfect. It already has a source column called Quantity—this came directly from the source data and is a good candidate for a measure. In addition, there is a calculated column, called Sales Amount, which can be used as a measure. Choose Order Details as the Table name. When you explicitly create a measure, as here, you won't see it if you flip to the PowerPivot window. However, of course, you could see Sales Amount, which is a calculated column used as a measure, and Year and Category. In addition, in the PowerPivot Field List, an explicit, calculated measure has a small calculator icon—a calculated column has no special symbol and looks just like any other column in a table.

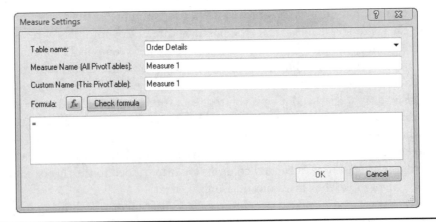

Figure 2-32   *Measure Settings dialog*

2. Enter **DAXMeasure** as the Measure Name. This is reflected in the Custom Name. The first name is the generic name for the measure. By default, this is the name of the measure in all pivot tables and charts. You can override this name on an individual pivot table basis by changing the Custom Name property. To do so, while viewing any pivot table or chart, click the measure in the field list of the PowerPivot Field List and then click Measure Settings on the PowerPivot ribbon. Any custom name you enter is then valid for that pivot table or chart.

3. In the Formula text box, enter either of the two following DAX formulas (as shown in Figure 2-33):

```
=SUM([Sales Amount])/CALCULATE(SUM([Sales Amount]),ALL('Order
Details'))
=SUM('Order Details'[Sales Amount])/
CALCULATE(SUM('Order Details'[Sales Amount]),ALL('Order Details'))
```

This formula (whichever version you used) is calculates the Sales Amount, of whatever is being viewed in the pivot table, divided by the total Sales Amount of all records in the Order Details table. The DAX syntax involved is covered thoroughly later in the book—so don't be too concerned if it's not exactly intuitive. For now, it's more important to concentrate upon the results. Remember to use letters first and then

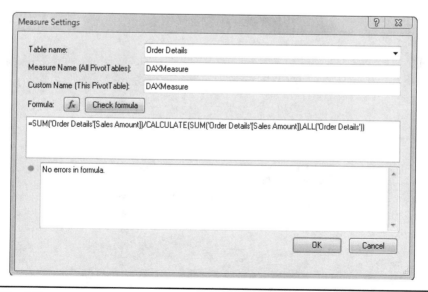

Figure 2-33 *DAX measure*

the TAB key as you type to fully exploit AutoComplete. Notice, also, how matching parentheses are highlighted as you type—this helps to eliminate parenthesis mismatch in your formulas. Click Check Formula to verify your syntax, and then click OK.

In the PowerPivot Field List, you should see the new measure under the Order Details table (you might need to expand the table in the field list, or right-click to see expansion options) as in Figure 2-34. If you need to edit the formula, select it in the PowerPivot Field List and click Measure Settings on the Excel PowerPivot ribbon. Our new explicit, calculated measure, DAXMeasure, has a small calculator icon. The calculated column, Sales Amount, does not. The new measure is also added to the Values drop-zone—if it's not, drag it from the PowerPivot Field List to the drop-zone.

Figure 2-34   *PowerPivot Field List*

Now, to populate the rest of the pivot table:

1. First, drag Sales Amount (Order Details table) from the field list in the PowerPivot Field List to the Values drop-zone, just below the DAXMeasure. It appears in the drop-zone as Sum of Sales Amount. Right-click and choose Edit Measure. Change the Custom Name to **DAXColumn** and click OK.

2. Click on the value for DAXColumn in the pivot table itself. Now click the PivotTable Tools tab to display the PivotTable Tools, Options ribbon. Verify that the Active Field in the Active Field group is DAXColumn and click Field Settings in the same group. In the subsequent Value Field Setting dialog, click the Number Format button to open the Format Cells dialog. Choose Currency as the format and click OK twice to exit both dialogs.

3. Drag Sales Amount a *second* time to the Values drop-zone, below the original. Rename it as before, but this time, call it GUIColumn. Right-click the value for GUIColumn in the pivot table, and move the mouse over Show Values As in the context menu. From the flyout menu, choose % of Grand Total.

4. Select the value for DAXMeasure in the pivot table, and from the PivotTable Tools ribbon, click Field Settings. Click the Number Format button in the dialog and choose Percentage before clicking OK twice. Your pivot table should look like Figure 2-35, although your currency symbol for the DAXColumn value may be $, or €, or otherwise.

5. From the Customers table in the PowerPivot Field List field list, drag first Country, then City to the Row Labels drop-zone—and observe the pivot table. Make sure that City is positioned below Country.

6. From the Products table, drag Category, then ProductName to the Column Labels drop-zone, and again watch the pivot table.

7. Right-click on Argentina in the pivot table and move the mouse over Expand/Collapse. In the flyout menu, choose Collapse Entire Field. Repeat this for Beverages in the pivot table.

	A	B	C	D
1	DAXMeasure	DAXColumn	GUIColumn	
2	100.00%	£1,354,458.59	100.00%	
3				
4				
5				

Sheet1 Sheet2 Sheet3

Figure 2-35 *Initial pivot table*

8. Drag Year from the Orders table to the Slicers Horizontal drop-zone. Do the same for the Category column from the Products table.

9. Finally, drag LastName from the Employees table to the Report Filter drop-zone. Hopefully, your pivot table is similar to Figure 2-36.

How many ways would you like to filter your BI report? Here are a few options—a later chapter (Chapter 5) covers pivot table filtering in more detail. Pivot table filtering is different from filtering the source data in the PowerPivot window—the latter restricts the data available in the pivot table. If you want to quickly experiment with filters, try these:

1. Click any year in the Year slicer. To select two years, hold down the CTRL key *after* having selected the first one. If you hold down the CTRL key *before* clicking the first one, you can toggle your choices in the slicer. To remove the current slice, click the small filter funnel icon at the top right of the slicer.

		Beverages			Condiments		
Row Labels	DAXMeasure	DAXColumn	GUIColumn	DAXMeasure	DAXColumn	GUIColumn
Argentina	0.13%	£1,798.00	0.13%	0.07%	£907.00	0.07%
Austria	1.95%	£26,452.05	1.95%	1.24%	£16,802.40	1.24%
Belgium	0.43%	£5,864.40	0.43%	0.20%	£2,714.70	0.20%
Brazil	2.98%	£40,400.50	2.98%	0.90%	£12,139.00	0.90%
Canada	1.02%	£13,829.70	1.02%	0.37%	£5,010.60	0.37%
Denmark	0.89%	£12,025.70	0.89%	0.33%	£4,455.40	0.33%
Finland	0.16%	£2,222.00	0.16%	0.14%	£1,873.00	0.14%
France	1.01%	£13,670.00	1.01%	0.53%	£7,148.40	0.53%
Germany	4.26%	£57,644.60	4.26%	1.28%	£17,395.10	1.28%
Ireland	0.25%	£3,339.40	0.25%	0.29%	£3,898.50	0.29%
Italy	0.09%	£1,155.00	0.09%	0.11%	£1,448.25	0.11%

Figure 2-36   *Completed pivot table*

2. Click any category in the Category slicer. You can slice on both Year and Category at the same time, if you wish.

3. Click the drop-down button next to the Row Labels caption and select a country or two. To see all of the countries again, click once more and choose Clear Filter from Country. You can also sort rows and columns through the filter button (for columns, the button is next to the Column Labels caption).

4. There is also a Report Filter called LastName. The filter button is in the adjacent cell with the caption All. Try an employee or two. To remove this filter, choose All from the drop-down.

Slicers, Report Filters, and Row/Column Labels filters are all activated differently! However, they all have the same ultimate effect—they change the context of the measures in the value section of the pivot table. They are also interdependent. For example, you can choose Beverages from the slicer or the Column Labels filter, and each updates the other. If you watch the DAXColumn, GUIColumn, and DAXMeasure values changing, it can be tricky at first to understand what's happening. It may be easier if you observe the figures for the Grand Total for Total DAXColumn, Total GUIColumn, and TotalDAXMeasure. The DAXColumn measure was created as a calculated column (a DAX formula) in the PowerPivot window. The GUIColumn measure was created from the DAXColumn using the mouse, in the GUI of the pivot table. The DAXMeasure measure was created directly as a calculated measure in the Excel workbook. There are so many possibilities for creating and filtering your BI!

NOTE

Observe how GUIColumn and DAXMeasure behave. With no filters, they are the same. When you impose a filter, they are often different. This is because the GUIColumn is sensitive to the current filter context. The DAXMeasure uses the DAX keyword ALL *to override the current filter context. These topics are discussed in more detail in Chapter 4.*

A Very Quick Pivot Chart

You are not limited to pivot tables to display your PowerPivot data. Pivot charts can add dramatic visualization to your business intelligence. If done sensibly, pivot charts can bring your pivot tables to life and immediately highlight interesting information. Of course, if pivot charts are overly elaborate, they can also obfuscate the data—you can easily turn your business intelligence back into relatively meaningless data. Our example, coming up shortly, is deliberately simple and hopefully clear.

There are three ways in which to add pivot charts. First, you can return to the PowerPivot window and choose the PivotTable drop-down from the Reports group of the Home ribbon. Then, from the drop-down, choose any option that mentions PivotChart or Charts. Second, you can use the same options from the PivotTable drop-down in the Report group of the PowerPivot ribbon in the Excel workbook. Both of these approaches generally create a new pivot chart that is not directly linked to an existing pivot table—in fact, a new pivot table is created as the basis for the pivot chart. The third method, instigated from the PivotTable Tools group on the Options ribbon in the Excel workbook, makes it easy to base the pivot chart on an existing pivot table. In this example, we'll use the latter, as it's so convenient:

1. Remove the GUIColumn and DAXMeasure columns from your pivot table. An easy way to do so is to right-click the column name in the Values drop-zone and choose Remove Field. You should have one value remaining, DAXColumn, which represents Sales Amount.

2. In the Category horizontal slicer, click Beverages and, while holding down the CTRL key, click Condiments. You can also drag with the mouse. Your pivot table should look like Figure 2-37.

3. Click the drop-down button next to the Row Labels caption. Click Select All to remove all the check marks, and turn on Canada and USA. Click OK to close the drop-down.

4. Click PivotTable Tools | Options to see its ribbon. If you can't see PivotTable Tools at the top of the Excel window, click anywhere inside the pivot table (clicking inside a slicer is not sufficient). In the Tools group, click PivotChart, accept the default of the first Column style of chart, and click OK.

5. Drag the pivot chart to a convenient location and, while holding down the CTRL key, click Confections in the horizontal slicer. My result is shown in Figure 2-38. Yours may differ somewhat if you have been experimenting with filters (for example, the LastName Report Filter or the Year slicer). That's not too important at this stage. What is important is that you have created, in just a few seconds, a very powerful visualization of your business intelligence.

Notice that many of the pivot table filters are replicated in the pivot chart. You can use either or both. The chart duplicates the Report Filter on LastName and the Column/Row Labels filters. The pivot table slicers are not reproduced in the pivot chart—simply use the ones above the pivot table. The Category filter in the chart is from the pivot table's Column Labels filter and is not the Category slicer, although the two are interdependent.

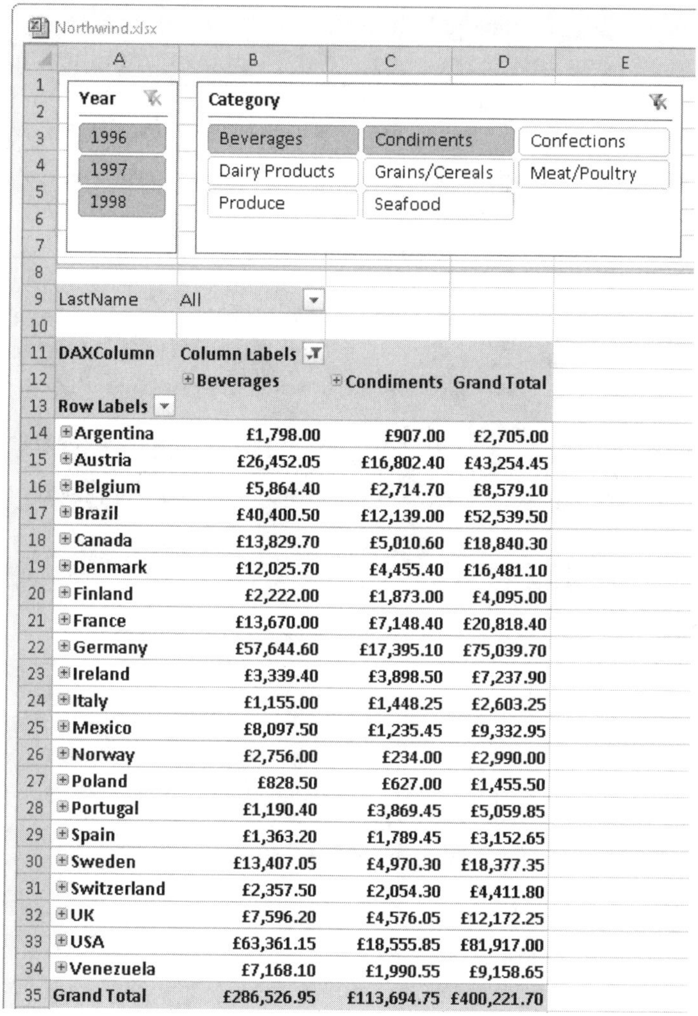

DAXColumn	Column Labels		
	Beverages	Condiments	Grand Total
Row Labels			
Argentina	£1,798.00	£907.00	£2,705.00
Austria	£26,452.05	£16,802.40	£43,254.45
Belgium	£5,864.40	£2,714.70	£8,579.10
Brazil	£40,400.50	£12,139.00	£52,539.50
Canada	£13,829.70	£5,010.60	£18,840.30
Denmark	£12,025.70	£4,455.40	£16,481.10
Finland	£2,222.00	£1,873.00	£4,095.00
France	£13,670.00	£7,148.40	£20,818.40
Germany	£57,644.60	£17,395.10	£75,039.70
Ireland	£3,339.40	£3,898.50	£7,237.90
Italy	£1,155.00	£1,448.25	£2,603.25
Mexico	£8,097.50	£1,235.45	£9,332.95
Norway	£2,756.00	£234.00	£2,990.00
Poland	£828.50	£627.00	£1,455.50
Portugal	£1,190.40	£3,869.45	£5,059.85
Spain	£1,363.20	£1,789.45	£3,152.65
Sweden	£13,407.05	£4,970.30	£18,377.35
Switzerland	£2,357.50	£2,054.30	£4,411.80
UK	£7,596.20	£4,576.05	£12,172.25
USA	£63,361.15	£18,555.85	£81,917.00
Venezuela	£7,168.10	£1,990.55	£9,158.65
Grand Total	£286,526.95	£113,694.75	£400,221.70

Figure 2-37 *Filtered pivot table*

Well done! In this PowerPivot overview chapter, you have already transformed raw source data into BI. Along the way, you've discovered some (but not all) of the major features of PowerPivot. Before the advent of PowerPivot, this would have taken you a little bit longer—and probably, it would not have been quite so straightforward. Within a few minutes, unfriendly and fragmented data has become both meaningful (information) and easily visualized and discovered (business intelligence).

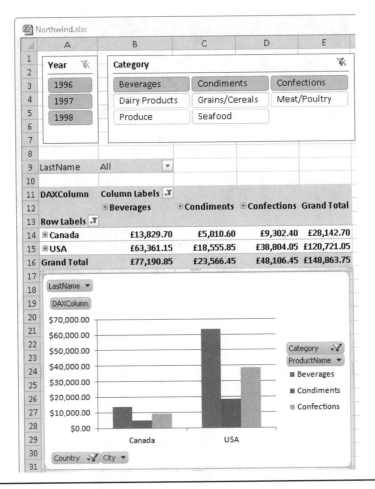

Figure 2-38 *A pivot chart*

Of course, there are other aspects to PowerPivot. For instance, there are many other ways of assembling data. Filtering warrants further investigation (you are not limited to filtering a pivot table or chart). You can also sort data and perform sophisticated analysis (for example, increases in sales from year to year with a couple of mouse clicks). Perhaps we should look further at relationships—you can even join data from relational tables to data from multidimensional cubes (that's quite tricky to do if you rely solely on SQL or MDX, but it's easy in PowerPivot)! And we have hardly begun to exploit the tremendous versatility of DAX. These topics (and more) are covered in subsequent chapters. But, hopefully, this overview chapter has revealed a few of the incredible possibilities. The next chapter is an in-depth guide to all that is PowerPivot.

Chapter 3

PowerPivot: In-Depth

This chapter goes a lot further than the previous two introductory chapters. It's a detailed and comprehensive guide to all of the ribbons: Excel PowerPivot ribbon, PowerPivot Home ribbon, PowerPivot Design ribbon, and PowerPivot Linked Table ribbon. All of the ribbon groups and buttons are discussed, some with step-by-step examples for you to follow. In the course of this chapter, you will become familiar with most of the dialog boxes and menus that are relevant to PowerPivot. This is essentially a grand tour of the PowerPivot graphical user interface. Everything you are likely to meet in a PowerPivot window is covered. The DAX language is introduced only briefly; Chapter 4 is specifically devoted to DAX. Many of the later chapters in the book provide a reference guide to DAX syntax. Pivot table manipulation and customization are covered in Chapter 5.

The main emphasis of this chapter is on how to assemble your data in PowerPivot. There is also a discussion of relationships between PowerPivot tables, including multidimensional to relational relationships. The main data sources used in this chapter are relational, multidimensional, flat files, Excel (including linked tables), and data feeds. There is even a little MDX!

▶   **Key concepts**   Importing data, relating data, refreshing data, filtering and sorting data, formatting data, DAX calculated column, MDX calculated measure, SQL and MDX query design, PowerPivot data in a pivot table

In this chapter, we take a more detailed look at some of the PowerPivot features. The last two chapters presented a quick start and an overview—this time, it's a more comprehensive and in-depth look, especially of what can be achieved largely by point-and-click. Don't worry, there is plenty of DAX in later chapters!

Most of the features you will use for PowerPivot and PowerPivot pivot tables are in four main areas. These are the PowerPivot ribbon in Excel; the Home and Design ribbons (you may also sometimes see a third Linked Table ribbon) in PowerPivot itself; the PowerPivot Field List in Excel; and the PivotTable Tools Options and Design ribbons in Excel. In general terms, the first two are used to assemble the necessary data and add a pivot table to a worksheet in Excel. The last two are used to place and customize the data in the pivot table. Chapter 5 will consider pivot reports (tables and charts) in depth, and will take a close look at the PowerPivot Field List and the PivotTable Tools Options and Design ribbons. This chapter concentrates on preparing the data, and it deals with the PowerPivot ribbon in Excel and the Home and Design and Linked Table ribbons in PowerPivot. Let's start with the PowerPivot ribbon in Excel.

PowerPivot Ribbon in Excel

Figure 3-1 shows the PowerPivot ribbon in Excel. This ribbon is divided into seven groups: Launch, Measures, Report, Excel Data, Options, Show/Hide, and Relationship. A couple of these groups contain more than one button or icon.

Launch Group

The Launch group contains a single button called PowerPivot Window. This opens a new PowerPivot window and creates an empty PowerPivot model in memory, if one is not already open. If you already have a PowerPivot window open, the button switches you into PowerPivot. In addition, you could also use the Windows task bar, or press ALT-TAB, to switch to PowerPivot, if it's already open.

Measures Group

The Measures group has three buttons. New Measure is used to create a new calculated measure for your pivot tables or charts in the current Excel workbook. You do so by entering a suitable DAX formula composed of one or more DAX functions. Delete Measure is used to remove an existing measure that you had already created with New Measure. Finally, the Measure Settings button allows you to modify the DAX formula you initially entered when creating a new measure. Chapter 4 gives you an overview of DAX formulas. Later, a whole section of the book (Part II) is devoted to a comprehensive reference to all DAX functions.

Report Group

The Report group has just the one button labeled PivotTable. This opens a drop-down menu that enables you to insert a pivot table or a pivot chart, or both, into an Excel worksheet. The menu is shown in Figure 3-2. The pivot report (table and/or chart) will be based on the data in your PowerPivot window. It duplicates the functionality of the PivotTable button in the Reports (yes, Reports, not Report!) group of the PowerPivot Home ribbon. Once you have your PowerPivot data, you can insert a pivot report into an Excel worksheet from either Excel or PowerPivot.

Figure 3-1   *PowerPivot ribbon in Excel*

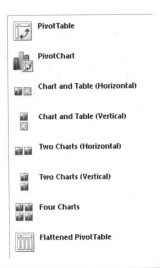

Figure 3-2 *PivotTable menu*

Excel Data Group

The Excel Data group consists of two buttons. The Create Linked Table button enables you to create a PowerPivot table from a table in an Excel worksheet. This only works with tables in the current Excel workbook. If you have a simple data range in a worksheet (as opposed to an Excel table), it will automatically be converted into an Excel table, complete with column headers. This has two implications. One, any data in the current workbook must be explicitly or implicitly converted to a table. Two, if you wish to import data into PowerPivot from an external Excel workbook, you must either use the From Other Sources button in the Get External Data group of the Home ribbon in PowerPivot itself, or copy and paste (more on external Excel workbooks later in this chapter). If you wish to try out linked tables with PowerPivot, here are a few very simple steps to get you started:

1. Enter some data into a cell in an Excel worksheet. You can enter a number or some text. For this example, we are not using a column header, although you could do so if you wanted.

2. With the focus on the same cell, go to the Home ribbon in Excel, and from the Styles group, click Format as Table and choose a style. In the ensuing dialog, click OK. Your data is now explicitly formatted as an Excel table, perhaps with a column heading of Column1.

3. To convert the Excel table into a PowerPivot table, go to the PowerPivot ribbon. Make sure the focus is within the table, and then click the Create Linked Table button in the Excel Data group. This switches you into the PowerPivot window.

If this is the first time you tried this, your PowerPivot table is probably called Table1. Notice the linked table symbol on the Table tab. If the original Excel table was created without column headings, the column in the PowerPivot table is called Column1. You can then right-click (or double-click) to rename either the PowerPivot table or the PowerPivot column heading.

4. Switch back to Excel and change the data you originally entered. You can go back to Excel by clicking Switch to Workbook on the Quick Access toolbar in PowerPivot. If you now switch back to PowerPivot, you can see that the data in the linked table has been automatically refreshed. This raises an interesting question: If PowerPivot tables are automatically updated by changes to data in an Excel linked table, why is there an Update All button in the Excel Data group? The answer lies in the PowerPivot window itself. When you add your first linked table to PowerPivot, it acquires a new third contextual ribbon called Linked Table. This has just one group, Linked Tables. One of the buttons in this group is labeled Update Mode. This button opens a small drop-down menu where you can set the update mode. The default is Automatic, which is why your PowerPivot table was refreshed when you made a change to the Excel table. The only other option is Manual. If you set it to manual, then you can use the Update All button in the PowerPivot ribbon in Excel. There is also an Update All button in the Linked Tables group of the Linked Table ribbon in PowerPivot itself. Both Update All buttons will refresh all data from *all* linked tables in PowerPivot. In PowerPivot itself, there is also an Update Selected button, but this refreshes only the current PowerPivot table.

5. The real world is the real world, and not a textbook. Errors occur—so here we are going to deliberately cause one. Delete the original table in the Excel worksheet— you can do so by selecting the table cell and its column header and pressing DEL. Now click the Update All button on the PowerPivot ribbon (you can also use the Update All button on the Linked Table ribbon in PowerPivot). Even if the update mode is set to automatic, this forces an immediate manual refresh of the linked table data in PowerPivot. Of course, the original Excel table no longer exists and the Errors in Linked Tables dialog opens. This dialog is shown in Figure 3-3.

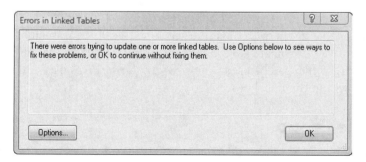

Figure 3-3   *Errors in Linked Tables dialog*

Figure 3-4   *Select Action dialog*

You could always click OK and ignore the error, but try the Options button. This opens another dialog called Select Action, which is shown in Figure 3-4. Your choices here include: Do Nothing, Change Excel Table Name, Remove Link to Excel Table, and Delete PowerPivot Table. The second option is disabled unless you had renamed (rather than deleted) the original Excel table. The first option ignores the error. The third option preserves the PowerPivot table but removes the link. The fourth option totally removes the table from PowerPivot. Select Delete PowerPivot Table and click OK. If you switch to the PowerPivot window, you can see that the table has disappeared.

Options Group

The Options group has a single button labeled Settings. This leads to the PowerPivot Options & Diagnostics dialog. In this dialog there are a number of advanced settings—it also displays the version number of your PowerPivot. The advanced settings are beyond the scope of this introductory book, but please note the check box on the Support & Diagnostics page labeled Enable PowerPivot Tracing for the Current Excel Session. If you enable this, a trace file is created. The trace file can then be opened in SQL Server Profiler—if you are a SQL Server administrator, you may already be aware that SQL Server Profiler can be used against SSAS. PowerPivot uses a hidden copy of SSAS running within the Excel process, so it works with SQL Server Profiler.

Show/Hide Group

There is a single Field List button in this group. Once you have a PowerPivot pivot report (table or chart) in your Excel worksheet and the focus is on the pivot report, you can toggle the PowerPivot Field List on and off. Pivot tables and PowerPivot Field Lists are covered in detail in Chapter 5.

Relationship Group

The Relationship group has a single item, Detection. This is useful when you import data into PowerPivot from a non-relational source or from multiple sources and you wish to relate PowerPivot tables. Relationships are covered later in this chapter when we discuss the PowerPivot Design ribbon, which has a Relationships group. When you click Detection in Excel, you can toggle automatic detection of relationships off and on. When Detection is turned on (the default setting), PowerPivot will try to find and automatically implement relationships between PowerPivot tables in the PowerPivot Field List. When you use the Relationships group on the PowerPivot Design ribbon, you manually create the relationships, if they don't already exist. It is recommended that you create relationships manually—it gives you that much more control, and the automatic detection may not find every relationship you require and may do so in a way that you don't want.

That concludes our tour of the PowerPivot ribbon in Excel. It's time to move on to the ribbons in the PowerPivot window itself. There are two main ribbons that are always visible: Home and Design. If you have a linked Excel table in PowerPivot, you will have a third contextual ribbon called Linked Table—it's only visible if the linked table is current. Let's start with the Home ribbon: You must be in the PowerPivot window and *not* the Excel workbook (as a reminder, use the PowerPivot Window button in the Excel PowerPivot ribbon to switch to PowerPivot).

Home Ribbon in PowerPivot

Whenever you open PowerPivot, the Home ribbon is the default ribbon. If PowerPivot is already open and you switch to PowerPivot from Excel, PowerPivot remembers the last ribbon, so you may need to click the Home tab to see the Home ribbon, if you had previously been looking at the Design ribbon (or the Linked Table ribbon, if you had been viewing a linked table in PowerPivot). The Home ribbon is shown in Figure 3-5.

Clipboard Group

The first button, Paste, creates a *new* PowerPivot table and copies in data from the Clipboard. This is yet another way of moving Excel data (though the Clipboard data doesn't necessarily have to originate in Excel) into PowerPivot. The second and third

Figure 3-5 *Home ribbon in PowerPivot*

buttons in the Clipboard group, Paste Append and Paste Replace, are only operative when you are viewing a PowerPivot table created through the Paste button. Please note that Paste Replace will replace the whole table; thus, if you have only one piece of data on the Clipboard, this will overwrite the entire table. The Copy button allows you to copy data between PowerPivot tables. After using Copy, you can use Paste to create a new table or Paste Append or Paste Replace to place the copied data into a table previously created through Paste. You can't copy and paste between existing PowerPivot tables, but you can paste into a new PowerPivot table. There is an additional use for Copy—you can subsequently paste into an Excel worksheet, if you want to perform traditional Excel analysis on the data, or into another application such as Word or PowerPoint.

Get External Data Group

The Get External Data group represents the core of PowerPivot. It includes all of the main data sources for your PowerPivot tables (with the exception of linked Excel tables and Clipboard data). It is of vital importance, so we'll devote some time to looking at its buttons and features. The buttons in this group (reading from top to bottom and left to right) are From Database, From Report, From Data Feeds, From Text, From Other Sources, and Refresh. All of these buttons, apart from the Refresh button, result in further dialogs or drop-downs. The Refresh button is disabled until you have imported some data. Let's start with From Database.

From Database

The From Database button results in three main options: SQL Server, Access, and Analysis Services or PowerPivot. As SQL Server appears first and is so popular, we'll consider it first. Even if you don't have SQL Server, I advise you to read the section—some topics covered (for example, query writing and filtering) are common to many of the PowerPivot data import options. The From Database drop-down menu is shown in Figure 3-6.

From SQL Server   The previous chapter has step-by-step instructions and a practical on how to import SQL Server tables—in case you jumped into the book at this point.

If you choose SQL Server, you have to provide a server name, a database name, and select the relevant tables and/or views (alternatively, you can write a Select statement

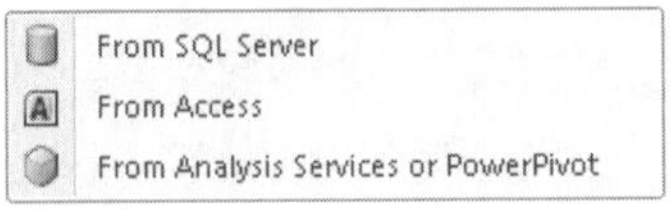

Figure 3-6   *From Database drop-down menu*

or type the name of a stored procedure that returns data). We looked at SQL Server imports in the previous chapter—but please notice that in the Select Tables and Views stage of the Table Import Wizard, there is a Preview & Filter button (the Select Tables and Views stage does not appear if you chose to write your own query). The Select Tables and Views dialog is shown in Figure 3-7. If you click the Preview & Filter button, it opens a Preview Selected Table dialog on the currently selected table. This dialog is shown in Figure 3-8. As well as showing a preview of the data, it allows you to turn off those columns you don't need (in effect, you are writing a Select column list). In addition, each column has a small drop-down button that lets you filter and/or sort the data—in effect, you are writing a SQL Where and/or Order By clause. If you change your mind about filtering the data, you can click the Clear Row Filters button or reopen the filter drop-down in the column heading and choose (Select All) or Clear Filter From. You can also filter and/or sort data retrospectively in the PowerPivot window or in a pivot table in Excel. Filtering data at this import stage or in the PowerPivot

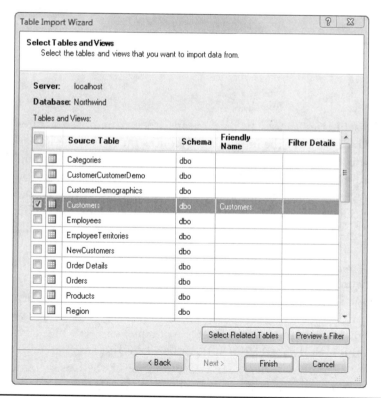

Figure 3-7   *Select Tables and Views dialog*

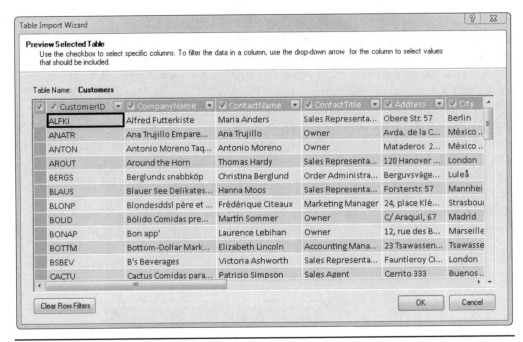

Figure 3-8 *Preview Selected Table dialog*

window (that is, filtering the source data) means you can't remove the filter later in a pivot table. Filtering data at the import stage reduces the size of the PowerPivot model. You can also add, change, or remove filters and sorts you impose during the Table Import Wizard by using the Table Properties button in the Properties group of the PowerPivot Design ribbon—so it's not a disaster if you get it wrong in the first place.

As just mentioned, you can opt to write your own queries instead of choosing tables and/or views. The query can be your own Select statement, or you can call a stored procedure that contains a Select statement and returns data. The choice is shown in the Choose How to Import the Data stage of the Table Import Wizard. This dialog is shown in Figure 3-9. If you turn on the option button for Write a Query That Will Specify the Data to Import, and click Next, you will be in the Specify a SQL Query dialog, which is shown in Figure 3-10. In this dialog you can give your query a name (this will be the name of your PowerPivot table) and type in your SQL Select statement. As this is SQL Server, the SQL will be T-SQL (Transact-SQL), which is the SQL dialect supported by SQL Server. Note, however, the Design button. This is easily missed, but it's very, very useful, especially if your SQL is a little rusty! Clicking this button opens a query designer in graphical mode. This graphical query designer for

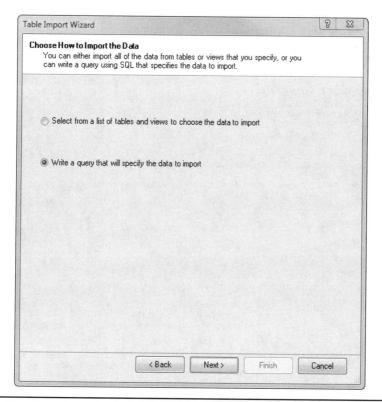

Figure 3-9 *Choose How to Import the Data dialog*

SQL is shown in Figure 3-11. The Edit as Text button, at the top left, toggles between graphical mode and text mode. If you make changes in text mode, you will lose any previous changes you made in graphical mode. The Import button allows you to use prewritten SQL script files. The Run Query button displays the results of your query in the Query Results pane at the bottom of the designer, so you can check whether your query is working as you want. This Query Results pane can be collapsed and expanded, as can the Selected Fields, Relationships, and Applied Filters panes at the right of the designer. The Database View pane to the left enables you to add tables or views or stored procedures to the query. In addition, you can choose particular columns from your tables or views. And, as a really nice touch, you can choose the columns you want from a stored procedure that returns data. The columns you choose are shown in the Selected Fields pane. In the same pane, the Aggregate column has a drop-down that you can use to create Group By columns and aggregate functions on other columns, such as Sum or Count.

Figure 3-10 *Specify a SQL Query dialog*

If you add two or more tables, the designer should pick up any relationships in your source data and display them in the Relationships pane. Should there be no relationships, you might try clicking Auto Detect to automatically add relationships. Alternatively, you can click the Add Relationship button (the third from the left) and choose your own fields for the join. If you do so, the Edit Fields button lets you change the columns used in the relationship. You can also add relationships between tables in PowerPivot later, but creating them at this point makes a fast PowerPivot even faster, as you are effectively denormalizing data before importing.

The Applied Filters pane has an Add Filter button (the first one on the left). This adds a Where clause to your query. Some of the options for the Where clause include Is (=) and Like. This feature and all of the other features in the query designer help you write your SQL. However, it's even more of a help if you already understand SQL, so you have some idea what it's doing for you! When you click OK to exit the designer, you can see the SQL generated in the Specify a SQL Query dialog. If you want to know a little more about writing SQL queries, please refer to Appendix A or to my book *Practical SQL Queries for Microsoft SQL Server 2008* (McGraw-Hill/Professional, 2010).

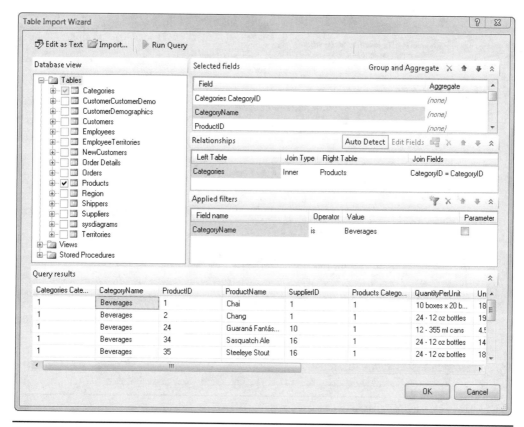

Figure 3-11   *SQL graphical query designer*

From Access   The previous chapter has step-by-step instructions and a practical on how to import Access tables—in case you jumped into the book at this point.

SQL Server is going to be a common choice for many readers' source data. Access is also likely to be very popular. As a reminder, you are not limited to only one type of data source—you can mix and match. For example, you might have a few PowerPivot tables from SQL Server *and* a few from Access. If you choose Access, in the first Connect to a Microsoft Access Database dialog, you will see a Browse button. The Connect to a Microsoft Access Database dialog is shown in Figure 3-12. Clicking this Browse button will assist you in locating your Access database without typing pathnames and filenames. The Browse button leads to an Open dialog. There is a drop-down at the bottom right that includes both .accdb (Access 2007 and 2010) and .mdb (pre-Access 2007) Access database types. Apart from that, importing from Access is very similar to importing from SQL Server. You get to decide whether to pick tables or to write your own queries.

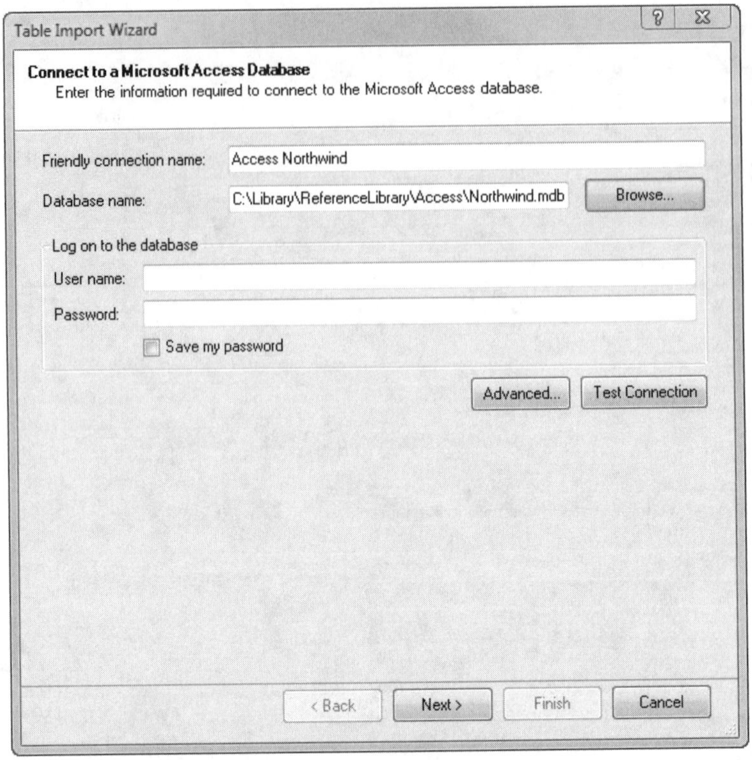

Figure 3-12 *Connect to a Microsoft Access Database dialog*

When you elect to pick tables, you will not see the schema names as you do with SQL Server. When you elect to write your own query, you have to type your own Access SQL; there is no handy graphical query designer as there is for SQL Server.

From Analysis Services or PowerPivot Importing from SSAS or PowerPivot was not covered in the previous chapter. And, as it's going to be so important to many readers, it's worth a detailed look here.

There are two important preliminary points to make. One (and you may be asking this if you are already familiar with SSAS cubes), why bother to create an on-the-fly PowerPivot cube when you already have a prebuilt SSAS cube? Two, why do SSAS and PowerPivot appear as import options on the same menu choice?

The beauty of importing from an SSAS cube is that you are no longer limited to cube data. You can combine SSAS multidimensional cube data with SQL Server relational data, for example, or with data from many other sources. Furthermore, you can create relationships between multidimensional and relational data, and, of course, display both in the same pivot table. Combining multidimensional and relational data is very difficult without PowerPivot. You have to know an awful lot of SQL and MDX! In PowerPivot, it only takes a few mouse clicks and maybe one or two simple DAX functions to create the mother of all data marts! PowerPivot uses a hidden copy of SSAS running in the Excel process space. As such, importing into PowerPivot from another PowerPivot or from SSAS are virtually the same under the hood. There is one proviso: In order to import PowerPivot tables into PowerPivot for Excel, the source PowerPivot must be PowerPivot for SharePoint (that is, from a PowerPivot workbook that has been published to a PowerPivot-enabled SharePoint document library) and *not* PowerPivot for Excel.

Here is a short step-by-step guide (you can try this if you have the SSAS Adventure Works database and cube) to importing into PowerPivot from SSAS:

1. On the Home ribbon in PowerPivot, click From Database in the Get External Data group.

2. From the ensuing drop-down, choose From Analysis Services or PowerPivot. This opens the Connect to Microsoft SQL Server Analysis Services dialog. In this dialog, you specify an SSAS server and database name. The dialog is shown in Figure 3-13. If you have the SSAS Adventure Works database, select it from the drop-down, or adapt the next few steps to your own SSAS database.

3. Click Next to open the Specify a MDX Query dialog where you can type an MDX query, if you want. The Specify a MDX Query dialog is shown in Figure 3-14. Or, at the bottom right in this dialog, click the Design button. You should be looking at a graphical MDX query designer. This is almost identical to the MDX designer in SQL Server Reporting Services (SSRS) and you may recognize it, except there is no option to switch into Data Mining eXtensions (DMX) from MDX, as there is in SSRS. The graphical query designer is shown in Figure 3-15. PowerPivot currently supports MDX, but not DMX. In the MDX query designer, there is an ellipsis button at the top left, just below the toolbar. This lets you change the cube, but not the database, context. For example, you may see a cube to which you have saved data mining content. Or, if you have SSAS Enterprise Edition, you may see one or more perspectives on a cube.

   Underneath you will see the Metadata pane. This shows the measures (or facts) and dimensions in the cube or perspective. In the Metadata pane there's a drop-down for Measure Group that lets you display all measure groups or a specific measure group. Choosing a specific measure group is quite useful—if you do so, the dimensions shown in the Metadata pane are only those that relate to that specific measure group. How dimensions relate to particular measure groups is determined on the Dimension Usage tab of the SSAS cube designer back in

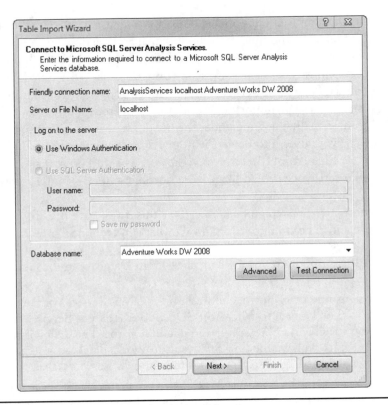

Figure 3-13   *Connect to Microsoft SQL Server Analysis Services dialog*

Business Intelligence Development Studio (BIDS). By showing only one measure group and its related dimensions, you avoid the possibility of creating a query that returns meaningless data. For example, in the Adventure Works cube, Resellers are not related to Internet Sales Amount—if you were to combine the two in a query, by default, you would end up with repeating data. When you add dimensions to the query, these are likely to be added to the Row Labels or Column Labels in a PowerPivot pivot table (they are also eminently suitable for adding to the Report Filter or Slicers Vertical or Slicers Horizontal). When you add measures, they are usually placed in the Values or central section of a pivot table.

4.   Let's add some dimensions (strictly speaking, for those of you who are SSAS veterans, we are going to add some dimension attribute hierarchy members) and some measures. Expand the Date dimension and then the Calendar folder. Drag the Date.Calendar Year attribute hierarchy (it's a blue rectangle, not a blue triangle/pyramid) into the central body of the query—you will see a caption, Drag Levels or Measures Here to Add to the Query. Incidentally, a level is part of a dimension attribute hierarchy (also part of a dimension user hierarchy).

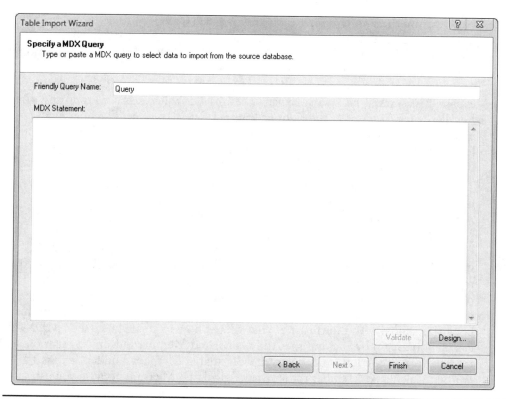

Figure 3-14   *Specify a MDX Query dialog*

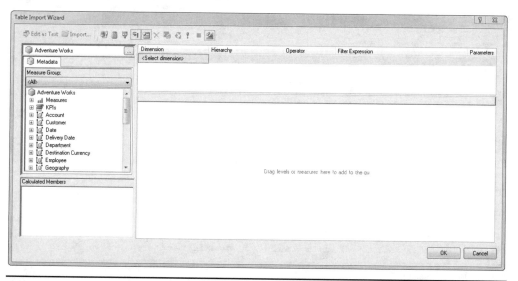

Figure 3-15   *MDX graphical query designer*

5. Now, expand the Product dimension and drag the Category attribute hierarchy just to the right of Calendar Year in the central section. Expand Measures and then expand the Internet Sales measure group folder. Drag Internet Sales Amount to the right of Category. The query can now execute (as the MDX is valid), and you will see years, product categories, and Internet Sales figures. Once again, expand Measures, if necessary. Expand the Reseller Sales measure group and drag Reseller Sales Amount to the right of Internet Sales Amount. The query will re-execute and you should see more year and category combinations—the null values for Internet Sales Amount are now displayed as you have non-null values for Reseller Sales Amount. The results are shown in Figure 3-16.

6. This is a good place to try out a calculated measure. You can have calculated measures as part of your cube design in BIDS—it's created using MDX. Alternatively, you can create calculated measures at this stage, again created using MDX. This is handy when you require an ad-hoc calculation. Or, if you are in a PowerPivot pivot table, you can create the measure there—then you use DAX, not MDX. All three methods are valid and all are feasible. You probably need to try all three! You need to get the right balance between reusability, flexibility, and performance—and that is going to involve some experimentation. SSAS cube design is beyond the scope of this book—but you will learn the DAX way in this book (hopefully!). And in this step, you will see how to create an ad-hoc MDX calculation. Begin by clicking the Add Calculated Member button on the toolbar; it's fourth from the left. This opens the Calculated Member Builder dialog. It's entitled Calculated Member rather than Calculated Measure because you can also create non-measure dimension members. This dialog is shown in Figure 3-17.

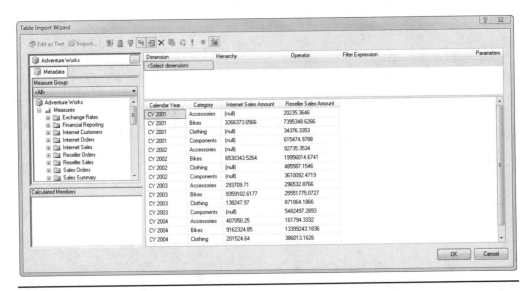

Figure 3-16 *MDX query results*

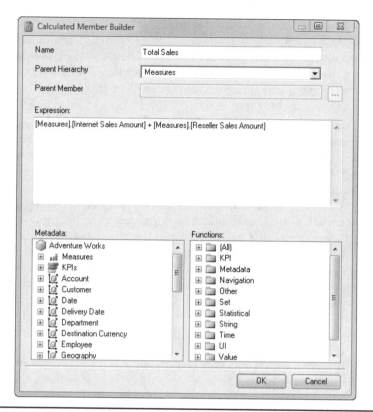

Figure 3-17   *Calculated Member Builder dialog*

7. In the Calculated Member Builder dialog, enter **Total Sales** as the Name and
    make sure the Parent Hierarchy is Measures. Expand Measures in the Metadata
    pane at the bottom left. Expand the Internet Sales measure group and double-
    click Internet Sales Amount. This adds `[Measures].[Internet Sales`
    `Amount]` to the Expression text box. Type a plus sign (+) after `[Measures]`
    `.[Internet Sales Amount]`. Expand the Reseller Sales measure group and
    double-click Reseller Sales Amount. The MDX formula in the Expression text
    box should look like this:

    ```
    [Measures].[Internet Sales Amount] + [Measures].[Reseller Sales Amount]
    ```

8. Click OK to exit the dialog, and your new measure appears in the Calculated
    Members pane at the bottom left of the query designer. Drag your new measure
    (Total Sales) to the right of Reseller Sales Amount in the central area of the query.
    You will have a new column that adds sales together by year by product category.

Well done, you have just written some MDX! The last button on the toolbar is for Design mode. Clicking this button toggles you between graphical mode and text mode where you can see the MDX. Please note that switching modes and making changes will overwrite changes made in the other mode. The MDX generated is perhaps overkill, so if you are new to MDX, don't be intimidated by the syntax. Click OK to exit the designer.

9. You are now back again in the Specify a MDX Query dialog of the Table Import Wizard. Here you can give your query a friendly name—this will be the name of the PowerPivot table. Click Validate to confirm that your syntax is valid, then click Finish, followed by Close. Your PowerPivot table is showing a subset of the cube data. You have converted multidimensional data into a flat, relational format. If you place this table into a PowerPivot pivot table in Excel, you are converting it back again into multidimensional data! We are going to extract the two dimensions and the measures out of the table as separate dimensions and measures. This raises a very important conceptual point. You are effectively creating a subset of an SSAS cube; you are creating a data mart from a data warehouse. By extracting from a few data marts (that is, PowerPivot tables from a cube), you can reassemble the marts into a new richer model in a PowerPivot pivot table in Excel. You are free to create your own BI, for you and your team, outside of the constraints of a predefined SSAS cube. Further, you can combine these data marts with data imported from relational sources—you can create your very own BI model, which may well be different from your corporate SSAS cube. This is the real beauty of PowerPivot—and this is why it's often called self-service BI, or personal BI, or instant BI. You have complete control and total flexibility, without having to understand star schemas and SSAS cube design. That said, there still remains a vital role for a centralized, enterprise-wide SSAS cube. Most organizations need *both* "traditional" SSAS cube BI and PowerPivot "self-service" BI. Before attempting the next step, you may want to right-click or double-click on the column headers in the PowerPivot table and give each column a friendlier name. Please note that the order of the columns may be different from your query—this is not at all important, as you can add them in any order you want to a pivot table.

10. On the Home ribbon in PowerPivot, click PivotTable in the Reports group and choose PivotTable from the drop-down menu. In the Create PivotTable dialog, accept the default of New Worksheet and click OK. The Create PivotTable dialog is shown in Figure 3-18. You are switched into an Excel worksheet, with an empty pivot table to the left and a PowerPivot Field List to the right.

11. In the PowerPivot Field List, drag the year to the Column Labels drop-zone. Drag the category to the Row Labels drop-zone. In turn, drag Internet Sales Amount, Reseller Sales Amount, and Total Sales to the Values drop-zone. Note the numbers appearing in the pivot table and the aggregate functions shown in the Values drop-zone. Are you wondering why all three aggregations are Count? Right-click each entry in the Values drop-zone, and from the context menu,

Figure 3-18 *Create PivotTable dialog*

choose Summarize By, then Sum. If you look at the pivot table, you will see that this has caused an error—the error message is telling you that you can't perform a Sum aggregation on string values. Often, PowerPivot will automatically convert data types for you. This is one occasion where it doesn't. Measures imported from cubes are always given a data type of Text, despite the data type of the measure in the cube design. If you understand BIDS, and you know how to "undeploy" or reverse-engineer the Adventure Works cube, you will see that the DataType for Internet Sales Amount and Reseller Sales Amount is Currency. SSAS data types are not fixed—you can override a sales amount with a string by using an MDX calculated member or the Scope statement in an MDX script. In essence, the data type is really Variant. PowerPivot has to play safe because this release does not support the Variant data type, and it imports SSAS cube measures as Text. This invalidates the measure for a Sum aggregation.

12. There are two ways to deal with this data type problem. One, you can use the DAX function VALUE(). Two, you can permanently reset the data type in PowerPivot. Here we adopt the second approach. Switch to PowerPivot and select the three measures columns. You can do this by using the SHIFT key with the mouse, or work on each column individually. From the Formatting group on the Home ribbon, choose Currency from the drop-down next to Data Type.

13. If you now switch back to Excel, there is a message at the top of the PowerPivot Field List. It informs you that the PowerPivot data has changed. Click the Refresh button next to the message. The measures should display correctly in the pivot table. If you scroll across, the totals for Internet Sales Amount, Reseller Sales Amount, and Total Sales are 29,358,677.22 and 80,450,596.98 and 109,809,274.20. The final resulting pivot table is shown in Figure 3-19.

That is very clever functionality. You could, of course, have connected a "normal" Excel pivot table directly to the SSAS cube (you can connect to only one cube at a time) without using PowerPivot at all. However, that is really not the point. To reiterate, if you use PowerPivot, you can combine multidimensional data from multiple SSAS cubes with data from relational sources or even from text files. You are no longer solely dependent on your SSAS developers and a single SSAS cube for your BI.

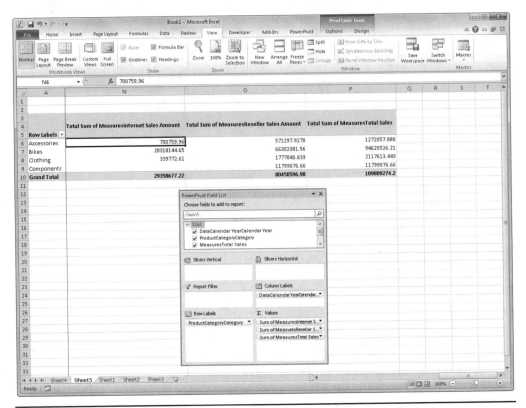

Figure 3-19 *PowerPivot pivot table using SSAS cube data*

You can even import data into PowerPivot from PowerPivot. However, the PowerPivot source must be PowerPivot for SharePoint, not PowerPivot for Excel. PowerPivot for SharePoint is not free, unlike PowerPivot for Excel. You will need SharePoint Server 2010, with Excel Services enabled, on a 64-bit machine with SQL Server Analysis Services 2008 R2 installed in SharePoint integrated mode (the latter is effectively PowerPivot for SharePoint). PowerPivot for SharePoint is not within the scope of this book. But, if you do have it, you can import data into your PowerPivot for Excel. To do so, you specify a URL to your PowerPivot for SharePoint workbook—rather than the server and database name that we tried for an SSAS connection. If you need to establish the URL of an object in SharePoint, you can refer to its properties.

If you want to know a little more about writing MDX queries, please refer to Appendix B or to my book *Practical MDX Queries for Microsoft SQL Server Analysis Services 2008* (McGraw-Hill/Professional, 2010). MDX queries extract data from SSAS cubes. SSAS also supports data mining models (a vital part of many BI solutions). To extract data from data mining models (either as Cases or Content or Prediction queries), you use DMX queries. This release of PowerPivot supports SQL and MDX but not DMX. In order to add SSAS data mining model data to your PowerPivot tables, you can embed the DMX within SQL. Appendix C shows how to write a few DMX queries and embed them inside SQL. If you want to learn DMX, please refer to my book *Practical DMX Queries for Microsoft SQL Server Analysis Services 2008* (McGraw-Hill/Professional, 2010).

From Report

The next item in the Get External Data group of the PowerPivot Home ribbon is From Report. If you click this, the Connect to a Microsoft SQL Server Reporting Services Report dialog opens, as shown in Figure 3-20. In this dialog, you have to enter a Report Path. To do so, click the Browse button to see the Open Report dialog. In the Name text box of this dialog, type the path to your Report Server or select a recently visited site. If SSRS is running in native mode, this is likely to be in the form of http://servername/reportserver. In SharePoint integrated mode, this is likely to be http://servername/<*document library*>. However, if SSRS is in native mode and you have SharePoint too, you might need to include the port number in the URL—it

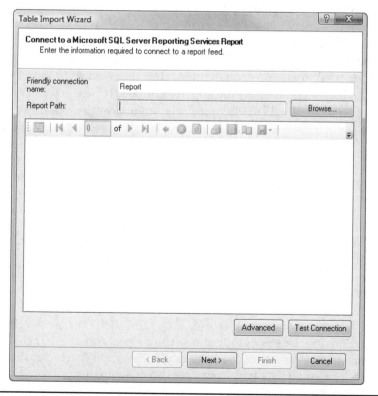

Figure 3-20   *Connect to a Microsoft SQL Server Reporting Services Report dialog*

is likely not to be the default of 80, which, by default, is reserved by SharePoint. Click Open—this will return a list of deployed SSRS reports from which to select a report—and then click Open again. If you are successful, your report will open in the small report viewer in the Connect to a Microsoft SQL Server Reporting Services Report dialog—this is where you can enter parameter values for parameterized reports. You can then complete the import of the report data into PowerPivot. There are a couple of provisos. One, the report must contain data that fits into the table format of PowerPivot. Two, the SSRS Report Server must be SQL Server Reporting Services 2008 R2—this will not work with SSRS 2008 (that's the release before 2008 R2)—but you can use SSRS 2008 reports that have subsequently been deployed to SSRS 2008 R2. If you do have SSRS 2008 R2, you can also *export* a report to PowerPivot from the Report Manager toolbar. This will automatically open Excel, let you choose an existing workbook or create a new workbook, and launch the PowerPivot Table Import Wizard. If you do have SSRS 2008 R2, you might like to create a report in BIDS or Report Builder 3, deploy the report, and try to import its data into PowerPivot.

From Data Feeds

A data feed provides live, streaming data from the Internet or from an intranet or extranet. If you import data into a PowerPivot table from a data feed (and remember to refresh the data often), your pivot tables will contain pretty dynamic data. Traditionally, BI provided fairly static and historic data. PowerPivot BI can be almost real time (I have seen this referred to as "real-enough time"). The data feed you connect to must be ATOM-compatible; RSS feeds are not supported in PowerPivot. You can even configure SSRS 2008 R2 reports to be ATOM-compatible and import them as data feeds. Here are a couple of steps, if you want to try importing into PowerPivot from a data feed:

1. Click From Data Feeds in the Get External Data group of the PowerPivot Home ribbon. This opens the Connect to a Data Feed dialog, which is shown in Figure 3-21. In this dialog, enter your Data Feed URL or the URL of a service document (.atomsvc) that lists data feeds, then click the Test Connection button, then click OK. PowerPivot remembers recently visited URLs, which makes selection easy. If you don't know a data feed URL, try http://services.odata.org/Northwind/Northwind.svc/—URLs can change, so this may not work by the time you read this book. I'm hoping it does, because it's a really good one—it's the Northwind database as a data feed.

2. If the connection is successful, click Next to see the Select Tables and Views dialog. Choose your source tables and, optionally, click Preview & Filter to filter the data. Filtering data feeds only allows the suppression of *entire* columns and not of individual rows. After choosing tables/views and maybe setting a filter, click Finish followed by Close. Your data should be in one or more PowerPivot tables, depending on how many tables/views were selected.

Figure 3-21   *Connect to a Data Feed dialog*

From Text

Use this option to import data from text or flat files. When you click From Text, it opens the Connect to Flat File dialog of the Table Import Wizard. The dialog is shown in Figure 3-22. You'll need to check that the Column Separator setting is correct and decide if the first row of your text file contains column headers or not. If you get these wrong, the file data will not display correctly in the dialog, in which case, you need to change them. There's a Browse button that allows you to locate your file, which will appear in the File Path field; the data from the file will be displayed in the lower section of the dialog. Once the data is shown, you can use the check boxes in the column headers to remove columns. Each column header also contains a small drop-down button. Use this to filter and/or sort the data to import. PowerPivot does its best to determine the correct data type for each column—you can assist PowerPivot by providing a schema.ini file. The filtering options may change from column to column as a result. For example, you may see an option for Text Filters or for Number Filters.

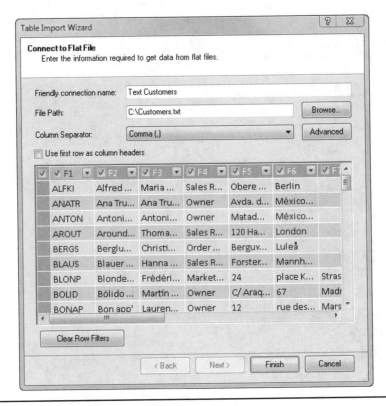

Figure 3-22 *Connect to Flat File dialog*

You can ascertain (and change) the data type of each column later with the Data Type drop-down in the Formatting group of the Home ribbon. You can also retrospectively change or remove any filters and/or sorts you choose at this stage from the Sort and Filter group of the Home ribbon, from the Table Properties button on the Design ribbon, or by using the drop-downs in the column headers in the resulting PowerPivot table. Filtering retrospectively does not affect the data stored in the PowerPivot model; it affects the display of data only. When you are done, click Finish, followed by Close.

If you would like to experiment with a text file import, find a suitable file. If you don't have a suitable file, here are a couple of suggestions (your own database software may well have an easier option for exporting to a text file). One, you can copy and paste from an existing PowerPivot table (perhaps originally imported from Access or Excel or SQL Server) into a text editor. Two, if you have SQL Server Integration Services (SSIS), you can load data into a text file from another source. Following are some hints on how to get both of these working.

To copy and paste, you need to be looking at an existing PowerPivot table with the focus within the table. Press CTRL-A to select the whole table, then click Copy in the Clipboard group of the Home ribbon. Open a text editor, such as Notepad, and paste in your data. Save and close the new text file. You can now use this as the import file for PowerPivot. Depending upon your text editor, you might have to change the Column Separator from Comma (,) to Tab (t).

To create a text file using SSIS, you need a new Integration Services Project in BIDS. Add a Data Flow Task to the Control Flow and then go to the Data Flow tab. Add a suitable source, such as OLE DB Source or Excel Source, and point it to your source data for the new text file—for example, you could use the Customers table in either a SQL Server or Access Northwind database. Add a Flat File Destination and drag the green data pipeline from the source to the destination. Double-click the Flat File Destination to configure it. You'll need a new Flat File connection manager. It's easier if you accept Delimited as the text file format; you'll also need to specify a file name for the new text file and decide whether the first row is going to contain column headers. When you've finished configuring your SSIS package, execute it to create a new text file. Then, you can use this as a data import source for PowerPivot.

From Other Sources

We are at the penultimate button in the Get External Data group of the PowerPivot Home ribbon. The From Other Sources button offers you a list of possible data sources for your PowerPivot tables. The list includes all of the options discussed earlier, even though the captions may be slightly different (Microsoft SQL Server, for example, is the same as SQL Server). The list is shown in Figure 3-23 and in Figure 3-24. Here we'll take a brief look at only those ones that are new—so Microsoft SQL Server and a couple of others won't be covered again. The list of import options is divided into sections. In the Relational Databases section (Figure 3-23) are Microsoft SQL Server, Microsoft SQL Azure, Microsoft SQL Server Parallel Data Warehouse, Microsoft Access, Oracle, Teradata, Sybase, Informix, IBM DB2, and Others (OLEDB/ODBC). In general, apart from the last one, they require a server name and login credentials. In addition, some require a database name. The last one, Others (OLEDB/ODBC), requires that you write your own connection string, if you don't have an existing DSN (data source name) file. PowerPivot will try, and often succeed, to display a list of tables from the connection—if it does, you can also write T-SQL queries against the source. Alternatively, you can write your own queries, using the default query language of the source. You may or may not have all of these data sources—it's a very comprehensive list! In addition, you may or may not have the necessary data providers required to connect to these sources. A couple of these data sources might be new to you. For example, SQL Azure is the great big SQL Server in the sky—it's a relational data

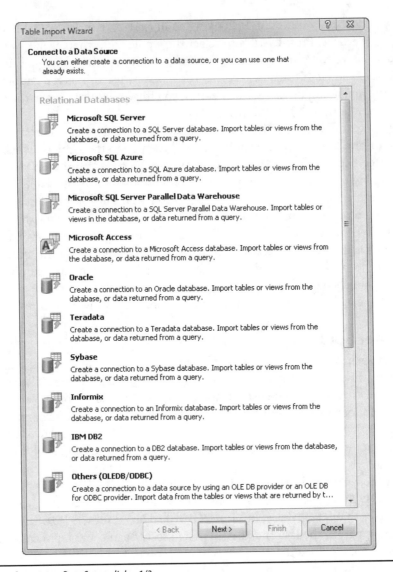

Figure 3-23   *Connect to a Data Source dialog 1/2*

source for those involved in cloud-based computing. Microsoft SQL Server Parallel Data Warehouse became available with Microsoft SQL Server 2008 R2. It's a massively parallel processing (MPP) implementation of SQL Server and is based on a hub-and-spoke architecture. In essence, Microsoft SQL Server Parallel Data Warehouse divides very large database tables across multiple servers so that load balancing and multiserver parallelism are possible.

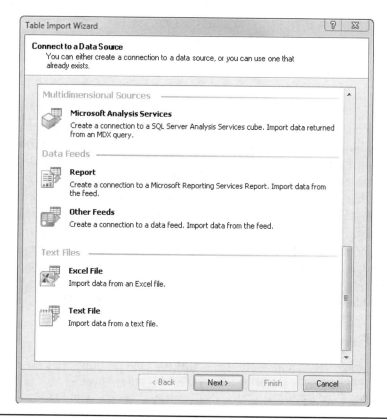

Figure 3-24   *Connect to a Data Source dialog 2/2*

There is also a Text Files section (Figure 3-24). It's in this section that you will find Excel. The previous chapter has step-by-step instructions and a practical on how to import from Excel, in case you jumped into the book at this point. If you are interested in how to import data from Excel worksheets into PowerPivot, refer back to the last chapter. Importing from Excel has one major difference from importing from relational sources—you have to create the relationships between tables manually. Again, there is a step-by-step example on this subject in Chapter 2. Later in this chapter, we take another look at relationships.

Refresh

The final button in the Get External Data group of the Home ribbon is labeled Refresh (there is also a Refresh option available through the Existing Connections button on the Design ribbon). Clicking this button opens a small drop-down menu that

Figure 3-25 *Refresh drop-down menu*

offers two choices: Refresh and Refresh All. The menu is shown in Figure 3-25. Both of these are of fundamental importance. When you import data into a PowerPivot table, you are creating a separate and independent copy of the original data (unless you use an Excel linked table). If the source data changes, the copy in PowerPivot is not updated, and it's likely that over time your source data and your PowerPivot data will get out of sync. If you click Refresh | Refresh, then the current table is re-imported and brought up-to-date. If you click Refresh | Refresh All, then *all* of your PowerPivot tables are re-imported and updated. PowerPivot is not a real-time system, and your pivot reports (tables and charts) can easily become stale if you don't use Refresh on a regular basis. Please note that the Refresh button is disabled until you import data into one or more PowerPivot tables (pasted data and linked tables alone do not enable the button).

Reports Group

The Reports group has a single button called PivotTable. It duplicates the functionality of the PivotTable button in the Report group of the PowerPivot ribbon in Excel. This is the button to use to create a pivot report on your PowerPivot tables back in Excel. You can insert a new pivot table (normal and flattened) or a pivot chart. There are additional choices to insert a pivot table and a pivot chart or two or more pivot charts. All of the choices are shown in Figure 3-26. When you insert more than one report, you can customize them differently if you wish. Working with pivot tables and pivot charts is covered in detail in Chapter 5.

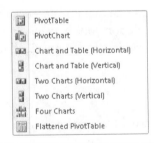

Figure 3-26 *PivotTable drop-down menu*

Formatting Group

The first option in the Formatting group is for checking and/or setting the Data Type of the current column in a PowerPivot table. For example, if you import a measure from an SSAS cube, its data type will be Text. You may want to reset this to a more appropriate type like Currency or Whole Number. If you get the data type right, it will display correctly in a pivot table and your DAX functions will operate successfully. It's not always strictly necessary to get the right data type for DAX functions—PowerPivot will often implicitly convert a column into a more appropriate data type. For example, if you have two numbers as data type Text and you attempt to add or sum them, DAX will automatically convert them into Decimal Number or Whole Number. However, you should be aware that this automatic implicit data conversion does not *always* take place. This is particularly true when the data originates in an SSAS cube. Therefore, it's probably good practice to check and explicitly set, if necessary, the data type for every column in every table. When you set the Data Type, you are changing how PowerPivot stores the data. The choices are shown in Figure 3-27.

The data types available are Text, Decimal Number, Whole Number, Currency, Date, and TRUE/FALSE. TRUE/FALSE is often referred to as a Boolean and corresponds to the data type of bit in SQL Server. The Date data type is of fundamental importance. Quite a few DAX functions are time or time intelligence functions—many of these require a column to be of data type Date and it's possibly better not to rely on automatic data type conversion.

The next button in the Formatting group is labeled Format. The Format options affect how the data is viewed in a pivot table—although a pivot table itself has its own formatting options, it's a good idea to get the formatting right at the PowerPivot stage. The format options available are dictated by the data type of the column. Only the Text format is available for a Text data type column and only TRUE/FALSE for a TRUE/FALSE data type. A data type of Date results in a wide range of date formats. A data type of Currency, Decimal Number, or Whole Number gives you a choice of General, Decimal Number, Whole Number, Currency, Accounting, Percentage, and Scientific formats.

Figure 3-27 *Data Type drop-down menu*

Hopefully, these are largely self-explanatory. The Accounting format displays negative figures in parentheses. The Scientific format displays figures in exponential format. When you set the Format, you are not changing how PowerPivot stores the data—it changes the display only.

Underneath the Format drop-down are five small buttons without captions. If you hover the mouse over each button in turn, however, you can see the tooltips: Apply Currency Format, Apply Percentage Format, Thousands Separator, Decrease Decimal, and Increase Decimal. You can use these to extend your choice in the Format drop-down—but in some cases, they will change your Format choice. The first button, Apply Currency Format, has a drop-down menu. This menu is shown in Figure 3-28. From the menu, you can easily apply some standard currency formats or choose the last entry—More Formats. More Formats opens the Currency Format dialog with another drop-down for Symbol. This gives a pretty formidable list of currency symbols—after my default currency symbol, my list starts with the Dari (Afghanistan) symbol and ends with the Divehi (Maldives) symbol—they are not in any kind of alphabetical order.

Sort and Filter Group

In the Sort and Filter group are four buttons. The first is labeled Sort A to Z or Sort Smallest to Largest, depending on the data type of the currently selected table column. The second is Sort Z to A, or Sort Largest to Smallest. The third button, Clear Sort, removes any sorting you have implemented. Finally, the fourth button, Clear All Filters, removes any filtering you have implemented. This last button is interesting, as there is nothing in the group to apply filtering in the first place! You can apply filtering in three different places in PowerPivot, and you can also apply filters to pivot reports in Excel. Clear All Filters removes PowerPivot filtering but not pivot table filtering. In PowerPivot, you can set up filters during the Table Import Wizard. Or you might use the Table Properties button in the Properties group of the PowerPivot Design ribbon. Alternatively, each column in a PowerPivot table has a small drop-down menu where you can filter (and sort too). This drop-down also has an option that will have a caption such as Date Filters or Number Filters or Text Filters—this enables you to impose complex and customized filtering. Clear Sort and Clear All Filters also undo these.

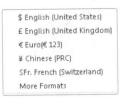

Figure 3-28   *Apply Currency Format drop-down menu*

View Group

The final group on the Home ribbon is the View group. Here there are two buttons: Freeze and Column Width. Freeze is handy when you scroll to the right of a table with many columns and have a column or columns that identify each row, such as a customer name. The columns you freeze are moved to the left and remain in view as you scroll— if you later unfreeze, the columns stay at the left. Before you click Freeze | Freeze, make sure you are in the correct column, or for multiple columns, make sure they are all selected. To select multiple columns, they must be adjacent: Hold down the SHIFT key after you have clicked in the first column and before you click on the last column (or drag with the mouse). In this release of PowerPivot, the CTRL key does not work, so you can't select non-adjacent columns to freeze. Once a column is frozen, you can undo the freeze by clicking Freeze | Unfreeze or by clicking Undo in the Edit group of the Design ribbon. The Column Width button opens the Column Width dialog, where you can resize a column (the width is expressed in pixels)—you can also accomplish this by dragging column dividers or by double-clicking dividers. The dialog is shown in Figure 3-29.

That concludes our tour of the PowerPivot Home ribbon. The next ribbon is the Design ribbon.

Design Ribbon in PowerPivot

To display the Design ribbon in PowerPivot, click the Design tab. If the ribbon opens over the top of your PowerPivot table and obscures the first couple of rows, double-click rather than single-click the Design tab. The Design ribbon contains the following groups: Columns, Calculations, Connections, Relationships, Properties, and Edit. Once again, let's work through these in sequence from left to right. The Design ribbon is shown in Figure 3-30.

Columns Group

In the Columns group there are three buttons: Hide and Unhide, Add, and Delete. There is a fundamental difference between hiding and deleting columns. If you delete

Figure 3-29 *Column Width dialog*

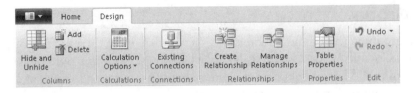

Figure 3-30 *Design ribbon in PowerPivot*

a column, you have lost it from PowerPivot and subsequently from any pivot report based on PowerPivot. You can't undelete by using the Undo button in the Edit group. However, you can add the column back by going through the Table Properties button in the Properties group and turning on the column's check box. Note that if you do this, the column gets added at the end of the table and not in its original position. If you imported from a table rather than writing a SQL query, this is another way to rearrange your columns. However, it's probably much easier to drag columns around in the table to change the order. Hiding a column merely removes the column from the display (in PowerPivot and/or in a pivot table based on the PowerPivot table). Hiding a column does not delete the column. Hidden columns can be referenced in DAX functions and formulas—deleted columns can't be used.

The Hide and Unhide button leads to the Hide and Unhide Columns dialog, which is shown in Figure 3-31. Here you can hide a column in PowerPivot and/or a pivot table back in Excel. If you have columns that are used in DAX calculated columns,

Figure 3-31 *Hide and Unhide Columns dialog*

it's possible you only want the PowerPivot Field List for the pivot table to show the final resulting column and not the original. This is especially useful if the column is a non-additive measure, such as price, that is only used to multiply by quantity to give a fully additive measure of the sales amount. To reshow a hidden column, click Hide and Unhide again or use the Undo button in the Edit group—the latter option is not available for long. If you close the PowerPivot window and reopen it, the Undo button is disabled. Clicking Add jumps you to a new column at the right-hand side of the table and activates the formula bar so you can enter a DAX formula. Alternatively, you can scroll to the far right to see a new column with a header of Add Column—if you click in this column, it also activates the formula bar. Clicking Add saves a scroll! The Delete button, as you might expect, deletes a column from a PowerPivot table. You can undelete by clicking the Table Properties button in the Properties group.

Calculations Group

There is just the one button, Calculation Options, in the Calculations group. The button has three options in its drop-down menu: Calculate Now (F9), Automatic Calculation Mode, and Manual Calculation Mode. This drop-down is shown in Figure 3-32. Your choice is between automatic and manual calculation mode. Automatic calculation mode is the default. If you change to manual calculation mode, you can then use Calculate Now (F9) or press the F9 key to force a calculation. If you are in manual mode, any changes to a calculated column result in the column being grayed-out and a "Calculation required" smart tag being displayed.

The calculation refers to one or more DAX calculated columns. A DAX calculated column is a new column that you add to a table and into which you enter a DAX formula consisting of one or more DAX expressions containing functions, operators, and literals. After you enter a DAX formula in the formula bar and press ENTER, the DAX formula evaluates for every single row in the table and the results are materialized. When you need to create many calculated columns with complex DAX formulas on many tables with millions of rows, this continual evaluation or calculation for every single calculated column at a time can interrupt your work for a few moments. You can postpone the calculations until you are ready by switching from Automatic Calculation Mode to Manual Calculation Mode. If you do so, remember to click Calculate Now (F9) or press the F9 key after you have finished the last formula.

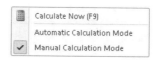

Figure 3-32   *Calculation Options drop-down menu*

Connections Group

Every single time you import data using the Get External Data group on the Home ribbon, you create a new connection. The sole Existing Connections button in the Connections group shows you all of these connections in the Existing Connections dialog, which is shown in Figure 3-33. This leads to a number of interesting possibilities. One, you can change the connection by clicking Edit. Two, you can use an existing Office Data Connection (.odc) file that was created previously by some other Excel/Office operation. Three, you can browse for other connection files by clicking Browse for More. Four, you can add tables or queries to an existing connection by clicking Open or double-clicking the connection.

The last point is worthy of more discussion. Often, you will use Get External Data and import a few tables from a particular source. Later, you may decide that you want another table from the same source. If you go back through Get External, you are creating a new connection to the same source. You can end up with many connections

Figure 3-33   *Existing Connections dialog*

to the same data source. If you go through Existing Connections and click Open, you can add new tables or queries to an existing connection. Having a single connection to a single source is much, much more efficient than having multiple connections to a single source. It also simplifies management of PowerPivot for Excel workbooks published to PowerPivot for SharePoint. If you do go for a single connection, you may see significant improvements in the speed of data import, especially if you re-import by clicking Refresh All from the Refresh button on the Home ribbon.

Relationships Group

There are two buttons in the Relationships group of the Design ribbon: Create Relationship and Manage Relationships. Create Relationship, naturally, is used to create relationships. Manage Relationships is used to edit or delete existing relationships. However, the Manage Relationships dialog also includes a Create button so that you can set up new relationships without having to go back to the Create Relationship button. If you are importing from a relational source that supports relationships, and relationships are defined in the source, PowerPivot might automatically create the relevant relationships for you—but this may not be so for arbitrary OLEDB/ODBC connections. If, however, you import from a non-relational source such as Excel or text files, you may want to define relationships. This has a number of benefits. It means you can use the important DAX functions RELATED() and RELATEDTABLE(). In addition, it helps you to have the correct data from multiple tables display correctly in a PowerPivot pivot report. The Create Relationship dialog is shown in Figure 3-34. The Manage Relationships dialog is shown in Figure 3-35.

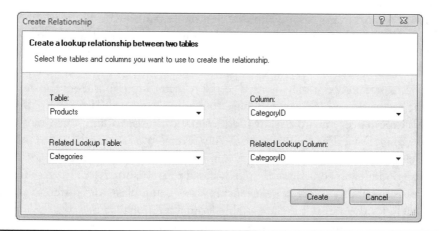

Figure 3-34   *Create Relationship dialog*

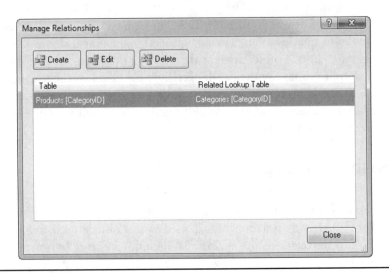

Figure 3-35   *Manage Relationships dialog*

If you import PowerPivot tables from disparate sources, then PowerPivot can't create the relationships automatically. This is also true when you import new tables on an existing connection—relationships with existing tables are not detected. If tables are related in some way, it's important that you tell PowerPivot. When you add tables to a pivot table, you could always try the Detection button in the Relationship group of the PowerPivot ribbon in Excel. But it's a good idea to explicitly and manually create relationships. If you omit them or the automatic detection algorithm gets it wrong, your pivot table may display inaccurate results.

Our Excel import example in Chapter 2 demonstrated how to set up relationships. If you skipped that chapter or the Excel part, it might be a good idea to refer back to it quickly. As a reminder, if you read Chapter 2, in PowerPivot relationships, in one-to-many relationships, the relationships go from the *many to the one*. If you have Access or SQL Server experience, you may be used to the relationship going from the one-side table to the many-side table—you will have to readjust your way of thinking. If you have SSAS experience, you are already used to relationships working this way around. If you get it wrong, PowerPivot will automatically reverse the relationship.

In this chapter, rather than repeating a step-by-step example from the last chapter, it might be a good idea to consider a more advanced relationship. A really great feature of PowerPivot is the ability to create relationships between tables from different sources. And this includes the ability to relate a table from a relational source to a table from a multidimensional source, such as an SSAS cube. This is truly personal BI! Here's a step-by-step example to relate relational data to multidimensional data (if you wish to click along rather than just read, you will need the SSAS Adventure Works database and cube and some familiarity with BIDS, in order to prepare a suitable dimension as a multidimensional source—and the SQL Server AdventureWorksDW2008 database as a relational source):

1. Reverse-engineer your SSAS Adventure Works database through File | New | Project | Import Analysis Services 2008 Database. You could, alternatively, open your Adventure Works SSAS solution. If you do so, please be careful. We are going to make changes to a dimension, so when you deploy, make sure you change the project name and the database name (right-click Project | Properties | Deployment | Target | Database). If you don't do this, you will overwrite the SSAS Adventure Works (assuming you have it)—and we are going to totally mess up a dimension, by way of illustration!

2. Open the Customer dimension (Customer.dim) from Solution Explorer. You should be in the Dimension Structure tab of the dimension designer. Remove the Country attribute hierarchy from the Attributes pane (right-click, then click Delete)—this also removes the Country level from the Customer Geography user hierarchy in the Hierarchies pane. We are going to relate this multidimensional database/cube dimension to a relational source to replace the deleted country attribute.

3. Drag the Geography Key attribute from the Customer (not from Geography) source in the Data Source View pane on the right into the Attributes pane at the left. Deploy and process the database with the changed dimension. To do this, right-click on the project, and choose Deploy. Remember your project/database name.

4. Go to PowerPivot, and from Get External Data choose From Database, From Analysis Services, or PowerPivot. Connect to your SSAS server and your new SSAS database. Click Next followed by Design to open the graphical query designer.

5. In the graphical query designer, expand the customer dimension and drag in the Geography Key attribute hierarchy (a blue rectangle) and the Customer Geography user hierarchy (a blue pyramid/triangle). Expand Measures and Internet Sales, and then drag in Internet Sales Amount to see data returned from the cube. Click OK, Finish, and Close. The query designer is shown in Figure 3-36.

6. Internet Sales Amount is a measure in the cube with a DataType property of Currency. You can verify this by selecting Internet Sales Amount in the Measures pane of the Cube Structure tab in the cube designer and looking at the Properties window. In PowerPivot it has a data type of Text. You can verify this by looking at the Data Type drop-down on the PowerPivot Home ribbon. Change the data type in PowerPivot to Currency. PowerPivot, to play it safe, always imports cube measures as Text.

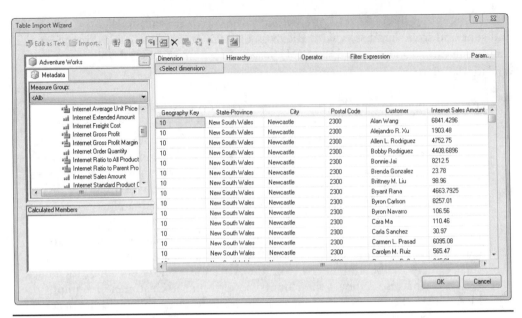

Figure 3-36   *MDX graphical query designer*

7.   From the Get External Data group on the Home ribbon, choose From
     Database, and then choose From SQL Server. Connect to your SQL Server
     AdventureWorksDW2008 database and click Next twice. Select DimGeography
     as the source table, and then click Finish, then Close.

8.   Now, for the core of this step-by-step example. Click Create Relationship on the
     Design ribbon. Remember that relationships go from the many to the one. The
     first (many) table is the table from SSAS. The second (one) table is the table from
     SQL Server (DimGeography). The key relating the tables is GeographyKey. Set
     up the relationship and click Create.

9.   Make sure you are looking at the first table (the one from SSAS) in PowerPivot.
     Click Add on the Design ribbon. This activates the formula bar. Enter the
     following DAX formula and press ENTER:

     =RELATED(DimGeography[EnglishCountryRegionName])

10. Rename the new column **Country** and verify that it shows the correct country for
     each row. You can check the country against the state-province column—you may
     have to scroll a long way down to get beyond California and the United States!
     The result is shown (with a frozen column and renamed columns) in Figure 3-37.

11. From the Home ribbon, click PivotTable, PivotTable, then OK. Back in Excel, use
     the PowerPivot Field List and drag the new calculated country column and then

State-Province	Customer	Internet Sales Amount	Country
Washington	Warren A. Wang	£1,763.97	United States
Washington	Warren Xu	£2,393.06	United States
Washington	Wendy Gill	£539.99	United States
Washington	Whitney C. Sanchez	£4.99	United States
Washington	William Rodriguez	£4.99	United States
Washington	Wyatt Goldstein	£37.27	United States
Washington	Wyatt Young	£1,249.84	United States
Washington	Xavier M. Kelly	£1,145.48	United States
Washington	Zoe Reed	£574.98	United States
England	Dale B. Andersen	£106.26	United Kingdom
England	Heidi Z. Arun	£3,165.4182	United Kingdom
England	Adriana A. Sai	£3,262.83	United Kingdom
England	Alisha Sun	£64.97	United Kingdom
England	Arthur G. Gonzalez	£2,398.05	United Kingdom
England	Barbara M. Wang	£5,160.08	United Kingdom
England	Byron Rubio	£64.97	United Kingdom
England	Calvin J. Goel	£179.95	United Kingdom
England	Clinton Gill	£553.97	United Kingdom
England	Daisy Ramos	£103.97	United Kingdom
England	Dana Muñoz	£21.49	United Kingdom
England	Donna D. She	£21.49	United Kingdom
England	Douglas Vance	£94.96	United Kingdom
England	Eddie Romero	£38.98	United Kingdom
England	Erik S. Diaz	£34.99	United Kingdom
England	Gilbert She	£53.47	United Kingdom

Figure 3-37   *SSAS data in PowerPivot with a DAX calculated column*

the city column from the first SSAS-based table into the Row Labels drop-zone. Drag the measure for Internet Sales Amount from the same table into the Values drop-zone and check that the aggregate function (Summarize By on the context menu) is Sum. The Field List is shown in Figure 3-38.

12. Right-click on Australia in the pivot table and choose Expand/Collapse | Collapse Entire Field. Expand Germany following the same procedure. The first city should be Berlin with sales of 260,930 (ignoring cents or pence), and total sales for all cities in all countries in the Grand Total row should be 29,358,677 (again ignoring cents or pence).

Wow! Well done, if it worked. That is really cool self-service BI. My result is shown in Figure 3-39.

Properties Group

The Properties group has only one button, with the caption Table Properties. Clicking this button opens the Edit Table Properties dialog, which is shown in Figure 3-40. There is quite a lot going on here, and the options vary according to the nature of the source table. For example, if your source is SQL Server, you can change the source table

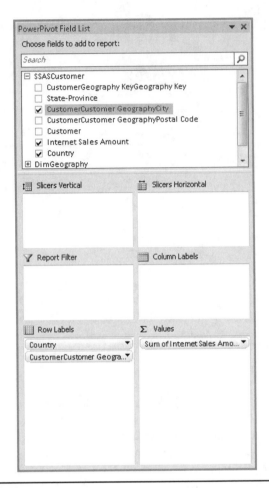

Figure 3-38   *PowerPivot Field List*

for the PowerPivot table—but you can't change the source database. The source table is the Source Name property. The column headers displayed can be from either the source itself or from PowerPivot—this makes a lot of sense if you have renamed the columns in PowerPivot. At the bottom right of the dialog, you can see when you last refreshed (synched or synchronized) the PowerPivot data from the source data. If you have any filters on the table, clicking Clear Row Filters will remove all filters. Note that this will not remove any sorts. To remove sorts, use Clear Sort from the small drop-down in the column headers. To change, add, or delete individual filters, you also use the small drop-down in the column hearers.

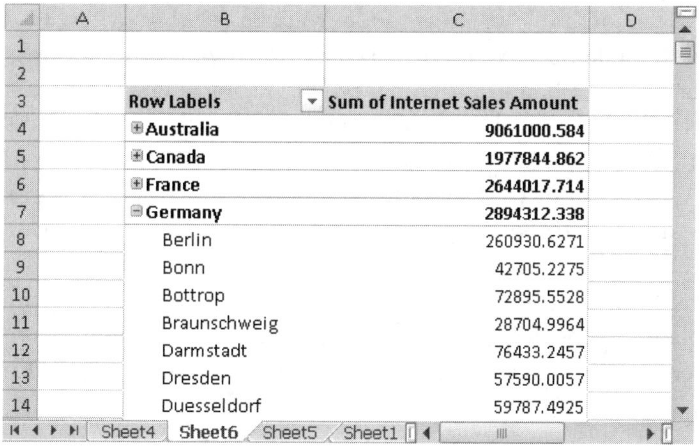

Figure 3-39   *PowerPivot pivot table*

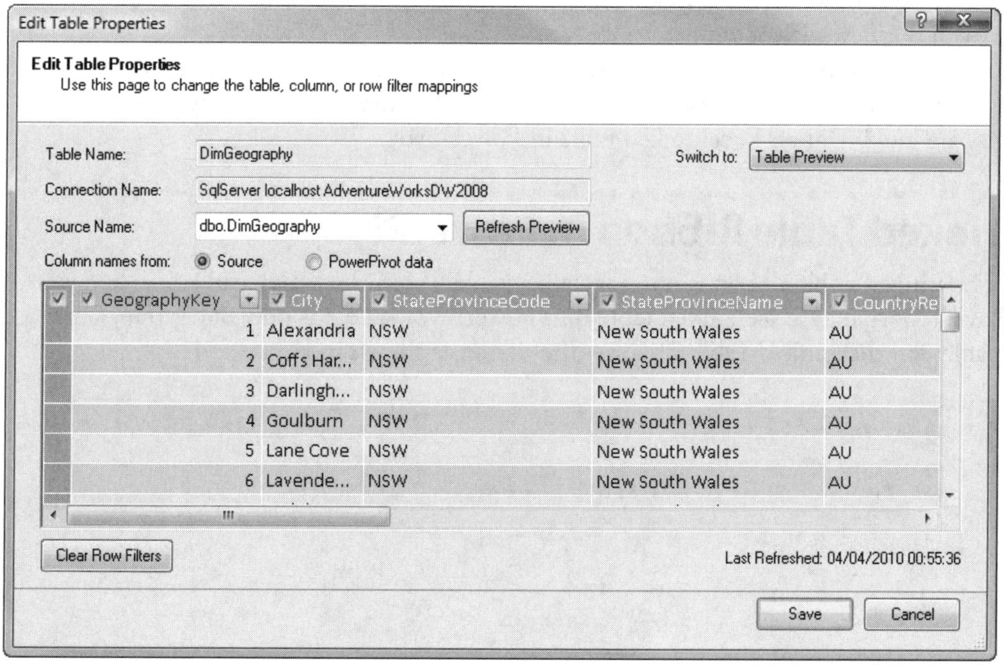

Figure 3-40   *Edit Table Properties dialog*

By default, you are in Table Preview mode. You can use the Switch To drop-down to toggle between Table Preview and Query Editor, provided you imported the table as a table rather than as a hand-crafted query. If the source data is an SSAS cube, you only have Query Editor—but there you can preview the table. Query Editor shows the syntax (for example, a SQL or MDX Select statement) that retrieves the data for the table. The Query Editor view has a Design button that results in a graphical query designer, from the Table Import Wizard, for your SQL or MDX. If you are using SQL rather than MDX, you will need to click Edit as Text to enable the graphical designer. Once in the graphical designer, you can use point-and-click and drag-and-drop to alter your initial table/query. Both SQL and MDX graphical query design were covered earlier in this chapter—if they are relevant to your needs, you may want to quickly refer back.

Edit Group

The final group of the PowerPivot Design ribbon is the Edit group. This has two drop-downs labeled Undo and Redo. Please be aware that you can't undo or redo many of the changes you make in PowerPivot. Also, the drop-downs are disabled if you close and reopen the PowerPivot window.

That's it for the Design ribbon, which is the second ribbon in PowerPivot. You may or may not have a third, contextual, ribbon called Linked Table. It's only visible when you are looking at an Excel linked table in PowerPivot.

Linked Table Ribbon in PowerPivot

The Linked Table ribbon is not normally visible. It only becomes available when you have imported an Excel linked table into PowerPivot. There is only one group, Linked Tables, on the Linked Table ribbon—the ribbon is shown in Figure 3-41.

Figure 3-41   *Linked Table ribbon in PowerPivot*

Figure 3-42   *Update Mode drop-down menu*

Linked Tables Group

The Linked Tables group includes buttons/drop-downs with the captions Update All, Update Selected, Excel Table, Go to Excel Table, and Update Mode. The Update Mode drop-down menu is shown in Figure 3-42. If you choose Manual, you must remember to click Update All or Update Selected to refresh PowerPivot if the original table in Excel changes. There is also an Update All button on the PowerPivot ribbon in Excel. To enable the Linked Table ribbon and these buttons, you first need to create an Excel linked table in PowerPivot. As a reminder, you do so by using the Create Linked Table button in the Excel Data group of the PowerPivot ribbon back in the Excel workbook itself (not the Get External Data group on the PowerPivot Home ribbon). How to do this was covered earlier in this chapter, in the "Excel Data Group" section, where we also saw how to use the buttons on the Linked Table ribbon in PowerPivot. If linked tables are an option for you, you may want to refer back.

That concludes our tour of the PowerPivot ribbons and graphical interface. The discussion has not covered all of the various possibilities of working—the emphasis has been on the PowerPivot ribbons and the PowerPivot ribbon in Excel. Quite often, the same functionality is available from context-sensitive menus accessed by a right-click. For example, you can freeze or hide a column by a simple right-click on the column header. The next chapter is an overview of DAX and how it can extend the already massive capabilities of PowerPivot available through the GUI.

Chapter 4

DAX: Overview

Data Analysis eXpressions (DAX) is a new language that makes its debut with PowerPivot for Excel. It is a language designed to use formulas, which in turn are based on one or more DAX functions. Some of its functions will look familiar to veteran Excel users, although there are differences between DAX and Excel functions. These differences are elaborated in this chapter. You will learn where and how to write DAX functions and formulas, and there are a number of examples to try. The all-important concept of filter context is discussed in detail. Other topics include data types and operator precedence. Two of the most popular functions, RELATED() and CALCULATE(), are covered in depth. The difference between DAX calculated columns and DAX measures is explained. Hopefully, there is enough DAX in this overview chapter to get you started. The second part of this book provides a comprehensive reference, with examples, of all the DAX functions.

> ► **Key concepts** What is DAX, where and how to write DAX, row context, filter context, data types, operator precedence, calculated columns, measures, RELATED() function, CALCULATE() function

What Is DAX?

In Chapter 1 and Chapter 2, there were very fleeting glimpses of a couple of DAX formulas. In this chapter, by contrast, there is rather more DAX. In particular, we examine the reasons for using DAX and take a look at some useful and popular DAX formulas. A DAX formula is made up of one or more DAX expressions, functions, operators, column values, table values, and literal values. DAX formulas can be used in the PowerPivot window and/or in a PowerPivot pivot report (table or chart) visualized in an Excel worksheet. In general terms, DAX extends PowerPivot to enhance its BI capabilities. DAX gives you a great deal of control flexibility—you are not limited by the composition of the source data. For many users, the already considerable functionality of PowerPivot and pivot tables may be more than enough. For other users, especially those of you with an interest in BI, DAX will give you almost unlimited possibilities.

DAX is not the same as SQL or MultiDimensional eXpressions (MDX), nor is it meant as a replacement for those languages. DAX is a new, dedicated BI language and is easier than the "traditional" BI query and script language, MDX—a lot of DAX syntax looks just like those good old familiar Excel formulas. There is a major difference between Excel functions and DAX functions: Excel functions normally operate on values in cells and ranges, while DAX functions can operate on columns, and tables, and measures as well as relationally across multiple tables. DAX is specifically designed for self-service or team BI. As such, you can use it to concatenate data, parse data, relate tables, denormalize data, create hierarchical drill-downs in a pivot table, perform time intelligence (for example, year-to-date sales or year-on-year sales growth), and much, much more. Many of these functions will be discussed in the course of this chapter.

NOTE

Nearly all of the examples in this chapter use Northwind data. If you want to experiment (and you don't have the data yet), as well as read, you can refer to Chapter 1 to see how to import SQL Server Northwind. Chapter 2 shows how to import Access Northwind or, alternatively, how to import Excel Northwind (available for download from this book's Web site), or even how to connect to a Northwind data feed.

Where to Write DAX

DAX formulas can be used to create calculated columns or calculated measures. A calculated column is defined in the PowerPivot window when you add a new column to a PowerPivot table. It doesn't matter which PowerPivot ribbon is current. A measure is defined in an Excel worksheet containing a pivot table and/or pivot chart based on PowerPivot tables. In order to create a measure, the focus must be in the pivot report or in the PowerPivot Field List—for the PowerPivot Field List to display, you must first have the focus on the pivot report. Then you can use the New Measure button in the Measures group of the PowerPivot ribbon in Excel. If another ribbon is current, you can always right-click a table in the field list and choose Add New Measure.

Calculated Columns

To create a calculated column, you must be in the PowerPivot window. As shown earlier in the book, one way of creating (or adding) a calculated column is to click the Add button in the Columns group of the Design ribbon. Or you can simply scroll until you see the first empty column, with the column header Add Column, and click in the column. You then enter your DAX formula in the formula bar and press ENTER—the formula bar lies between the ribbon and the table. If you create or modify a calculated column, and you already have a pivot table, the PowerPivot Field List will alert you to the fact and present a Refresh button so the pivot table and field list can be updated with the change.

Context of a Calculated Column

Every row in the table will contain the result of the DAX formula in the calculated column, even if the result is an error or a blank value. The context of the calculated column result is at the row level in the table. Calculated columns have *row context*. The result of the column for each row is usually fixed, although a refresh of the source data may result in a change if the source data has changed. Some people refer to calculated columns as *static* data.

Evaluation and Materialization of a Calculated Column

As soon as you've finished the formula and pressed ENTER, the column result is evaluated for each row. This is true if you are in the default automatic calculation mode. If you switch to manual calculation mode, the result is not evaluated until you press F9 or choose Calculate Now (as a reminder, this option is available in the Calculation Options drop-down—Design ribbon, Calculations group). Whether the evaluation is performed automatically or manually, once the evaluation is complete, the results are materialized. In other words, the calculated column is now a static part of your PowerPivot table and looks and behaves just like a normal, imported column. Calculated columns are often used to extend or manipulate the data you've already imported. Just like regular columns, calculated columns are used as rows, columns, filters, or slicers in a pivot table. Popular examples of calculated columns include parsing an existing column, concatenating existing columns, or denormalizing data by referencing a column in another PowerPivot table.

Where to Use a Calculated Column in a Pivot Table

In the PowerPivot Field List, a calculated column looks just like a normal imported column. *Normally*, you add it to any drop-zone, apart from Values. It's often used to describe or qualify the data that you do have in Values. It's also often used to filter the data that you do have in the Values drop-zone. Consequently, consider adding a calculated column to Slicers Vertical, Slicers Horizontal, Report Filter, Column Labels, or Row Labels. You saw examples of this in Chapters 1 and 2, in the Year and Category calculated columns.

That said, you *can* add a calculated column to the Values drop-zone, if it's suitable. A suitable candidate is a calculated column that can be sensibly aggregated in some way, for example by a Sum or a Count. Often suitable columns will be numeric—indeed, they may look like metrics (measures or facts). If you add a calculated column to the Values drop-zone, PowerPivot implicitly creates a measure, while leaving the original column unchanged. This works, but it's often better to create a measure explicitly yourself, using the New Measure button on the PowerPivot ribbon in Excel. That gives you so much more control and flexibility. In Chapter 2, you saw examples of both approaches. If you followed the practicals and still have your workbook, you may want to take a quick look. We created a calculated column called Sales Amount. This was added to the Values drop-zone and PowerPivot aggregated it with a Sum—an implicit measure directly from a calculated column. It got renamed to DAXColumn. There was also an explicit measure, created with the New Measure button, DAXMeasure. Incidentally, this too was based on the same calculated column, but its syntax was much richer, and that is ultimately what gives you more control. In general, it's recommended that you create explicit measures rather than have regular or calculated columns double up as implicit measures. You'll see explicitly calculated measures shortly (they are usually simply referred to as measures). If that's not enough, you can use the GUI to create implicit measures, as well! In Chapter 2, we created such an implicit measure, GUIColumn.

For those readers with an SSAS and cube background (and if you don't have this background, please feel free to skip this paragraph), a calculated column is an attribute in a non-measure dimension—it can be used for creating user hierarchies just like an SSAS attribute hierarchy. The results for every row are its members. As a non-measure dimension, it would normally be added to Row Labels, for example, and not to the Values drop-zone in the field list. It would, also, normally not be aggregated. However, you *could* add it to the Values drop-zone. If the column is numeric it will, by default, be summed. If it's non-numeric, it will normally be counted. When you do add it to the Values drop-zone, PowerPivot will implicitly create a measure with an appropriate aggregation function that references the column. This is what happened to the Sales Amount calculated column (renamed DAXColumn) in Chapter 2.

Referring to Calculated Columns

When you reference a calculated or a regular column in a DAX formula, you must include the column name inside square brackets, for example, [Year]. If you are creating a calculated column based on a calculated or regular column in another table, the referenced column must be prefaced with the table name, for example, Orders[Year] or 'Orders'[Year]. The single quotes around the table name are optional, unless there is a space or special character in the table name. Calculated column names must be unique within a table, but you can use the same name for a column within different tables. If you do so, the column name will be given a suffix in the GUI.

Examples of Calculated Columns

These examples are reproduced (with one addition) from Chapter 2:

```
='Order Details'[Quantity] * 'Order Details'[UnitPrice]
=[Quantity] * [UnitPrice]
=YEAR('Orders'[OrderDate])
=YEAR(Orders[OrderDate])
=YEAR([OrderDate])
=RELATED('Categories'[CategoryName])
```

The fourth example is an addition to the formulas reproduced from Chapter 2. The first and second examples are equivalent. The third, fourth, and fifth examples are equivalent. Most DAX functions can appear in calculated column or measure formulas. However, as RELATED() requires a row context, it is most often used for a calculated column or as an input to another DAX function. RELATED(), an extremely useful function, is covered in more detail shortly.

Measures

To create a measure, you must be in the Excel workbook (not the PowerPivot window) and you must have an existing pivot report with the focus either in the report or its PowerPivot Field List. You then click the New Measure button on the PowerPivot ribbon, or right-click a table in the field list and choose Add New Measure. Either action opens the Measure Settings dialog. In this dialog, you enter your DAX formula in the Formula text box. When you finish the formula, it's a good idea to click Check Formula (to verify your syntax) before clicking OK to exit the dialog.

Context of a Measure

A measure has no context until it's added to the Values drop-zone. Then its context is determined by the other attributes in the pivot table. The context of a measure is given by your choices in Slicers Vertical, Slicers Horizontal, Report Filter, Column Labels, and Row Labels. As an example, if you select only 1996 from a slicer based on Year, the values of the measure displayed (that is, a measure that has been added to the Values drop-zone) are those relevant to 1996 and not any other year or years. This is the standard behavior of a measure. Its values are governed by the filters you implement in the pivot table. Measures have *filter context*. As such, the values of a measure in a pivot table will often change as you slice and filter. Measures are often said to be *dynamic*.

One of the most powerful aspects of DAX is the ability to alter the filter context at will. The CALCULATE() function lets you add to or subtract from the existing filter context. You can change or override the current filters or remove the filters completely. If you remove the current filters completely, you are effectively turning a dynamic measure into a static, fixed measure. In the example in the upcoming section "Examples of Measures," the function ALL() modifies the CALCULATE() function to remove any current filter context on the Order Details table. In plain words, this means that the value in any particular cell is unchanged no matter how you slice, dice, or filter the date. Sometimes, overriding the filter context (totally or partially) is just what you need. Sometimes, honoring the current filter is just what you need. Later in this chapter, you'll see examples of both. Hopefully, then, it will begin to make sense. The filter context is one of the more difficult concepts in PowerPivot.

Evaluation and Non-Materialization of a Measure

A measure is not evaluated until it is added to the Values drop-zone. As you add columns to Column Labels and Row Labels and drill down and drill up, the measure gets re-evaluated for every single cell in the pivot table individually. If you filter in these labels, in a Report Filter, and/or in a slicer, re-evaluation will occur. The evaluations are not stored permanently in a PowerPivot table; they are never materialized. This is another reason why measures as referred to as *dynamic* data.

Where to Use a Measure in a Pivot Table

In the PowerPivot Field List, a calculated measure has a small calculator icon to distinguish it from normal and calculated columns. You can *only* add the measure to the Values drop-zone. You can't, for example, add it to Row Labels or to a slicer. In Chapter 2, you saw just such a measure: DAXMeasure.

For those readers with an SSAS and cube background (and if you don't have this background, please feel free to skip this paragraph), a measure is a member of a measure group. A measure is always an aggregation, and its value is determined by how you slice and dice (filter context). A measure in PowerPivot is always a measure. You can't change it into a degenerate or fact dimension—that's why it can only be added to the Values drop-zone in the field list and not to Column Labels, for example.

Referring to Measures

Measure names, like column names, must be referenced using square brackets, for example, [DAXMeasure]. You may reference a measure, for instance, when you build a measure based on another measure. Measures are assigned to a parent table; however, as measure names must be unique across *all* tables, it's not necessary to preface a measure name with a table name.

Examples of Measures

These examples are reproduced from Chapter 2.

```
=SUM([Sales Amount])/CALCULATE(SUM([Sales Amount]),ALL('Order Details'))
=SUM('Order Details'[Sales Amount])/
CALCULATE(SUM('Order Details'[Sales Amount]),ALL('Order Details'))
```

Both examples are equivalent. There is yet another way of writing these examples—there is a shortcut that allows you to omit the CALCULATE() function. Although most DAX functions can be a part of both calculated column and measure formulas, the CALCULATE() function is normally used for a measure. This is for two reasons.

One, it is often used to return a number or metric of interest. Two, as it is used to modify the filter context, it is most appropriate in the Values drop-zone as a measure. CALCULATE() is covered shortly—it's a very popular function.

How to Write DAX

Whether a calculated column or a measure (in the formula bar in PowerPivot or in the Measure Settings dialog in the Excel worksheet), you can choose to type everything in your DAX formula. Or preferably, you will avail yourself of AutoComplete. AutoComplete not only saves typing, but obviates typos and syntax errors. Here's a very simple DAX formula for a calculated column (actually, just a single function that you met earlier), and this example demonstrates how to take advantage of AutoComplete:

1.   The completed formula is:

    ```
    =YEAR(Orders[OrderDate])
    ```

2.   First, activate the formula bar by adding a new column to the Orders PowerPivot table. You have two choices to start the formula. Either type an equal sign (=) or use the small function button immediately to the left of the typing area in the formula bar. The latter opens the Insert Function dialog, which is shown in Figure 4-1. From the Select a Category drop-down, choose Date & Time. From the Select a Function drop-down, choose Year and click OK. This method enters an

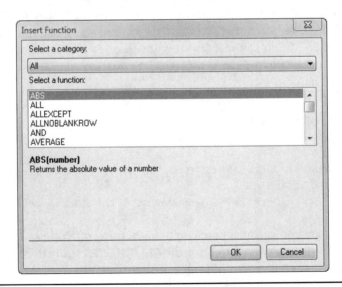

Figure 4-1   *Insert Function dialog*

equal sign for you, followed by the function and an opening parenthesis. If you typed the equal sign instead, press "y" to open a list of functions beginning with that letter. Use the arrow keys, if necessary, to highlight YEAR and press TAB. This enters the function name followed by a parenthesis. If you both type an equal sign and use the Insert Function dialog, PowerPivot is clever enough not to insert a second equal sign.

3. Type the letter "o" and use the arrow keys, or mouse, to select Orders[OrderDate]. Press TAB to insert this column name.

4. Type a closing parenthesis and notice how it and the first opening parenthesis are highlighted. This is very useful as it helps you to balance left and right parentheses in more complex formulas.

5. To check your syntax, click the small check mark button in the formula bar. To accept and apply your syntax, press ENTER. To back out, press ESC or click the small cross button.

Should you require more room in which to work, you can drag the lower edge of the formula bar downward. If you want your formula to appear on more than one line, press ALT-ENTER.

Working on a DAX formula as a measure is similar. First you click the New Measure button in the PowerPivot ribbon in Excel. This opens the Measure Settings dialog, which is shown in Figure 4-2.

In this dialog you can also access the Insert Function dialog—the function button is just to the right of the Formula caption. You check syntax by clicking the Check Formula button. You can back out by pressing ESC or clicking Cancel. You can enlarge the typing area by resizing the whole dialog. You apply the formula by pressing ENTER or clicking OK.

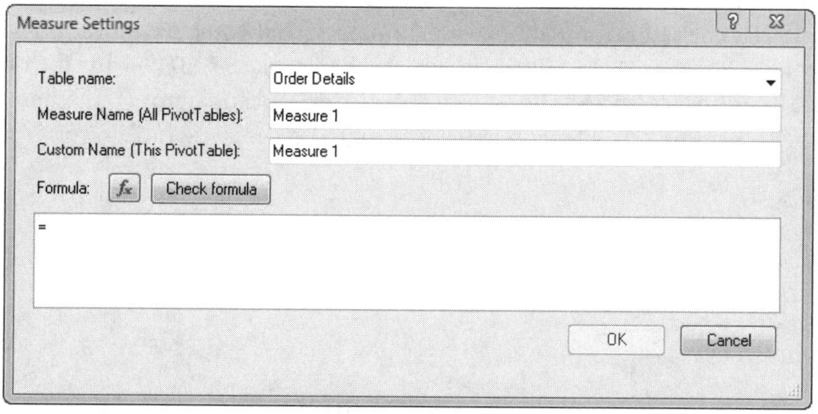

Figure 4-2   *Measure Settings dialog*

Operators and Operator Precedence

DAX has a range of arithmetic, comparison, concatenation, and logical operators. The arithmetic operators include addition (+), subtraction (−), multiplication (*), division (/), and exponentiation (^). If you have more than one arithmetic operator, you need to be aware of operator precedence and how to control it. Multiplication and division are performed before addition and subtraction, for example. The precedence rules are similar to those in many other languages. If you wish to override the order of precedence, you must enclose the part you want to evaluate first inside parentheses. Here are a couple of examples (you might want to try these as calculated columns on any table, or as measures):

```
=7 + 3 * 2
=(7 + 3) * 2
```

The first example results in 13, the second in 20. In the first example, the default precedence order means 3 is multiplied by 2 first, and then added to 7. In the second example, the parentheses force 7 and 3 to be added together first, and then multiplied by 2.

To perform concatenation, you can use the DAX function CONCATENATE(). This is limited to two parameters, so if you wish to concatenate more than two values, you have to use a nested CONCATENATE(). Perhaps a neater alternative is to use the ampersand (&) concatenation operator. The next two examples produce the same result (please note the use of double quotes to delineate literal string values):

```
=CONCATENATE("Hello",CONCATENATE("big","world"))
="Hello" & "big" & "world"
```

The two logical operators, AND and OR, are not keywords but, rather, the functions AND() and OR(). Each is limited to two parameters, so if you have more you will need a nested AND() or OR(). Alternatively, you can replace AND() with the double-ampersand operator (&&) and OR() with the double-pipe operator (||)—these are not limited to two parameters.. Here are a few calculated column examples:

```
=AND(1=1,2=2)
=AND(1=1,2=3)
=OR(1=1,2=3)
=AND(1=1,AND(2=2,3=3))
=1=1 && 2=2 && 3=4
=1=1 || 2=2 || 3=4
```

Note that the logical operators return either TRUE or FALSE.

Data Types

Quite often, functions require input of a certain data type. If the data type is wrong, the function will fail. Fortunately, if it's feasible, PowerPivot will often attempt an implicit conversion of the data type. There are no explicit conversion functions as such, with the possible exceptions of VALUE() (*not* VALUES()), FORMAT(), DATEVALUE(), and TIMEVALUE(). Here are two calculated column examples for you to try on OrderID column (Whole Number) of the Orders table:

```
=SUM(Orders[OrderID])
=RIGHT(Orders[OrderID],2)
```

Both of these work. The first is fine, as SUM() expects a numeric input. The second is possible, even though RIGHT() expects a text parameter, as PowerPivot does an implicit conversion from numeric to string. Now change the data type of the OrderID column to Text (Home ribbon, Formatting group, Data Type drop-down) and try the next two formulas (same as before, but in a different order to save on redoing the RIGHT() function formula):

```
=RIGHT(Orders[OrderID],2)
=SUM(Orders[OrderID])
```

Only the first one works. SUM() fails because it expects a numeric parameter, and, this time, there was no implicit data conversion. If you click in the column, you should see a smart tag that explains the error. Therefore, it's very important that you get the data types for your columns correct as implicit conversion does not always work. Don't forget to reset the OrderID column back to a data type of Whole Number.

Null Values

In relational databases, such as SQL Server, a missing value is treated as a Null value. Operations involving a Null generally return a Null, although it is possible to change this default behavior in SQL Server. In multidimensional databases, such as SSAS, missing values are treated as zeros or empty strings, depending on the source data type. PowerPivot is much closer to the latter approach—a missing value is classified as a Blank. Adding a number to a blank value returns the number, rather than another Blank or a Null. You can generate a Blank through the BLANK() function. You can generate a whole column of Blank values by double-clicking an Add Column column header in a table and renaming the column. You can test for a Blank with the ISBLANK() function. You may want to try the following formula (results shown in Figure 4-3) as a calculated column on the Customers table:

```
=IF(ISBLANK(Customers[Region]),BLANK() & "No region","Region")
```

CompanyName ▾	Address ▾	City ▾	Region ▾	PostalCode ▾	Country ▾	Phone ▾	Fax ▾	CalculatedColumn1 ▾
Alfred Futterkiste	Obere Str. ...	Berlin		12209	Germany	030-0074...	030-0...	No region
Ana Trujillo Empa...	Avda. de l...	México...		05021	Mexico	(5) 555-4...	(5) 55...	No region
Antonio Moreno ...	Matadero...	México...		05023	Mexico	(5) 555-3...		No region
Around the Horn	120 Hanov...	London		WA1 1DP	UK	(171) 55...	(171) ...	No region
Berglunds snabbk...	Berguvsvä...	Luleå		S-958 22	Sweden	0921-12...	0921-...	No region
Blauer See Delika...	Forsterstr...	Mann...		68306	Germany	0621-084...	0621-...	No region
Blondesddsl père...	24, place ...	Strasb...		67000	France	88.60.15...	88.60...	No region
Bólido Comidas p...	C/ Araquil...	Madrid		28023	Spain	(91) 555 ...	(91) 5...	No region
Bon app'	12, rue de...	Marse...		13008	France	91.24.45...	91.24...	No region
Bottom-Dollar M...	23 Tsawas...	Tsawa...	BC	T2F 8M4	Canada	(604) 55...	(604) ...	Region
B's Beverages	Fauntlero...	London		EC2 5NT	UK	(171) 55...		No region
Cactus Comidas p...	Cerrito 333	Buen...		1010	Argentina	(1) 135-5...	(1) 13...	No region

Figure 4-3   *A calculated column*

This formula demonstrates a couple of points about Blank values. The Region column of the SQL Server Northwind database contains quite a few Nulls. If your Northwind import is from SQL Server, these Null values are changed into Blank values. The ISBLANK() function is testing for Blank values. The IF() function is seeing if ISBLANK() returned TRUE or FALSE. If it's not TRUE, the output is the string "Region." If it is TRUE, the output is the string "No region" concatenated to a Blank—generated by the BLANK() function. This concatenation results in the string "No region" and not in another Blank. You can also add a number to a Blank and the result will be the number. This behavior is different from the default behavior of a Null in a relational database such as SQL Server.

Why Use the RELATED() Function?

The RELATED() function is frequently used in calculated columns. This section shows just why it is so popular.

First of all, here's what RELATED() does, in multidimensional terms. RELATED() denormalizes attributes from multiple dimensions into a single, de-snowflaked dimension and creates a natural user hierarchy within that single dimension. Wow! No wonder it's popular! It is similar to the Excel VLOOKUP() function, but far more versatile. VLOOKUP(), for example, requires a specific arrangement of columns and only references the first one—RELATED() can access any column in a related table.

Secondly, here's what it does, in somewhat plainer English: It makes viewing a pivot table easier, faster, more intuitive, and much more likely to reveal true business intelligence. It means the consumer of the pivot table needs to know nothing about databases or about relationships between tables—RELATED() makes relationships completely transparent. Maybe it's worth a look.

An important point to make is that for RELATED() to work its magic and hide relationships, you have to have table relationships in the first place! The same is true for its sibling function, RELATEDTABLE(). But let's go right back to the beginning and start with no relationship between the Products and the Categories tables from the Northwind database. Here's a step-by-step example that demonstrates the value of relationships and the RELATED() function:

1. Delete the relationship between the Products and Categories tables—from the Design ribbon, choose Relationships group | Manage Relationships button—and select the relationship before clicking Delete, followed by clicking OK on the warning, and then Close in the Manage Relationships dialog. The Manage Relationships dialog, with the relationship to delete selected, is shown in Figure 4-4.

2. Also, delete the existing RELATED() function by deleting the Category calculated column in the Products table.

3. Insert a pivot table into a new worksheet—choose Home ribbon | Reports group | PivotTable button | PivotTable from the drop-down, and click OK.

4. In the Excel worksheet, put Quantity from Order Details in Values, CategoryName from Categories, and then ProductName from Products in Row Labels. Ignore any warning message in the field list about relationships being needed, and take a look at the data. If you were to heed the message and let PowerPivot create required relationships, you would not see the mismatch of data we are about to consider. There are a couple of strange things going on. If you look under Beverages, you can see Alice Mutton, which is not a

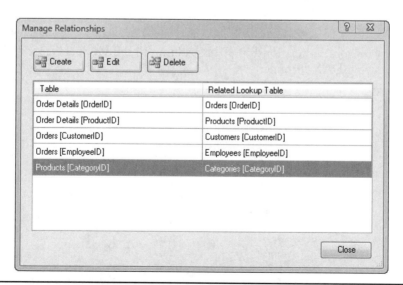

Figure 4-4 *Manage Relationships dialog*

beverage, and Chai, which is. Under Meat/Poultry, you can see Alice Mutton in its correct place, but also Chai, which is in the wrong place. As there is no relationship between categories and products, something called a cross-join with no possibility of an inner join (in SQL-speak), or a Crossjoin() with no possibility of Autoexists (in MDX-speak), has occurred. The pivot table is showing every possible combination of categories and products, even if we know that many of the combinations are invalid. As the Products table is still related to the Order Details table (through the common ProductID column), the break between categories and products also means a break between categories and the quantity sold. There is no relationship between CategoryName and Quantity. If there is no relationship between a row label (or column label) and a value, a pivot table will display total figures repeated. That's why the Grand Total is 51317 and the subtotals for Beverages and Meat/Poultry also show 51317. If you ever get repeating figures like this in your own pivot tables, you know you've got the relationships wrong. This example is shown in Figure 4-5. This analysis raises a fundamental issue—how do you know when a product is under the wrong category. I had no idea that Chai was a beverage and that Alice Mutton was meat/poultry (although the word mutton might provide a clue—but then again, the Indian delicacy "Bombay duck" is a fish)! If you aren't (or your end user isn't) familiar with every single item of data, you must go back and check the data in the source. In this example, you might use the following query, against SQL Server or Access, to establish that Chai is a beverage and Alice Mutton is meat/poultry:

```
select ProductName, CategoryName
from Products as P
inner join Categories as C
on P.CategoryID = C.CategoryID
```

5. Let's try to "force" a relationship. Add a column to the Products table and enter the following DAX formula:

```
=RELATED(Categories[CategoryName])
```

	A	B	C	D
1	Row Labels	Sum of Quantity		
2	⊞ Beverages	51317		
3	⊞ Condiments	51317		
4	⊞ Confections	51317		
5	⊞ Dairy Products	51317		
6	⊞ Grains/Cereals	51317		
7	⊞ Meat/Poultry	51317		
8	⊞ Produce	51317		
9	⊞ Seafood	51317		
10	Grand Total	51317		

Figure 4-5 *Repeating data indicating missing relationships*

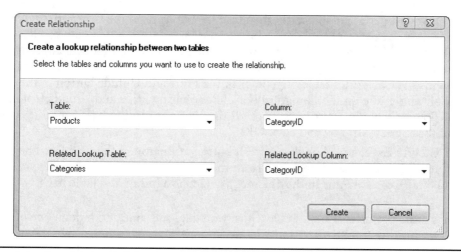

Figure 4-6   *Create Relationship dialog*

6. This will fail, and the smart tag will tell you why. We need a relationship before we can use RELATED(). Accept the error for now and rename the column to Category.

7. Re-establish our deleted relationship—first, from the Design ribbon, choose Relationships group | Create Relationship button. In the Create Relationship dialog, relate the Products table to the Categories table on the CategoryID column before clicking Create. The Create Relationship dialog is shown in Figure 4-6. Your Category column, using the RELATED() function, should now be working.

8. Switch to Excel and click the Refresh button at the top of the field list. Replace CategoryName from the Categories table with Category from the Products table. Make sure that Category is above ProductName in the Row Labels drop-zone. Now your pivot table is looking good. The result is shown in Figure 4-7. The subtotals appear reasonable and Alice Mutton is under Meat/Poultry only and Chai can only be seen under Beverages.

	A	B	C	D
1	**Row Labels** ▾	**Sum of Quantity**		
2	⊞ Beverages	9532		
3	⊞ Condiments	5298		
4	⊞ Confections	7906		
5	⊞ Dairy Products	9149		
6	⊞ Grains/Cereals	4562		
7	⊞ Meat/Poultry	4199		
8	⊞ Produce	2990		
9	⊞ Seafood	7681		
10	**Grand Total**	51317		

Sheet1 / Sheet2 / S

Figure 4-7   *Non-repeating data*

9. But you can even go one better than this! You don't need the Categories table in the field list—it's only going to confuse your business user. After all, you have just denormalized its data (that is, the category name) into the Products table. Switch to PowerPivot. Hide all the columns of the Categories table from the pivot table. With the Categories table current, click the Hide and Unhide button in the Columns group on the Design ribbon. The resulting Hide and Unhide Columns dialog is shown in Figure 4-8. Turn off the check box in the In PivotTable column of the (Select All) row and click OK.

10. Switch to Excel and click the Refresh button at the top of the field list. The Categories table has disappeared from the PowerPivot Field List. When you hide all of a table's columns in this manner, you are also hiding the table itself.

That's quite powerful stuff. You have put two tables into one and hidden one of them. This greatly simplifies the end-user experience. Your users don't need to know about the Categories table and whether it has relationships or not—indeed, they may not even understand relationships. In addition, they now have a nice drill-down from category to product. If you are familiar with SSAS cube design, you have just simulated a natural user hierarchy in one table based on attributes from two tables. You have hidden the original attribute (CategoryName) that now populates a new level (Category) in your new, simulated natural user hierarchy.

You can easily extend this. You can create a drill-down hierarchy in one table based on three or more tables. For example, you could display the category for each order line

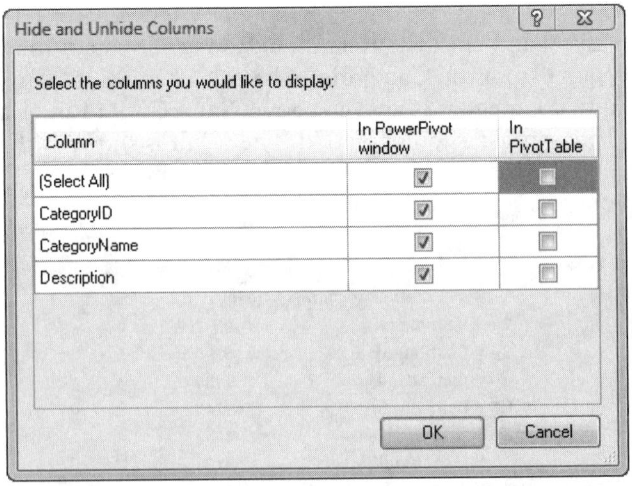

Column	In PowerPivot window	In PivotTable
(Select All)	✓	☐
CategoryID	✓	☐
CategoryName	✓	☐
Description	✓	☐

Hide and Unhide Columns

Select the columns you would like to display:

OK   Cancel

Figure 4-8   *Hide and Unhide Columns dialog*

in the Orders Details table. Your column would need to reference the Products table, which in turn references the Categories table. This is, in effect, a double jump. The next two lines of code show how (the first goes in the Products table; the second goes in the Order Details table and assumes that the first one is named Category):

```
=RELATED(Categories[CategoryName])
=RELATED(Products[Category])
```

This is all very nice, but there is one proviso. You can't relate a table to itself in PowerPivot, and therefore, you can't use RELATED() if it references a column in the same table. Thus, you can't create a hierarchy directly in the Employees table. This is a self-join table, in a relational source, with the Reports To column referencing the EmployeeID column. During the import of this table (assuming a relational source), if you click the Details hyperlink in the Messages column of the Data Preparation row, you will see the message that self-joins are not supported. To get around this problem, you are probably going to have to write some SQL that joins the table to itself and unravels the hierarchy. You might use a common table expression (CTE) to do so.

RELATED() has a sibling function, RELATEDTABLE(). In general, RELATED() would appear in a child table (the many side of a relationship) and pull back a column from a parent table. For example, you could add the category name to a products table. In general, RELATEDTABLE() would appear in the parent table and reference the matching rows in the child table. As it may well return more than one matching row, RELATEDTABLE() returns a table rather than a column. As such, it can't be used to populate a column directly. However, it can be fed into another DAX function that accepts a table as a parameter. The so-called X-functions do just that. Here's an example:

```
=COUNTX(RELATEDTABLE('Order Details'),'Order Details'[OrderID])
```

If you have a calculated column in the Orders table, this will show how many order lines there were in each order.

Why Use the CALCULATE() Function?

The CALCULATE() function is very popular in measures. Here, we examine why this might be so.

Measures have filter context. As the user filters (Report Filter and/or Row Labels or Column Labels) and/or slices (Slicers Vertical or Slicers Horizontal), they change the context in which the measures are shown in the pivot table. By default, the measure values will change to reflect the current context—measures are re-evaluated every time the context is changed. This may or may not be the result you desire.

The CALCULATE() function gives you total control over the way filters affect the measures. You can use the function to honor an existing filter, you can ignore the filter altogether, you can change the filter, you can honor the filter only in part, or you can create a new filter context that is completely different from the filter context implemented by the user in the pivot table GUI. Wow again!

In slightly simpler language, CALCULATE() lets you control how measures (added to the Values drop-zone) change or don't change as the user manipulates the pivot table. Here's a step-by-step example to get you started:

1. Create a new pivot table, or remove all entries from the PowerPivot Field List drop-zones for an existing pivot table.

2. Add Category (from the Products table) to Row Labels. Add Year (from Orders) to Slicers Horizontal. Add Country (from Customers) also to Slicers Horizontal. Add Quantity (from Order Details) to Values—its default name should be Sum of Quantity. The resulting pivot table is shown in Figure 4-9.

3. Notice the grand total is 51317. Use the slicer to show just 1996—the total is now 9581 (please be aware that there are different incarnations of Northwind with differing years and sales figures—you may adjust the exercise to reflect your totals and years). Remove the Year slice and slice on Austria from the Country slicer; the total is now 5167. Then, try both 1996 and Austria; the result is 949. Then remove the slices. You have just been changing the filter context of the measure (an implicit measure based on a table column, Quantity) in the pivot table.

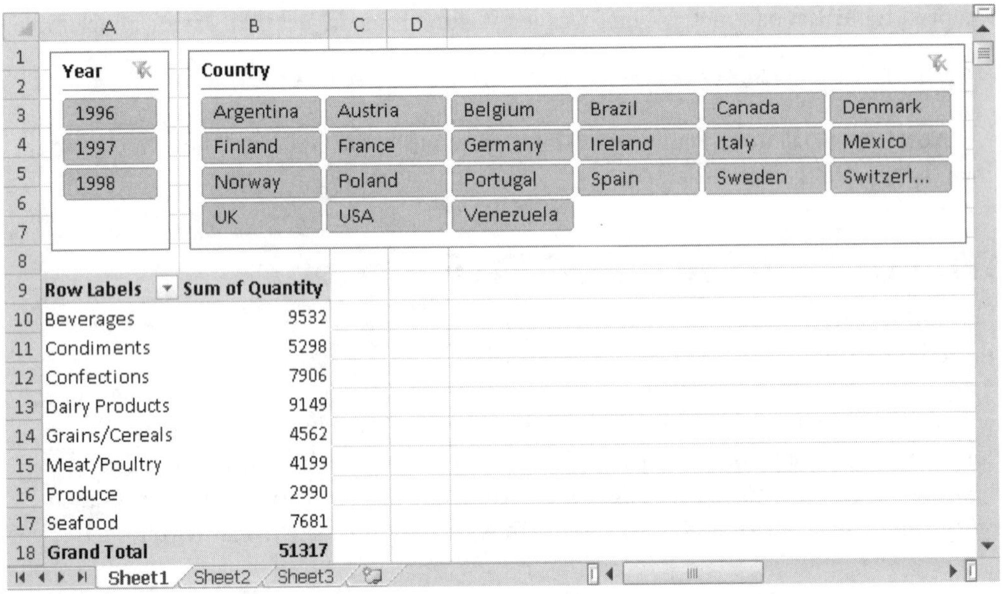

Figure 4-9   *Pivot table example*

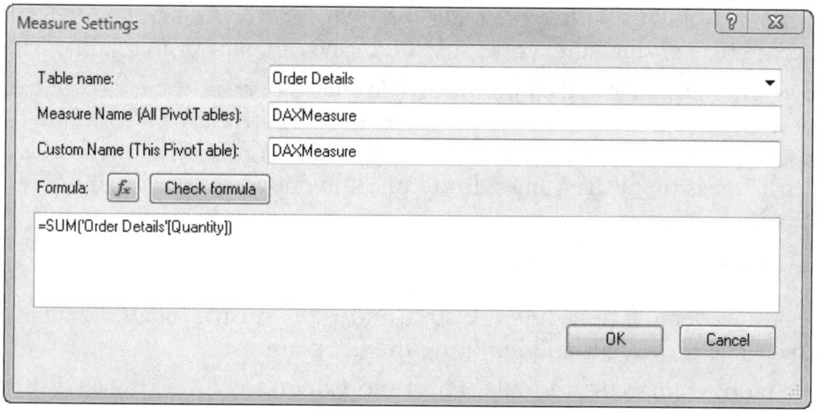

Figure 4-10   *Measure Settings dialog*

4. With the focus in the pivot table, click the New Measure button in the Measures group on the PowerPivot ribbon. In the Measure Settings dialog, make sure the Table name is Order Details; for Measure name, enter **DAXMeasure**; in Formula, enter the following DAX formula; and click Check Formula. Your dialog should look like Figure 4-10. Click OK. Your pivot table now resembles Figure 4-11.

```
=SUM('Order Details'[Quantity])
```

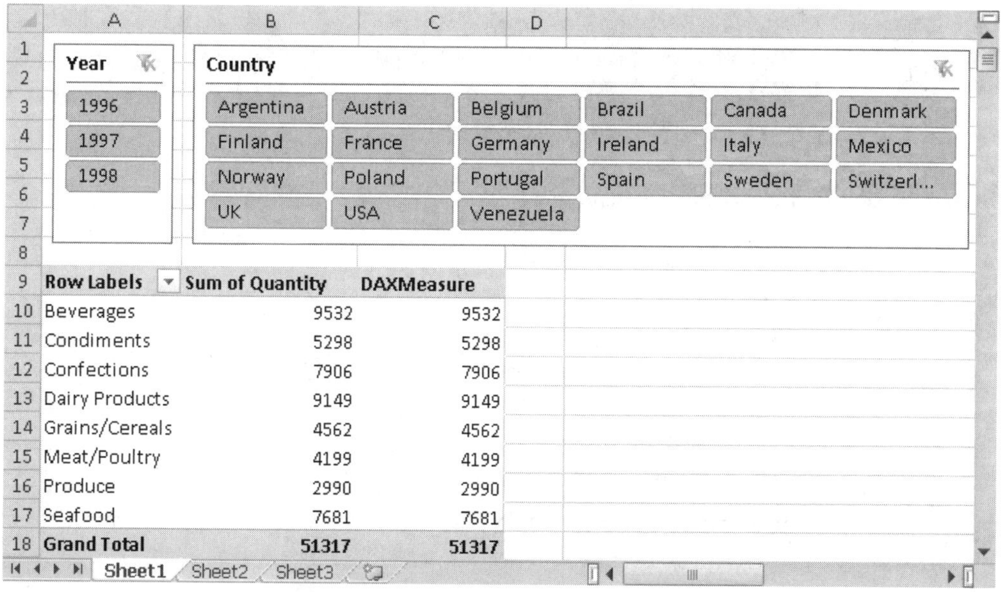

Figure 4-11   *Pivot table with a measure based on a DAX formula*

5. Check the overall total, then the totals for 1996, for Austria, and for 1996 and Austria. Your new measure written in DAX is no different from the implicit measure.

6. Change the DAX formula. One way to do this is to click the Measure Settings button, while the focus is in the pivot table. Alternatively, you can right-click the measure in the field list and choose Edit Formula. Yet another method is to right-click the measure in the Values drop-zone and choose Edit Measure. The new syntax is as follows:

```
=CALCULATE(SUM('Order Details'[Quantity]))
```

7. Check the overall figure, 1996, Austria, and 1996/Austria again. There is no change. The measure is still honoring the filter context.

8. Once more, change the formula. This time, extend the CALCULATE() function as shown here:

```
=CALCULATE(SUM('Order Details'[Quantity]),ALL(Customers[Country]))
```

Try with no slicer (that is, no filter), just 1996 with all countries, just Austria with all years, and just 1996 with Austria. The four results are shown in Figure 4-12 (No filter), Figure 4-13 (Year filter), Figure 4-14 (Country filter), and Figure 4-15 (Year and Country filter). These are the first of three sets of four results in this exercise.

Year	Country				
1996	Argentina	Austria	Belgium	Brazil	Canada	Denmark
1997	Finland	France	Germany	Ireland	Italy	Mexico
1998	Norway	Poland	Portugal	Spain	Sweden	Switzerl...
	UK	USA	Venezuela			

Row Labels	Sum of Quantity	DAXMeasure
Beverages	9532	9532
Condiments	5298	5298
Confections	7906	7906
Dairy Products	9149	9149
Grains/Cereals	4562	4562
Meat/Poultry	4199	4199
Produce	2990	2990
Seafood	7681	7681
Grand Total	**51317**	**51317**

Figure 4-12   *No filter context 1/3*

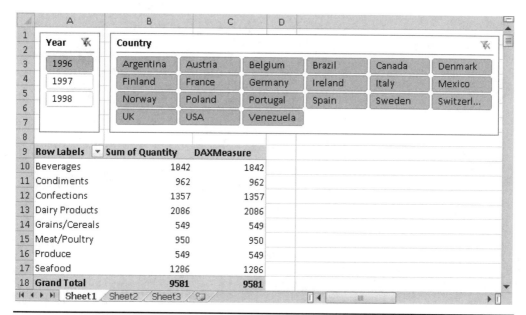

Figure 4-13   *Year filter context 1/3*

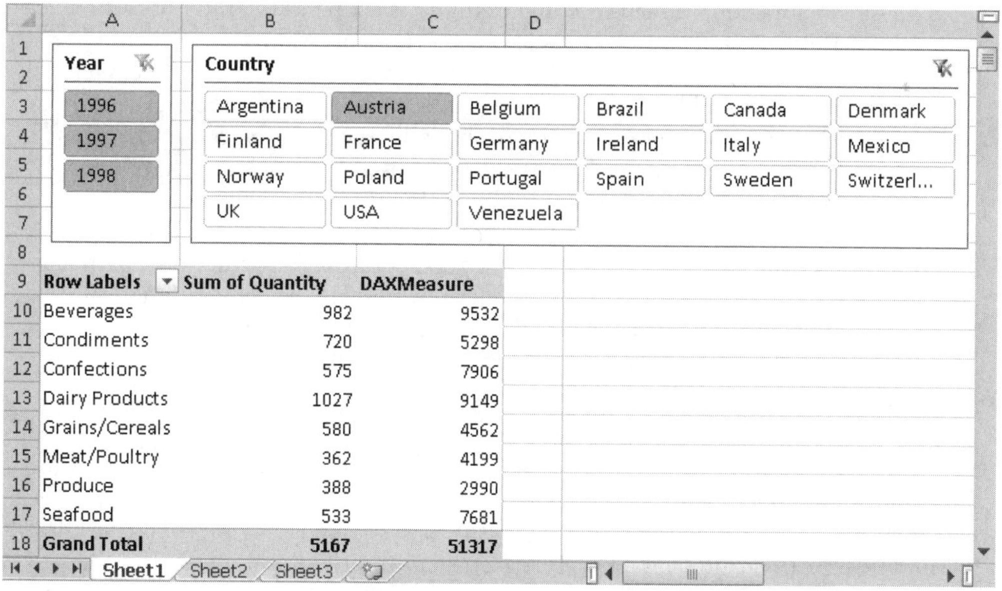

Figure 4-14   *Country filter context 1/3*

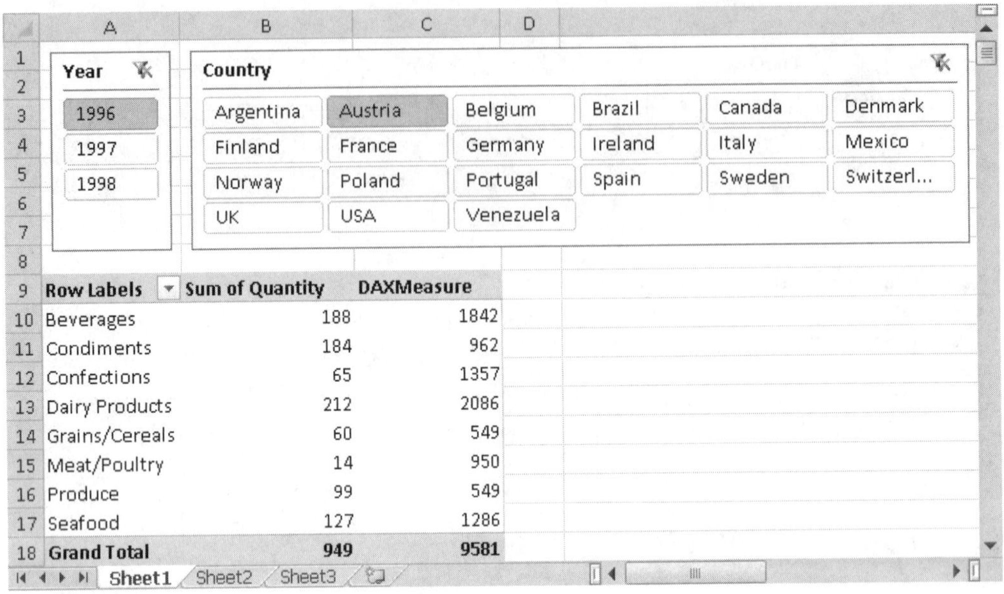

Figure 4-15 *Year and Country filter context 1/3*

This is the core of DAX. If you understand what's happening, you understand DAX. The `ALL()` function, in the preceding example, is acting as the filter or `SetFilter` parameter of the `CALCULATE()` function. `ALL()` is overriding the current filter context. The filter parameter is optional and you can have more than one. Here, it's telling the pivot table to ignore any filter on country (for example, Austria) that the user may choose. It's always going to show the figure for *all* countries—thanks to the `ALL()` function. Why might this be very useful? There are a number of important reasons. For example, you can have highly customized and flexible measures that display exactly what you want. Or, you might want to control the scope of the end user—so that, even if they add countries and filter on a particular country, the figures they see are still for all countries. You are programmatically overriding the user actions in the GUI. Or you might have measures based on this measure, and those new measures require the data for all countries.

9. Let's experiment. Change the formula as follows:

```
=CALCULATE(SUM('Order Details'[Quantity]),ALL(Orders[Year]))
```

Now as you filter, the Year slicer is totally ignored, but the Country filter is operative again. Some of the possible results are shown in Figure 4-16 (No filter), Figure 4-17 (Year filter), Figure 4-18 (Country filter), and Figure 4-19 (Year and Country filter). Take some time to digest the figures and understand what is happening.

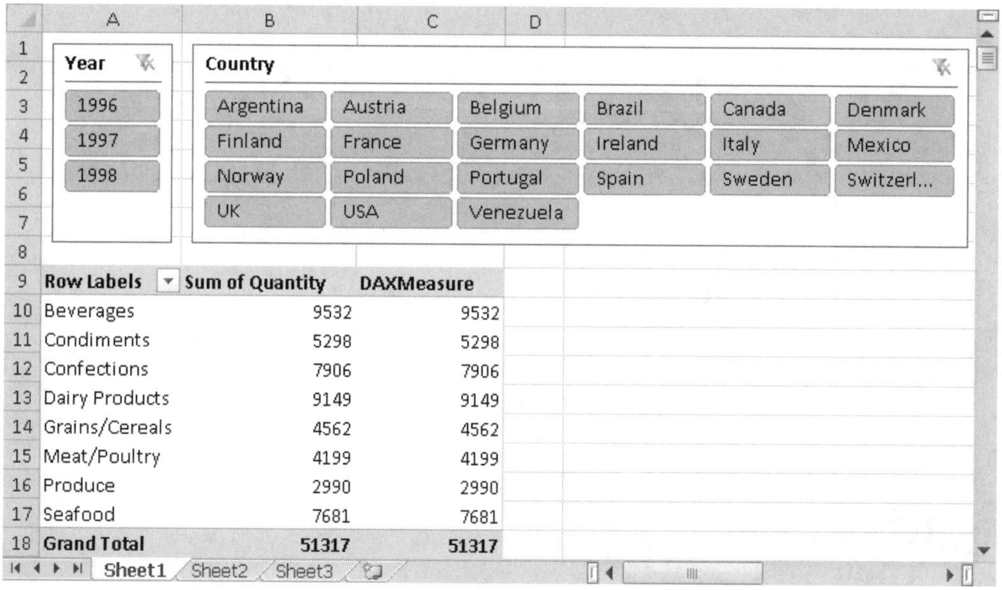

Figure 4-16 *No filter context 2/3*

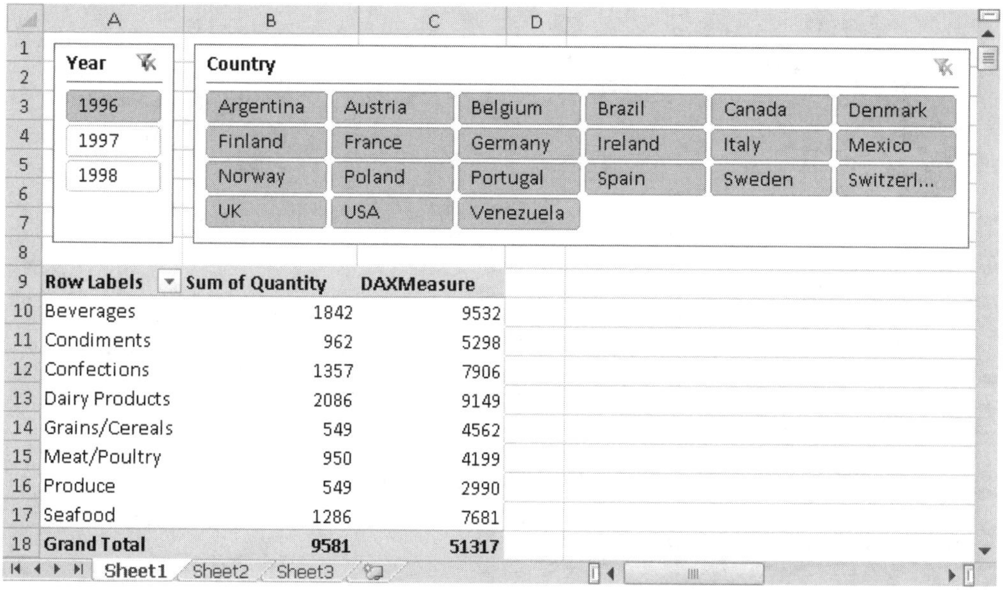

Figure 4-17 *Year filter context 2/3*

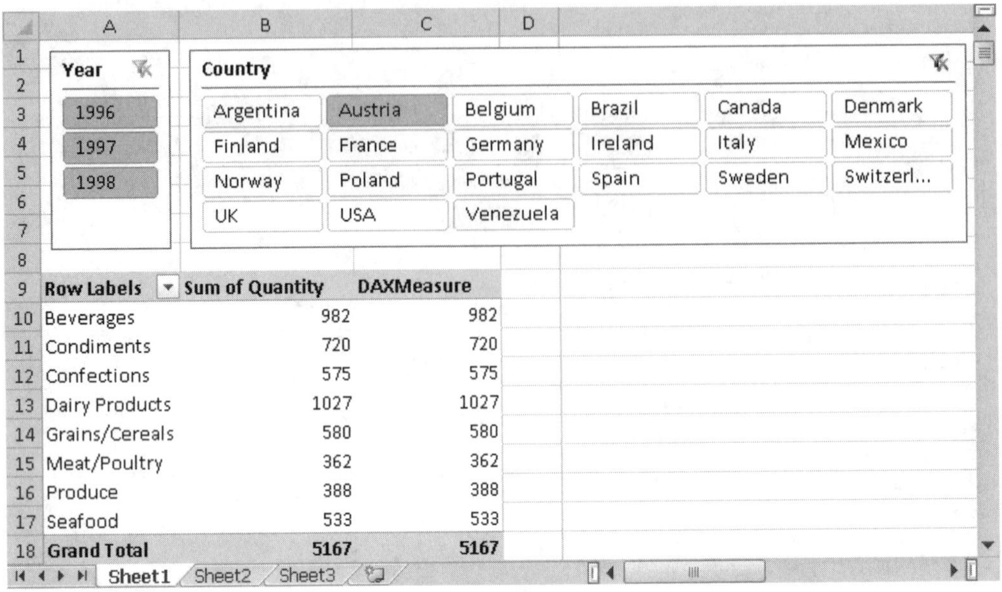

Figure 4-18 *Country filter context 2/3*

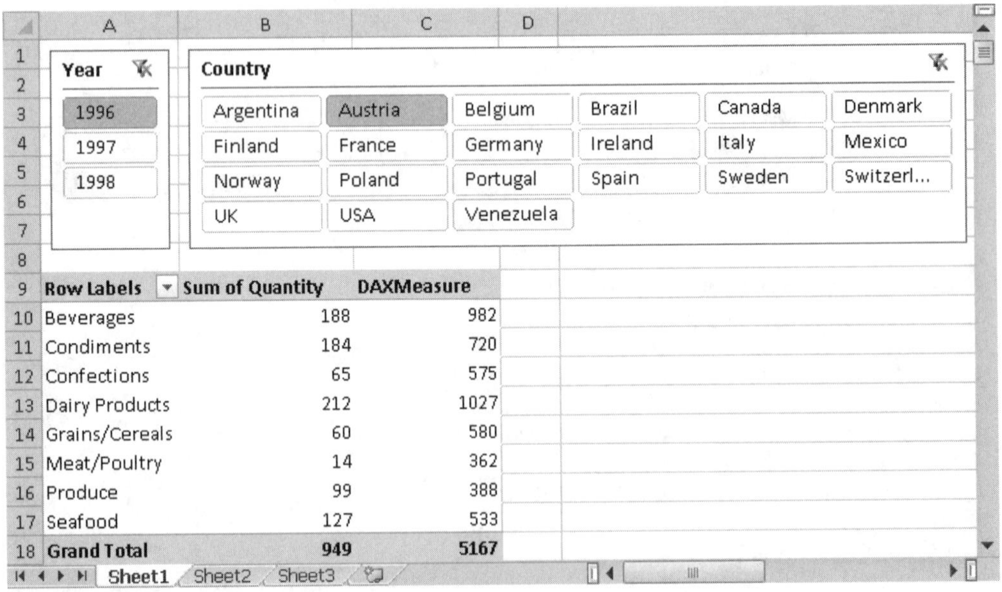

Figure 4-19 *Year and Country filter context 2/3*

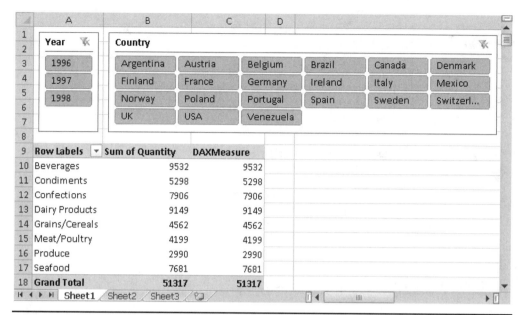

Figure 4-20   *No filter context 3/3*

10. And here's yet another change to the formula (some results are shown in Figure 4-20 (No filter), Figure 4-21 (Year filter), Figure 4-22 (Country filter), and Figure 4-23 (Year and Country filter)):

```
=CALCULATE(SUM('Order Details'[Quantity]),
ALL(Orders[Year]),ALL(Customers[Country]))
```

You have removed the filter context for both Year and Country. No matter which years and/or countries are chosen, the totals remain the same. The ALL() function is repeated for both slicers/filters. However, you can have many slicers. You can also filter from Report Filter or from Column Labels or from Row Filters. If you had ten possible filters, you would need to repeat the ALL() function ten times. The next step shows a very convenient alternative.

11. Change the formula as follows:

```
=CALCULATE(SUM('Order Details'[Quantity]),
ALLEXCEPT('Order Details',Products[Category]))
```

Try slicing on 1996 and/or Austria again. The results are unchanged from the previous step. The ALLEXCEPT() function is causing the measure to ignore *all* filters on the Order Details table (including the Quantity) *except* any filter based on product category.

Row Labels	Sum of Quantity	DAXMeasure
Beverages	1842	9532
Condiments	962	5298
Confections	1357	7906
Dairy Products	2086	9149
Grains/Cereals	549	4562
Meat/Poultry	950	4199
Produce	549	2990
Seafood	1286	7681
Grand Total	**9581**	**51317**

Figure 4-21 *Year filter context 3/3*

Row Labels	Sum of Quantity	DAXMeasure
Beverages	982	9532
Condiments	720	5298
Confections	575	7906
Dairy Products	1027	9149
Grains/Cereals	580	4562
Meat/Poultry	362	4199
Produce	388	2990
Seafood	533	7681
Grand Total	**5167**	**51317**

Figure 4-22 *Country filter context 3/3*

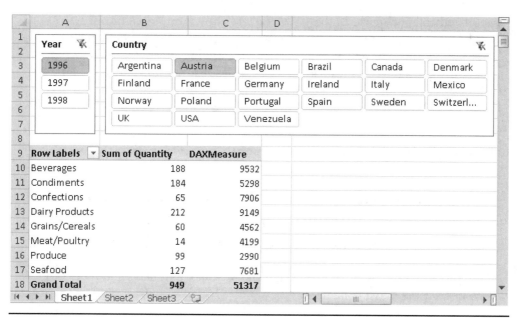

Figure 4-23   *Year and Country filter context 3/3*

12. This final step is given with a little less guidance. Try each of the following five formulas in turn and observe the totals in the pivot table as you slice/filter on 1996 and/or Austria:

```
=CALCULATE(SUM('Order Details'[Quantity]),
FILTER(Orders,Orders[Year]=1996))
=CALCULATE(SUM('Order Details'[Quantity]),Orders[Year]=1996)
=CALCULATE(SUM('Order Details'[Quantity]),Customers[Country]="Austria")
=CALCULATE(SUM('Order Details'[Quantity]),
Customers[Country]="Austria",Orders[Year]=1996)
=CALCULATE(SUM('Order Details'[Quantity]),
Customers[Country]="Austria" || Customers[Country]="Mexico",
Orders[Year]=1996)
```

The first and second examples superficially produce the same result until you slice on 1997—the choice is yours (FILTER() returns a fixed table). The second example is more efficient than the first as it is evaluated only for the cells in the current context; FILTER() evaluates against the whole Orders table. The fifth example includes Mexico as well as Austria.

The CALCULATE() function, in our examples, has been using the SUM() function on the Quantity. You could write the SUM() function as a separate measure and base CALCULATE() on this new measure. In that case, the SUM() function would be encapsulated and not appear in the CALCULATE() function. When CALCULATE() is based directly on another measure, you can omit CALCULATE() itself, but the filter parameters must be enclosed inside parentheses. The measure itself acts as a function. If you want to try, create a measure called QuantitySum and amend the last CALCULATE() example in Step 12. Here are the two DAX formulas you will need:

```
=SUM('Order Details'[Quantity])
=CALCULATE([QuantitySum],
Customers[Country]="Austria" || Customers[Country]="Mexico",
Orders[Year]=1996)
```

Now change the CALCULATE() formula, as shown next, to use the shorthand:

```
=[QuantitySum](Customers[Country]="Austria" ||
Customers[Country]="Mexico",Orders[Year]=1996)
```

Please note that the filter parameters are enclosed in parentheses and there is no comma (,) after the measure name.

This section has been a fairly detailed introduction to the CALCULATE() function. To reiterate, CALCULATE() can be used to control the filter context of measures within a PowerPivot pivot table.

Where to Go from Here

This chapter has been an overview of and introduction to DAX. As such, only a very few functions have been covered. In particular, the very useful date and time functions have not been mentioned. These functions enable you to build time intelligence—for example, year-on-year changes and year-to-date figures. The second part of this book (Part II, DAX) delves much more deeply into DAX. It looks at *every* DAX function. Among many other techniques, it demonstrates how to include time intelligence in your PowerPivot pivot tables.

Chapter 5

Pivot Tables and Pivot Charts: Overview

Thin chapter is concerned with looking at pivot reports, that is, pivot tables and pivot charts. The chapter is an overview; a whole book could easily be written about pivot tables in Excel—and another one just on pivot charts! The emphasis here is on creating pivot tables and charts. The most important focus is on how to add data to a pivot report using the PowerPivot Field List. But, once this is done, there are dozens of context menus, drop-down menus, and quite a few ribbons with dozens of buttons. Some of these are explored in this chapter, especially where they are particularly relevant to working with PowerPivot. These menu options and buttons help you organize, control, and format your pivot reports. By the end of the chapter, you should be in a position to create meaningful and attractive pivot tables and charts.

▶ **Key concepts**   Creating pivot tables, creating pivot charts, linking pivot charts to pivot tables, using the PowerPivot Field List with pivot tables, using the PowerPivot Field List with pivot charts, organizing pivot reports, controlling pivot reports, formatting pivot reports

Background to Pivot Reports

A *pivot report* is either a pivot table or a pivot chart. A pivot table shows data as values or figures. A pivot chart is a graphical representation of data. Both, of course, have their place in business intelligence. You might use a pivot chart to monitor your business, with its easy high-level visualization of business metrics. You might use a pivot table to analyze those metrics in a little more depth and detail. Often, you might want both, perhaps with the chart reflecting the data in the table. Alternatively, your chart may well show different data from your table. In addition, you can have multiple pivot tables and charts. Excel and PowerPivot provide many options for inserting pivot reports. The number of options available can be a little overwhelming at first. There are so many options, as there are different types of pivot reports supported by Excel.

A pivot report can be based directly on worksheet data—you could use the PivotTable button on the Insert ribbon to do this. Or, you might want a pivot report based directly on an SSAS cube. You can accomplish this through the From Other Sources button on the Data ribbon. Yet again, you can have a pivot report based on a PowerPivot model. In that case you might insert the report through the PivotTable button on the PowerPivot ribbon, or through the PivotTable button on the Home ribbon in the PowerPivot window.

There are also a number of options for inserting a pivot table and a related or an unrelated pivot chart. In addition, there are different ways of inserting supporting objects, such as slicers. To help cut through the complexity, this chapter is devoted only to pivot reports based on PowerPivot models. Furthermore, pivot tables and pivot charts will be considered separately—the longer section on pivot tables coming first. The later section on pivot charts will demonstrate how to link a chart to a table and how to have an independent chart. And, where there are alternative methods of reaching the same goal, the easiest and most direct alternative will be shown.

Pivot Tables

When you want to create a pivot report, the choice is between a pivot table and a pivot chart, or both together. You can, of course, add further tables and charts retrospectively, whether related or unrelated to the first reports inserted. Here, we discuss how to insert a single pivot table.

Creating a Pivot Table

As the pivot tables shown in this book are based on a PowerPivot model, you must first have some data in the PowerPivot model. Once the data is assembled, you are ready to view it in a pivot table. If you change the PowerPivot model later, you can easily update the field list by clicking the Refresh button that will appear at the top of the PowerPivot Field List for the pivot table.

There are two main ways of inserting a pivot table (as stated earlier, this chapter concentrates on the most direct and easiest alternatives and, for the sake of clarity, does not mention every single possibility). One way to create a pivot table is to click the PivotTable button in the Reports group on the Home ribbon in PowerPivot. The second way is to click the PivotTable button in the Report group on the PowerPivot ribbon in Excel. Both of these result in the same drop-down menu. This menu is shown in Figure 5-1.

In this menu, there are two choices for inserting a stand-alone pivot table (that is, a pivot table without a related pivot chart). One option is called PivotTable and the other Flattened PivotTable. There have been many examples of the former throughout this book—but, to show the comparison between a "normal" and a flattened pivot table, Figure 5-2 shows a typical result after choosing PivotTable. Figure 5-3 shows a typical result after choosing Flattened PivotTable.

A flattened pivot table looks more like an Excel table. It's flattened, or completely expanded, and there is no option to collapse column or row labels. A simpler display sacrifices the ability to drill up or drill down.

Before the pivot table is inserted, the Create PivotTable dialog allows you to decide upon the location of the pivot table. This dialog is shown in Figure 5-4.

Figure 5-1   *Inserting a pivot table menu*

	A	B	C	D	E
1	Sales	Column Labels ▼			
2	Row Labels ▼	1996	1997	1998	Grand Total
3	Argentina		1816.6	6302.5	8119.1
4	Austria	29352	63151.98	46992.65	139496.63
5	Belgium	6438.8	12087.1	16609.08	35134.98
6	Brazil	23849.3	44550.51	46568.67	114968.48
7	Canada	7949.6	34970.1	12414.4	55334.1
8	Denmark	3011.8	27192.65	4577.8	34782.25
9	Finland	3210.8	14280.65	2287	19778.45
10	France	17629.9	47905.8	19963.06	85498.76
11	Germany	37804.6	124170.33	82665.7	244640.63
12	Ireland	10562	23959.05	22796.34	57317.39
13	Italy	1004.2	8448.95	7252	16705.15
14	Mexico	4687.9	14840.65	4544.9	24073.45
15	Norway	1058.4	700	3976.75	5735.15
16	Poland	459	1207.85	1865.1	3531.95
17	Portugal	2482	7284.75	2701.9	12468.65
18	Spain	3100.4	8053.05	8278.44	19431.89
19	Sweden	7414.6	28024.7	24084.4	59523.7
20	Switzerland	4289.7	18702.5	9927.3	32919.5
21	UK	9654	27832.6	23129.91	60616.51
22	USA	41907.8	121037.7	100621.48	263566.98
23	Venezuela	10431.7	28171.23	22211.96	60814.89
24	Grand Total	226298.5	658388.75	469771.34	1354458.59

◄ ◄ ► ►◄ PowerPivot

Figure 5-2   *Unflattened pivot table*

⊿	A	B	C	D	E	F
1						
2						
3		Sales	Year ▼			
4		Country ▼	1996	1997	1998	
5		Argentina		1816.6	6302.5	
6		Austria	29352	63151.98	46992.65	
7		Belgium	6438.8	12087.1	16609.08	
8		Brazil	23849.3	44550.51	46568.67	
9		Canada	7949.6	34970.1	12414.4	
10		Denmark	3011.8	27192.65	4577.8	
11		Finland	3210.8	14280.65	2287	
12		France	17629.9	47905.8	19963.06	
13		Germany	37804.6	124170.33	82665.7	
14		Ireland	10562	23959.05	22796.34	
15		Italy	1004.2	8448.95	7252	
16		Mexico	4687.9	14840.65	4544.9	
17		Norway	1058.4	700	3976.75	
18		Poland	459	1207.85	1865.1	
19		Portugal	2482	7284.75	2701.9	
20		Spain	3100.4	8053.05	8278.44	
21		Sweden	7414.6	28024.7	24084.4	
22		Switzerland	4289.7	18702.5	9927.3	
23		UK	9654	27832.6	23129.91	
24		USA	41907.8	121037.7	100621.48	
25		Venezuela	10431.7	28171.23	22211.96	
26						

⊮ ◀ ▶ ⊯   Flat / PowerPivot / ⸬ /   ◀   ⫶   ▶

Figure 5-3   *Flattened pivot table*

Create PivotTable   ？ ✕

◉ New Worksheet

◯ Existing Worksheet

Location: 'PowerPivot'!$A$1

OK   Cancel

Figure 5-4   *Create PivotTable dialog*

PowerPivot Field List for Pivot Tables

Once the pivot table has been inserted into an Excel worksheet, you control the data that appears through the PowerPivot Field List. This field list has a slightly different appearance when you are working with a pivot chart. In this section, we are concentrating on the PowerPivot Field List that accompanies a pivot table. An example of a PowerPivot Field List is shown in Figure 5-5.

Often, the PowerPivot Field List will simply disappear. It's sensitive to context, so it only shows when the focus is within a pivot table. If you have a Report Filter, you can also place the focus there to display a hidden field list. Placing the focus on a slicer does not cause a hidden field list to appear. If you still can't see the PowerPivot Field List, make sure the Field List toggle button, in the Show/Hide group on the PowerPivot ribbon, is turned on.

Let's spend a little time looking at the PowerPivot Field List. By default, it's docked on the right-hand side of the worksheet containing the pivot table. You can undock it simply by dragging on its title bar so that it becomes free-floating. You can then dock it on any side of the worksheet by dragging far enough. Alternatively, if it's free-floating, you can redock it in the last docked position by double-clicking its title bar. If you click

Figure 5-5   *PowerPivot Field List for a pivot table*

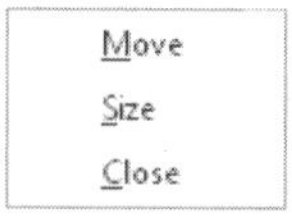

Move
Size
Close

Figure 5-6   *PowerPivot Field List drop-down menu*

the Close button at the right of the title bar, the PowerPivot Field List gets hidden, even if the focus is in the pivot table. To redisplay it, click the Field List button on the PowerPivot ribbon. Immediately to the left of the Close button is a small button that opens a drop-down menu. This menu gives you choices for moving, sizing, or closing the field list. The menu is shown in Figure 5-6. Of course, it's possible to resize the field list by dragging its left-hand border (assuming it's docked on the right-hand side of the worksheet).

Just below the title bar is a text box for searching the field list. However, there may well be another entry between the title bar and the search text box. This area is sometimes referred to as the *message area*. There are two possible messages that are displayed in this message area. One informs you that relationships are needed between tables. This can happen if suitable table relationships have not been established in the PowerPivot window. The message can only appear if the Detection toggle button, in the Relationship group of the PowerPivot ribbon, is turned on (this is the default state). If the message ("Relationship may be needed") does appear, clicking the Create button causes PowerPivot to attempt to find and create the required relationship. A lack of suitable relationships between tables in the PowerPivot model may result in inaccurate and misleading data appearing in the pivot table. This relationship message is shown in Figure 5-7.

The second message that may show occurs when the PowerPivot model is changed after the pivot table has been created. For example, you may have returned to the PowerPivot window and created a new calculated column in a table, or added a new table to the model. To the right of the message ("PowerPivot data was modified") is a Refresh button. Clicking this button updates the PowerPivot Field List to reflect the changes made in the PowerPivot model. This message is shown in Figure 5-8.

If there is a message in the message area, the search text box is underneath the message. If there's no message, the search box is immediately underneath the title bar. This text box is used to search for tables, regular columns, calculated columns, or calculated measures in the table and column list area of the PowerPivot Field List. This is handy when there are many tables and columns and measures. If you search for a column or a measure, and its containing table is collapsed, the search will automatically expand the table to reveal its columns and measures. If there are multiple potential results, the arrow buttons step through the entries. Figure 5-9 shows the result of searching for the ShipCountry column.

Figure 5-7   *"Relationship needed" message*

Figure 5-8   *"Data modified" message*

Figure 5-9   *Searching the PowerPivot Field List*

Apart from a few of the features already discussed, the PowerPivot Field List does not contain ribbons or buttons or left-click menus. However, there are a number of context-sensitive, right-click menus. As they are context-sensitive, these pop-up menus may well present different choices. The next few sections take a look at these context menus.

Table Context Menu

To see the table context menu, right-click on any table that appears in the table and column list section of the PowerPivot Field List. The menu is shown in Figure 5-10. The first four choices in this menu are for expanding or collapsing either the selected table or all tables. The fifth entry, Add New Measure, is very useful. If you choose this option, the new calculated measure will automatically default to the selected table. It means that you don't have to change the Table name property in the subsequent Measure Settings dialog. The Measure Settings dialog is shown in Figure 5-11.

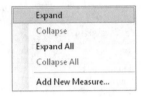

Figure 5-10   *Table context menu*

Column Context Menu

You can have both regular and calculated columns in the PowerPivot Field List. As a reminder, a regular column is part of the data imported into the PowerPivot model—a calculated column is added later using a DAX formula. Both types of columns look the same in the PowerPivot Field List, and both have the same context menu. If it's important to distinguish between regular and calculated columns, you can adopt a naming convention. The context menu for a column is shown in Figure 5-12. The second, third, and fourth choices in the menu are disabled; they are relevant to calculated measures only. The final six entries in the menu allow you to add the column to one of the six drop-zones at the foot of the PowerPivot Field list. You can, of course, accomplish that simply by dragging to the required drop-zone. Adding a column to the Values drop-zone implicitly allows it to function as a measure. By default, a numeric column will be summed, and a non-numeric column counted (unless it can be implicitly converted into a number, like OrderID in our Northwind model). Adding a column to any other drop-zone leaves it as a column (or a non-measure dimension attribute, if you know your SSAS).

Figure 5-11   *Measure Settings dialog*

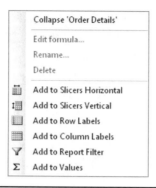

Figure 5-12   *Column context menu*

Calculated Measure Context Menu

An *explicit measure*, or calculated measure, is distinguished from regular and calculated columns by the small calculator icon after its name. Unlike for a column, the second, third, and fourth options in the context menu are enabled for an explicit measure. Clicking Edit Formula opens the Measure Settings dialog, so you can amend the DAX formula for the measure. The only drop-zone available for a measure is Values. You can't place a measure in any of the other five drop-zones. The context menu for a measure is shown in Figure 5-13.

Drop-Zone Entry Context Menu (Apart from Values)

There are six drop-zones in the PowerPivot Field List, corresponding to the areas in or around a pivot table. The drop-zones are Slicers Vertical, Slicers Horizontal, Report Filter, Column Labels, Row Labels, and Values. The Values drop-zone (corresponding to the data area in a pivot table) is subtly different from the other five. As such, it's covered separately in the next section. Measures can only be added to the Values

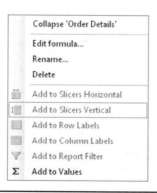

Figure 5-13   *Measure context menu*

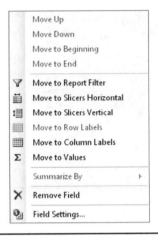

Figure 5-14 *Drop-zone entry context menu (apart from Values)*

drop-zone and not to any of the other five. None of the six drop-zones has its own context menu, but context menus are enabled for any entry in the drop-zone. For non-Values drop-zones, the entries can only be regular or calculated columns. For the Values drop-zone, the entry may be a column or a measure.

Figure 5-14 shows the context menu when you right-click on a column in any drop-zone (apart from Values). The first group of four choices allows you to change the position of the entry within the current drop-zone (assuming you have more than one entry). You can achieve the same thing by simply dragging the entry up or down. The second group of six entries lets you move the column to another drop-zone. Again, you can also do this by simply dragging from one drop-zone to another. The eleventh option, Summarize By, is disabled—it only applies to columns in the Values drop-zone. The Field Settings option opens the Field Settings dialog, where you can change the Custom Name property for the column. The Field Settings dialog is shown in Figure 5-15.

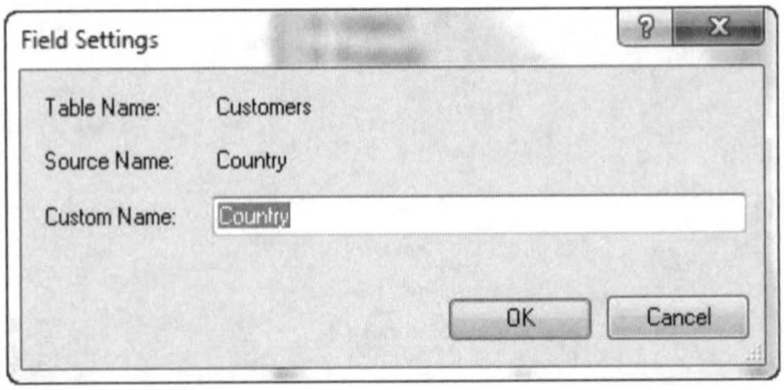

Figure 5-15 *Field Settings dialog*

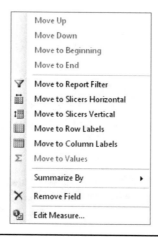

Figure 5-16   *Drop-zone entry context menu (Values only)*

Drop-Zone Entry Context Menu (Values Only)

An entry in the Values drop-zone can be either a measure or a column (regular or calculated). The context menu (shown in Figure 5-16) for each type of entry is slightly different. If it's a measure, the menu does not allow you to move the entry to another drop-zone. Also, if it's a measure, the Summarize By option is disabled—your aggregation will be part of the DAX formula for the measure. Right-clicking on a measure and choosing Edit Measure opens the Measure Settings dialog for that measure, as shown in Figure 5-17. Right-clicking on a column and choosing Edit Measure opens the Measure Settings dialog for that column—this is shown in Figure 5-18.

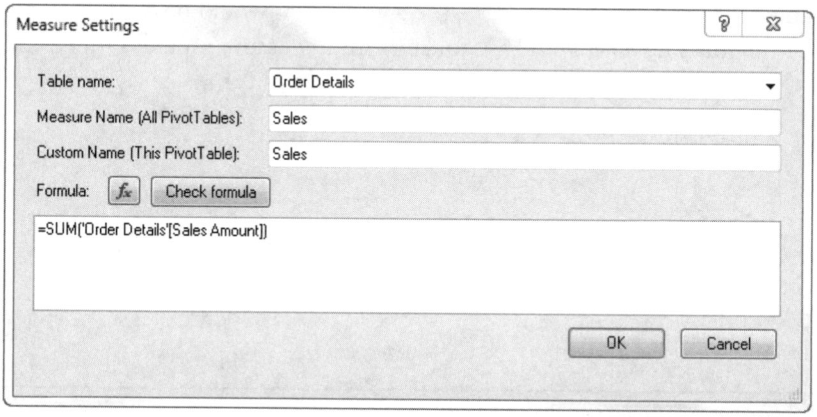

Figure 5-17   *Measure Settings dialog for a measure*

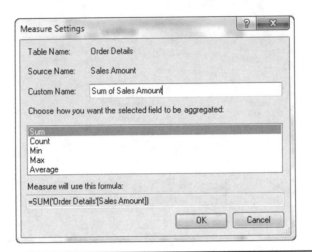

Figure 5-18 *Measure Settings dialog for a column*

The Measure Settings dialog for a column lets you change the aggregation function for that column—clicking Summarize By does the same. The Measure Settings dialog for a column lets you change the name for that column. For example, if you add the Sales Amount column from the Order Details table to the Values drop-zone, it's called Sum of Sales Amount, and you may want to change this back to Sales Amount. The Summarize By option in the context menu is only enabled for columns. This leads to a fly-out menu (shown in Figure 5-19), which presents another way to change the aggregation on a column. The aggregation choices are Sum, Count, Min, Max, and Average. The only one that makes sense for a non-numeric column is Count. All of these aggregations are also available for measures—in that case, the aggregation would be defined in the DAX formula for the measure. Using a DAX formula for a measure provides much more flexibility than using Summarize By for a numeric column.

Figure 5-19 *Summarize By fly-out menu for a column*

Slicers for Pivot Tables

Adding slicers to a pivot table is best done in the PowerPivot Field list by placing columns in either Slicers Vertical or Slicers Horizontal. You can also add slicers from the Insert ribbon, but the slicer does not get added to the PowerPivot Field List. Yet another alternative is to add a slicer from the PivotTable Tools/Options ribbon.

Slicers too have their own context menu. This menu (shown in Figure 5-20) has a large number of options—only the most interesting from a PowerPivot perspective are discussed here. There are three options for sorting the buttons in a slicer and one option for removing a filter. You can also control the sort order of the buttons by choosing Slicer Settings. A filter can be removed more simply by clicking the filter button at the top right of the slicer.

Choosing Size and Properties opens the Size and Properties dialog. The Position and Layout page has a useful setting, called Number of Columns. This page of the dialog is shown in Figure 5-21. Selecting Slicer Settings in the context menu opens the Slicer Settings dialog. This dialog is shown in Figure 5-22. In the Slicer Settings dialog you can control how the items in the slicer are sorted. In addition, you can decide whether to have a header or not, and its caption. There are further options that apply to items with no data—by default, these appear as buttons without a caption in the slicer. You may want these to be hidden in your slicer.

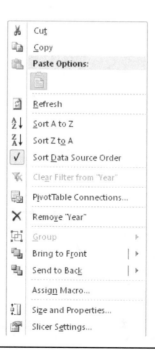

Figure 5-20   *Slicer context menu*

Figure 5-21   *Position and Layout page of the Size and Properties dialog*

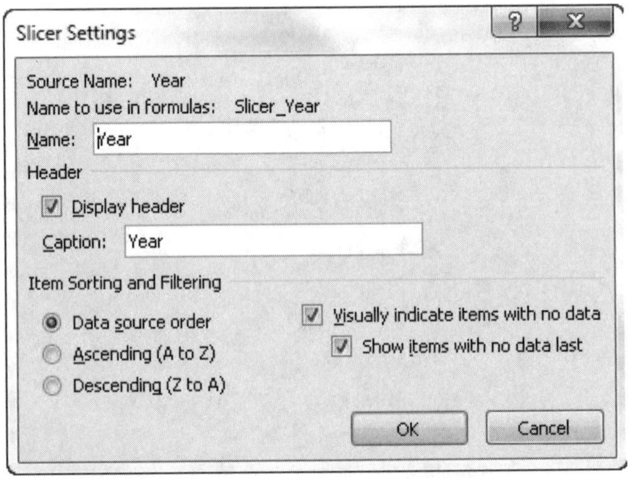

Figure 5-22   *Slicer Settings dialog*

Pivot Table Menus and Ribbons

The pivot table itself has context menus too. Lots of them! Whole books have been written, and will be written, about using and customizing pivot tables. In a single chapter, not every single avenue can be followed. Instead, the emphasis is on those options that are most useful and interesting from a PowerPivot perspective. For the purposes of this section, a pivot table is defined as the areas corresponding to the Report Filter, Column Labels, Row Labels, and Values drop-zones of the PowerPivot Field List. As pivot table areas, they all have context menus and/or drop-down menus. In addition, there are ribbons that both duplicate and extend some of the options available through the menus. To avoid undue repetition, not every alternative is explored—the emphasis here is on ease of implementation. The following sections detail some of the drop-down menu options, context menu options, and ribbon button functionality for PowerPivot pivot tables.

Report Filter Drop-Down Menu

When you add a column to the Report Filter drop-zone in the PowerPivot Field List, a filter will appear immediately above the main body of the pivot table. You can add more than one Report Filter, if you wish. Each filter consists of two cells. The first cell shows the column name, while the second cell shows the current filter on that column. By default, the filter is All. The second cell contains a small button that leads to a drop-down menu. The sole purpose of this menu is to enable you to set a filter context for the data in the pivot table. In many ways, a Report Filter is similar to a slicer. The drop-down menu for a Report Filter can have one of two possible formats. The appearance is governed by the Select Multiple Items check box at the bottom of the menu. The two possible formats are shown in Figures 5-23 and 5-24.

Figure 5-23   *Report Filter drop-down menu without multiselect*

Figure 5-24   *Report Filter drop-down menu with multiselect*

The example shown is for the LastName column from the Employees table in Northwind. There are only a few entries to browse before making a decision about a filter. When you have lots of entries, the search box at the top of the menu is very useful.

Column Labels/Row Labels Drop-Down Menu

When you add a column to Column Labels, a cell with the caption Column Labels appears in the pivot table. This cell has a small button that opens the Column Labels drop-down menu. The same is true when you add a column to Row Labels. Both of the drop-downs are the same—an example (using the Country column from the Customers table) is shown in Figure 5-25. Please note that it is possible to hide the cell, and then the drop-down menu is unavailable. Its visibility is determined by the setting for Display Field Captions and Filter Drop Downs on the Display tab of the PivotTable Options dialog. This dialog is accessed through the Options button in the PivotTable group of the PivotTable Tools/Options ribbon.

This drop-down menu is more feature-rich than the one for a Report Filter. It allows you to sort, not just filter—and the filter options are more sophisticated. The menu is divided into three sections. The first section contains three options and is devoted to sorting. The second section, to do with filtering, also has three options. The third section includes a search box and all the labels (or captions) for the column. In the first section, you can sort in an ascending or descending order. If you require more control over sorting, click More Sort Options. This opens the Sort dialog shown in Figure 5-26. In the example demonstrated here (on the Country column from the Customers table), the sort has been defined as descending on the value of the Sales Amount in the data area.

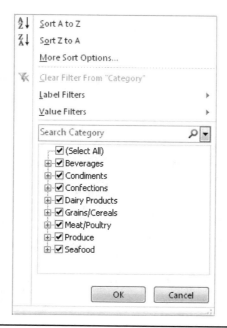

Figure 5-25   *Column Labels/Row Labels drop-down menu*

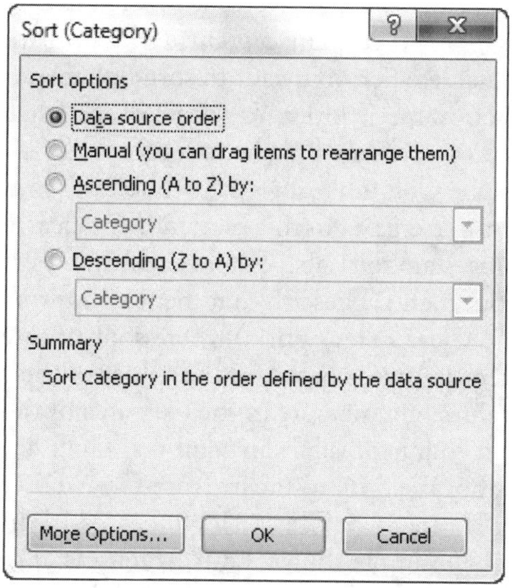

Figure 5-26   *Sort dialog*

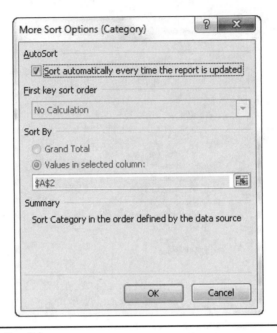

Figure 5-27 *More Sort Options dialog*

This dialog has a More Options button that leads to a More Sort Options dialog. This dialog is shown in Figure 5-27. It contains a really useful drop-down labeled First Key Sort Order—this is invaluable when you want to sort alphabetic months of the year or days of the week in their numeric order. You can sort months, for example, from January to December, and override an alphabetic sort.

The second section of the Column Labels/Row Labels drop-down menu is for filtering. The first of the three entries in this section is for clearing any existing filter. The second and third entries are for Label Filters and Value Filters, respectively. Each of these has its own fly-out menu. These fly-out menus, in turn, have options that lead to dialogs (apart from the Clear Filter option) where sophisticated filtering can be implemented. Label Filters are filters based on the values of the column. Value Filters are filters based on the values of a measure in the data area of the pivot table—although you can also base them on counts of values in columns. The Label Filters fly-out is shown in Figure 5-28. All of the options (apart from Clear Filter) lead to the Label Filter dialog as shown in Figure 5-29. This dialog includes 14 different comparison operators or phrases. In the example shown, both Argentina and Austria will be removed from the list of countries. To remove Label Filters, click Clear Filter in the Column Labels/Row Labels drop-down menu.

Figure 5-28   *Label Filters fly-out menu*

The Value Filters fly-out menu is shown in Figure 5-30. All of the options (apart from Clear Filter) result in a dialog. This dialog is entitled Value Filter for eight of the nine options that open a dialog. The Top 10 option opens the Top 10 Filter dialog. In either of these two dialogs, you can filter the column or row labels by the value of a measure in the data area of the pivot table. The Value Filter dialog is shown in Figure 5-31. The dialog has a total of eight comparison operators or phrases. The Top 10 Filter dialog is shown in Figure 5-32. This dialog is where you choose to view the top or bottom performers in relation to a particular measure.

Figure 5-29   *Label Filter dialog*

Figure 5-30 *Value Filters fly-out menu*

Label Filters and Value Filters are mutually exclusive. You can't have both Label Filters *and* Value Filters. Strictly speaking, that's not quite true. You can have both Label Filters and Value Filters, but not through the GUI. You have to write the MDX (not DAX!) to create a named set. This alternative is available through the Fields, Items, & Sets button in the Calculations group of the PivotTable Tools/Options ribbon. This is an advanced topic and is introduced in Chapter 12.

The final section of the Column Labels/Row Labels drop-down menu is for searching for entries and implementing filtering by selecting/deselecting check boxes. There is also a context menu for entries in rows and columns. This, too, allows you to sort and filter. The important options in this menu are covered elsewhere in this chapter—there are often alternative ways of reaching the same goal in a pivot table.

Data Area Context Menu

When you add a column or measure to the Values drop-zone, it appears in the data area of the pivot tables. Usually, you would want to add a numeric column or measure. If it's a non-numeric column, the only useful aggregation is that of Count. The net result is

Figure 5-31 *Value Filter dialog*

Top 10 Filter (Category)

Show

| Top | 10 | Items | by | Sum of Sales Amount |

OK   Cancel

Figure 5-32   *Top 10 Filter dialog*

one or more figures or values in the data area. If you right-click on a cell containing a value, a context menu appears. This is shown in Figure 5-33.

This menu includes many options. Some of these lead to dialogs, some to fly-out menus. Some of the options are very powerful indeed—Show Values As is particularly powerful and can transform your pivot tables from business intelligence into business wisdom! Show Values As, therefore, is covered in great detail shortly, in the practical later in this section. Not all of the options in the context menu are covered here. Some are available through a ribbon as well and will be mentioned when we reach the section of this chapter on ribbons. Some are fairly obvious, for example, Copy or Remove, and will not be discussed. The Additional Actions option is only relevant for pivot tables based directly on SSAS cubes and not for those based on PowerPivot models, at least in this release of PowerPivot. The ones remaining, and covered here, include Format Cells, Number Format, Sort, and Show Values As.

Figure 5-33   *Data area context menu*

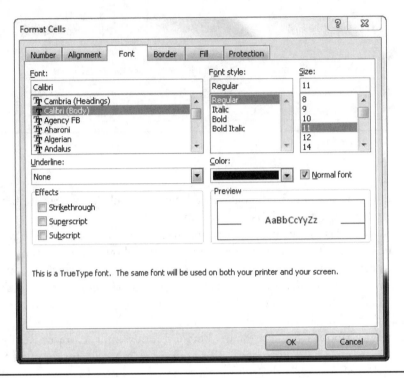

Figure 5-34 *Format Cells dialog—Font tab*

The Format Cells option opens the Format Cells dialog. This dialog is shown in Figure 5-34 with the Font tab selected. One thing you might consider doing here is choosing a color for the data values. Format Cells only works on the current cell. If you want to format all the cells containing the value, use Number Format instead. Alternatively, you can go through the Field Settings button in the Active Field group of the PivotTable Tools/Options ribbon.

Unlike Format Cells, Number Format affects all of the cells that contain the measure. Number Format also leads to the Format Cells dialog, but only the Number tab is available. This tab of the dialog is shown in Figure 5-35. This option is valuable when you want to quickly apply a numeric format, such as Currency or Percentage, to *all* the values of a particular measure or column in the data area.

The Sort option has a fly-out menu. This is useful for quickly sorting from smallest to largest (or vice versa) on a measure. If you have the same measure in multiple columns (because you have a column in Column Labels), the sort is applied to the rows based on values in the current column. The Sort fly-out menu is shown in Figure 5-36.

Figure 5-35 *Format Cells dialog—Number tab*

The Show Values As option also has a fly-out menu. This menu, in itself, has many options. These are among the most useful and powerful options in a pivot table, and they can greatly enhance your business intelligence. Consequently, you may want to follow along with the following practical. The exercises assume you have the Northwind PowerPivot model. Chapter 1 showed how to build this model on a SQL Server Northwind source. Chapter 2 showed how to import Northwind from Access, from Excel (you can download the one for Excel from this book's Web site), or from a data feed.

Figure 5-36 *Sort fly-out menu*

You'll also need a couple of calculated columns that have been used in a few chapters in this book. These are the Year column in the Orders table and the Sales Amount column in the Order Details table. As a reminder, their respective DAX formulas are:

```
=YEAR(Orders[OrderDate])
```

```
='Order Details'[Quantity] * 'Order Details'[UnitPrice]
```

There are various incarnations of Northwind, so your results may differ from mine. That's not too important; what is important is to see how to implement some real BI. So, here are the step-by-step instructions:

1. Add Year (from Orders) to Column Labels and add Country (from Customers) to Row Labels.

2. Add Sales Amount (from Order Details) to Values. Right-click its entry in Values and choose Edit Measure. In the Measure Settings dialog, change the measure's name from Sum of Sales Amount to Sales Amount.

3. Drag Sales Amount, again, from the Order Details table to Values and position it below the first entry. Right-click and choose Edit Measure. Call this second entry Calculation. Your PowerPivot Field List should look like Figure 5-37, and your pivot table like Figure 5-38.

Figure 5-37 *PowerPivot Field List*

	A	B	C	D	E
1		Column Labels ▼			
2		1996		1997	
3	Row Labels ▼	Sales Amount	Calculation	Sales Amount	Calculation
4	Argentina			1816.6	1816.6
5	Austria	29352	29352	63151.98	63151.98
6	Belgium	6438.8	6438.8	12087.1	12087.1
7	Brazil	23849.3	23849.3	44550.51	44550.51
8	Canada	7949.6	7949.6	34970.1	34970.1
9	Denmark	3011.8	3011.8	27192.65	27192.65
10	Finland	3210.8	3210.8	14280.65	14280.65
11	France	17629.9	17629.9	47905.8	47905.8
12	Germany	37804.6	37804.6	124170.33	124170.33
13	Ireland	10562	10562	23959.05	23959.05
14	Italy	1004.2	1004.2	8448.95	8448.95
15	Mexico	4687.9	4687.9	14840.65	14840.65
16	Norway	1058.4	1058.4	700	700
17	Poland	459	459	1207.85	1207.85
18	Portugal	2482	2482	7284.75	7284.75
19	Spain	3100.4	3100.4	8053.05	8053.05
20	Sweden	7414.6	7414.6	28024.7	28024.7
21	Switzerland	4289.7	4289.7	18702.5	18702.5
22	UK	9654	9654	27832.6	27832.6
23	USA	41907.8	41907.8	121037.7	121037.7
24	Venezuela	10431.7	10431.7	28171.23	28171.23
25	**Grand Total**	226298.5	226298.5	658388.75	658388.75

Figure 5-38   *Pivot table*

4.   Right-click on any value in the Calculation column in the pivot table. This opens the data area context menu. From the menu, choose Show Values As to show its fly-out menu. This menu is shown in Figure 5-39.

5.   From the fly-out, choose % of Grand Total. The result is shown in Figure 5-40; the screenshot does not show all of the results. According to my version of Northwind, Germany was a pretty good market in 1997.

6.   Repeat the previous two steps, but this time, choose % of Parent Row Total. Figure 5-41 shows the result. The USA was the top market in 1996, being responsible for nearly a fifth of all sales. Please note that the Grand Total row at the bottom is showing 100%.

7.   This time, try % Difference From. Unlike the previous two examples, this one has an ellipsis and opens a dialog, called Show Values As. The dialog is shown in Figure 5-42.

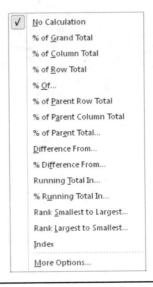

✓	No Calculation
	% of Grand Total
	% of Column Total
	% of Row Total
	% Of…
	% of Parent Row Total
	% of Parent Column Total
	% of Parent Total…
	Difference From…
	% Difference From…
	Running Total In…
	% Running Total In…
	Rank Smallest to Largest…
	Rank Largest to Smallest…
	Index
	More Options…

Figure 5-39   *Show Values As fly-out menu*

	A	B	C	D	E
1		Column Labels ▾			
2		1996		1997	
3	Row Labels ▾	Sales Amount	Calculation	Sales Amount	Calculation
4	Argentina		0.00%	1816.6	0.13%
5	Austria	29352	2.17%	63151.98	4.66%
6	Belgium	6438.8	0.48%	12087.1	0.89%
7	Brazil	23849.3	1.76%	44550.51	3.29%
8	Canada	7949.6	0.59%	34970.1	2.58%
9	Denmark	3011.8	0.22%	27192.65	2.01%
10	Finland	3210.8	0.24%	14280.65	1.05%
11	France	17629.9	1.30%	47905.8	3.54%
12	Germany	37804.6	2.79%	124170.33	9.17%
13	Ireland	10562	0.78%	23959.05	1.77%
14	Italy	1004.2	0.07%	8448.95	0.62%
15	Mexico	4687.9	0.35%	14840.65	1.10%
16	Norway	1058.4	0.08%	700	0.05%
17	Poland	459	0.03%	1207.85	0.09%
18	Portugal	2482	0.18%	7284.75	0.54%
19	Spain	3100.4	0.23%	8053.05	0.59%
20	Sweden	7414.6	0.55%	28024.7	2.07%
21	Switzerland	4289.7	0.32%	18702.5	1.38%
22	UK	9654	0.71%	27832.6	2.05%
23	USA	41907.8	3.09%	121037.7	8.94%
24	Venezuela	10431.7	0.77%	28171.23	2.08%
25	Grand Total	226298.5	16.71%	658388.75	48.61%

PowerPivot

Figure 5-40   *% of Grand Total*

	A	B	C	D	E
1		Column Labels ▼			
2		1996		1997	
3	Row Labels ▼	Sales Amount	Calculation	Sales Amount	Calculation
4	Argentina		0.00%	1816.6	0.28%
5	Austria	29352	12.97%	63151.98	9.59%
6	Belgium	6438.8	2.85%	12087.1	1.84%
7	Brazil	23849.3	10.54%	44550.51	6.77%
8	Canada	7949.6	3.51%	34970.1	5.31%
9	Denmark	3011.8	1.33%	27192.65	4.13%
10	Finland	3210.8	1.42%	14280.65	2.17%
11	France	17629.9	7.79%	47905.8	7.28%
12	Germany	37804.6	16.71%	124170.33	18.86%
13	Ireland	10562	4.67%	23959.05	3.64%
14	Italy	1004.2	0.44%	8448.95	1.28%
15	Mexico	4687.9	2.07%	14840.65	2.25%
16	Norway	1058.4	0.47%	700	0.11%
17	Poland	459	0.20%	1207.85	0.18%
18	Portugal	2482	1.10%	7284.75	1.11%
19	Spain	3100.4	1.37%	8053.05	1.22%
20	Sweden	7414.6	3.28%	28024.7	4.26%
21	Switzerland	4289.7	1.90%	18702.5	2.84%
22	UK	9654	4.27%	27832.6	4.23%
23	USA	41907.8	18.52%	121037.7	18.38%
24	Venezuela	10431.7	4.61%	28171.23	4.28%
25	Grand Total	226298.5	100.00%	658388.75	100.00%

◄ ◄ ► ► PowerPivot

Figure 5-41 *% of Parent Row Total*

8.   In this dialog, select Year as the Base Field, and (previous) as the Base Item, before clicking OK. My result is shown in Figure 5-43. The result of the calculation for 1996 is blank as there were no sales in the previous year, 1995. Sales in Denmark showed a dramatic increase from 1996 to 1997.

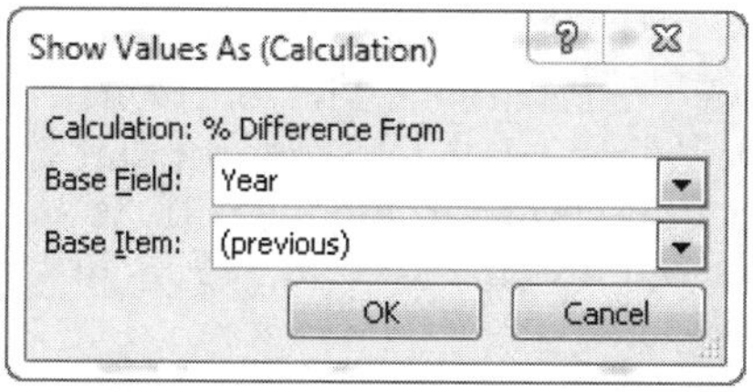

Figure 5-42 *Show Values As dialog*

	Column Labels			
	1996		1997	
Row Labels	Sales Amount	Calculation	Sales Amount	Calculation
Argentina			1816.6	
Austria	29352		63151.98	115.15%
Belgium	6438.8		12087.1	87.72%
Brazil	23849.3		44550.51	86.80%
Canada	7949.6		34970.1	339.90%
Denmark	3011.8		27192.65	802.87%
Finland	3210.8		14280.65	344.77%
France	17629.9		47905.8	171.73%
Germany	37804.6		124170.33	228.45%
Ireland	10562		23959.05	126.84%
Italy	1004.2		8448.95	741.36%
Mexico	4687.9		14840.65	216.57%
Norway	1058.4		700	-33.86%
Poland	459		1207.85	163.15%
Portugal	2482		7284.75	193.50%
Spain	3100.4		8053.05	159.74%
Sweden	7414.6		28024.7	277.97%
Switzerland	4289.7		18702.5	335.99%
UK	9654		27832.6	188.30%
USA	41907.8		121037.7	188.82%
Venezuela	10431.7		28171.23	170.05%
Grand Total	226298.5		658388.75	190.94%

PowerPivot

Figure 5-43 *% Difference From*

9. Often, you may want to see running totals. This next example may prove quite useful. From the fly-out menu, choose Running Total In. You can right-click on any value for Calculation, including blanks. Once again, you'll see the Show Values As dialog, but, this time, there is only one setting. Make Year the Base Field, before clicking OK. The result is shown in Figure 5-44. The running total for Argentina in 1996 is zero, as its sales were blank that year. In general, if it's a numeric calculation, blanks are treated as zeros.

10. Let's have a look at one final example. This time, choose Rank Largest to Smallest. In the Show Values As dialog, confirm that Country is the Base Field, and click OK. The result is shown in Figure 5-45. Is our sales team doing well in Sweden? It's climbed from number 10 to 8 to 5, in just two years!

Hopefully, these few examples demonstrate a little of the tremendous BI potential of pivot tables. There are, perhaps, two observations to make. One, you are not limited

	A	B	C	D	E
1		Column Labels ▾			
2		1996		1997	
3	Row Labels ▾	Sales Amount	Calculation	Sales Amount	Calculation
4	Argentina		0	1816.6	1816.6
5	Austria	29352	29352	63151.98	92503.98
6	Belgium	6438.8	6438.8	12087.1	18525.9
7	Brazil	23849.3	23849.3	44550.51	68399.81
8	Canada	7949.6	7949.6	34970.1	42919.7
9	Denmark	3011.8	3011.8	27192.65	30204.45
10	Finland	3210.8	3210.8	14280.65	17491.45
11	France	17629.9	17629.9	47905.8	65535.7
12	Germany	37804.6	37804.6	124170.33	161974.93
13	Ireland	10562	10562	23959.05	34521.05
14	Italy	1004.2	1004.2	8448.95	9453.15
15	Mexico	4687.9	4687.9	14840.65	19528.55
16	Norway	1058.4	1058.4	700	1758.4
17	Poland	459	459	1207.85	1666.85
18	Portugal	2482	2482	7284.75	9766.75
19	Spain	3100.4	3100.4	8053.05	11153.45
20	Sweden	7414.6	7414.6	28024.7	35439.3
21	Switzerland	4289.7	4289.7	18702.5	22992.2
22	UK	9654	9654	27832.6	37486.6
23	USA	41907.8	41907.8	121037.7	162945.5
24	Venezuela	10431.7	10431.7	28171.23	38602.93
25	Grand Total	226298.5	226298.5	658388.75	884687.25

Figure 5-44 *Running Total In*

to just the one calculation at a time. If you want more than one, simply add the relevant column or measure more times to the Values drop-zone, and perform a different calculation on each one. Two, if a pivot table has so many possibilities, why do we need DAX? If these examples are BI, calculations based on DAX formulas are BI on steroids. For example, if your sales amounts were in different currencies, you could apply a conversion factor, based on the country name, to convert sales into a common currency before ranking.

PivotTable Tools/Options Ribbon

The previous section demonstrated how to use a pivot table. This section and the next few sections discuss a few of the options available for customizing the appearance of a pivot table. It involves a quick look at a couple of Excel ribbons. We start with the PivotTable Tools/Options ribbon, which is shown in Figure 5-46. Not every single

Row Labels	1996 Sales Amount	Calculation	1997 Sales Amount	Calculation	1998 Sales Amount	Calculation
Argentina			1816.6	19	6302.5	15
Austria	29352	3	63151.98	3	46992.65	3
Belgium	6438.8	11	12087.1	15	16609.08	10
Brazil	23849.3	4	44550.51	5	46568.67	4
Canada	7949.6	9	34970.1	6	12414.4	11
Denmark	3011.8	16	27192.65	10	4577.8	16
Finland	3210.8	14	14280.65	14	2287	20
France	17629.9	5	47905.8	4	19963.06	9
Germany	37804.6	2	124170.33	1	82665.7	2
Ireland	10562	6	23959.05	11	22796.34	7
Italy	1004.2	19	8448.95	16	7252	14
Mexico	4687.9	12	14840.65	13	4544.9	17
Norway	1058.4	18	700	21	3976.75	18
Poland	459	20	1207.85	20	1865.1	21
Portugal	2482	17	7284.75	18	2701.9	19
Spain	3100.4	15	8053.05	17	8278.44	13
Sweden	7414.6	10	28024.7	8	24084.4	5
Switzerland	4289.7	13	18702.5	12	9927.3	12
UK	9654	8	27832.6	9	23129.91	6
USA	41907.8	1	121037.7	2	100621.48	1
Venezuela	10431.7	7	28171.23	7	22211.96	8
Grand Total	226298.5		658388.75		469771.34	

Figure 5-45   *Rank Largest to Smallest*

item on this ribbon (and others) will be explored. Some ribbon buttons and menus have alternatives discussed elsewhere, or are simply not relevant—for example, OLAP Tools | Offline OLAP is not going to work. And some are even going to cause confusion—for example, the Field List button creates a second (non-PowerPivot) field list, and Insert Slicer creates a slicer that does not appear in the PowerPivot Field List drop-zones.

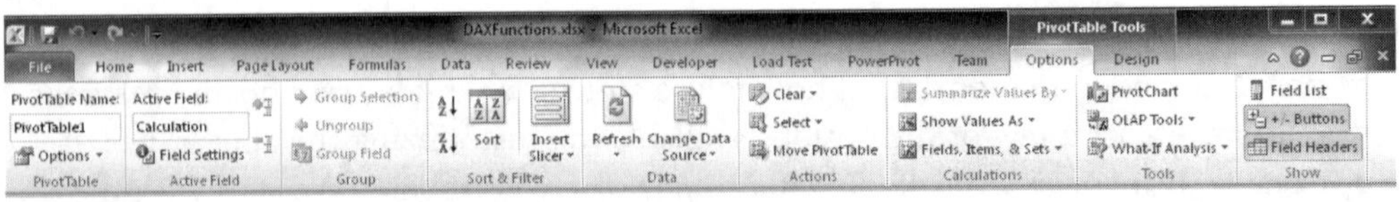

Figure 5-46   *PivotTable Tools/Options ribbon*

PivotTable Group   This is the first group on the ribbon. If you click Options followed by Options, once again, you open the PivotTable Options dialog. This has a number of tabs, a couple of which will be examined here. The first tab is Layout & Format, and is shown in Figure 5-47.

Two useful options on this tab are in the Format section. They are labeled "For Error Values Show" and "For Empty Cells Show." You may, for instance, wish empty or blank cells to display a zero, or perhaps a string such as "NA."

The next tab, shown in Figure 5-48, is the Totals & Filters tab.

This tab includes a Grand Totals section that allows you to toggle grand totals for both rows and columns. This functionality is duplicated on the PivotTable Tools/ Design ribbon, where it is, perhaps, more accessible.

The third tab is the Display tab. This tab is shown in Figure 5-49.

A handy (or dangerous!) option on this tab is to suppress the Column Labels and Row Labels drop-down menus. This option is perhaps easier to access through the Field Headers button in the Show group of the ribbon.

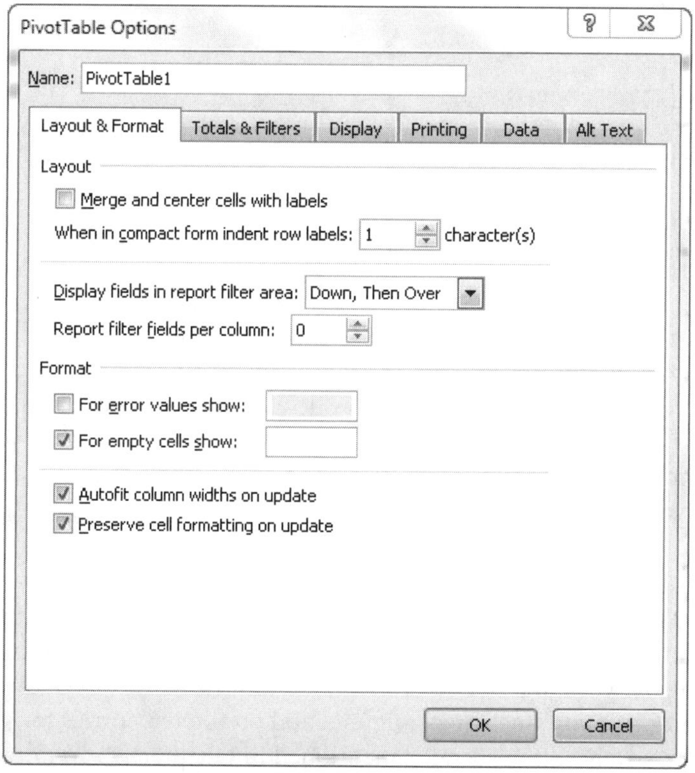

Figure 5-47   *PivotTable Options dialog—Layout & Format tab*

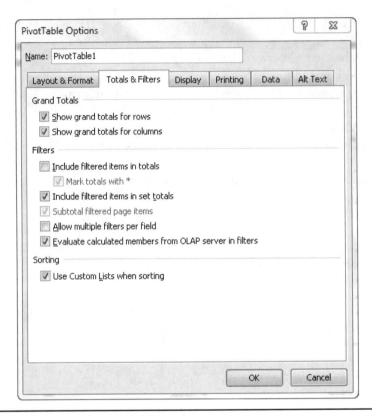

Figure 5-48 *PivotTable Options dialog—Totals & Filters tab*

Actions Group   The Clear button has a Clear All option in its drop-down menu. Clear All removes all the entries from the PowerPivot Field List and is a quick way to start redesigning your pivot table. It does not delete the pivot table from the worksheet. The Select button has an Entire PivotTable option in its drop-down. If you follow this with the correct sequence of clicks, you can not only clear the pivot table, but also remove the pivot table altogether. The sequence required is Home ribbon | Cells group Delete button | Delete Cells.

Calculations Group   The Fields, Items, & Sets button opens a drop-down menu. From this menu you can open the New Set dialog. In this dialog you can create new sets graphically or by writing MDX. A *set* is a customizable list of values from a column. You can exploit this to produce preconfigured and prefiltered entries for your pivot table. This is an advanced topic, and is mentioned in Chapter 12. To implement this, it

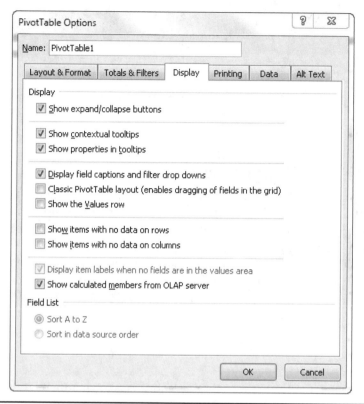

Figure 5-49 *PivotTable Options dialog—Display tab*

helps if you have some experience with SSAS cubes and MDX (not DAX). When you create a set, it appears as a column under a parent node called Sets in the PowerPivot Field List, and from there it can be added to a pivot table or pivot chart.

Tools Group   This group includes the all-important PivotChart button. Use this to insert a pivot chart that is linked to the current pivot table.

Show Group   Please try not to click the Field List button in this group! If you do, you will end up with two field lists for your pivot table. The +/− Buttons button is a toggle that disables or re-enables the + and − buttons that you see when you drill down on Column Labels or Row Labels. If you disable these buttons, you can still expand and collapse by right-clicking. The Field Headers button hides or shows the Column Labels and Row Labels captions and drop-downs.

Figure 5-50 *PivotTable Tools/Design ribbon*

PivotTable Tools/Design Ribbon

This is the second of the two PivotTable Tools ribbons. It is shown in Figure 5-50.

As its name suggests, the Design ribbon is where you set the appearance of a pivot table. The appearance is quite important, not only from a cosmetic perspective, but also to hide or show data. If you would like to experiment, place Year in Column Labels, Country then City in Row Labels, and Sales Amount in Values. Use the Row Labels drop-down to filter the country and show Argentina and Austria only. Your pivot table should look something like Figure 5-51. The screenshot is using all the default settings, before any design changes.

Layout Group   The Subtotals button opens a drop-down menu. This menu is shown in Figure 5-52.

From this menu, try turning off subtotals and then showing them at the bottom. The final result is shown in Figure 5-53. When you are finished, set subtotals back to display at the top.

Sum of Sales Amount	Column Labels			
Row Labels	1996	1997	1998	Grand Total
⊟ Argentina		1816.6	6302.5	8119.1
Buenos Aires		1816.6	6302.5	8119.1
⊟ Austria	29352	63151.98	46992.65	139496.63
Graz	17170.4	53467.38	42598.9	113236.68
Salzburg	12181.6	9684.6	4393.75	26259.95
Grand Total	29352	64968.58	53295.15	147615.73

Figure 5-51 *Pivot table filtered on Argentina and Austria*

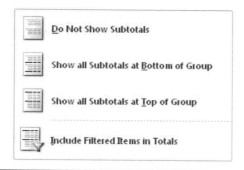

Figure 5-52   *Subtotals drop-down menu*

If you observe the grand totals at the bottom, they are equal to the total of the subtotals for Argentina and Austria. Now, from the same drop-down, choose to include filtered items in totals. The result is shown in Figure 5-54. The grand totals now include the subtotals for those countries that are filtered out, as well as those for Argentina and Austria. If you are from an SSAS background, you have just disabled visual totals. When you are finished, reverse the process, and exclude filtered items.

The Grand Totals button also has a drop-down menu. This is shown in Figure 5-55.

If you turn off grand totals for rows and columns, your pivot table looks like Figure 5-56. When you are done, re-enable the grand totals for rows and columns.

	A	B	C	D	E	F
1	Sum of Sales Amount	Column Labels				
2	Row Labels	1996	1997	1998	Grand Total	
3	Argentina					
4	Buenos Aires		1816.6	6302.5	8119.1	
5	Argentina Total		1816.6	6302.5	8119.1	
6	Austria					
7	Graz	17170.4	53467.38	42598.9	113236.68	
8	Salzburg	12181.6	9684.6	4393.75	26259.95	
9	Austria Total	29352	63151.98	46992.65	139496.63	
10	Grand Total	29352	64968.58	53295.15	147615.73	

PowerPivot

Figure 5-53   *Subtotals at the bottom*

	A	B	C	D	E	F
1	Sum of Sales Amount	Column Labels ▼				
2	Row Labels ▼	1996	1997	1998	Grand Total *	
3	⊟Argentina					
4	Buenos Aires		1816.6	6302.5	8119.1	
5	Argentina Total *		1816.6	6302.5	8119.1	
6	⊟Austria					
7	Graz	17170.4	53467.38	42598.9	113236.68	
8	Salzburg	12181.6	9684.6	4393.75	26259.95	
9	Austria Total *	29352	63151.98	46992.65	139496.63	
10	Grand Total *	226298.5	658388.75	469771.34	1354458.59	

Figure 5-54 *Filtered items included in totals*

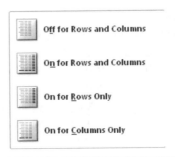

Figure 5-55 *Grand Totals drop-down menu*

	A	B	C	D	E	F
1	Sum of Sales Amount	Column Labels ▼				
2	Row Labels ▼	1996	1997	1998		
3	⊟Argentina					
4	Buenos Aires		1816.6	6302.5		
5	Argentina Total		1816.6	6302.5		
6	⊟Austria					
7	Graz	17170.4	53467.38	42598.9		
8	Salzburg	12181.6	9684.6	4393.75		
9	Austria Total	29352	63151.98	46992.65		
10						

Figure 5-56 *Grand Totals turned off for rows and columns*

Figure 5-57 *Report Layout drop-down menu*

The Report Layout button drop-down is shown in Figure 5-57. From this drop-down, try tabular layout followed by outline layout. The final result is shown in Figure 5-58. This format creates extra columns for labels. After you finish experimenting, revert back to the default compact layout.

The Blank Rows button drop-down is shown in Figure 5-59. Try inserting a blank line after each item—the result is shown in Figure 5-60. You may want to reset your pivot table by turning off blank lines when you are finished.

PivotTable Style Options   In this group, you might like to try out the four check boxes. Notice how Banded Rows and Banded Columns amend the overall style of the pivot table in the PivotTable Styles group.

PivotTable Styles   This group has a single button with a drop-down. If you open the drop-down, and hover the mouse over a style, you have a live preview of the effect of the style on your pivot table. At the bottom of the drop-down, you have options to remove your current style or even to create your own styles.

Page Layout and View Ribbons

The Page Layout ribbon has a Sheet Options group and the View ribbon has a Show group. Check boxes in these groups can be used to suppress gridlines and headings in the worksheet. Only the View/Show group has an option to hide the Excel formula bar. You may want to hide items before sharing your worksheet and pivot table. A perfect way to share your PowerPivot pivot table is to save or publish to PowerPivot for SharePoint. You can achieve this by clicking File | Save & Send | Save to SharePoint.

	A	B	C	D	E	F	G
1	Sum of Sales Amount		Year				
2	Country	City	1996	1997	1998	Grand Total	
3	Argentina			1816.6	6302.5	8119.1	
4		Buenos Aires		1816.6	6302.5	8119.1	
5	Austria		29352	63151.98	46992.65	139496.63	
6		Graz	17170.4	53467.38	42598.9	113236.68	
7		Salzburg	12181.6	9684.6	4393.75	26259.95	
8	Grand Total		29352	64968.58	53295.15	147615.73	
9							
10							

Figure 5-58 *Pivot table in outline form*

Home Ribbon

On the Home ribbon there is a Format As Table button in the Styles group. You can use this to alter the overall appearance of the pivot table. If you do so, it may change the pivot table styles in the PivotTable Tools/Design ribbon.

Also in the Styles group is the Conditional Formatting button. This is a very powerful and useful feature, so you may want to follow these quick step-by-step instructions:

1. Start by preparing a pivot table that resembles the one shown in Figure 5-61. Or, you could easily adapt the steps to your own pivot table. The example shown here has been filtered to show only Argentina and Austria as countries. In addition, the Column Labels and Row Labels have been hidden—through the Field Headers button on the PivotTable Tools/Options ribbon.

2. Click on a subtotal value for any year, for any country. You can even use the blank entry for Argentina in 1996.

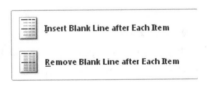

Figure 5-59 *Blank Rows drop-down menu*

	A	B	C	D	E	F	
1	Sum of Sales Amount	Column Labels ▼					
2	Row Labels ▼	1996	1997	1998	Grand Total		
3	⊟ Argentina		1816.6	6302.5	8119.1		
4	Buenos Aires		1816.6	6302.5	8119.1		
5							
6	⊟ Austria	29352	63151.98	46992.65	139496.63		
7	Graz	17170.4	53467.38	42598.9	113236.68		
8	Salzburg	12181.6	9684.6	4393.75	26259.95		
9							
10	Grand Total	29352	64968.58	53295.15	147615.73		

Figure 5-60   *Pivot table with blank lines*

3. Click the Conditional Formatting button in the Styles group of the Home ribbon. This opens a drop-down menu, which is shown in Figure 5-62.

4. From this drop-down, hover the mouse over Data Bars to see its fly-out menu, as shown in Figure 5-63.

5. In this fly-out menu click More Rules, at the bottom of the menu, to open the New Formatting Rule dialog. The dialog is shown in Figure 5-64.

6. Toward the top of this dialog are three option buttons. Turn on the third of these—this means the conditional formatting will be applied to every subtotal for every country and every year. Click OK and you should see colored data bars in the pivot table. In my example, the one for Argentina in 1997 is quite narrow, while the one for Austria in the same year is much wider. You have quick visual cues to the size of the values.

	A	B	C	D	E	F	
1	Sum of Sales Amount						
2		1996	1997	1998	Grand Total		
3	⊟ Argentina		1816.6	6302.5	8119.1		
4	Buenos Aires		1816.6	6302.5	8119.1		
5	⊟ Austria	29352	63151.98	46992.65	139496.63		
6	Graz	17170.4	53467.38	42598.9	113236.68		
7	Salzburg	12181.6	9684.6	4393.75	26259.95		
8	Grand Total	29352	64968.58	53295.15	147615.73		

Figure 5-61   *Pivot table without conditional formatting*

Figure 5-62 *Conditional Formatting drop-down menu*

7. Select any cell for the subtotal for a city. Repeat steps 3 through 6, but choose a different color in the New Formatting Rule dialog—the color for the fill in the Bar Appearance section of the dialog. Remember to turn on the third option button, before clicking OK. The final effect can be seen in Figure 5-65, although the two colors don't display well in monochrome printing!

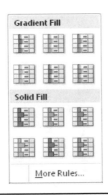

Figure 5-63 *Data Bars fly-out menu*

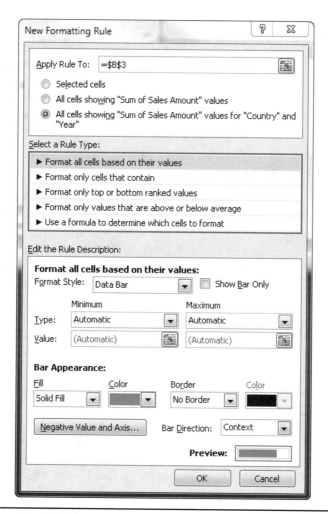

Figure 5-64   *New Formatting Rule dialog*

	A	B	C	D	E	F
1	**Sum of Sales Amount**					
2		1996	1997	1998	**Grand Total**	
3	⊟ **Argentina**		1816.6	6302.5	8119.1	
4	Buenos Aires		1816.6	6302.5	8119.1	
5	⊟ **Austria**	29352	63151.98	46992.65	139496.63	
6	Graz	17170.4	53467.38	42598.9	113236.68	
7	Salzburg	12181.6	9684.6	4393.75	26259.95	
8	**Grand Total**	29352	64968.58	53295.15	147615.73	

Figure 5-65   *Pivot table with conditional formatting*

Pivot Charts

You are probably not surprised to learn that there are many different ways of creating a pivot chart. How you do so is dictated by your requirements. Do you want a single chart or multiple charts? Should a chart be linked to an existing pivot table or created from scratch? Would you like to create a pivot chart and a pivot table at the same time? If you create them at the same time, how do you link or separate them?

Creating a Pivot Chart

A pivot chart always works in conjunction with a pivot table. If you create a pivot chart, and it's not linked to a pivot table, a separate pivot table is created on a separate worksheet to underlie the pivot chart. You can create a pivot chart, against your current PowerPivot model, from the PivotTable button on the Excel PowerPivot ribbon, or on the PowerPivot Home ribbon. When you do so, you can create one, two, or four charts. If you opt for a single pivot chart, you can decide whether you want a pivot table at the same time, or not. If you create both a pivot chart and a table, they are independent—changes to the data in one do not affect the other one. Instead, another pivot table, linked to the pivot chart, is automatically added to another worksheet. You end up with one chart and two tables, the pivot table on the same worksheet as the pivot chart being independent. When you insert more than one chart, each chart has its own PowerPivot Field List and its own linked pivot table. Each of the latter also has its own PowerPivot Field List.

Another approach is to start just with a pivot table, using the PivotTable button in Excel or the PowerPivot window, and adding the pivot chart later. Should you adopt this approach, then the pivot chart you create can be independent of the pivot table or linked. To insert a pivot chart that is not linked, use the PivotTable button in Excel or PowerPivot again. To insert a pivot chart that is linked to your table, use the PivotChart button in the Tools group on the PivotTable Tools/Options ribbon in Excel.

Linking a pivot chart to an existing pivot table is quite useful for BI. It enables you to analyze the same scenario graphically and with numbers at the same time. The pivot chart will have its own PowerPivot Field List, but it will be interdependent with the pivot table PowerPivot Field List—if you make changes in one field list, it will update the other one. The next set of step-by-step instructions shows a linked pivot table and chart.

PowerPivot Field List for Pivot Charts

The PowerPivot Field List for a pivot chart is shown in Figure 5-66.

This field list is pretty similar to the field list you see for a pivot table, apart from two of the six drop-zones—Column Labels and Row Labels. Column Labels has a new title, Legend Fields (Series). The Row Labels drop-zone has become Axis Fields (Categories).

Figure 5-66   *PowerPivot Field List for a pivot chart*

The Values drop-zone corresponds to the y-axis or value axis of a chart. The Axis Fields drop-zone corresponds to the x-axis or categories axis of a chart, while the Legend Fields drop-zone corresponds to the legend or series of a chart. A short practical in the section "Pivot Chart Menus and Ribbons" demonstrates these areas of a pivot chart.

Slicers for Pivot Charts

Slicers behave the same way for both pivot tables and pivot charts. If the chart and table are linked, they both share the same slicer. In the situation of a linked table and chart, adding a slicer results in a shared common slicer for both the table and the chart—the slicer is not duplicated in the worksheet.

Pivot Chart Menus and Ribbons

A pivot chart has many context menus. Right-clicking on different areas of the chart leads to different context-sensitive pop-up menus. There are also four main ribbons dedicated to pivot charts. Rather than list all of the context menus, and their literally hundreds of options, one or two will be examined in the course of the following practical. After the practical there's a brief introduction to the pivot chart ribbons—if you don't have a pivot chart first, you won't see these ribbons.

To create a pivot chart, based on an existing pivot table:

1. You can use any pivot table as the base for your pivot chart. The example here has Sales Amount as Values, Year as Column Labels, and Country and City as Row Labels. You can see my starting point in Figure 5-67. I have hidden the Column Labels and Row Labels drop-down menus. It's also filtered to show only Argentina and Austria.

2. Make sure the focus is in the pivot table and click the PivotChart button in the Tools group of the PivotTable Tools/Options ribbon. This opens the Insert Chart dialog, which is shown in Figure 5-68.

3. Accept the clustered column default and click OK. The chart is added to the current worksheet—you may want to drag it so it's to the right of the pivot table. If you don't, when you remove the filter on Argentina and Austria, the chart may obscure part of the table. For the purposes of a screenshot only, I have dragged the chart immediately below the table—this is probably not a good position! The pivot chart and its linked pivot table are shown in Figure 5-69.

4. Click in both the chart and the table. The field list for each has the same entries in the drop-zones and two of the drop-zones have different captions. If you make changes to one, the other is updated automatically. Maybe you could add a slicer to one (for example, the Category column from the Products table, =RELATED (Categories [CategoryName]))? The slicer appears in both field lists, but only once in the worksheet. When you remove the slicer from one field list, it will disappear from the other.

	A	B	C	D	E	F
1	Sum of Sales Amount					
2		1996	1997	1998	Grand Total	
3	⊟ Argentina		1816.6	6302.5	8119.1	
4	Buenos Aires		1816.6	6302.5	8119.1	
5	⊟ Austria	29352	63151.98	46992.65	139496.63	
6	Graz	17170.4	53467.38	42598.9	113236.68	
7	Salzburg	12181.6	9684.6	4393.75	26259.95	
8	Grand Total	29352	64968.58	53295.15	147615.73	

Figure 5-67 *Pivot table for a pivot chart*

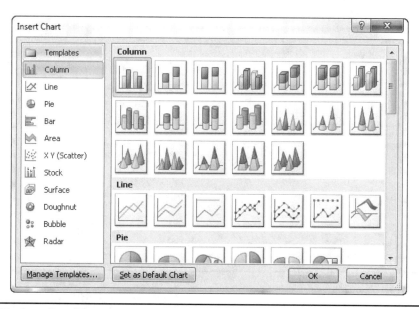

Figure 5-68   *Insert Chart dialog*

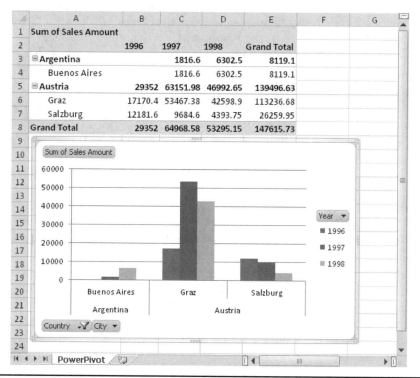

Figure 5-69   *Pivot chart and linked pivot table*

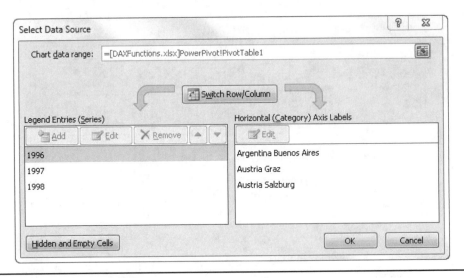

Figure 5-70 *Select Data Source dialog*

5. Right-click on a blank area of the chart and choose Select Data from the context menu. If that option is not in the context menu, you have right-clicked somewhere apart from a blank area! Alternatively, you can click the Select Data button in the Data group of the PivotChart Tools/Design ribbon. Hopefully, you are looking at the Select Data Source dialog, as shown in Figure 5-70.

6. In this dialog, click the Switch Row/Column button and then OK. Observe the effect on both the chart and the table. This is called "pivoting"—which is why pivot reports are called pivot reports. Repeat the previous step and this one to revert to the original design.

7. Experiment by right-clicking on various areas of the chart. If you right-click on a button, you can hide the buttons. Right-clicking on a blank area is a quick way to change a chart type. Right-clicking on the chart itself allows you to format the plot area. There are hundreds of options! Other areas where you might want to right-click are the grid lines, the legend, the vertical axis, the horizontal axis, and a column in the chart. All of these have one or more format options on the context menu. These options, in turn, open dialogs with hundreds of settings available.

8. If your chart is still looking reasonable, add Quantity from the Order Details table to the Values drop-zone, in either field list. Some of the Quantity values are quite difficult to see in the chart, as they are a lot smaller than the Sales Amount values. Right-click on the values on the x-axis, and choose Format Axis. This opens the Format Axis dialogs as shown in Figure 5-71.

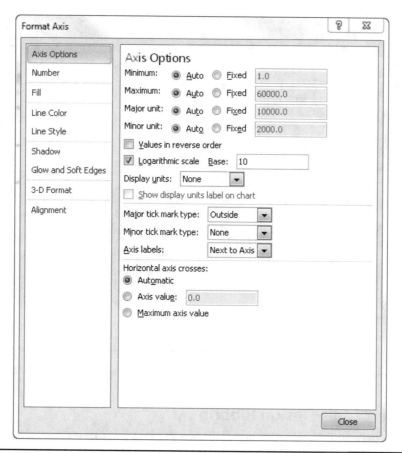

Figure 5-71   *Format Axis dialog*

9.   In this dialog, select the Logarithmic scale check box on the Axis Options page and click Close. Now the Quantity values are easier to see, as the vertical scale is logarithmic. Figure 5-72 shows the result.

10.   Feel free to experiment. Maybe try changing the chart type. If you want to delete the pivot chart, left-click to shows its borders, and press DELETE. The chart will be deleted, but the original table will remain.

The next section is a very brief look at the four pivot chart ribbons and the Insert ribbon. Only the most important and pertinent features are mentioned.

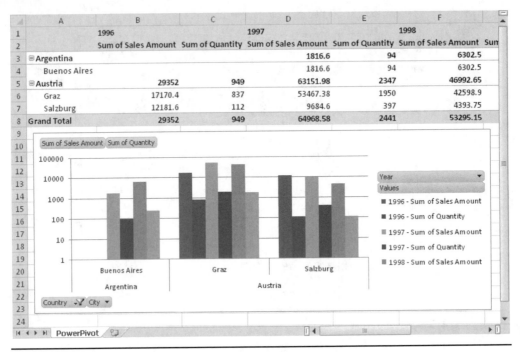

Figure 5-72   *Pivot chart with logarithmic scale*

PivotChart Tools/Design Ribbon

The PivotChart Tools/Design ribbon is shown in Figure 5-73.

Type Group   The Change Chart Type button opens the Change Chart Type dialog. This (apart from its title) is the same as the Insert Chart dialog that you met earlier. Naturally enough, you can use this to alter the fundamental design of your chart. The Save As Template button allows you to save a chart as a template—when you create charts, you can, optionally, base them on previously saved templates (these have a .crtx file extension).

Figure 5-73   *PivotChart Tools/Design ribbon*

Data Group   Switch Row/Column is a really cool button. It flips or "pivots" your pivot chart (and any linked pivot table) by swapping the Legend Fields and the Axis Fields. You can do the same through the Select Data button.

Chart Layouts Group   The Chart Layouts button in this group has a drop-down menu. Use this to alter the overall appearance of a chart. This is an easy way to add titles to your charts and reposition the legend.

Chart Styles Group   The Chart Styles button in this group opens a drop-down menu. This is handy for altering the color scheme of your chart.

PivotChart Tools/Layout Ribbon
The PivotChart Tools/Layout ribbon is shown in Figure 5-74.

Current Selection Group   Pivot charts have so many options for design that it's easy to create a mess! The Reset to Match Style button can undo a lot of harm and harmonize your design changes. The Format Selection button is an alternative to right-clicking within the chart and choosing format options from context menus.

Labels Group   This group contains five buttons. These are for showing, hiding, and positioning the chart legend, labels, and titles.

Axes Group   Use this group to control both axes and gridlines. The Axes button has different options from the Axis button in the Labels group. This one has more to do with position, the latter has more to do with captions.

Background Group   The Background group has buttons to format the plot area, chart walls, and chart floors, and for rotating a chart.

Figure 5-74   *PivotChart Tools/Layout ribbon*

Figure 5-75 *PivotChart Tools/Format ribbon*

Analysis Group This group includes a Trendline button. Some of the options for trend lines are quite advanced—for example, adding exponential trend lines or moving average trend lines.

PivotChart Tools/Format Ribbon

The PivotChart Tools/Format ribbon is shown in Figure 5-75.

Shape Styles Group The single button, Shape Styles, is context-sensitive. Use this to format the background of the chart, the legend, or the columns in a column chart.

WordArt Styles Group Use the first drop-down in this group to create amazing fonts and font colors for the text in your charts.

PivotChart Tools/Analyze Ribbon

The PivotChart Tools/Analyze ribbon is shown in Figure 5-76.

Data Group The Clear button opens a drop-down menu. This menu has two options for clearing filters on the chart or for clearing all. If you choose Clear All, it will remove the chart. Please be careful—it will also remove any linked pivot table. If your chart is linked to a table, then click on the chart and press DELETE—this removes the chart without removing the linked table.

Figure 5-76 *PivotChart Tools/Analyze ribbon*

Show/Hide Group   The Field Buttons button can be used to selectively remove buttons from the pivot chart. It also has a Hide All option, which removes all buttons. To re-establish all buttons, click Hide All again. Try not to use the Field List button— if you do, you will have a second (and non-PowerPivot) field list for the chart. This second field list also persists for any linked pivot table.

Insert Ribbon

The Insert ribbon has quite a few groups and buttons. Only the Charts group is discussed here, as it is the most relevant to chart design.

Charts Group   The buttons in this group allow you to change the chart type if the pivot chart has the focus. It duplicates the functionality of the Change Chart Type button in the Type group of the PivotChart Tools/Design ribbon. You can also change the chart type by right-clicking on the pivot chart. If the pivot chart does not have the focus, the buttons will create a new chart. The diagonal arrow button at the bottom right opens either the Change Chart Type or the Insert Chart dialog.

That concludes this chapter. You have had an overview of pivot tables and pivot charts, especially in the context of PowerPivot.

Part II

DAX

Chapter 6

Fundamental Functions: Filter, Logical, and Miscellaneous Functions

This is a wide-ranging chapter on some of the fundamental DAX functions. It includes syntax and examples for all of the Filter functions and all of the Logical functions. In addition, it discusses some other functions—for example, those that are often referred to as Information or IS() functions. An example is ISBLANK(). There is also one Text function, BLANK(), which has been added here because of its close relationship to ISBLANK(). The Filter functions, in particular, are extremely powerful. Among other things, they allow you to override the filter context that a user chooses in a pivot table. They help to display classic BI values such as "percentage of parent" or "percentage of all." Some of the examples are shown as calculated columns, others as measures. With measures, in particular, your results may differ from those shown in the screenshots, as there are a few different incarnations of Northwind—not always with the same data!

▶ **Key concepts**   Filtering data, overriding and changing filter context, denormalizing data, testing data, conditional testing, examining data, dealing with errors

▶ **Keywords**   ALL(), ALLEXCEPT(), ALLNOBLANKROW(), AND(), BLANK(), CALCULATE(), CALCULATETABLE(), DISTINCT(), EARLIER(), EARLIEST(), FALSE(), FILTER(), IF(), IFERROR(), ISBLANK(), ISERROR(), ISLOGICAL(), ISNONTEXT(), ISNUMBER(), ISTEXT(), NOT(), OR(), RELATED(), RELATEDTABLE(), TRUE(), VALUES()

▶ **Preparation**   Some of the examples in this chapter (and all the other chapters on DAX functions) refer to calculated columns created earlier on our Northwind sample. If you don't have Northwind data in a PowerPivot model, instructions of how to import Northwind from SQL Server are given in Chapter 1. If you do not have SQL Server or SQL Server Northwind, you may want to import the Access version of Northwind—instructions are in Chapter 2. Alternatively, you can download an Excel version of Northwind from this book's Web site—if you do, you'll need to set up relationships between the tables, and again, Chapter 2 shows you how. The calculated columns you'll need, if you want to try out the examples, were created in Chapter 1 and Chapter 2. As a reminder, they are the Year column in the Orders table, the Sales Amount column in the Order Details table, and the Category column in the Products table. Here are their respective DAX formulas:

```
=YEAR(Orders[OrderDate])
='Order Details'[Quantity] * 'Order Details'[UnitPrice]
=RELATED(Categories[CategoryName])
```

ALL() 1/7

ALL() can be used to modify the filter context of a measure. Consequently, the examples over the next few pages concentrate on measures. In particular, ALL() is frequently used to modify the filter context for a CALCULATE() function. As such, many of the following examples are going to use CALCULATE() as well as ALL(). CALCULATE() itself has a separate entry later in the chapter. Before we investigate further, here are three measures in this example that are always modified by the filter context. The first is called Num (for numerator), the second Den (for denominator), and the third NumOverDen (for numerator divided by denominator). All three measures have been added to the Order Details table. The Employees LastName column is on the Row Labels, and there are slicers on Year and Category.

ALL() is a Filter function. The examples are measures. Your figures may differ if you have a different release of Northwind from the one used here.

Syntax

```
=SUM('Order Details'[Sales Amount])
=SUM('Order Details'[Sales Amount])
=SUM('Order Details'[Sales Amount])/SUM('Order Details'[Sales Amount])
```

Result

Row Labels	Num	Den	NumOverDen
Buchanan	75567.75	75567.75	1
Callahan	133301.03	133301.03	1
Davolio	202143.71	202143.71	1
Dodsworth	82964	82964	1
Fuller	177749.26	177749.26	1
King	141295.99	141295.99	1
Leverling	213051.3	213051.3	1
Peacock	250187.45	250187.45	1
Suyama	78198.1	78198.1	1
Grand Total	1354458.59	1354458.59	1

Slicers: Year (1996, 1997, 1998); Category (Beverages, Condiments, Confections, Dairy Products, Grains/Cereals, Meat/Poultry, Produce, Seafood)

Analysis

If you slice on Year and/or Category, notice how the numerator and denominator both change. They reflect the current filter context. As they are both equal, the third measure is always 1. With measures, it is often a requirement that you allow the numerator and denominator to behave differently. This is useful for calculating ratios in particular.

By overriding the current filter context, you can return figures for percentage of all or percentage of parent. The next few formulas investigate how to override the filter context.

The first two measures could also be written as follows:

```
=SUMX('Order Details','Order Details'[Sales Amount])
```

ALL() 2/7

The second and third measures have been changed. They now incorporate the CALCULATE() function. CALCULATE() enables you to override the filter context—although not in these examples.

ALL() is a Filter function. The examples are measures. Your figures may differ if you have a different release of Northwind from the one used here.

Syntax

```
=SUM('Order Details'[Sales Amount])
=CALCULATE(SUM('Order Details'[Sales Amount]))
=SUM('Order Details'[Sales Amount])/
CALCULATE(SUM('Order Details'[Sales Amount]))
```

Result

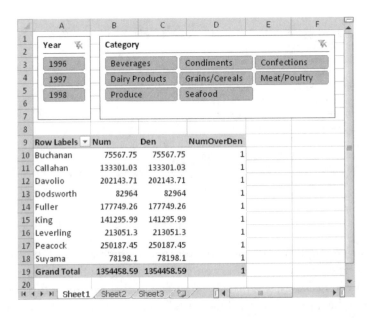

Analysis

The introduction of the CALCULATE() function has had no effect on the pivot table. The slicers still change the numerator and the denominator identically. CALCULATE() by itself makes no difference. Its real power lies in its ability to accept parameters after the expression to aggregate sales. These additional parameters are called the filter or SetFilter parameters. One such parameter includes the ALL() function. The next formula shows how to use it and what it does.

ALL() 3/7

The ALL() function in the denominator has a table as its own parameter. It can also accept columns instead of a reference to a table.

ALL() is a Filter function. The examples are measures. Your figures may differ if you have a different release of Northwind from the one used here.

Syntax

```
=SUM('Order Details'[Sales Amount])
=CALCULATE(SUM('Order Details'[Sales Amount]),ALL(Orders))
=SUM('Order Details'[Sales Amount])/
CALCULATE(SUM('Order Details'[Sales Amount]),ALL(Orders))
```

Result

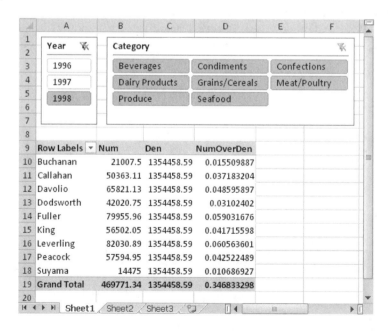

Analysis

To examine the purpose of ALL(), try slicing on Year and/or on Category. The Category slicer affects both the numerator and the denominator. The Year slicer affects only the numerator. The denominator continues to show the sales for all dates—although that figure will vary by product category. The Year column is part of the Orders table. The ALL() function is saying "consider all rows from the Orders table"; consequently, all years are included in the calculation. The only filter that is operative is that on product category, in this example. The ALL() function has overridden the Year slicer in the denominator. The numerator is still affected by the Year slicer. In the result, the sales of all categories made by Buchanan in 1998 were about 1.5 percent of the sales of all categories by all employees for all time. The figures for each employee in the denominator are the same, as the employee is part of the Orders table (it has a foreign key of EmployeeID)—and the ALL() function is ignoring all context on that table.

ALL() 4/7

In these examples, the table used in the ALL() function has been changed from Orders to Products.

ALL() is a Filter function. The examples are measures. Your figures may differ if you have a different release of Northwind from the one used here.

Syntax

```
=SUM('Order Details'[Sales Amount])
=CALCULATE(SUM('Order Details'[Sales Amount]),ALL(Products))
=SUM('Order Details'[Sales Amount])/
CALCULATE(SUM('Order Details'[Sales Amount]),ALL(Products))
```

Result

	A	B	C	D	E	F
1	Year 🔻	Category				🔻
2						
3	1996	Beverages	Condiments		Confections	
4	1997	Dairy Products	Grains/Cereals		Meat/Poultry	
5	1998	Produce	Seafood			
6						
7						
8						
9	Row Labels ▾	Num	Den	NumOverDen		
10	Buchanan	13517.5	75567.75	0.178879218		
11	Callahan	18640.8	133301.03	0.13983988		
12	Davolio	48832	202143.71	0.241570712		
13	Dodsworth	20513.6	82964	0.247259052		
14	Fuller	42029.4	177749.26	0.236453305		
15	King	33517	141295.99	0.237211261		
16	Leverling	46506.55	213051.3	0.218288037		
17	Peacock	52842.35	250187.45	0.211211034		
18	Suyama	10127.75	78198.1	0.129514016		
19	Grand Total	286526.95	1354458.59	0.211543529		
20						

Sheet1 / Sheet2 / Sheet3

Analysis

This time, the Category filter is ignored in the denominator, as it's part of the Products table—the table parameter in the ALL() function. The Year slicer, however, does affect the denominator. In the result, Buchanan's sales of Beverages were nearly 18 percent of his sales of all categories. The ALL() function is invaluable for working out percentage of parent or percentage of total. The figures for each employee in the denominator are different here, as the employee is not part of the Products table.

ALL() 5/7

In these examples, there are two ALL() functions. Each takes a different table as a parameter.

ALL() is a Filter function. The examples are measures. Your figures may differ if you have a different release of Northwind from the one used here.

Syntax

```
=SUM('Order Details'[Sales Amount])
=CALCULATE(SUM('Order Details'[Sales Amount]),ALL(Products),ALL(Orders))
=SUM('Order Details'[Sales Amount])/
CALCULATE(SUM('Order Details'[Sales Amount]),ALL(Products),ALL(Orders))
```

Result

	A	B	C	D	E	F
1						
2	Year		Category			
3	1996		Beverages	Condiments	Confections	
4	1997		Dairy Products	Grains/Cereals	Meat/Poultry	
5	1998		Produce	Seafood		
6						
7						
8						
9	Row Labels	Num	Den	NumOverDen		
10	Buchanan	1596.5	1354458.59	0.0011787		
11	Callahan	8774.5	1354458.59	0.006478234		
12	Davolio	25556	1354458.59	0.018868056		
13	Dodsworth	12877.5	1354458.59	0.009507489		
14	Fuller	30523.5	1354458.59	0.022535573		
15	King	6886.5	1354458.59	0.005084319		
16	Leverling	20909	1354458.59	0.015437164		
17	Peacock	12321	1354458.59	0.009096624		
18	Suyama	2779.25	1354458.59	0.002051927		
19	Grand Total	122223.75	1354458.59	0.090238085		
20						

Sheet1 / Sheet2 / Sheet3

Analysis

Neither of the two slicers has any effect on the denominator. Indeed, the employee context is ignored too, as the employee is part of the Orders table. The denominator is always going to be the same. However, the year, category, and employee all dictate the context of the numerator. This is how to show a percentage of the grand total. Buchanan's sales of Beverages in 1998 were about 0.11 percent of the total sales of all categories by all employees for all years.

ALL() 6/7

This is an important variation on the ALL() function. There is only the single ALL() here, but it has the table that contains the source measure as one of its columns.

ALL() is a Filter function. The examples are measures. Your figures may differ if you have a different release of Northwind from the one used here.

Syntax

```
=SUM('Order Details'[Sales Amount])
=CALCULATE(SUM('Order Details'[Sales Amount]),ALL('Order Details'))
=SUM('Order Details'[Sales Amount])/
CALCULATE(SUM('Order Details'[Sales Amount]),ALL('Order Details'))
```

Result

Row Labels	Num	Den	NumOverDen
Buchanan	1596.5	1354458.59	0.0011787
Callahan	8774.5	1354458.59	0.006478234
Davolio	25556	1354458.59	0.018868056
Dodsworth	12877.5	1354458.59	0.009507489
Fuller	30523.5	1354458.59	0.022535573
King	6886.5	1354458.59	0.005084319
Leverling	20909	1354458.59	0.015437164
Peacock	12321	1354458.59	0.009096624
Suyama	2779.25	1354458.59	0.002051927
Grand Total	122223.75	1354458.59	0.090238085

Analysis

Superficially, the result is identical to those in the previous examples. If you dig deeper, there is a fundamental difference. The previous example ignored any context on the Orders and the Products tables. However, you might add a column from another table (to a slicer or to Report Filter, Column Labels, or Row Labels), and that could change the filter context. Our example here will ignore *any* filters on Sales Amount, which is part of the Order Details table. Such an approach can give the percentage of the grand total, no matter how the end user adds table columns to the pivot table and slices and filters. Unfortunately, we have run out of tables—so with Northwind it's difficult to prove! If you revert to the previous example and maybe filter on customer, it would have no effect as the customer is part of the Orders table (as the CustomerID foreign key). The same argument applies to the Categories table; there is a foreign key of

CategoryID in the Products table. Maybe you might want to adapt this example and the previous one to your own data—assuming you have more tables than we have here.

ALL() 7/7

To demonstrate these formulas, you may want to add a ProductName slicer (the column is in the Products table). The ALL() function now has a column, rather than a table, parameter.

ALL() is a Filter function. The examples are measures. Your figures may differ if you have a different release of Northwind from the one used here.

Syntax

```
=SUM('Order Details'[Sales Amount])
=CALCULATE(SUM('Order Details'[Sales Amount]),
ALL(Products[ProductName]))
=SUM('Order Details'[Sales Amount])/
CALCULATE(SUM('Order Details'[Sales Amount]),ALL(Products[ProductName]))
```

Result

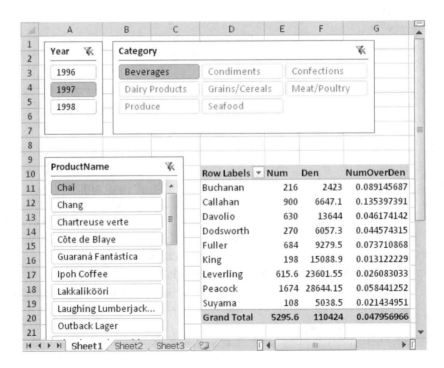

Analysis

There are a lot of interesting things going on here. The Category and ProductName slicers are cascading—the selection in the former dictates the products shown in the latter. If you select a product first, it automatically selects the right category and makes the category the first one in the Category slicer. You can control this behavior in the Slicer Settings dialog. If you then select a different category, you end up with an empty pivot table as there is no relationship between the product and an inappropriate category—you have to remove the filter in the products slicer.

From a DAX perspective, the important change is the column parameter to the ALL() function. The Category slicer alters the denominator; the ProductName slicer does not. The SetFilter argument is saying, "implement all filters except those on product name." The user can select a product category and the figures in the pivot table will be updated, both numerator and denominator. When the user selects a product, only the numerator gets updated. This technique is handy for showing percentage of parent. In 1997, Buchanan's sales of Chai were about 8.9 percent of his sales of all Beverages.

ALLEXCEPT() 1/2

The ALLEXCEPT() function is another function that returns a table and can be used as a SetFilter argument for the CALCULATE() function. Its own parameters are a table name followed by one or more column names. Before we look at ALLEXCEPT(), here are three formulas for a numerator, denominator, and a numerator divided by a denominator.

ALLEXCEPT() is a Filter function. The examples are measures. Your figures may differ if you have a different release of Northwind from the one used here.

Syntax

```
=SUM('Order Details'[Sales Amount])
=CALCULATE(SUM('Order Details'[Sales Amount]))
=SUM('Order Details'[Sales Amount])/
CALCULATE(SUM('Order Details'[Sales Amount]))
```

Result

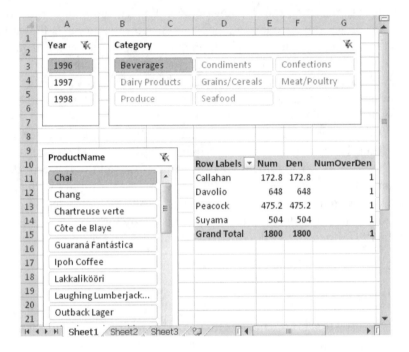

Analysis

All three slicers change the filter context. As you slice, the denominator is constantly changing too. Please notice that if there are no sales for an employee, the default behavior is to hide the employee.

ALLEXCEPT() 2/2

Now we introduce ALLEXCEPT() into the measures.

ALLEXCEPT() is a Filter function. The examples are measures. Your figures may differ if you have a different release of Northwind from the one used here.

Syntax

```
=SUM('Order Details'[Sales Amount])
=CALCULATE(SUM('Order Details'[Sales Amount]),
ALLEXCEPT(Products,Products[Category]))
=SUM('Order Details'[Sales Amount])/
CALCULATE(SUM('Order Details'[Sales Amount]),
ALLEXCEPT(Products,Products[Category]))
```

Result

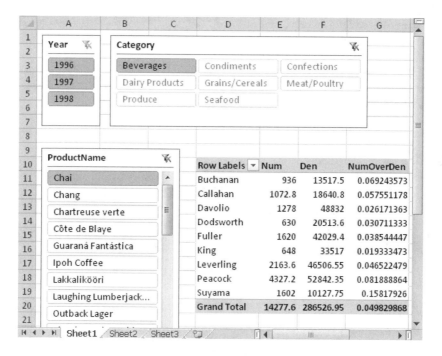

Analysis

The Category slicer affects the denominator; the ProductName slicer does not. The ALLEXCEPT() syntax is asking to override all filters on the Products table, except that on category. Another way of writing this is to use the ALL() function and then a comma-separated list of all the columns in the Products table apart from Category. ALLEXCEPT() is a convenient shorthand when you only want to respect the filter context of one or two columns in a table, but override it on all the other columns. If there are no sales for an employee, the employee is still shown—this is because the denominator is never null.

ALLNOBLANKROW()

For these examples, the ProductName slicer has been removed.

ALLNOBLANKROW() is a Filter function. The examples are measures. Your figures may differ if you have a different release of Northwind from the one used here.

Syntax

```
=SUM('Order Details'[Sales Amount])
=CALCULATE(SUM('Order Details'[Sales Amount]),
ALLNOBLANKROW(Employees[LastName]))
=SUM('Order Details'[Sales Amount])/
CALCULATE(SUM('Order Details'[Sales Amount]),
ALLNOBLANKROW(Employees[LastName]))
```

Result

	A	B	C	D	E	F
1	Year		Category			
2						
3	1996		Beverages	Condiments	Confections	
4	1997		Dairy Products	Grains/Cereals	Meat/Poultry	
5	1998		Produce	Seafood		
6						
7						
8						
9						
10	Row Labels ▼	Num	Den	NumOverDen		
11	Buchanan		19458.3			
12	Callahan	1458.4	19458.3	0.074950021		
13	Davolio	2762	19458.3	0.141944569		
14	Dodsworth	2808	19458.3	0.144308598		
15	Fuller	3721.6	19458.3	0.191260285		
16	King	1385.6	19458.3	0.071208687		
17	Leverling	1660.8	19458.3	0.085351752		
18	Peacock	5289.9	19458.3	0.271858282		
19	Suyama	372	19458.3	0.019117806		
20	Grand Total	19458.3	19458.3	1		
21						

Sheet1 / Sheet2 / Sheet3

Analysis

ALLNOBLANKROW() is similar to ALL(). However, ALL() will also return the Unknown member, a blank row—ALLNOBLANKROW() does not. This extra blank row is created by PowerPivot where you have a referential integrity violation from a table on the many side of a relationship. For example, you might have an order assigned to an employee who does not exist in the Employees table.

AND()

AND() is a function and not an operator. Many of the DAX functions have the same name as Excel functions and they tend to behave in a similar manner.

AND() is a Logical function. The examples are calculated columns on any table.

Syntax

```
=AND(1=1,2=2)
=AND(1=1,2=3)
=AND(1=1,AND(2=2,3=3))
=1=1 && 2=2 && 3=4
```

Result

CalculatedColumn1	CalculatedColumn2	CalculatedColumn3	CalculatedColumn4	Add Column
TRUE	FALSE	TRUE	FALSE	
TRUE	FALSE	TRUE	FALSE	
TRUE	FALSE	TRUE	FALSE	
TRUE	FALSE	TRUE	FALSE	
TRUE	FALSE	TRUE	FALSE	
TRUE	FALSE	TRUE	FALSE	
TRUE	FALSE	TRUE	FALSE	
TRUE	FALSE	TRUE	FALSE	

Analysis

The AND() function tests to see if two conditions are true. If both are true, it returns TRUE. If either or both are false, it returns FALSE. AND() accepts a maximum of two conditions, which is different from the Excel AND() function. Should you want to test more than two conditions, then you must use a nested AND(). This is shown in the third example. Alternatively, you can replace the AND() function with the double ampersand (&&) operator as in the last example.

BLANK()

Officially, BLANK() is a Text function. It's included here because it's such a fundamental and important function. It's also closely related to the ISBLANK() Logical function, which is shown later in this chapter.

BLANK() is a Text function. The example is a calculated column on the Customers table.

Syntax

```
=IF(ISBLANK(Customers[Region]),BLANK() & "No region","Region")
```

Result

CompanyName	Region	PostalCode	Country	Phone	Fax	CalculatedColumn1	Add Column
Alfreds Futterkiste		12209	Germany	030-007...	030-0...	No region	
Ana Trujillo Empa...		05021	Mexico	(5) 555-...	(5) 5...	No region	
Antonio Moreno ...		05023	Mexico	(5) 555-...		No region	
Around the Horn		WA1 1DP	UK	(171) 55...	(171)...	No region	
Berglunds snabb...		S-958 22	Sweden	0921-12 ...	0921-...	No region	
Blauer See Delik...		68306	Germany	0621-08...	0621-...	No region	
Blondesddsl pèr...		67000	France	88.60.15...	88.60...	No region	
Bólido Comidas p...		28023	Spain	(91) 555 ...	(91) ...	No region	
Bon app'		13008	France	91.24.45...	91.24...	No region	
Bottom-Dollar M...	BC	T2F 8M4	Canada	(604) 55...	(604)...	Region	

Analysis

BLANK() returns a blank or an empty value. ISBLANK() tests for a blank. In DAX, a blank is subtly different from a null in most databases (although in SQL Server, you can change the default behavior of nulls). As this example demonstrates, a blank is treated as an empty string in text calculations. In arithmetic calculations it is treated as a zero. Here, the concatenation of a blank to a string does not result in a blank.

CALCULATE()

Earlier in this chapter, there were quite a few examples of CALCULATE(). It is one of the most frequently used DAX functions. Its importance lies in its ability to change, ignore, or augment a filter context in a pivot table. We have seen CALCULATE() used with ALL() and ALLEXCEPT(). Here is another way of entering a SetFilter argument to the function. The first measure is called Num and the second Den. CALCULATE() was previously discussed in some depth in Chapter 4.

CALCULATE() is a Filter function. The examples are measures. Your figures may differ if you have a different release of Northwind from the one used here.

Syntax

```
=CALCULATE(AVERAGE('Order Details'[Sales Amount]))
=CALCULATE(AVERAGE('Order Details'[Sales Amount]),
Employees[LastName] = "Davolio")
=FORMAT([Num]/[Den],"Percent")
```

Result

Analysis

The denominator has a fixed context on employee name. All other filters will affect the denominator, but it will always be for Davolio, no matter how you slice on Year or Category. The result shows that her average sales were less than half of those of Buchanan for Beverages in 1996. FORMAT() is a Text function. It converts a value (numeric or date, for instance) into a string and applies formatting. Please note that, rather than repeat the first two formulas again in the third one, the measures have been referred to by name. Like column names, measure names must be enclosed in square brackets. Because a measure name must be unique within a PowerPivot model, there is no need to preface the measure name with a table name. By having measures refer to other measures, you can cut down on the syntax involved. There is also another shorthand that allows you to omit the CALCULATE() function altogether. The following three measures give the same result—but the second one is much shorter. It is using the first measure as a function. The parameter to the function (as it's a parameter, it has to be in parentheses) is the SetFilter argument of the CALCULATE() function. The following three measures can effectively replace the measures that were originally used in this example:

```
=CALCULATE(AVERAGE('Order Details'[Sales Amount]))
=[Num](Employees[LastName] = "Davolio")
=FORMAT([Num]/[Den],"Percent")
```

CALCULATETABLE()

CALCULATE() returns scalar values, while CALCULATETABLE() returns a table. You can't display tables in calculated columns nor as measures in a pivot table. As such, CALCULATETABLE() is used as an input into other functions that expect a table parameter. The functions that take a table parameter include the X-functions. The examples here use SUMX(), which adds together the values in the specified column in a table—the table name must precede the column name in SUMX().

CALCULATETABLE() is a Filter function. The examples are calculated columns on the Categories table.

Syntax

```
=SUMX(RELATEDTABLE(Products),Products[UnitsInStock])
=SUMX(CALCULATETABLE(RELATEDTABLE(Products),
Products[Discontinued]=FALSE),Products[UnitsInStock])
=Categories[CalculatedColumn1] - Categories[CalculatedColumn2]
```

Result

CategoryName	CalculatedColumn1	CalculatedColumn2	CalculatedColumn3	Add Column
Beverages	559	539	20	
Condiments	507	507	0	
Confections	386	386	0	
Dairy Products	393	393	0	
Grains/Cereals	308	282	26	
Meat/Poultry	165	136	29	
Produce	100	74	26	
Seafood	701	701	0	

Analysis

CALCULATETABLE() appears in the second calculated column. Like CALCULATE(), it can accept filter arguments. The filter in the example restricts the returned rows to only those for products that aren't discontinued. RELATEDTABLE() returns matching rows from a table that has a relationship to the current table. In the Products table, there are a total of 559 units of Beverage products in stock. Of these, 539 are for products that aren't discontinued. The third column simply works out the difference between the two totals.

DISTINCT()

Here there are three measures. Two of them demonstrate possible uses of the DISTINCT() function. The first measure doesn't include DISTINCT(), but is shown for comparison purposes. DISTINCT() returns a table and, therefore, is used as input into other functions that accept a table as an argument.

DISTINCT() is a Filter function. The examples are measures. Your figures may differ if you have a different release of Northwind from the one used here.

Syntax

```
=COUNTA((Orders[CustomerID]))
=COUNTROWS(DISTINCT(Orders[CustomerID]))
=CALCULATE(COUNTROWS(DISTINCT(Orders[CustomerID])),ALL(Orders[Year]))
```

Result

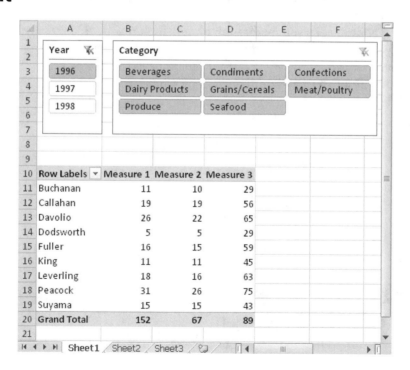

Analysis

The first measure counts all of the values of CustomerID in the Orders table. Because employees are on the rows, this count is filtered by employee. The measure contains a COUNTA() function. The second measure includes a COUNTROWS() function, which requires a table input. DISTINCT() returns the table and counts the *unique* values of CustomerID—it eliminates duplicates. Again, it is filtered at the employee level. In the third measure, any filter on year is overridden. In the result, Buchanan had 11 customers in 1996. Of these, 10 were unique, and his total number of customers over all time is 29. If you subtract the second measure from the first, you can obtain the number of repeat customers. COUNTA() and COUNTROWS() are discussed in the next chapter. DISTINCT() is very similar to another function, VALUES(), except the latter may also return an Unknown member. VALUES() is covered later in this chapter.

EARLIER()

There are two functions, EARLIER() and EARLIEST(), that enable you to compare column values across rows in PowerPivot tables. These functions have a number of applications. For example, you might wish to rank each row by some particular value. Or you may want to compare column values across rows for a particular product. Both applications are shown in the two calculated columns in this example.

EARLIER() is a Filter function. The examples are calculated columns on the Order Details table.

Syntax

```
=MAXX(FILTER('Order Details','Order Details'[ProductID] =
EARLIER('Order Details'[ProductID])),'Order Details'[Quantity])
=COUNTROWS(FILTER('Order Details','Order Details'[Quantity] >
EARLIER('Order Details'[Quantity]))) + 1
```

Result

OrderID	ProductID	Quantity	CalculatedColumn1	CalculatedColumn2	Add Column
10508	39	10	130	1548	
10521	35	3	100	2041	
10530	76	50	90	160	
10546	35	30	100	498	
10553	35	6	100	1832	
10566	76	10	90	1548	
10569	76	30	90	498	
10575	76	10	90	1548	

Analysis

The two examples are subtly different. The first one has a filter, with an equality test on the ProductID column. It will iterate through all the entries for a particular product, and return the maximum quantity ordered for a particular product. It will start on the first row and find all other rows with the same product. It will then move on to the second row and repeat the process. In this manner, it will traverse every single row in the table. The second example does not distinguish between different products. If it finds a row that has a larger quantity ordered than any other row, then the COUNTROWS() function will return zero. If we add 1 to this, that row will be ranked in first place. FILTER() is covered later in this chapter. MAXX() and COUNTROWS() are discussed in the next chapter. There is an optional second parameter to EARLIER(). If omitted, it defaults to 1, which means "compare to the immediate previous pass only." Theoretically, the maximum number of scans of all the table rows is n^2 where n is the number of rows. You may need to be aware of possible performance implications, when using EARLIER() and EARLIEST(). Here is another example; it shows how many employees report to a particular employee:

```
=COUNTROWS(FILTER(Employees,[ReportsTo]=EARLIER([EmployeeID],1)))
```

If you try this on the Employees table, you should find that only Fuller and Buchanan are managers.

EARLIEST()

EARLIEST() is very similar to EARLIER(). The same two examples are shown here, and the result is the same. EARLIEST() allows for more recursion than EARLIER(). Recursion levels are beyond the scope of this introductory book. However, you might like to know that EARLIEST() fetches the outermost row context where there are nested contexts. This can occur where you have multiple, nested aggregation functions.

EARLIEST() is a Filter function. The examples are calculated columns on the Order Details table.

Syntax

```
=MAXX(FILTER('Order Details','Order Details'[ProductID] =
EARLIEST('Order Details'[ProductID])),'Order Details'[Quantity])
=COUNTROWS(FILTER('Order Details','Order Details'[Quantity] >
EARLIEST('Order Details'[Quantity]))) + 1
```

Result

OrderID	ProductID	Quantity	CalculatedColumn1	CalculatedColumn2	Add Column
10508	39	10	130	1548	
10521	35	3	100	2041	
10530	76	50	90	160	
10546	35	30	100	498	
10553	35	6	100	1832	
10566	76	10	90	1548	
10569	76	30	90	498	
10575	76	10	90	1548	

Analysis

For the first calculated column result, it may be informative to filter on a particular product and sort descending on Quantity. When that's done, compare the value in the calculated column to the Quantity column. The DAX formula is showing the maximum quantity sold of each product. To understand the second calculated column result, it's helpful not to filter on product but to sort ascending on the calculated column and relate its value to that in the first calculated column. This time, the DAX is ranking rows by the quantity sold. If there's a tie, then the next rank value will not be a consecutive number.

FALSE()

EARLIER() and EARLIEST() are not the easiest of DAX functions! FALSE() is a little more straightforward.

FALSE() is a Logical function. The example is a calculated column on the Customers table.

Syntax

=IF(ISBLANK(Customers[Region]),FALSE(),TRUE())

Result

CompanyName	Region	PostalCode	Country	Phone	Fax	CalculatedColumn1	Add Column
Alfreds Futterkiste		12209	Germany	030-007...	030-0...	FALSE	
Ana Trujillo Empa...		05021	Mexico	(5) 555-...	(5) 5...	FALSE	
Antonio Moreno ...		05023	Mexico	(5) 555-...		FALSE	
Around the Horn		WA1 1DP	UK	(171) 55...	(171)...	FALSE	
Berglunds snabb...		S-958 22	Sweden	0921-12 ...	0921-...	FALSE	
Blauer See Delik...		68306	Germany	0621-08...	0621-...	FALSE	
Blondesddsl pèr...		67000	France	88.60.15...	88.60...	FALSE	
Bólido Comidas p...		28023	Spain	(91) 555 ...	(91) ...	FALSE	
Bon app'		13008	France	91.24.45...	91.24...	FALSE	
Bottom-Dollar M...	BC	T2F 8M4	Canada	(604) 55...	(604)...	TRUE	

Analysis

FALSE() quite simply returns a value of FALSE. Here, it's shown in conjunction with the IF() and ISBLANK() functions. Both of those functions are coming up shortly, in this chapter.

FILTER()

FILTER() returns a table and is consequently used as an input to another function. Its main purpose is to return a set of rows that meet a specified condition. FILTER() is shown here in calculated column examples. It can also be passed into a CALCULATE() function as a SetFilter argument.

FILTER() is a Filter function. The examples are calculated columns on the Categories table.

Syntax

```
=SUMX(FILTER(RELATEDTABLE(Products),Products[UnitPrice]>0),
Products[UnitsInStock])
=SUMX(FILTER(RELATEDTABLE(Products),Products[UnitPrice]>30),
Products[UnitsInStock])
=SUMX(FILTER(RELATEDTABLE(Products),Products[UnitPrice]>30 &&
Products[Discontinued]=TRUE()),Products[UnitsInStock])
=SUMX(FILTER(RELATEDTABLE(Products),Products[UnitPrice]>30 ||
Products[Discontinued]=TRUE()),Products[UnitsInStock])
```

Result

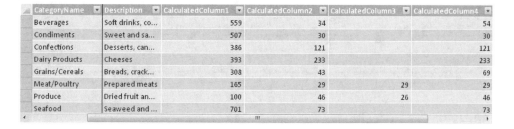

CategoryName	Description	CalculatedColumn1	CalculatedColumn2	CalculatedColumn3	CalculatedColumn4
Beverages	Soft drinks, co...	559	34		54
Condiments	Sweet and sa...	507	30		30
Confections	Desserts, can...	386	121		121
Dairy Products	Cheeses	393	233		233
Grains/Cereals	Breads, crack...	308	43		69
Meat/Poultry	Prepared meats	165	29	29	29
Produce	Dried fruit an...	100	46	26	46
Seafood	Seaweed and ...	701	73		73

Analysis

The SUMX() function is operating on the UnitsInStock column in the Products table. The RELATEDTABLE() function is returning all products that match the current product category. The double ampersand (&&) means AND, while the double pipe symbol (||) means OR. If you compare the second and third columns, you can see that all Meat/Poultry products that cost more than 30 are discontinued. RELATEDTABLE() follows later in this chapter. SUMX() is mentioned in the next chapter (Chapter 7) and in a later chapter on Math & Trig functions (Chapter 11).

IF()

The IF() function tests a condition. If the condition is true, then the first value is returned; otherwise, the second value is returned. Both return values must be the same data type—the third example here results in an error. You can nest the IF() function to implement complex branching.

IF() is a Logical function. The examples are calculated columns on the Customers table.

Syntax

```
=IF(ISBLANK(Customers[Region]),FALSE(),TRUE())
=IF(ISBLANK(Customers[Region]),
IF(Customers[City]="London","London",Customers[Country]),
Customers[Region])
=IF(ISBLANK(Customers[Region]),FALSE(),Customers[Region])
```

Result

CompanyName	City	Region	Country	CalculatedColumn1	CalculatedColumn2	CalculatedColu...
Ana Trujillo Empa...	México D.F.		Mexico	FALSE	Mexico	#ERROR
Antonio Moreno ...	México D.F.		Mexico	FALSE	Mexico	#ERROR
Around the Horn	London		UK	FALSE	London	#ERROR
Berglunds snabb...	Luleå		Sweden	FALSE	Sweden	#ERROR
Blauer See Delik...	Mannheim		Germany	FALSE	Germany	#ERROR
Blondesddsl pèr...	Strasbourg		France	FALSE	France	#ERROR
Bólido Comidas p...	Madrid		Spain	FALSE	Spain	#ERROR
Bon app'	Marseille		France	FALSE	France	#ERROR
Bottom-Dollar M...	Tsawassen	BC	Canada	TRUE	BC	#ERROR
B's Beverages	London		UK	FALSE	London	#ERROR

Analysis

The second calculated column shows the Region, if there is one. If not, it shows the Country—apart from the city of London, where the city name is used instead of the country name. SSAS developers may recognize a ragged hierarchy here.

IFERROR()

Like the IF() function, the IFERROR() function returns one of two values. Also, like the IF() function, the two values must be of the same data type—otherwise, IFERROR() generates an error itself. Unlike IF(), the first of the two return values is itself a test. If the first value is going to result in an error, then the second value is returned instead.

IFERROR() is a Logical function. The examples are calculated columns on the Products table.

Syntax

```
=Products[UnitsInStock]/Products[UnitsOnOrder]
=IFERROR(Products[UnitsInStock]/Products[UnitsOnOrder],0)
```

Result

ProductName	UnitsInStock	UnitsOnOrder	CalculatedColumn1	CalculatedColumn2
Chai	39	0	Infinity	0
Chang	17	40	0.425	0.425
Aniseed Syrup	13	70	0.185714285714286	0.185714285714286
Chef Anton's Ca...	53	0	Infinity	0
Chef Anton's G...	0	0	NaN	0
Grandma's Boys...	120	0	Infinity	0
Uncle Bob's Org...	15	0	Infinity	0
Northwoods Cr...	6	0	Infinity	0
Mishi Kobe Niku	29	0	Infinity	0
Ikura	31	0	Infinity	0

Analysis

The first calculated column is going to give one of two possible errors for certain rows. Dividing a zero by zero gives NaN (not a number), while dividing a non-zero by zero results in Infinity. IFERROR() is a convenient shorthand for the IF() function together with the ISERROR() function. The latter is shown later in this chapter.

ISBLANK()

ISBLANK() tests for blank values. We met it earlier, when looking at the BLANK() Text function.

ISBLANK() is an Information function. The example is a calculated column on the Customers table.

Syntax

```
=IF(ISBLANK(Customers[Region]),BLANK() & "No region","Region")
```

Result

CompanyName	Region	PostalCode	Country	Phone	Fax	CalculatedColumn1	Add Column
Alfreds Futterkiste		12209	Germany	030-007...	030-0...	No region	
Ana Trujillo Empa...		05021	Mexico	(5) 555-...	(5) 5...	No region	
Antonio Moreno ...		05023	Mexico	(5) 555-...		No region	
Around the Horn		WA1 1DP	UK	(171) 55...	(171)...	No region	
Berglunds snabb...		S-958 22	Sweden	0921-12 ...	0921-...	No region	
Blauer See Delik...		68306	Germany	0621-08...	0621-...	No region	
Blondesddsl pèr...		67000	France	88.60.15...	88.60...	No region	
Bólido Comidas p...		28023	Spain	(91) 555 ...	(91) ...	No region	
Bon app'		13008	France	91.24.45...	91.24...	No region	
Bottom-Dollar M...	BC	T2F 8M4	Canada	(604) 55...	(604)...	Region	

Analysis

ISBLANK() returns either TRUE or FALSE. Here, it's combined with the IF() function. Please note that the concatenation of a string with BLANK() does not give a blank.

ISERROR()

All of the IS() family of functions return TRUE or FALSE. They are often used in conjunction with IF(). Here, we are testing for an error condition.

ISERROR() is an Information function. The examples are calculated columns on the Products table.

Syntax

```
=Products[UnitsInStock]/Products[UnitsOnOrder]
=ISERROR(Products[UnitsInStock]/Products[UnitsOnOrder])
=IF(ISERROR(Products[UnitsInStock]/Products[UnitsOnOrder]),0,
Products[UnitsInStock]/Products[UnitsOnOrder])
```

Result

ProductName	UnitsInStock	UnitsOnOrder	CalculatedColumn1	CalculatedColumn2	CalculatedColumn3
Chai	39	0	Infinity	TRUE	0
Chang	17	40	0.425	FALSE	0.425
Aniseed Syrup	13	70	0.185714285714286	FALSE	0.185714285714286
Chef Anton's Ca...	53	0	Infinity	TRUE	0
Chef Anton's G...	0	0	NaN	TRUE	0
Grandma's Boys...	120	0	Infinity	TRUE	0
Uncle Bob's Org...	15	0	Infinity	TRUE	0
Northwoods Cr...	6	0	Infinity	TRUE	0
Mishi Kobe Niku	29	0	Infinity	TRUE	0
Ikura	31	0	Infinity	TRUE	0

Analysis

The third example combines ISERROR() with IF(). You might want to compare this to the IFERROR() function. As a reminder, NaN means "not a number."

ISLOGICAL()

ISLOGICAL() is another IS() or Information function. It tests for a TRUE or FALSE value and returns TRUE or FALSE.

ISLOGICAL() is an Information function. The example is a calculated column on the Products table.

Syntax

```
=ISLOGICAL(Products[Discontinued])
```

Result

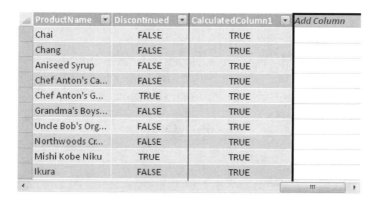

ProductName	Discontinued	CalculatedColumn1	Add Column
Chai	FALSE	TRUE	
Chang	FALSE	TRUE	
Aniseed Syrup	FALSE	TRUE	
Chef Anton's Ca...	FALSE	TRUE	
Chef Anton's G...	TRUE	TRUE	
Grandma's Boys...	FALSE	TRUE	
Uncle Bob's Org...	FALSE	TRUE	
Northwoods Cr...	FALSE	TRUE	
Mishi Kobe Niku	TRUE	TRUE	
Ikura	FALSE	TRUE	

Analysis

The Discontinued column in the Products table has a data type of TRUE/FALSE.

ISNONTEXT()

ISNONTEXT() has its converse in ISTEXT(). Please be careful with ISNONTEXT()— if it returns TRUE, it does not necessarily mean the column contains numbers. If the column has a data type of TRUE/FALSE or contains only blanks, for example, ISNONTEXT() will show TRUE. If you want to test specifically for a number, use ISNUMBER() instead.

ISNONTEXT() is an Information function. The example is a calculated column on the Products table.

Syntax

```
=ISNONTEXT(Products[UnitPrice])
```

Result

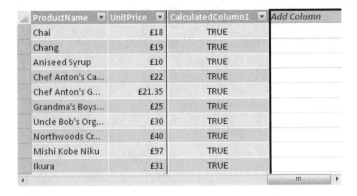

ProductName	UnitPrice	CalculatedColumn1	Add Column
Chai	£18	TRUE	
Chang	£19	TRUE	
Aniseed Syrup	£10	TRUE	
Chef Anton's Ca...	£22	TRUE	
Chef Anton's G...	£21.35	TRUE	
Grandma's Boys...	£25	TRUE	
Uncle Bob's Org...	£30	TRUE	
Northwoods Cr...	£40	TRUE	
Mishi Kobe Niku	£97	TRUE	
Ikura	£31	TRUE	

Analysis

The UnitPrice column in the Products table has a data type of Currency. You may want to test the data type of a column before attempting manipulation of the data. The Math & Trig functions, for example, don't operate on text values.

ISNUMBER()

ISNUMBER() checks whether a column contains numeric data.

ISNUMBER() is an Information function. The example is a calculated column on the Products table.

Syntax

```
=ISNUMBER(Products[UnitPrice])
```

Result

ProductName	UnitPrice	CalculatedColumn1	Add Column
Chai	£18	TRUE	
Chang	£19	TRUE	
Aniseed Syrup	£10	TRUE	
Chef Anton's Ca...	£22	TRUE	
Chef Anton's G...	£21.35	TRUE	
Grandma's Boys...	£25	TRUE	
Uncle Bob's Org...	£30	TRUE	
Northwoods Cr...	£40	TRUE	
Mishi Kobe Niku	£97	TRUE	
Ikura	£31	TRUE	

Analysis

Although the UnitPrice column in the Products table has a data type of Currency, it still qualifies as a numeric column.

ISTEXT()

This is the last of the IS() or Information functions. Again, it simply returns TRUE or FALSE.

ISTEXT() is an Information function. The example is a calculated column on the Products table.

Syntax

```
=ISTEXT(Products[UnitPrice])
```

Result

ProductName	UnitPrice	CalculatedColumn2	Add Column
Chai	£18	FALSE	
Chang	£19	FALSE	
Aniseed Syrup	£10	FALSE	
Chef Anton's Ca...	£22	FALSE	
Chef Anton's G...	£21.35	FALSE	
Grandma's Boys...	£25	FALSE	
Uncle Bob's Org...	£30	FALSE	
Northwoods Cr...	£40	FALSE	
Mishi Kobe Niku	£97	FALSE	
Ikura	£31	FALSE	

Analysis

This is a useful test to perform before trying to apply some of the Text functions to the values in a column.

NOT()

NOT() changes TRUE to FALSE and the reverse.

NOT() is a Logical function. The examples are calculated columns on the Products table.

Syntax

```
=IF(Products[UnitPrice] < 50, "Cheap","Expensive")
=IF(NOT(Products[UnitPrice] > 50), "Cheap","Expensive")
```

Result

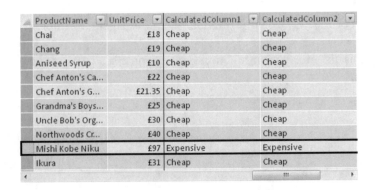

ProductName	UnitPrice	CalculatedColumn1	CalculatedColumn2
Chai	£18	Cheap	Cheap
Chang	£19	Cheap	Cheap
Aniseed Syrup	£10	Cheap	Cheap
Chef Anton's Ca...	£22	Cheap	Cheap
Chef Anton's G...	£21.35	Cheap	Cheap
Grandma's Boys...	£25	Cheap	Cheap
Uncle Bob's Org...	£30	Cheap	Cheap
Northwoods Cr...	£40	Cheap	Cheap
Mishi Kobe Niku	£97	Expensive	Expensive
Ikura	£31	Cheap	Cheap

Analysis

Mishi Kobe Niku is quite pricey!

OR()

OR(), as opposed to AND(), will result in TRUE if either of the two conditions is true. AND() only returns TRUE if both conditions are true.

OR() is a Logical function. The examples are calculated columns on any table.

Syntax

```
=OR(1=1,2=3)
=1=1 || 2=2 || 3=4
```

Result

Analysis

OR() accepts a maximum of two tests, which is different from the equivalent Excel OR() function. If you want more, then you can nest an OR() within an OR()—or you can use the double pipe (||) symbol, as shown in the second example.

RELATED()

RELATED() is one of the most popular DAX functions. It's going to help you denormalize your data and make browsing pivot tables so much easier and more intuitive. RELATED() was discussed in some detail in Chapter 4.

RELATED() is a Filter function. The first two examples are calculated columns on the Orders table. The third example is a calculated column on the Order Details table, the result of which is not shown in the screenshot.

Syntax

```
=RELATED(Employees[LastName])
=RELATED('Order Details'[Quantity])
=RELATED(Employees[LastName])
```

Result

OrderID	CalculatedColumn1	CalculatedColu...	Add Column
10248	Buchanan	#ERROR	
10249	Suyama	#ERROR	
10250	Peacock	#ERROR	
10251	Leverling	#ERROR	
10252	Peacock	#ERROR	
10253	Leverling	#ERROR	
10254	Buchanan	#ERROR	
10255	Dodsworth	#ERROR	
10256	Leverling	#ERROR	
10257	Peacock	#ERROR	

Analysis

The first example returns the employee responsible for a particular order. It's getting data from another table. In order for this to work, you must have defined a relationship between the two tables involved. Setting up relationships was examined in Chapter 2 and in Chapter 3. The RELATED() function must appear in the table on the many side of a relationship—it's doing a lookup of a value. The second example fails because, this time, the Orders table is on the one side of the relationship. The third example will work—it's jumping tables. The starting point is the Order Details table. This is related to the Orders table, which, in turn, is related to the Employees table. The net effect is to show the employee responsible for each order line.

RELATEDTABLE()

RELATED() must appear in a table on the many side of a relationship. RELATEDTABLE() can appear in either the many-side or the one-side table in a relationship. Generally, it is more useful on the one side. As it returns a table, it can't be used directly. Instead, it's fed into another DAX function that accepts a table as a parameter. The examples here pass the rows returned by RELATEDTABLE() into the COUNTROWS() function.

RELATEDTABLE() is a Filter function. The first example is a calculated column on the Employees table. The second example is a calculated column on the Products table. Only the result from the first example is shown in the screenshot.

Syntax

```
=COUNTROWS(RELATEDTABLE(Orders))
=COUNTROWS(RELATEDTABLE(Employees))
```

Result

LastName	Notes	ReportsTo	CalculatedColumn1	Add Column
Davolio	Educati...	2	123	
Fuller	Andrew...		96	
Leverling	Janet ha...	2	127	
Peacock	Margare...	2	156	
Buchanan	Steven ...	2	42	
Suyama	Michael...	5	67	
King	Robert ...	5	72	
Callahan	Laura re...	2	104	
Dodsworth	Anne ha...	5	43	

Analysis

The first example is the more useful. The RELATEDTABLE() function is in a calculated column on the one side of a direct relationship. The outcome is a count of the number of orders for each employee. The second example (result not in screenshot) shows the number of employees responsible for each order line. COUNTROWS() is covered in the next chapter.

TRUE()

The function TRUE() returns the value TRUE.

TRUE() is a Logical function. The example is a calculated column on the Customers table.

Syntax

```
=IF(ISBLANK(Customers[Region]),FALSE(),TRUE())
```

Result

CompanyName	Region	PostalCode	Country	Phone	Fax	CalculatedColumn1	Add Column
Alfreds Futterkiste		12209	Germany	030-007...	030-0...	FALSE	
Ana Trujillo Empa...		05021	Mexico	(5) 555-...	(5) 5...	FALSE	
Antonio Moreno ...		05023	Mexico	(5) 555-...		FALSE	
Around the Horn		WA1 1DP	UK	(171) 55...	(171)...	FALSE	
Berglunds snabb...		S-958 22	Sweden	0921-12 ...	0921-...	FALSE	
Blauer See Delik...		68306	Germany	0621-08...	0621-...	FALSE	
Blondesddsl père...		67000	France	88.60.15...	88.60...	FALSE	
Bólido Comidas p...		28023	Spain	(91) 555 ...	(91) ...	FALSE	
Bon app'		13008	France	91.24.45...	91.24...	FALSE	
Bottom-Dollar M...	BC	T2F 8M4	Canada	(604) 55...	(604)...	TRUE	

Analysis

We've met this example a few times. For instance, it was used earlier in this chapter for the FALSE() function.

VALUES()

This is the final function in this chapter. Please note that VALUES() can't be used directly to give a value for a calculated column or a measure, as it returns a table of rows. Don't confuse VALUES() with VALUE()—the latter is a Text function for converting strings into numbers.

VALUES() is a Filter function. The examples are measures. Your figures may differ if you have a different release of Northwind from the one used here.

Syntax

```
=COUNTROWS('Order Details')
=COUNTROWS(DISTINCT('Order Details'[ProductID]))
=COUNTROWS(VALUES('Order Details'[ProductID]))
=CALCULATE(COUNTROWS(VALUES('Order Details'[ProductID])),
ALL('Order Details'))
=[Measure 3]/[Measure 4]
```

Result

Row Labels	Measure 1	Measure 2	Measure 3	Measure 4	Measure 5
Buchanan	5	4	4	77	0.051948052
Callahan	7	6	6	77	0.077922078
Davolio	12	7	7	77	0.090909091
Dodsworth	5	4	4	77	0.051948052
Fuller	7	6	6	77	0.077922078
King	5	5	5	77	0.064935065
Leverling	5	5	5	77	0.064935065
Peacock	26	12	12	77	0.155844156
Suyama	6	4	4	77	0.051948052
Grand Total	78	12	12	77	0.155844156

Year slicer: 1996, 1997, 1998 (1996 selected)

Category slicer: Beverages (selected), Condiments, Confections, Dairy Products, Grains/Cereals, Meat/Poultry, Produce, Seafood

Analysis

These are fairly complex examples with which to finish the chapter. The first example shows how many order lines (as opposed to orders) are attributable to each employee. If you look at the Order Details table in the PowerPivot window, you can see there are 2155 rows, which matches the Grand Total (to see that figure, remove any slice on Year or Category). The second and third examples tell us how many distinct products were sold by each employee. The fourth calculated column is showing the total number of distinct products in all the order lines. Because it's using ALL('Order Details'), it overrides all filter contexts including that of employee. The final calculated column is a "percentage of all" column—the denominator is fixed. In 1996, Buchanan had five order lines for products belonging to the Beverages category. Of these, four were unique products—in other words, two of the order lines must have been for the same product. The total number of unique products (regardless of category) appearing in order lines is 77. If you prefer a "percentage of parent" answer showing the total number of unique products by category, change the fourth formula to this:

```
=CALCULATE(COUNTROWS(VALUES('Order Details'[ProductID])),ALL('Orders'))
```

If you try this, in 1996, Buchanan sold 4 out of a possible 12 products from the Beverages category.

Like DISTINCT(), VALUES() eliminates duplicate values. Unlike DISTINCT(), it will include the Unknown member if there is one. Unknown members can occur as a result of referential integrity violations between related tables. This is possible if the data from one table is refreshed independently of the data in a related table. In our sample Northwind data, there are no Unknown members, so the second and third examples presented give the same answers. CALCULATE() and ALL() are examined earlier in this chapter. COUNTROWS() is covered in the next chapter.

Chapter 7

Aggregate Functions: Statistical Functions and SUM()/SUMX() Functions

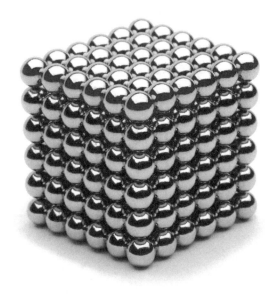

The aggregate functions include the Statistical functions and both SUM() and SUMX() from the Math & Trig functions. Such functions often result in numeric values. The functions can be used equally well as calculated columns or as measures. If used as calculated columns, they are often added to the Values drop-zone in the PowerPivot Field List and displayed in the central data area of a pivot table. They are ideally suited for producing totals and subtotals. In this chapter, the alphabetical order of the functions has not been observed completely. For example, AVERAGEX() appears before AVERAGEA(), but after AVERAGE()—this is to highlight the difference between a base column function, such as AVERAGE(), and its table function equivalent, AVERAGEX(). AVERAGEA(), another column function, then follows. In general, the X-functions, for instance, AVERAGEX(), accept a table argument. The base functions, like AVERAGE(), accept a column argument, and they operate on numeric or date values. The A-functions, for example, AVERAGEA(), also accept a column argument, but they usually work on every value in a column, even text and blank values.

▶ **Key concepts**   Aggregating data, averaging data, counting rows, summing data, finding minimum and maximum values

▶ **Keywords**   AVERAGE(), AVERAGEX(), AVERAGEA(), COUNT(), COUNTX(), COUNTA(), COUNTAX(), COUNTBLANK(), COUNTROWS(), MAX(), MAXX(), MAXA(), MIN(), MINX(), MINA(), SUM(), SUMX()

AVERAGE()

AVERAGE() finds the mean of all the numeric values in the specified column. The average of date values is returned as a serial number.

This example is a calculated column in the Order Details table.

Syntax

```
='Order Details'[Sales Amount] - AVERAGE('Order Details'[Sales Amount])
```

Result

OrderID	ProductID	Sales Amount	CalculatedColumn1
10508	39	£180	(£448.5191)
10521	35	£54	(£574.5191)
10530	76	£900	£271.4809
10546	35	£540	(£88.5191)
10553	35	£108	(£520.5191)
10566	76	£180	(£448.5191)
10569	76	£540	(£88.5191)
10575	76	£180	(£448.5191)

Analysis

The example calculates the deviation from the mean for the sales on each order line. Blank or TRUE/FALSE values are ignored. Zeros count toward the total number of rows. You can't calculate AVERAGE() on a column that contains text. The AVERAGE() function only accepts a column—the following expression is invalid as an input:

```
=AVERAGE('Order Details'[Quantity] * 'Order Details'[UnitPrice])
```

AVERAGEX()

This is an X-function. It takes a table as its first parameter—if you try a column instead, you'll receive an error. The second parameter is the column, or expression with scalar result, that you wish to average.

This example is a calculated column in the Employees table.

Syntax

```
=AVERAGEX(RELATEDTABLE(Orders),Orders[Freight])
```

Result

LastName	Notes	ReportsTo	CalculatedColumn1
Davolio	Educati...	2	£71.8426
Fuller	Andrew...		£90.5876
Leverling	Janet ha...	2	£85.7066
Peacock	Margare...	2	£72.7317
Buchanan	Steven ...	2	£93.3026
Suyama	Michael...	5	£56.4249
King	Robert ...	5	£92.5756
Callahan	Laura re...	2	£71.9988

Analysis

Here, RELATEDTABLE() is used to generate a table, which is then passed into AVERAGEX() as the first argument. The second argument causes AVERAGEX() to calculate the mean freight charge of all orders gained by each employee. Michael Suyama has the lowest freight charges.

AVERAGEA()

Here we see the first of the A-functions. Unlike the X-functions, the A-functions require a column as their first parameter. Also, unlike the X-functions, the A-functions take only a single parameter. In those respects, AVERAGEA() is similar to the base function, AVERAGE(). However, there is a major difference between the base functions and the A-functions—the A-functions can cope with non-numeric and non-date data.

These examples are calculated columns in the Products table.

Syntax

```
=AVERAGE(Products[Discontinued])
=AVERAGEA(Products[Discontinued])
```

Result

ProductName	CalculatedColumn1	CalculatedColumn2
Chai	#ERROR	0.103896103896104
Chang	#ERROR	0.103896103896104
Aniseed Syrup	#ERROR	0.103896103896104
Chef Anton's Ca...	#ERROR	0.103896103896104
Chef Anton's G...	#ERROR	0.103896103896104
Grandma's Boys...	#ERROR	0.103896103896104
Uncle Bob's Org...	#ERROR	0.103896103896104
Northwoods Cr...	#ERROR	0.103896103896104

Analysis

The Discontinued column has a data type of TRUE/FALSE. The first example, AVERAGE(), generates an error. AVERAGEA() does not give an error. A TRUE counts as 1 and a FALSE as 0. A text value would also count as 0. If you multiply the result here by 77 (the total number of rows), the answer is 8. This indicates that 8 products are discontinued. The COUNTROWS() function would give you the total number of rows in a table. You could achieve the same answer (8) with the following formulas:

```
=COUNTROWS(FILTER(Products,[Discontinued]=TRUE))
=COUNTAX(FILTER(Products,[Discontinued]=TRUE),[Discontinued]) COUNTAX()
and COUNTROWS() are examined in this chapter, and FILTER() was discussed
in the last chapter.
```

COUNT()

COUNT() is a base aggregate function. Just as with AVERAGE(), there are A-function and X-function variations. In addition, there is also an AX-function version as well.

This example is a calculated column in the Order Details table.

Syntax

```
=COUNT('Order Details'[Discount])
```

Result

OrderID	ProductID	CalculatedColumn1
10508	39	2155
10521	35	2155
10530	76	2155
10546	35	2155
10553	35	2155
10566	76	2155
10569	76	2155
10575	76	2155

Analysis

The result is 2155. This does not necessarily mean there are 2155 rows in the table. Rather, it indicates that 2155 rows contain a number (or date) in the specified column. To return the number of rows in the table, COUNTROWS() is better, as COUNT() does not count non-numeric or non-date values. In this case, every row in the Discount column contains a number, so it does represent the total count of the rows in the table.

COUNTX()

This is the X-function version of the base COUNT() function.

This example is a calculated column in the Employees table.

Syntax

```
=COUNTX(RELATEDTABLE(Orders),Orders[EmployeeID])
```

Result

LastName	ReportsTo	CalculatedColumn1
Davolio	2	123
Fuller		96
Leverling	2	127
Peacock	2	156
Buchanan	2	42
Suyama	5	67
King	5	72
Callahan	2	104

Analysis

The answer shows how many orders were attributable to each employee. It works as the EmployeeID column is numeric. COUNTX ( ) also works on dates. If you want to count non-numeric or non-date values in a table, try COUNTAX ( ). If you wish to count the same in a column, use COUNTA ( ). These two functions are covered next.

COUNTA()

This time, it's the A-function version of COUNT ( ).

These examples are calculated columns in the Products table.

Syntax

```
=COUNT(Products[Discontinued])
=COUNTA(Products[Discontinued])
```

Result

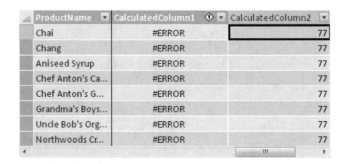

ProductName	CalculatedColumn1	CalculatedColumn2
Chai	#ERROR	77
Chang	#ERROR	77
Aniseed Syrup	#ERROR	77
Chef Anton's Ca...	#ERROR	77
Chef Anton's G...	#ERROR	77
Grandma's Boys...	#ERROR	77
Uncle Bob's Org...	#ERROR	77
Northwoods Cr...	#ERROR	77

Analysis

The Discontinued column has a data type of TRUE/FALSE. Consequently, the first example results in an error as it uses COUNT(). But COUNTA() is rather more successful.

COUNTAX()

COUNTAX() is the AX-function variety of COUNT(). The A means count non-numeric and non-date values, and the X means count a table-column rather than just a column.

These examples are calculated columns in the Products table.

Syntax

```
=COUNTX(Products,Products[Discontinued])
=COUNTAX(Products,Products[Discontinued])
```

Result

ProductName	CalculatedColumn1	CalculatedColumn2
Chai	#ERROR	77
Chang	#ERROR	77
Aniseed Syrup	#ERROR	77
Chef Anton's Ca...	#ERROR	77
Chef Anton's G...	#ERROR	77
Grandma's Boys...	#ERROR	77
Uncle Bob's Org...	#ERROR	77
Northwoods Cr...	#ERROR	77

Analysis

The first formula fails as the Discontinued column is a TRUE/FALSE column. The second formula produces the same result as the following formula:

```
=COUNTA(Products[Discontinued])
```

COUNTA() is simpler. COUNTAX() is more powerful, as you can apply it to another related table (using RELATEDTABLE()) or to a filtered table (using FILTER()).

COUNTBLANK()

This is yet another counting function. COUNTBLANK(), as its name suggests, counts the blank values in a column.

This example is a calculated column in the Customers table.

Syntax

```
=COUNTBLANK(Customers[Region])
```

Result

CompanyName	Phone	Fax	CalculatedColumn1
Alfreds Futterkiste	030-007...	030-0...	60
Ana Trujillo Empa...	(5) 555-...	(5) 5...	60
Antonio Moreno ...	(5) 555-...		60
Around the Horn	(171) 55...	(171)...	60
Berglunds snabb...	0921-12 ...	0921-...	60
Blauer See Delik...	0621-08...	0621-...	60
Blondesddsl pèr...	88.60.15...	88.60...	60
Bólido Comidas p...	(91) 555 ...	(91) ...	60

Analysis

There are 60 customers that have a blank entry in the Region column. Zeros are not blanks, and are not counted.

COUNTROWS()

Here we have the last of the counting functions in this chapter.

These examples are calculated columns in the Employees table.

Syntax

```
=COUNTROWS(Orders)
=COUNTX(RELATEDTABLE(Orders),Orders[EmployeeID])
=(Employees[CalculatedColumn2] / Employees[CalculatedColumn1]) * 100
```

Result

LastName	CalculatedColumn1	CalculatedColumn2	CalculatedColumn3
Davolio	830	123	14.8192771084337
Fuller	830	96	11.566265060241
Leverling	830	127	15.3012048192771
Peacock	830	156	18.7951807228916
Buchanan	830	42	5.06024096385542
Suyama	830	67	8.07228915662651
King	830	72	8.67469879518072
Callahan	830	104	12.5301204819277

Analysis

Davolio had nearly 15 percent of the orders. COUNTROWS() tells you the total number of rows in the Orders table. COUNTX() tells you the total number of rows in the Orders table in the row context of the current employee. The second example could be replaced with

```
=COUNTROWS(RELATEDTABLE(Orders))
```

However, COUNTX() is more flexible, as it lets you specify a specific column to count.

MAX()

MAX() returns the maximum value in a column.

This example is a calculated column in the Orders table.

Syntax

```
=MAX(Orders[Freight])
```

Result

OrderID	ShipPostalCode	ShipCountry	Year	CalculatedColumn1
10249	44087	Germany	1996	£1,007.64
10260	50739	Germany	1996	£1,007.64
10267	80805	Germany	1996	£1,007.64
10273	01307	Germany	1996	£1,007.64
10277	04179	Germany	1996	£1,007.64
10279	60528	Germany	1996	£1,007.64
10284	60528	Germany	1996	£1,007.64
10285	01307	Germany	1996	£1,007.64

Analysis

MAX () can handle numbers or dates. For other data types, use MAXA (). The result shows the largest freight charge for any order.

MAXX()

The X-function version of MAX (), MAXX (), returns the maximum numeric or date value in a table column. The column itself can be the result of an expression, as shown in this example. There is no MAXAX () function.

This example is a calculated column in the Orders table.

Syntax

```
=MAXX(RELATEDTABLE('Order Details'),
'Order Details'[Quantity] * 'Order Details'[UnitPrice])
```

Result

OrderID	ShipPostalCode	ShipCountry	Year	CalculatedColumn1
10249	44087	Germany	1996	£1,696
10260	50739	Germany	1996	£780
10267	80805	Germany	1996	£3,080
10273	01307	Germany	1996	£882
10277	04179	Germany	1996	£728
10279	60528	Germany	1996	£468
10284	60528	Germany	1996	£544
10285	01307	Germany	1996	£943.2

Analysis

This example uses an expression for the second, column, parameter of MAXX (). You could also reference either a regular or a calculated column—here you might try the Sales Amount calculated column. The result shows the maximum sales amount from the order lines for each order.

MAXA()

MAXA () can cope with values that are neither numeric nor dates.

These examples are calculated columns in the Products table.

Syntax

```
=MAX(Products[Discontinued])
=MAXA(Products[Discontinued])
```

Result

ProductName	CalculatedColumn1	CalculatedColumn2
Chai	#ERROR	1
Chang	#ERROR	1
Aniseed Syrup	#ERROR	1
Chef Anton's Ca...	#ERROR	1
Chef Anton's G...	#ERROR	1
Grandma's Boys...	#ERROR	1
Uncle Bob's Org...	#ERROR	1
Northwoods Cr...	#ERROR	1

Analysis

The first example is for MAX()—it causes an error. The second example uses MAXA() and handles the TRUE/FALSE Discontinued column. A value of TRUE counts as 1, while blanks, text, and FALSE count as zero.

MIN()

MIN() works on numeric or date columns.

This example is a calculated column in the Orders table.

Syntax

```
=MIN(Orders[Freight])
```

Result

OrderID	ShipCountry	Year	CalculatedColumn1
10249	Germany	1996	£0.02
10260	Germany	1996	£0.02
10267	Germany	1996	£0.02
10273	Germany	1996	£0.02
10277	Germany	1996	£0.02
10279	Germany	1996	£0.02
10284	Germany	1996	£0.02
10285	Germany	1996	£0.02

Analysis

The minimum freight charge for any order is only two cents (or two pence). The currency unit is determined by the regional settings in Control Panel and by the settings in the Formatting group of the PowerPivot Home ribbon.

MINX()

MINX() is the X-function table version of MIN().
   This example is a calculated column in the Orders table.

Syntax

```
=MINX(RELATEDTABLE('Order Details'),'Order Details'[Quantity] * 'Order
Details'[UnitPrice])
```

Result

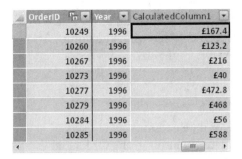

OrderID	Year	CalculatedColumn1
10249	1996	£167.4
10260	1996	£123.2
10267	1996	£216
10273	1996	£40
10277	1996	£472.8
10279	1996	£468
10284	1996	£56
10285	1996	£588

Analysis

The formula returns the minimum sales amount of all the order lines belonging to a particular order.

MINA()

Here we have the A-function variation on the MIN() function.
   These examples are calculated columns in the Products table.

Syntax

```
=MIN(Products[Discontinued])
=MINA(Products[Discontinued])
```

Result

Analysis

The first example results in an error as the Discontinued column values are neither numeric nor dates. In the second example, TRUE is counted as 1 and FALSE as zero. MINA(), therefore, returns zero.

SUM() 1/2

This function, SUM(), and its related function SUMX(), are officially Math & Trig functions. You can verify this in the Insert Function dialog. However, they are also introduced in this chapter as they do perform an aggregation.

This example is a calculated column in the Order Details table.

Syntax

```
=SUM('Order Details'[Sales Amount])
```

Result

Analysis

The formula is working out the total value of all sales in the Order Details table. You might divide into the Sales Amount calculated column to ascertain the percentage contribution of each order line to overall sales.

SUM() 2/2

It probably bears reiterating that DAX functions and formulas can (in most cases) be used in either calculated columns or measures. In the previous example, SUM() was a calculated column.

This example is a measure.

Syntax

```
=SUM('Order Details'[Sales Amount])
```

Result

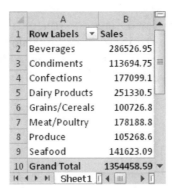

Analysis

The pivot table in the result depicts total sales by product category, and the grand total for sales for all categories.

SUMX()

SUMX() is the X-function version of SUM(). It requires a table as its first parameter.

This example is a calculated column in the Categories table.

Syntax

```
=SUMX(RELATEDTABLE(Products),Products[UnitsInStock])
```

Result

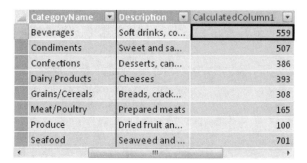

Analysis

The first argument must be a table or another function that returns a table. The second argument is the column you wish to aggregate. Here, the result shows the total number of stock items for each product category.

Chapter 8

Date & Time Functions 1/2: Basic Functions

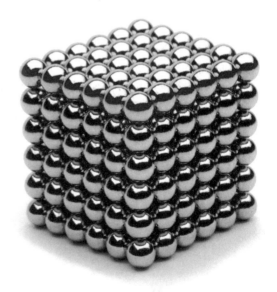

For the purpose of clarity, the Date & Time functions in DAX have been divided into two chapters. This is the first of those two chapters and deals with the more basic date and time functions. The next chapter is devoted to a group of Date & Time functions that are often referred to as time intelligence functions. The basic functions are often simpler and more forgiving. The time intelligence functions usually require that you have put some thought into how your dates are stored in the PowerPivot model. The emphasis in this chapter is on parsing, manipulating, and returning dates. The basic functions generally return dates and times. The time intelligence functions generally return measures or values associated with dates and times.

Please note that the display of dates and times is determined by your regional settings in Control Panel and the choices you make in the Formatting group of the PowerPivot Home ribbon. Dates and times displayed in a pivot table can also be customized to your liking. PowerPivot uses a special date data type, unlike Excel itself, which conforms to the Gregorian calendar.

Also, please be aware that there are different incarnations of the Northwind database. They often contain slightly different dates, and your results (if they use the Northwind Orders table and OrderDate column) may not always match the results shown in screenshots in this chapter.

▶ **Key concepts** Converting numbers and text to dates, parsing dates, manipulating dates, returning the current date and time

▶ **Keywords** DATE(), DATEVALUE(), DAY(), EDATE(), EOMONTH(), HOUR(), MINUTE(), MONTH(), NOW(), SECOND(), TIME(), TIMEVALUE(), TODAY(), WEEKDAY(), WEEKNUM(), YEAR(), YEARFRAC()

DATE()

DATE() accepts a comma-separated list of three numbers (year, month, day) and returns a date, with a data type of date. You can also have three strings, provided the strings can be converted into appropriate numbers.

The examples are for calculated columns in any table.

Syntax

```
=DATE(2001,12,31)
=DATE(01,12,31)
```

Result

OrderID	OrderDate	ShippedDate	CalculatedColumn1
10249	05-Jul-96	10-Jul-96	December 31, 2001
10260	19-Jul-96	29-Jul-96	December 31, 2001
10267	29-Jul-96	06-Aug-96	December 31, 2001
10273	05-Aug-96	12-Aug-96	December 31, 2001
10277	09-Aug-96	13-Aug-96	December 31, 2001
10279	13-Aug-96	16-Aug-96	December 31, 2001
10284	19-Aug-96	27-Aug-96	December 31, 2001
10285	20-Aug-96	26-Aug-96	December 31, 2001
10286	21-Aug-96	30-Aug-96	December 31, 2001
10301	09-Sep-96	17-Sep-96	December 31, 2001

Analysis

The result shown is from the first formula. If you recall, you can control the formatting of dates and times. To do so, use the Format drop-down menu in the Formatting group of the Home ribbon in PowerPivot. Please be careful with DATE(); the second example results in 1901, not 2001. It's probably a good idea to display four-digit years. DATE() accepts numbers as inputs. If your input is one string, use DATEVALUE() instead, as follows:

```
=DATEVALUE("2001/12/31")
```

However, DATE() will work with three separate strings (it implicitly converts them to numbers), as here:

```
=DATE("2001","12","31")
```

DATEVALUE() is covered next in this chapter.

DATEVALUE()

Like DATE(), DATEVALUE() returns a date as a date data type. Unlike DATE(), it takes a string or a text column as its single parameter. The string or text column must conform to certain rules—the following example fails.

The examples are for calculated columns in any table.

Syntax

```
=DATEVALUE("2001/12/31")
=DATEVALUE("20011231")
```

Result

OrderID	OrderDate	ShippedDate	CalculatedColumn1
10249	05-Jul-96	10-Jul-96	December 31, 2001
10260	19-Jul-96	29-Jul-96	December 31, 2001
10267	29-Jul-96	06-Aug-96	December 31, 2001
10273	05-Aug-96	12-Aug-96	December 31, 2001
10277	09-Aug-96	13-Aug-96	December 31, 2001
10279	13-Aug-96	16-Aug-96	December 31, 2001
10284	19-Aug-96	27-Aug-96	December 31, 2001
10285	20-Aug-96	26-Aug-96	December 31, 2001
10286	21-Aug-96	30-Aug-96	December 31, 2001
10301	09-Sep-96	17-Sep-96	December 31, 2001

Analysis

The first formula is successful and the result is shown in the screenshot. The second one gives an error. You can use Text functions to manipulate the string into a valid format for DATEVALUE(), or alternatively, try Text functions and the DATE() function:

```
=DATE(LEFT("20011231",4),MID("20011231",5,2),RIGHT("20011231",2))
```

LEFT(), MID(), and RIGHT() are Text functions and are covered in Chapter 10.

DAY()

DAY() returns the day of the month. This function and some of the other Date & Time functions are useful for creating date drill-down columns in your pivot tables.

The example is for a calculated column in the Orders table.

Syntax

```
=DAY(Orders[OrderDate])
```

Result

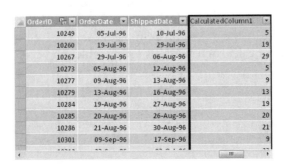

OrderID	OrderDate	ShippedDate	CalculatedColumn1
10249	05-Jul-96	10-Jul-96	5
10260	19-Jul-96	29-Jul-96	19
10267	29-Jul-96	06-Aug-96	29
10273	05-Aug-96	12-Aug-96	5
10277	09-Aug-96	13-Aug-96	9
10279	13-Aug-96	16-Aug-96	13
10284	19-Aug-96	27-Aug-96	19
10285	20-Aug-96	26-Aug-96	20
10286	21-Aug-96	30-Aug-96	21
10301	09-Sep-96	17-Sep-96	9

Analysis

In this formula, DAY() is parsing a regular column of data type date. DAY() can also accept a text parameter:

```
=DAY("2001/12/31")
```

EDATE()

If you need a date that is so many months in the future (or the past), EDATE() is the function to use. For dates in the past, make the second parameter negative.

The example is for a calculated column in the Orders table.

Syntax

```
=EDATE(Orders[OrderDate],6)
```

Result

OrderID	OrderDate	ShippedDate	CalculatedColumn1
10249	05-Jul-96	10-Jul-96	05-Jan-97
10260	19-Jul-96	29-Jul-96	19-Jan-97
10267	29-Jul-96	06-Aug-96	29-Jan-97
10273	05-Aug-96	12-Aug-96	05-Feb-97
10277	09-Aug-96	13-Aug-96	09-Feb-97
10279	13-Aug-96	16-Aug-96	13-Feb-97
10284	19-Aug-96	27-Aug-96	19-Feb-97
10285	20-Aug-96	26-Aug-96	20-Feb-97
10286	21-Aug-96	30-Aug-96	21-Feb-97
10301	09-Sep-96	17-Sep-96	09-Mar-97

Analysis

Your business rule may be that orders must ship within six months of the order date. You might use this formula and compare it to the actual ShippedDate column in the Orders table. That way, you can see that you shipped on time (or not!).

EOMONTH()

This EOMONTH() function is a handy alternative to EDATE(). Not only does it jump into the future (or the past), but it then returns the last day of the month in that future (or past) date. This is an ideal function for working out maturity dates.

The example is for a calculated column in the Orders table.

Syntax

```
=EOMONTH(Orders[OrderDate],6)
```

Result

Analysis

If you compare the result to that of the EDATE() one in the previous example, you'll see that EOMONTH() is giving the month-end dates—EO means EndOf.

HOUR()

HOUR() simply returns a number between 0 and 23. It accepts a date column, a time value, or a string as its single input parameter.

The first example is for a calculated column in any table. The second example is for a calculated column in the Orders table.

Syntax

```
=HOUR(NOW())
=HOUR(Orders[OrderDate])
```

Result

Analysis

The result shown is from the first example. Your result, of course, may be different. NOW(), which is described later in this chapter, returns the current date *and* time. The second example returns zero—that's because the OrderDate column has no time component, so it defaults to midnight. HOUR() can also work on strings:

```
=HOUR("2001/12/31 5:19 PM")
```

MINUTE()

As HOUR() gives the hour, MINUTE(), unsurprisingly, gives the minute, between 0 and 59. The example is for a calculated column in any table.

Syntax

```
=MINUTE(NOW())
```

Result

Analysis

Again, your result may vary from the screenshot here. MINUTE() can also work with a string parameter:

```
=MINUTE("2001/12/31 5:19 PM")
```

MONTH()

MONTH() returns the month from a date—as a number, between 1 and 12, not as a month name.

The example is for a calculated column in the Orders table.

Syntax

```
=MONTH(Orders[OrderDate])
```

Result

OrderID	OrderDate	ShippedDate	CalculatedColumn1
10249	05-Jul-96	10-Jul-96	7
10260	19-Jul-96	29-Jul-96	7
10267	29-Jul-96	06-Aug-96	7
10273	05-Aug-96	12-Aug-96	8
10277	09-Aug-96	13-Aug-96	8
10279	13-Aug-96	16-Aug-96	8
10284	19-Aug-96	27-Aug-96	8
10285	20-Aug-96	26-Aug-96	8
10286	21-Aug-96	30-Aug-96	8
10301	09-Sep-96	17-Sep-96	9

Analysis

MONTH() also operates on a suitably formatted string:

```
=MONTH("2001/12/31 5:19 PM")
=MONTH("2001/12/31")
```

The calculated column that contains the returned month number is often added to Column Labels or Row Labels in a pivot table. It's frequently combined with a year column and a quarter column to give drill-down on dates. There is, however, a potential drawback—the months appear as numbers rather than month names. Many users prefer to see the month names. Unfortunately, there is no DAX function in this first release of PowerPivot to give you the month name directly. There are at least two solutions, if the month name is not already part of your source data. One, you can write your own DAX formula to generate the month name. It might begin something like the following:

```
=IF(MONTH(Orders[OrderDate])=1,"January",
IF(MONTH(Orders[OrderDate])=2,"February",
```

and so on. Alternatively, you could do this:

```
=IF(MONTH(Orders[OrderDate])=1,"Jan",
IF(MONTH(Orders[OrderDate])=2,"Feb",
```

and so on.

Two, you can write a query when you import the data, if it's from a suitable source. For a SQL Server source, you might try one of these:

```
select datename(mm,orderdate) as MonthName from orders
select left(datename(mm,orderdate),3) as MonthName from orders
```

This, in turn, raises another interesting problem. If you add the month name to Row Labels or Column labels in a pivot table, the month names are sorted alphabetically (April, August, and so on). Fortunately, there is a GUI solution. First, right-click on a month name in the pivot table. Choose Sort, More Sort Options to open the Sort dialog. In this dialog, click More Options to open the More Sort Options dialog. In this second dialog, under AutoSort, turn off Sort Automatically Every Time the Report Is Updated. Then, from the First Key sort order drop-down, choose the entry beginning Jan or January (whichever is appropriate). Click OK twice to exit the two dialogs. Right-click once again on the month name in the pivot table, and choose Sort, followed by Sort A to Z.

NOW()

NOW() returns the current date and time. This is in contrast with TODAY(), which only returns the date.

The example is for a calculated column in any table.

Syntax

`=NOW()`

Result

OrderID	OrderDate	ShippedDate	CalculatedColumn1
10249	05-Jul-96	10-Jul-96	26-Apr-10 23:33:41
10260	19-Jul-96	29-Jul-96	26-Apr-10 23:33:41
10267	29-Jul-96	06-Aug-96	26-Apr-10 23:33:41
10273	05-Aug-96	12-Aug-96	26-Apr-10 23:33:41
10277	09-Aug-96	13-Aug-96	26-Apr-10 23:33:41
10279	13-Aug-96	16-Aug-96	26-Apr-10 23:33:41
10284	19-Aug-96	27-Aug-96	26-Apr-10 23:33:41
10285	20-Aug-96	26-Aug-96	26-Apr-10 23:33:41
10286	21-Aug-96	30-Aug-96	26-Apr-10 23:33:41
10301	09-Sep-96	17-Sep-96	26-Apr-10 23:33:41

Analysis

If you refresh the data in the table containing the column, the return value of NOW() will be updated. A refresh causes a recalculation. The same applies if you are in Manual Calculation mode and you choose Calculate Now. The TODAY() function appears later in this chapter.

There Is No QUARTER()

Partly in order to conform to existing Excel functions, there is no QUARTER() function in DAX. This example presents just one of a few possible solutions to extract the quarter from a date.

The example is for a calculated column in the Orders table.

Syntax

```
=IF(MONTH(Orders[OrderDate])<=3,1,IF(MONTH(Orders[OrderDate])<=6,2,
IF(MONTH(Orders[OrderDate])<=9,3,4)))
```

Result

OrderID	OrderDate	ShippedDate	CalculatedColumn1
10279	13-Aug-96	16-Aug-96	3
10284	19-Aug-96	27-Aug-96	3
10285	20-Aug-96	26-Aug-96	3
10286	21-Aug-96	30-Aug-96	3
10301	09-Sep-96	17-Sep-96	3
10312	23-Sep-96	03-Oct-96	3
10313	24-Sep-96	04-Oct-96	3
10323	07-Oct-96	14-Oct-96	4
10325	09-Oct-96	14-Oct-96	4
10337	24-Oct-96	29-Oct-96	4

Analysis

You might also try the CONCATENATE() function to prepend the letter "Q" to the quarter number. CONCATENATE() is a Text function and is discussed in Chapter 10. Or you might want to try this approach:

```
=IF(MONTH(Orders[OrderDate])<=3,"Q1",
IF(MONTH(Orders[OrderDate])<=6,"Q2",IF(MONTH(Orders[OrderDate])<=9,"Q3","
Q4")))
```

As an alternative to a DAX formula, you may want to return the quarter as part of an import query. Here are two possible SQL Server solutions:

```
select datepart(qq,orderdate) as MonthName from orders
select 'Q' + cast(datepart(qq,orderdate) as char) as MonthName
from orders
```

SECOND()

SECOND() operates on date columns or on strings to give the second, from 0 to 59.
The example is for a calculated column in any table.

Syntax

```
=SECOND("2001/12/31 5:19:45 PM")
```

Result

OrderID	OrderDate	ShippedDate	CalculatedColumn1
10249	05-Jul-96	10-Jul-96	45
10260	19-Jul-96	29-Jul-96	45
10267	29-Jul-96	06-Aug-96	45
10273	05-Aug-96	12-Aug-96	45
10277	09-Aug-96	13-Aug-96	45
10279	13-Aug-96	16-Aug-96	45
10284	19-Aug-96	27-Aug-96	45
10285	20-Aug-96	26-Aug-96	45
10286	21-Aug-96	30-Aug-96	45
10301	09-Sep-96	17-Sep-96	45

Analysis

If you try this on the OrderDate column in the Orders table, it will result in zeros. The OrderDate column is the date only, without any time element. As such, it defaults to midnight exactly—down to the second.

TIME()

TIME() converts a comma-separated list of numbers into a time. All three of the examples have the same result.

The examples are for calculated columns in any table.

Syntax

```
=TIME(17,0,0)
=TIME(41,0,0)
=TIME(0,1020,0)
```

Result

OrderID	OrderDate	ShippedDate	CalculatedColumn1
10249	05-Jul-96	10-Jul-96	5:00:00 PM
10260	19-Jul-96	29-Jul-96	5:00:00 PM
10267	29-Jul-96	06-Aug-96	5:00:00 PM
10273	05-Aug-96	12-Aug-96	5:00:00 PM
10277	09-Aug-96	13-Aug-96	5:00:00 PM
10279	13-Aug-96	16-Aug-96	5:00:00 PM
10284	19-Aug-96	27-Aug-96	5:00:00 PM
10285	20-Aug-96	26-Aug-96	5:00:00 PM
10286	21-Aug-96	30-Aug-96	5:00:00 PM
10301	09-Sep-96	17-Sep-96	5:00:00 PM

Analysis

You may need to change the format to see the same result. The second function subtracts 24 from 41 to give 17. The third one divides 1020 by 60, again to give 17. Try not to use the result as a date—the date will be 30 Dec 1899! The TIME() function will also implicitly convert text values into numbers:

```
=TIME("0","1020","0")
```

TIMEVALUE()

TIME() can work on a list of three text values. TIMEVALUE() is designed for a single string.

The examples are for calculated columns in any table.

Syntax

```
=TIMEVALUE("17:00:00")
=TIMEVALUE("5:00:00 PM")
```

Result

OrderID	OrderDate	ShippedDate	CalculatedColumn1
10249	05-Jul-96	10-Jul-96	5:00:00 PM
10260	19-Jul-96	29-Jul-96	5:00:00 PM
10267	29-Jul-96	06-Aug-96	5:00:00 PM
10273	05-Aug-96	12-Aug-96	5:00:00 PM
10277	09-Aug-96	13-Aug-96	5:00:00 PM
10279	13-Aug-96	16-Aug-96	5:00:00 PM
10284	19-Aug-96	27-Aug-96	5:00:00 PM
10285	20-Aug-96	26-Aug-96	5:00:00 PM
10286	21-Aug-96	30-Aug-96	5:00:00 PM
10301	09-Sep-96	17-Sep-96	5:00:00 PM

Analysis

The result has a date data type. Once again, you may want to adjust the format of the result.

TODAY()

NOW() results in the current date and time. TODAY() simply returns the current date. The example is for a calculated column in any table.

Syntax

```
=TODAY() + 10
```

Result

OrderID	OrderDate	ShippedDate	CalculatedColumn1
10249	05-Jul-96	10-Jul-96	6-May-10
10260	19-Jul-96	29-Jul-96	6-May-10
10267	29-Jul-96	06-Aug-96	6-May-10
10273	05-Aug-96	12-Aug-96	6-May-10
10277	09-Aug-96	13-Aug-96	6-May-10
10279	13-Aug-96	16-Aug-96	6-May-10
10284	19-Aug-96	27-Aug-96	6-May-10
10285	20-Aug-96	26-Aug-96	6-May-10
10286	21-Aug-96	30-Aug-96	6-May-10
10301	09-Sep-96	17-Sep-96	6-May-10

Analysis

The example adds ten days to today's date. Your result is going to be different! The date's time element will be midnight.

WEEKDAY()

If you want to ascertain the day of the week as a number, try WEEKDAY(). By default, Sunday is the first day of the week. This corresponds to the explicit second parameter in the second example.

The examples are for calculated columns in the Orders table.

Syntax

```
=WEEKDAY(Orders[OrderDate])
=WEEKDAY(Orders[OrderDate],1)
```

Result

OrderID	OrderDate	ShippedDate	CalculatedColumn1
10249	05-Jul-96	10-Jul-96	6
10260	19-Jul-96	29-Jul-96	6
10267	29-Jul-96	06-Aug-96	2
10273	05-Aug-96	12-Aug-96	2
10277	09-Aug-96	13-Aug-96	6
10279	13-Aug-96	16-Aug-96	3
10284	19-Aug-96	27-Aug-96	2
10285	20-Aug-96	26-Aug-96	3
10286	21-Aug-96	30-Aug-96	4
10301	09-Sep-96	17-Sep-96	2

Analysis

Both of the examples have the same answer. The default for the first day of the week is Sunday. The second example makes the default explicit. The return value is a number from 1 to 7. Should the first day of your week be Monday, try the following formula (the return value will be a number between 0 and 6):

```
=WEEKDAY(Orders[OrderDate],2)
```

WEEKNUM()

WEEKNUM() is used for the week number of the year.
The examples are for calculated columns in the Orders table.

Syntax

```
=WEEKNUM(Orders[OrderDate])
=WEEKNUM(Orders[OrderDate],1)
```

Result

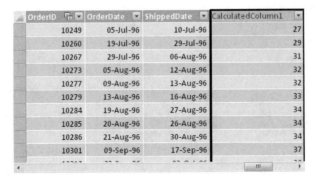

Analysis

You should receive the same result from both examples. The week number is influenced by the day of the week that starts the week. The default value is 1 for Sunday. If your week begins on a Monday, this is the formula:

```
=WEEKNUM(Orders[OrderDate],2)
```

YEAR()

YEAR() returns the year (calendar year) from a date.

The example is a calculated column in the Orders table.

Syntax

```
=YEAR(Orders[OrderDate])
```

Result

Analysis

YEAR() brings back the calendar year. If you want the fiscal year, you are going to have to write a more complex DAX formula, or calculate the fiscal year on the source data by importing as a query. YEAR() also supports a text parameter:

```
=YEAR("2001/12/31")
```

YEARFRAC()

If you have a date interval, YEARFRAC() will calculate the fraction, or proportion, of the year that the interval represents. The two dates that delimit the interval are passed as two parameters into the function.

The examples are for calculated columns in the Orders table.

Syntax

```
=ROUND(YEARFRAC(Orders[OrderDate],Orders[ShippedDate]) * 100,2)
=ROUND(YEARFRAC(Orders[OrderDate],Orders[ShippedDate],0) * 100,2)
```

Result

OrderID	OrderDate	ShippedDate	CalculatedColumn1
10249	05-Jul-96	10-Jul-96	1.39
10260	19-Jul-96	29-Jul-96	2.78
10267	29-Jul-96	06-Aug-96	1.94
10273	05-Aug-96	12-Aug-96	1.94
10277	09-Aug-96	13-Aug-96	1.11
10279	13-Aug-96	16-Aug-96	0.83
10284	19-Aug-96	27-Aug-96	2.22
10285	20-Aug-96	26-Aug-96	1.67
10286	21-Aug-96	30-Aug-96	2.5
10301	09-Sep-96	17-Sep-96	2.22

Analysis

The two formulas are identical in outcome. The second one contains the optional Basis parameter—the default is 0 (US 30/60), a year of 360 days divided into twelve 30-day months. If you observe orders 10267 and 10273, they have the same answer. The Basis parameter determines which of five methods are employed to calculate the fraction. For a full explanation, please refer to SQL Server Books Online (BOL). The following example uses a Basis of 3 (Actual 365).

Now try the following formula with a 3 switch, a 365-day year with months having their real number of days:

```
=ROUND(YEARFRAC(Orders[OrderDate],Orders[ShippedDate],3) * 100,2)
```

If you look at orders 10267 and 10273, this time, the YEARFRAC() results are different. ROUND() is a Math & Trig function used here to tidy up the results. ROUND() is examined in a Chapter 11.

Chapter 9

Date & Time Functions 2/2: Time Intelligence Functions

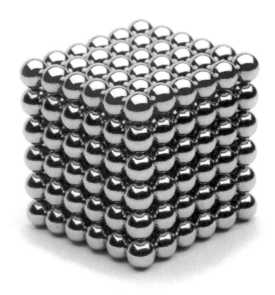

This is the second chapter dealing with DAX Date & Time functions. The previous chapter discusses some of the basic Date and Time functions. In this chapter, the emphasis is on the time intelligence Date and Time functions. The time intelligence functions are primarily used to *navigate* dates. In particular, they allow you to jump ahead or back in time and retrieve relevant data. This is useful if you wish to compare your data across or between time periods. Practical applications would include year-on-year changes. They allow you to compare the present date, in your filter context, with past and future dates. In addition, these functions can help you define ranges of dates or dates up to a particular date. A practical application here might be year-to-date sales. The basic functions generally return dates and times. The time intelligence functions generally return measures or values associated with dates and times, or ranges of periods used by other functions to calculate these values.

- ▶ **Key concepts** Jumping backward and forward in time, navigating time, establishing date ranges, returning dates up to the current date, year-on-year changes, year-to-date totals

- ▶ **Keywords** CLOSINGBALANCEMONTH(), CLOSINGBALANCEQUARTER(), CLOSINGBALANCEYEAR(), DATEADD(), DATESBETWEEN(), DATESINPERIOD(), DATESMTD(), DATESQTD(), DATESYTD(), ENDOFMONTH(), ENDOFQUARTER(), ENDOFYEAR(), FIRSTDATE(), FIRSTNONBLANK(), LASTDATE(), LASTNONBLANK(), NEXTDAY(), NEXTMONTH(), NEXTQUARTER(), NEXTYEAR(), OPENINGBALANCEMONTH(), OPENINGBALANCEQUARTER(), OPENINGBALANCEYEAR(), PARALLELPERIOD(), PREVIOUSDAY(), PREVIOUSMONTH(), PREVIOUSQUARTER(), PREVIOUSYEAR(), SAMEPERIODLASTYEAR(), STARTOFMONTH(), STARTOFQUARTER(), STARTOFYEAR(), TOTALMTD(), TOTALQTD(), TOTALYTD()

- ▶ **Preparation** There are 35 time intelligence functions in DAX, and 35 in this chapter. Most of them require that you have regular or calculated columns in your PowerPivot model to cover standard time periods—that is, in addition to a standard date column. If you wish to try the examples, please add the following calculated columns to the Orders table in the Northwind PowerPivot model. Instructions on how to create this model from a SQL Server source Northwind are in Chapter 1. Instructions on how to do so from an Access, Excel, or data feed Northwind are in Chapter 2. You will need calculated columns for the year, quarter, and month of orders. If you worked through some of the earlier chapters, you may already have a column for the year. Here are the DAX formulas for Year,

Month, and Quarter, respectively (the Quarter column references the Month column, so you have to complete Month before Quarter):

```
=YEAR(Orders[OrderDate])
```

```
=MONTH(Orders[OrderDate])
```

```
=IF(Orders[Month]<4,"Q1",IF(Orders[Month]<7,"Q2",IF(Orders[Month]<10,
"Q3","Q4")))
```

Time intelligence requires that you prepare your date data carefully. In particular, some of the functions only return intuitive results if your dates are contiguous and you have the same time periods in every year. Indeed, the recommendation is that you create a separate table just to hold dates (this is sometimes called a time or date *dimension*). These topics are discussed fully in Chapter 12, which deals with common PowerPivot and DAX solutions and problems. As it exists at present, the Northwind PowerPivot model does not meet all of the requirements on dates to return meaningful answers to some of the DAX formulas in this chapter. Specifically, it is not suitable for 13 of the 35 functions. In quite a comprehensive book, these are the first and only occasions on which faithful old Northwind has let us down—on just 13 DAX functions. There are three possible solutions—but two of them require that you have SQL Server.

The first solution is to use the ContosoRetailDW SQL Server sample database (and import the DimDate and FactSales tables)—in that database, the dates are already suitable for all the DAX time intelligence functions. That is the solution adopted here—so, some functions use ContosoRetailDW, and the relevant formulas for 13 functions are flagged as using that database. You can download ContosoRetailDW from www .microsoft.com (search on ContosoRetailDW).

The second approach is to use the AdventureWorksDW2008 SQL Server sample database (and import the DimDate and FactInternetSales tables). However, that requires a bit of further work as the date column relating the two tables is an integer and not a date.

The third solution is to create a new table in your PowerPivot model for Northwind (Excel or Access or data feed version, not just SQL Server version) to hold dates and relate the OrderDate column in the Orders table to the date column in the new table. The new table should hold contiguous dates from the first day of the first year for orders to the last day of the last year. You can use Fill | Series from the Editing group on the Excel Home ribbon to create the date table. You can then import, or link, into your PowerPivot model. Guidance on how to set up AdventureWorksDW2008 and Northwind dates is given in Chapter 12.

For now, for just a few functions in this chapter, we are going to use the ContosoRetailDW database.

Here are the steps to import suitable tables from ContosoRetailDW:

1. Either from a new PowerPivot model, or from an existing Northwind PowerPivot model, connect to SQL Server and to the ContosoRetailDW database.
2. Import two tables: DimDate and FactSales.
3. On the Design ribbon, click Manage Relationships and verify that FactSales is related to DimDate through the DateKey (called Datekey in DimDate) column.

CLOSINGBALANCEMONTH()

Please note that the Year, Quarter, Month, and OrderDate columns from the Orders table have been added to the Row Labels in the pivot table. The Quantity column from Order Details has been added to the Values drop-zone before creating the measures for our examples. There are slicers on Year and Category. CLOSINGBALANCEMONTH() returns the last value for the current month context when combined with a calculation function. Often, this will be the value for the last day of the current month. In general, all of the CLOSINGBALANCE() and OPENINGBALANCE() family of functions accept an expression as the first parameter and return a scalar value. You can also have an optional third parameter—a SetFilter parameter, as shown in the second example.

The examples are measures. The measures have been added to the Order Details table. Unless otherwise explicitly stated, the functions and formulas in this chapter use the Northwind PowerPivot model. As there are various incarnations of Northwind, your figures may differ from those shown here.

Syntax

```
=CLOSINGBALANCEMONTH(SUM('Order Details'[Quantity]),Orders[OrderDate])
```

```
=CLOSINGBALANCEMONTH(SUM('Order Details'[Quantity]),Orders[OrderDate],
ALL(Products[Category]))
```

```
=IF(COUNTROWS(VALUES(Orders[OrderDate])) > 1,
CLOSINGBALANCEMONTH(SUM('Order Details'[Quantity]),
Orders[OrderDate],ALL(Products[Category])))
```

```
=CALCULATE(SUM('Order Details'[Quantity]),LASTDATE(Orders[OrderDate]))
```

Result

	A	B	C	D	E	F
1						
2	Year	Category				
3						
4	1996	Beverages	Condiments	Confections		
5	1997	Dairy Products	Grains/Cereals	Meat/Poultry		
6	1998	Produce	Seafood			
7						
8						
9						
10	Row Labels	Sum of Quantity	Measure 1	Measure 2	Measure 3	Measure 4
11	⊞ 1996	1842	35	139	139	35
12	⊞ 1997	3996	20	38	38	20
13	⊟ 1998	3694	42	178	178	42
14	⊞ Q1	2381	6	245	245	6
15	⊟ Q2	1313	42	178	178	42
16	⊞ 4	1092	42	151	151	42
17	⊟ 5	221	42	178	178	42
18	May 01, 98	35	42	178		35
19	May 04, 98	56	42	178		56
20	May 05, 98	88	42	178		88
21	May 06, 98	42	42	178		42
22	Grand Total	9532	42	178	178	42

Sheet1 / Sheet2 / Sheet3

Analysis

The time intelligence functions require that the date column has a `date` data type. Many of the functions accept a `SetFilter` parameter, as the second and third examples show. The first formula results in 42 for 1998, Q2 of 1998, month 5 of 1998, and May 6. This is the closing balance, at the month level, for all of those periods. The figure for 1996 is 35. If you expand, you will see that the quantity sold on December 31 of that year is 35. The second example ignores the filter set in the Category slicer. The third example suppresses the result at the daily level—`VALUES()` always has more than one row at aggregate levels. The fourth example uses `LASTDATE()` to produce a similar result, but not at the daily level. `LASTDATE()` is covered later in this chapter.

CLOSINGBALANCEQUARTER()

`CLOSINGBALANCEQUARTER()` returns the last value for the current quarter context if a calculation formula is also used.

The example is a measure on the Order Details table.

Syntax

```
=CLOSINGBALANCEQUARTER(SUM('Order Details'[Quantity]),Orders[OrderDate])
```

Result

Analysis

Superficially, these results are similar to those of the previous function with the Category slicer overridden. However, the figure for month 4 of 1998 has disappeared. This function is only going to show the values for the last month in a quarter—based on the last day of the period. The previous function showed values for all months. If no value exists, the function will return a blank.

CLOSINGBALANCEYEAR()

CLOSINGBALANCEYEAR() returns the last value for the current year context when used with a calculation. With this function, and OPENINGBALANCEYEAR(), there is an optional fourth parameter for the year-end date—the default is December 31. This is useful if you are not working with regular calendar years.

The example is a measure on the Order Details table.

Syntax

```
=CLOSINGBALANCEYEAR(SUM('Order Details'[Quantity]),Orders[OrderDate])
```

Result

	A	B	C	D	E	F
1						
2	Year	Category				
3						
4	1996	Beverages	Condiments	Confections		
5	1997	Dairy Products	Grains/Cereals	Meat/Poultry		
6	1998	Produce	Seafood			
7						
8						
9						
10	Row Labels	Sum of Quantity	Measure 1			
11	⊞1996	9581	139			
12	⊞1997	25489	38			
13	⊟1998	16247	178			
14	⊞Q1	10646				
15	⊟Q2	5601	178			
16	⊞4	4680				
17	⊟5	921	178			
18	May 01, 98	277	178			
19	May 04, 98	101	178			
20	May 05, 98	365	178			
21	May 06, 98	178	178			
22	Grand Total	51317	178			

Sheet1 Sheet2 Sheet3

Analysis

This time, the value for Q1 of 1998 has gone—it is not the last quarter in that year. Incidentally, CLOSINGBALANCEYEAR() on a year returns the same figure as OPENINGBALANCEYEAR() from the next year. OPENINGBALANCEYEAR() is covered later in this chapter.

DATEADD()

DATEADD() allows you to navigate backward or forward in time. It's useful for making comparisons across time.

The first example is a calculated column on the Orders table. The second, third, and fourth formulas are measures and use ContosoRetailDW. The resulting screenshot is for the second, third, and fourth examples. Before creating the first measure for ContosoRetailDW, add SalesAmount from FactSales to the Values drop-zone. Also, place CalendarYear, CalendarQuarter, CalendarMonth, and Datekey from DimDate on the Row Labels of the pivot table. When you create the measures, place them in the FactSales table. If you tried the previous function, you may want to remove the slicers from that example—otherwise, you may receive a "Relationship needed" warning.

Syntax

```
=DATEADD(Orders[OrderDate],-1,YEAR)

=CALCULATE(SUM(FactSales[SalesAmount]),
DATEADD(DimDate[Datekey],-1,YEAR))

=SUM(FactSales[SalesAmount])/CALCULATE(SUM(FactSales[SalesAmount]),
DATEADD(DimDate[Datekey],-1,YEAR))

=IF(CALCULATE(SUM(FactSales[SalesAmount]),
DATEADD(DimDate[Datekey],-1,YEAR)),
SUM(FactSales[SalesAmount])/CALCULATE(SUM(FactSales[SalesAmount]),
DATEADD(DimDate[Datekey],-1,YEAR)),BLANK())
```

Result

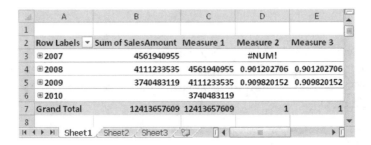

Row Labels	Sum of SalesAmount	Measure 1	Measure 2	Measure 3
⊞ 2007	4561940955		#NUM!	
⊞ 2008	4111233535	4561940955	0.901202706	0.901202706
⊞ 2009	3740483119	4111233535	0.909820152	0.909820152
⊞ 2010		3740483119		
Grand Total	12413657609	12413657609	1	1

Analysis

The second formula shows sales of the previous year. The third formula expresses the current year as a ratio of the previous year. The fourth formula returns a blank instead of a division-by-zero error. Please note that the third parameter here for DATEADD() is YEAR and not YEAR(). The last formula is quite complex. You may want to break it down into separate measures as follows:

```
=SUM(FactSales[SalesAmount])

=CALCULATE([Measure 1],DATEADD(DimDate[Datekey],-1,YEAR))

=IF([Measure 2],[Measure 1]/[Measure 2],BLANK())
```

You can further simplify the CALCULATE() function by using the measure itself as a function. If you try this, the SetFilter argument must be in parentheses and there is no comma after the measure. Here's an example:

```
[Measure 1](DATEADD(DimDate[Datekey],-1,YEAR))
```

DATESBETWEEN()

Sales Amount from the Order Details table has been added to the Values drop-zone before creating the measures. You will also need the Year, Quarter, Month, and OrderDate columns from the Orders table. DATESBETWEEN() returns a range of dates. The first parameter is the date column. The second and third parameters are the start and end dates. The range of dates returned is inclusive of the start and end dates.

The examples are measures on the Order Details table.

Syntax

```
=CALCULATE(SUM('Order Details'[Sales Amount]),
DATESBETWEEN(Orders[OrderDate],DATE(1997,12,1),DATE(1997,12,3)))

=CALCULATE(SUM('Order Details'[Sales Amount]),
DATESBETWEEN(Orders[OrderDate],DATE(1998,5,4),BLANK()))

=CALCULATE(SUM('Order Details'[Sales Amount]),
DATESBETWEEN(Orders[OrderDate],BLANK(),DATE(1996,7,5)))
```

Result

	A	B	C	D	E
2	**Year** 🔽	**Category**			🔽
4	1996	Beverages	Condiments	Confections	
5	1997	Dairy Products	Grains/Cereals	Meat/Poultry	
6	1998	Produce	Seafood		
10	**Row Labels** 🔽	**Sum of Sales Amount**	**Measure 1**	**Measure 2**	**Measure 3**
11	⊞ 1996	226298.5			2303.4
12	⊞ 1997	658388.75	11426.5		
13	⊟ 1998	469771.34		13995.05	
14	⊞ Q1	315242.12			
15	⊟ Q2	154529.22		13995.05	
16	⊞ 4	134630.56			
17	⊟ 5	19898.66		13995.05	
18	May 01, 98	5903.61		13995.05	
19	May 04, 98	2831.65		13995.05	
20	May 05, 98	7901.5		13995.05	
21	May 06, 98	3261.9		13995.05	
22	**Grand Total**	1354458.59	11426.5	13995.05	2303.4

◄ ◄ ► ►◄ Sheet1 / Sheet2 / Sheet3 / 🔄

Analysis

BLANK(), as a start date, means from before the first date. BLANK(), as an end date, means after the last date. The second example (Measure 2) shows the total from May 4, 1998, to the end of time. The only year with a value for this formula is 1998.

DATESINPERIOD()

DATESINPERIOD() also gives a range of dates. Instead of start and end dates, as in DATESBETWEEN(), you use a start date and then a number of intervals. A positive number takes you forward in time, and a negative number takes you back in time.

The example is a measure on the Order Details table.

Syntax

```
=CALCULATE(SUM('Order Details'[Sales Amount]),
DATESINPERIOD(Orders[OrderDate],DATE(1996,7,4),5,DAY))
```

Result

	A	B	C	D	E
1					
2	Year	Category			
3					
4	1996	Beverages	Condiments	Confections	
5	1997	Dairy Products	Grains/Cereals	Meat/Poultry	
6	1998	Produce	Seafood		
7					
8					
9					
10	Row Labels	Sum of Sales Amount	Measure 1		
11	⊟1996	226298.5	4787.2		
12	⊟Q3	84437.5	4787.2		
13	⊟7	30192.1	4787.2		
14	Jul 04, 96	440	4787.2		
15	Jul 05, 96	1863.4	4787.2		
16	Jul 08, 96	2483.8	4787.2		
17	Jul 09, 96	3730	4787.2		
18	Jul 10, 96	1444.8	4787.2		
19	Jul 11, 96	625.2	4787.2		
20	Jul 12, 96	2490.5	4787.2		
21	Jul 15, 96	517.8	4787.2		
22	Jul 16, 96	1119.9	4787.2		

Sheet1 / Sheet2 / Sheet3

Analysis

The start date here is July 4, 1996, and the number of intervals is 5. July 9 does not qualify for the range—the potential dates are July 4, 5, 6, 7, and 8. July 6 and 7 are not present, so the SUM() is for July 4, 5, and 8. Please note that the fourth interval parameter for DATESINPERIOD() here is DAY and not DAY().

DATESMTD()

DATESMTD() returns all of the dates in the current month up to and including the current date.

The example is a measure on the Order Details table.

Syntax

```
=CALCULATE(SUM('Order Details'[Sales Amount]),
DATESMTD(Orders[OrderDate]))
```

Result

Row Labels	Sum of Sales Amount	Measure 1
⊞ 1996	226298.5	50953.4
⊞ 1997	658388.75	77476.26
⊟ 1998	469771.34	19898.66
⊞ Q1	315242.12	109825.45
⊟ Q2	154529.22	19898.66
⊞ 4	134630.56	134630.56
⊟ 5	19898.66	19898.66
May 01, 98	5903.61	5903.61
May 04, 98	2831.65	8735.26
May 05, 98	7901.5	16636.76
May 06, 98	3261.9	19898.66
Grand Total	1354458.59	19898.66

Analysis

This is effectively a running total that is restarted every month. The quarterly totals are equal to those of the last month in the quarter. There is also a convenient alternative in TOTALMTD():

```
=TOTALMTD(SUM('Order Details'[Sales Amount]),(Orders[OrderDate]))
```

TOTALMTD() is covered later in the chapter.

DATESQTD()

DATESQTD() returns all the dates in the current quarter up to and including the current date.

The example is a measure on the Order Details table.

Syntax

```
=CALCULATE(SUM('Order Details'[Sales Amount]),
DATESQTD(Orders[OrderDate]))
```

Result

	A	B	C	D	E
1					
2	Year	Category			
3					
4	1996	Beverages	Condiments	Confections	
5	1997	Dairy Products	Grains/Cereals	Meat/Poultry	
6	1998	Produce	Seafood		
7					
8					
9					
10	Row Labels	Sum of Sales Amount	Measure 1		
11	⊞1996	226298.5	141861		
12	⊞1997	658388.75	193718.12		
13	⊟1998	469771.34	154529.22		
14	⊞Q1	315242.12	315242.12		
15	⊟Q2	154529.22	154529.22		
16	⊞4	134630.56	134630.56		
17	⊟5	19898.66	19898.66		
18	May 01, 98	5903.61	5903.61		
19	May 04, 98	2831.65	8735.26		
20	May 05, 98	7901.5	16636.76		
21	May 06, 98	3261.9	19898.66		
22	Grand Total	1354458.59	154529.22		

Sheet1 / Sheet2 / Sheet3

Analysis

This time, the quarterly totals are equal to the sum of all the months in the quarter. If you don't want the lower-level totals to reset, you could override the date filter context:

```
=CALCULATE(SUM('Order Details'[Sales Amount]),
DATESQTD(Orders[OrderDate]),ALL(Orders))
```

You could also use TOTALQTD() to achieve the same result—the syntax is a little more concise. TOTALQTD() is mentioned later in this chapter.

DATESYTD()

DATESYTD() returns all the dates in the current year up to and including the current date. There is also an optional second parameter for specifying the year-end date.

The examples are measures on the Order Details table.

Syntax

```
=CALCULATE(SUM('Order Details'[Sales Amount]),
DATESYTD(Orders[OrderDate]))

=CALCULATE(SUM('Order Details'[Sales Amount]),
DATESYTD(Orders[OrderDate]),ALL(Orders))
```

Result

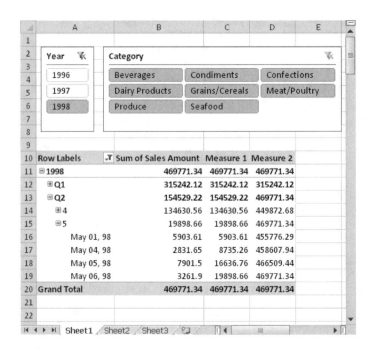

Analysis

Both examples give the same answer at the yearly level. The second example prevents the lower-level running totals from resetting. You can achieve the same result with TOTALYTD(), which is covered later in this chapter.

ENDOFMONTH()

ENDOFMONTH() returns the last date of the month.

The example is a measure on the Order Details table.

Syntax

```
=CALCULATE(SUM('Order Details'[Sales Amount]),
ENDOFMONTH((Orders[OrderDate]))))
```

Result

Row Labels	Sum of Sales Amount	Measure 1
⊞ 1996	226298.5	1765.6
⊞ 1997	658388.75	590.5
⊟ 1998	469771.34	3261.9
⊞ Q1	315242.12	7897.6
⊟ Q2	154529.22	3261.9
⊞ 4	134630.56	2729.5
⊟ 5	19898.66	3261.9
May 01, 98	5903.61	3261.9
May 04, 98	2831.65	3261.9
May 05, 98	7901.5	3261.9
May 06, 98	3261.9	3261.9
Grand Total	1354458.59	3261.9

Year: 1996, 1997, 1998

Category: Beverages, Condiments, Confections, Dairy Products, Grains/Cereals, Meat/Poultry, Produce, Seafood

Analysis

The value for the last day of a month becomes the month value. The value of the last day of the last month of a quarter becomes the quarter value. The value of the last day of the last month of the last quarter of a year becomes the year value.

ENDOFQUARTER()

ENDOFQUARTER() returns the last date of the quarter.

The example is a measure on the Order Details table.

Syntax

```
=CALCULATE(SUM('Order Details'[Sales Amount]),
ENDOFQUARTER(Orders[OrderDate]))
```

Result

▲	A	B	C	D	E
1					
2	Year ▼	Category			▼
3					
4	1996	Beverages	Condiments	Confections	
5	1997	Dairy Products	Grains/Cereals	Meat/Poultry	
6	1998	Produce	Seafood		
7					
8					
9					
10	Row Labels ▼	Sum of Sales Amount	Measure 1		
11	⊞1996	226298.5	1765.6		
12	⊞1997	658388.75	590.5		
13	⊟1998	469771.34	3261.9		
14	⊞Q1	315242.12	7897.6		
15	⊟Q2	154529.22	3261.9		
16	⊞4	134630.56			
17	⊟5	19898.66	3261.9		
18	May 01, 98	5903.61	3261.9		
19	May 04, 98	2831.65	3261.9		
20	May 05, 98	7901.5	3261.9		
21	May 06, 98	3261.9	3261.9		
22	Grand Total	1354458.59	3261.9		

Sheet1 Sheet2 Sheet3

Analysis

The result is similar to that of ENDOFMONTH() except that values for months that are not at the end of a quarter are missing.

ENDOFYEAR()

ENDOFYEAR() returns the last date of the year.

The example is a measure on the Order Details table.

Syntax

```
=CALCULATE(SUM('Order Details'[Sales Amount]),
ENDOFYEAR(Orders[OrderDate]))
```

Result

	A	B	C	D	E
1					
2	Year 🔽	Category			🔽
3					
4	1996	Beverages	Condiments	Confections	
5	1997	Dairy Products	Grains/Cereals	Meat/Poultry	
6	1998	Produce	Seafood		
7					
8					
9					
10	Row Labels 🔽	Sum of Sales Amount	Measure 1		
11	⊞1996	226298.5	1765.6		
12	⊞1997	658388.75	590.5		
13	⊟1998	469771.34	3261.9		
14	⊞Q1	315242.12			
15	⊟Q2	154529.22	3261.9		
16	⊞4	134630.56			
17	⊟5	19898.66	3261.9		
18	May 01, 98	5903.61	3261.9		
19	May 04, 98	2831.65	3261.9		
20	May 05, 98	7901.5	3261.9		
21	May 06, 98	3261.9	3261.9		
22	Grand Total	1354458.59	3261.9		

Sheet1 Sheet2 Sheet3

Analysis

Again, this is similar, but now some quarterly values are missing, except for the last quarter of each year.

FIRSTDATE()

FIRSTDATE() returns the first date in the current context.
The example is a measure on the Order Details table.

Syntax

```
=CALCULATE(SUM('Order Details'[Sales Amount]),
FIRSTDATE(Orders[OrderDate]))
```

Result

Row Labels	Sum of Sales Amount	Measure 1
⊞ 1996	226298.5	440
⊞ 1997	658388.75	6931.6
⊟ 1998	469771.34	1987
⊞ Q1	315242.12	1987
⊟ Q2	154529.22	14397.85
⊞ 4	134630.56	14397.85
⊟ 5	19898.66	5903.61
May 01, 98	5903.61	5903.61
May 04, 98	2831.65	2831.65
May 05, 98	7901.5	7901.5
May 06, 98	3261.9	3261.9
Grand Total	1354458.59	440

Year: 1996, 1997, 1998

Category: Beverages, Condiments, Confections, Dairy Products, Grains/Cereals, Meat/Poultry, Produce, Seafood

Analysis

The figure for May 1998 is the same as that for May 1, 1998. If the value for May 1 were blank, the value for May would also be blank. Similarly, the figure for 1998 will be the same as that for the first quarter in 1998, and so on.

FIRSTNONBLANK()

FIRSTNONBLANK() is similar to FIRSTDATE() except it finds the first value that is not blank. FIRSTNONBLANK() can be used on other columns, not just dates.

The example is a measure on the Order Details table.

Syntax

```
=CALCULATE(SUM('Order Details'[Sales Amount]),
FIRSTNONBLANK(Orders[OrderDate],SUM('Order Details'[Sales Amount])))
```

Result

	Sum of Sales Amount	Measure 1
Row Labels ▼		
⊞1996	226298.5	440
⊞1997	658388.75	6931.6
⊟1998	469771.34	1987
⊞Q1	315242.12	1987
⊟Q2	154529.22	14397.85
⊞4	134630.56	14397.85
⊟5	19898.66	5903.61
May 01, 98	5903.61	5903.61
May 04, 98	2831.65	2831.65
May 05, 98	7901.5	7901.5
May 06, 98	3261.9	3261.9
Grand Total	1354458.59	440

Slicers — Year: 1996, 1997, 1998. Category: Beverages, Condiments, Confections, Dairy Products, Grains/Cereals, Meat/Poultry, Produce, Seafood.

Analysis

The figure for May 1998 is the same as that for May 1, 1998. If the value for May 1 were blank, the value for May would be the first non-blank value found in May.

LASTDATE()

LASTDATE() returns the last date in the current context.

The examples are measures on the Order Details table.

Syntax

```
=CALCULATE(SUM('Order Details'[Sales Amount]),
LASTDATE(Orders[OrderDate]))

=CALCULATE(SUM('Order Details'[Sales Amount]),
LASTDATE(Orders[OrderDate])) - CALCULATE(SUM('Order Details'[Sales
Amount]),
FIRSTDATE(Orders[OrderDate]))

=CALCULATE(SUM('Order Details'[Sales Amount]),
DATESBETWEEN(Orders[OrderDate],BLANK(),LASTDATE(Orders[OrderDate])))

=CALCULATE(SUM('Order Details'[Sales Amount]),
DATESBETWEEN(Orders[OrderDate],BLANK(),LASTDATE(Orders[OrderDate])),
ALL(Products))
```

Result

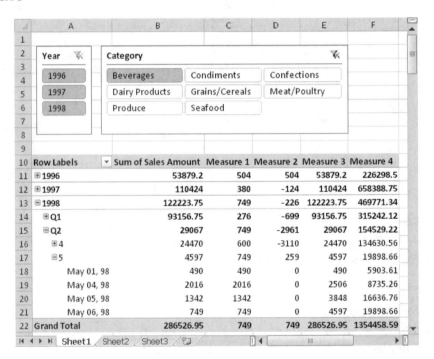

Analysis

LASTDATE(), FIRSTDATE(), and BLANK() are often used to establish date ranges. There are a few examples here. Try them one at a time to understand what the DAX is doing. The second example shows the increase (or decrease) from the first to the last day within the current context. In 1997, sales on the last day of the year for Beverages were 124 down on the first day. The last example ignores the Category slicer.

LASTNONBLANK()

LASTNONBLANK() is similar to LASTDATE(). However, if the value for the last date is blank, it will search backward in time until it finds the first non-blank value.

The example is a measure on the Order Details table.

Syntax

```
=CALCULATE(SUM('Order Details'[Sales Amount]),
LASTNONBLANK(Orders[OrderDate],SUM('Order Details'[Sales Amount])))
```

Result

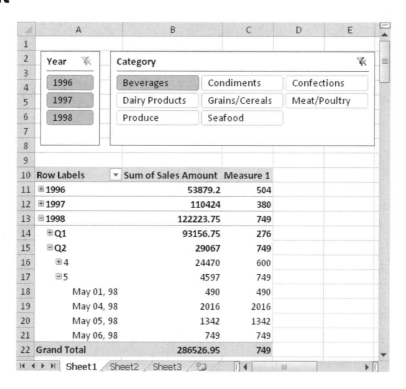

Analysis

The last non-blank value for 1998 is 749, when sliced by Beverages. The last non-blank values for Q2 and May are also 749. However, the last non-blank value for Q1 1998 is 276.

NEXTDAY()

NEXTDAY() retrieves the value from the next day when used with a calculation function. NEXTDAY(), itself, returns the date of the next day.

The example is a measure on the Order Details table.

Syntax

```
=CALCULATE(SUM('Order Details'[Sales Amount]),
NEXTDAY(Orders[OrderDate]))
```

Result

Analysis

There is no value for May 1, 1998, as May 2 does not exist or is a blank. NEXTDAY() does not cross higher-level boundaries.

NEXTMONTH()

NEXTMONTH() retrieves the value from the next month when used in conjunction with a calculation function.

The example is a measure on the FactSales table. The formula uses ContosoRetailDW. Before creating the measure, add SalesAmount from FactSales to the Values drop-zone. Also, place CalendarYear, CalendarQuarter, CalendarMonth, and Datekey on the Row Labels of the pivot table. When you create the measure, place it in the FactSales table.

Syntax

=CALCULATE(SUM('FactSales'[SalesAmount]),NEXTMONTH(DimDate[Datekey]))

Result

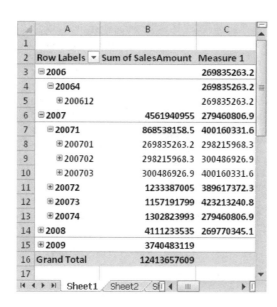

Analysis

The entry for 2009 is blank because the entry for 200912 is blank. The latter is blank as there is no 201001.

NEXTQUARTER()

NEXTQUARTER() retrieves the value from the next quarter if it's used with a calculation function.

The example is a measure on FactSales. The formula uses ContosoRetailDW.

Syntax

=CALCULATE(SUM('FactSales'[SalesAmount]),NEXTQUARTER(DimDate[Datekey]))

Result

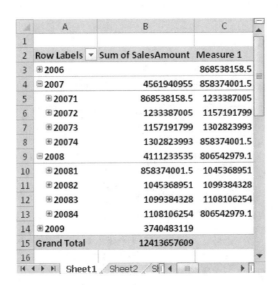

	A	B	C
1			
2	Row Labels ▼	Sum of SalesAmount	Measure 1
3	⊞ 2006		868538158.5
4	⊟ 2007	4561940955	858374001.5
5	⊞ 20071	868538158.5	1233387005
6	⊞ 20072	1233387005	1157191799
7	⊞ 20073	1157191799	1302823993
8	⊞ 20074	1302823993	858374001.5
9	⊟ 2008	4111233535	806542979.1
10	⊞ 20081	858374001.5	1045368951
11	⊞ 20082	1045368951	1099384328
12	⊞ 20083	1099384328	1108106254
13	⊞ 20084	1108106254	806542979.1
14	⊞ 2009	3740483119	
15	Grand Total	12413657609	
16			

Sheet1 Sheet2 Sh

Analysis

Once again, there is no entry for 2009.

NEXTYEAR()

NEXTYEAR() retrieves the value from the next year when used in conjunction with a calculation function.

The example is a measure on FactSales. The formula uses ContosoRetailDW.

Syntax

=CALCULATE(SUM('FactSales'[SalesAmount]),NEXTYEAR(DimDate[Datekey]))

Result

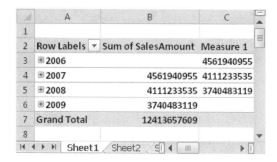

Analysis

And again, there is no total for 2009. Also, note that 2006 (when there are no sales) is shown as the measure does have a value—it's the total for 2007.

OPENINGBALANCEMONTH()

OPENINGBALANCEMONTH() retrieves the closing balance from the previous month. The balance is defined by the first, expression, parameter of the function. There is an optional third parameter for defining a filter.

The example is a measure on FactSales. The formula uses ContosoRetailDW.

Syntax

=OPENINGBALANCEMONTH(SUM(FactSales[SalesAmount]),DimDate[Datekey])

Result

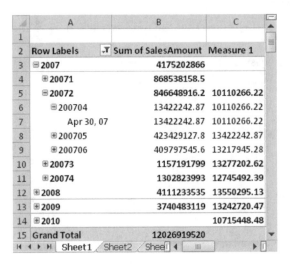

Analysis

The opening balance for 200705 is the same as the closing balance for 200704, which is the sales value for April 30, 2007.

OPENINGBALANCEQUARTER()

OPENINGBALANCEQUARTER() retrieves the closing balance from the previous quarter. Again, you can have a SetFilter argument as an optional third parameter.

The example is a measure on FactSales. The formula uses ContosoRetailDW.

Syntax

```
=OPENINGBALANCEQUARTER(SUM(FactSales[SalesAmount]),DimDate[Datekey])
```

Result

	A	B	C
1			
2	Row Labels	Sum of SalesAmount	Measure 1
3	⊟2007	4271564294	
4	⊟20071	578161497.8	
5	⊞200701	269835263.2	
6	⊞200702	298215968.3	
7	⊟200703	10110266.22	
8	Mar 31, 07	10110266.22	
9	⊞20072	1233387005	10110266.22
10	⊞20073	1157191799	13277202.62
11	⊞20074	1302823993	12745492.39
12	⊞2008	4111233535	13550295.13
13	⊞2009	3740483119	13242720.47
14	⊞2010		10715448.48
15	Grand Total	12123280948	
16			

Sheet1 / Sheet2 / Shee

Analysis

The value of 20072 is the same as the closing balance of 20071, which is the value for March 31, 2007.

OPENINGBALANCEYEAR()

OPENINGBALANCEYEAR() retrieves the closing balance from the previous year. You can also have an optional third parameter for defining a filter. A fourth parameter allows you to specify the year-end date—the default is December 31.

The example is a measure on FactSales. The formula uses ContosoRetailDW.

Syntax

```
=OPENINGBALANCEYEAR(SUM(FactSales[SalesAmount]),DimDate[Datekey])
```

Result

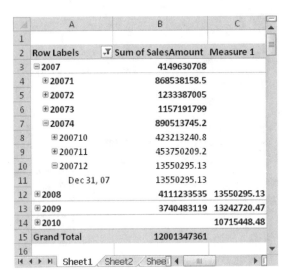

Analysis

The opening balance for 2008 is equal to the closing balance for 2007. That, in turn, is the value for December 31, 2007.

PARALLELPERIOD()

PARALLELPERIOD() jumps ahead or back in time.

The examples are measures on FactSales. The formulas use ContosoRetailDW.

Syntax

```
=CALCULATE(SUM('FactSales'[SalesAmount]),
PARALLELPERIOD(DimDate[Datekey],-1,MONTH))
```

```
=CALCULATE(SUM('FactSales'[SalesAmount]),
PARALLELPERIOD(DimDate[Datekey],1,QUARTER))
```

```
=CALCULATE(SUM('FactSales'[SalesAmount]),
PARALLELPERIOD(DimDate[Datekey],1,YEAR))
```

Result

	A	B	C	D	E
1					
2	Row Labels	Sum of SalesAmount	Measure 1	Measure 2	Measure 3
3	⊞2006			868538158.5	4561940955
4	⊟2007	4149630708	4136080412	4551776798	4111233535
5	⊞20071	868538158.5	568051231.6	1233387005	4111233535
6	⊞20072	1233387005	1124076386	1157191799	4111233535
7	⊞20073	1157191799	1187844745	1302823993	4111233535
8	⊟20074	890513745.2	1256108050	858374001.5	4111233535
9	⊞200710	423213240.8	379144599.6	858374001.5	4111233535
10	⊞200711	453750209.2	423213240.8	858374001.5	4111233535
11	⊞200712	13550295.13	453750209.2	858374001.5	4111233535
12	⊞2008	4111233535	4138307904	4059402512	3740483119
13	⊞2009	3740483119	3808534879	2933940140	
14	⊞2010		330734413.5		
15	Grand Total	12001347361	12413657609	12413657609	12413657609
16					

Sheet1 / Sheet2 / Sheet3

Analysis

If the second parameter is negative, PARALLELPERIOD() goes back in time. The third parameter can be YEAR, QUARTER, or MONTH (please note these are enumerated constants and not strings), but not DAY. PARALLELPERIOD() is similar to DATEADD(). However, the former always returns full periods and not partial periods. You can demonstrate the difference by comparing the quarterly results for 2010 from the following two examples:

```
=CALCULATE(SUM('FactSales'[SalesAmount]),
PARALLELPERIOD(DimDate[Datekey],-1,YEAR))
```

```
=CALCULATE(SUM('FactSales'[SalesAmount]),
DATEADD(DimDate[Datekey],-1,YEAR))
```

PREVIOUSDAY()

PREVIOUSDAY() gives the value from the previous day when combined with a calculation function.

The example is a measure on the Order Details table.

Syntax

```
=CALCULATE(SUM('Order Details'[Sales Amount]),
PREVIOUSDAY(Orders[OrderDate]))
```

Result

	A	B	C	D	E
1					
2	Year	Category			
3					
4	1996	Beverages	Condiments	Confections	
5	1997	Dairy Products	Grains/Cereals	Meat/Poultry	
6	1998	Produce	Seafood		
7					
8					
9					
10	Row Labels	Sum of Sales Amount	Measure 1		
11	⊞1996	226298.5			
12	⊞1997	658388.75			
13	⊟1998	469771.34			
14	⊞Q1	315242.12			
15	⊟Q2	154529.22			
16	⊞4	134630.56			
17	⊟5	19898.66			
18	May 01, 98	5903.61			
19	May 04, 98	2831.65			
20	May 05, 98	7901.5	2831.65		
21	May 06, 98	3261.9	7901.5		
22	Grand Total	1354458.59			

Sheet1 / Sheet2 / Sheet3

Analysis

PREVIOUSDAY(), by itself, simply returns a date.

PREVIOUSMONTH()

PREVIOUSMONTH() gives the value from the previous month if used with a calculation function.

The example is a measure on FactSales. The formula uses ContosoRetailDW.

Syntax

```
=CALCULATE(SUM(FactSales[SalesAmount]),PREVIOUSMONTH(DimDate[Datekey]))
```

Result

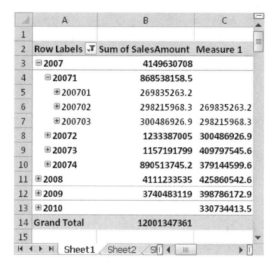

Analysis

The figure for 200702 is the sales amount for 200701.

PREVIOUSQUARTER()

PREVIOUSQUARTER() gives the value from the previous quarter when you use it with a calculation function.

The example is a measure on FactSales. The formula uses ContosoRetailDW.

Syntax

```
=CALCULATE(SUM(FactSales[SalesAmount]),
PREVIOUSQUARTER(DimDate[Datekey]))
```

Result

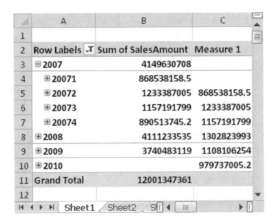

Analysis

The result for 20072 is the sales value for 20071.

PREVIOUSYEAR()

PREVIOUSYEAR() gives the value from the previous year if combined with a calculation function. There is an optional second parameter for the year-end date—the default is December 31.

The example is a measure on FactSales. The formula uses ContosoRetailDW.

Syntax

```
=CALCULATE(SUM(FactSales[SalesAmount]),PREVIOUSYEAR(DimDate[Datekey]))
```

Result

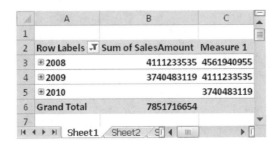

Analysis

The answer for 2009 is the same as the sales for 2008.

SAMEPERIODLASTYEAR()

SAMEPERIODLASTYEAR() jumps back one year. However, it does so at every date level. The examples are measures on FactSales. The formulas use ContosoRetailDW.

Syntax

```
=CALCULATE(SUM(FactSales[SalesAmount]),
SAMEPERIODLASTYEAR(DimDate[Datekey]))

=CALCULATE(SUM(FactSales[SalesAmount])) -
CALCULATE(SUM(FactSales[SalesAmount]),
SAMEPERIODLASTYEAR(DimDate[Datekey]))
```

Result

	A	B	C	D
1	Row Labels	Sum of SalesAmount	Measure 1	Measure 2
2	⊟2007	4561940955		4561940955
3	⊟20071	868538158.5		868538158.5
4	⊞200701	269835263.2		269835263.2
5	⊞200702	298215968.3		298215968.3
6	⊞200703	300486926.9		300486926.9
7	⊞20072	1233387005		1233387005
8	⊞20073	1157191799		1157191799
9	⊞20074	1302823993		1302823993
10	⊟2008	4111233535	4561940955	-450707420.3
11	⊟20081	858374001.5	868538158.5	-10164156.96
12	⊞200801	279460806.9	269835263.2	9625543.643
13	⊞200802	288852634	298215968.3	-9363334.325
14	⊞200803	290060560.6	300486926.9	-10426366.28
15	⊞20082	1045368951	1233387005	-188018054.2
16	⊞20083	1099384328	1157191799	-57807470.89
17	⊞20084	1108106254	1302823993	-194717738.3
18	⊞2009	3740483119	4111233535	-370750415.5
19	⊞2010		3740483119	-3740483119
20	Grand Total	12413657609	12413657609	0
21				

Sheet1 Sheet2 Sheet3

Analysis

The first formula retrieves the sales for one year ago, but it does so at the day, month, quarter, and year levels. This makes SAMEPERIODLASTYEAR() an extremely powerful function. The second formula works out the year-on-year change for *any* date. You can achieve the same results using DATEADD().

STARTOFMONTH()

STARTOFMONTH() is the converse of ENDOFMONTH(). It returns the first day of the month.

The example is a measure on the Order Details table.

Syntax

```
=CALCULATE(SUM('Order Details'[Sales Amount]),
STARTOFMONTH((Orders[OrderDate]))))
```

Result

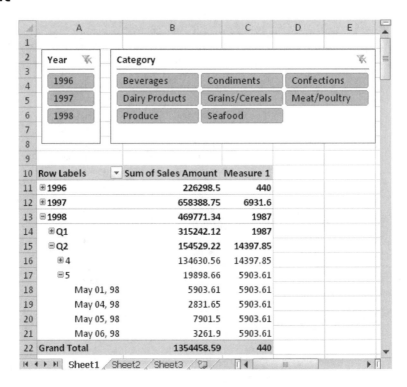

Analysis

The value for May 1998 is the same as that of May 1, 1998. The value for Q2 1998 is the same as that of April 1998, not May 1998.

STARTOFQUARTER()

STARTOFQUARTER() returns the first day of the quarter.

The example is a measure on FactSales. The formula uses ContosoRetailDW.

Syntax

=CALCULATE(SUM(FactSales[SalesAmount]),STARTOFQUARTER(DimDate[Datekey]))

Result

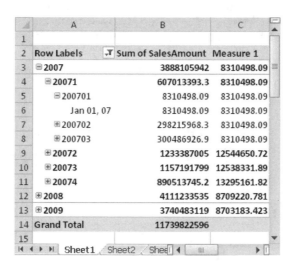

	A	B	C
1			
2	Row Labels	Sum of SalesAmount	Measure 1
3	⊟ 2007	3888105942	8310498.09
4	⊟ 20071	607013393.3	8310498.09
5	⊟ 200701	8310498.09	8310498.09
6	Jan 01, 07	8310498.09	8310498.09
7	⊞ 200702	298215968.3	8310498.09
8	⊞ 200703	300486926.9	8310498.09
9	⊞ 20072	1233387005	12544650.72
10	⊞ 20073	1157191799	12538331.89
11	⊞ 20074	890513745.2	13295161.82
12	⊞ 2008	4111233535	8709220.781
13	⊞ 2009	3740483119	8703183.423
14	Grand Total	11739822596	
15			

Sheet1 Sheet2 Shee

Analysis

The result for 20071 is the same as the sales for January 1, 2007.

STARTOFYEAR()

STARTOFYEAR() returns the first day of the year. An optional second parameter lets you specify a year-end date.

The example is a measure on FactSales. The formula uses ContosoRetailDW.

Syntax

=CALCULATE(SUM(FactSales[SalesAmount]),STARTOFYEAR(DimDate[Datekey]))

Result

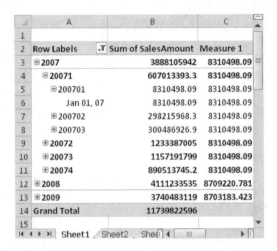

Analysis

The figures within each year reflect the sales for January 1. It might be fruitful to compare the values for quarters (apart from first quarters) with the results from the last formula.

TOTALMTD()

TOTALMTD() evaluates an expression over all the days of the month, up to and including the current context day. The second parameter is the date column. You can define a filter as an optional third parameter.

The example is a measure on the Order Details table.

Syntax

=TOTALMTD(SUM('Order Details'[Sales Amount]),Orders[OrderDate])

Result

	A	B	C	D	E
1					
2	Year	Category			
3					
4	1996	Beverages	Condiments	Confections	
5	1997	Dairy Products	Grains/Cereals	Meat/Poultry	
6	1998	Produce	Seafood		
7					
8					
9					
10	Row Labels	Sum of Sales Amount	Measure 1		
11	⊞ 1996	226298.5	50953.4		
12	⊞ 1997	658388.75	77476.26		
13	⊟ 1998	469771.34	19898.66		
14	⊞ Q1	315242.12	109825.45		
15	⊟ Q2	154529.22	19898.66		
16	⊞ 4	134630.56	134630.56		
17	⊟ 5	19898.66	19898.66		
18	May 01, 98	5903.61	5903.61		
19	May 04, 98	2831.65	8735.26		
20	May 05, 98	7901.5	16636.76		
21	May 06, 98	3261.9	19898.66		
22	Grand Total	1354458.59	19898.66		

Sheet1 Sheet2 Sheet3

Analysis

The totals for the year, the last quarter, and the last month are equal to the total for the last day of the last month in the last quarter. The result is the same as the result of this formula:

```
=CALCULATE(SUM('Order Details'[Sales Amount]),
DATESMTD(Orders[OrderDate]))
```

TOTALQTD()

TOTALQTD() returns all the days of the quarter, up to and including the current context day when used with a calculation function. The first example has a third filter parameter.

The examples are measures on the Order Details table.

Syntax

```
=TOTALQTD(SUM('Order Details'[Sales Amount]),Orders[OrderDate],ALL(Orders))
```

```
=TOTALQTD(SUM('Order Details'[Sales Amount]),Orders[OrderDate])
```

Result

	A	B	C	D	E	F
1						
2	Year	Category				
3						
4	1996	Beverages	Condiments	Confections		
5	1997	Dairy Products	Grains/Cereals	Meat/Poultry		
6	1998	Produce	Seafood			
7						
8						
9						
10	Row Labels ▾	Sum of Sales Amount	Measure 1	Measure 2		
11	⊞ 1996	226298.5	141861	141861		
12	⊞ 1997	658388.75	193718.12	193718.12		
13	⊟ 1998	469771.34	154529.22	154529.22		
14	⊞ Q1	315242.12	315242.12	315242.12		
15	⊟ Q2	154529.22	154529.22	154529.22		
16	⊞ 4	134630.56	134630.56	134630.56		
17	⊞ 5	19898.66	154529.22	19898.66		
18	Grand Total	1354458.59	154529.22	154529.22		
19						
20						
21						
22						

Sheet1 / Sheet2 / Sheet3

Analysis

The two examples are subtly different. Take a look at the contrasting sales figures for May 1998. The first formula does not reset the aggregation as it crosses monthly boundaries, but the second one does. The first formula overrides the date filter context as the OrderDate column is in the Orders table.

TOTALYTD()

TOTALYTD() returns all the days of the year, up to and including the current context day when used with a calculation function. The example uses an optional filter argument as the third parameter. A fourth parameter allows you to specify a year-end date.

The example is a measure on the Order Details table.

Syntax

```
=TOTALYTD(SUM('Order Details'[Sales Amount]),
Orders[OrderDate],ALL(Orders))
```

Result

Row Labels	Sum of Sales Amount	Measure 1
⊞1996	226298.5	226298.5
⊞1997	658388.75	658388.75
⊟1998	469771.34	469771.34
⊞Q1	315242.12	315242.12
⊟Q2	154529.22	469771.34
⊞4	134630.56	449872.68
⊞5	19898.66	469771.34
Grand Total	1354458.59	469771.34

Year: 1996, 1997, 1998

Category: Beverages, Condiments, Confections, Dairy Products, Grains/Cereals, Meat/Poultry, Produce, Seafood

Analysis

The total for Q2 1998 is that of Q1 and Q2. The total for 1998 is the same as the total for Q2. The Grand Total is the same as that for 1998.

Well done! You have completed a long chapter! This is the last of the 35 time intelligence functions.

Chapter 10

Text Functions

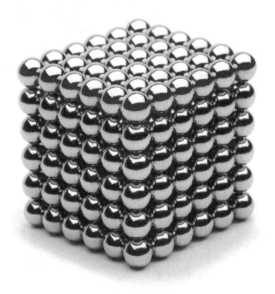

This chapter deals with text (or string) manipulation. Most of the text functions are the same as their Excel function equivalents; however, they accept text or column parameters rather than worksheet cells or ranges. Many of these text functions return text, and as such are usually more suitable for creating calculated columns in PowerPivot tables rather than measures—text values can't be added together to give subtotals and totals in a pivot table (unless you do a COUNT()). Having said that, if the text value can be converted into a number (for example the string "123"), then it may be used as an additive measure. Usually, PowerPivot will implicitly do the conversion, but you can always do it explicitly with the VALUE() function. Please note that the FORMAT() text function also operates against numbers as well as against text.

- ▶ **Key concepts**   Comparing and finding strings, concatenating and parsing strings, changing and formatting strings

- ▶ **Keywords**   CONCATENATE(), EXACT(), FIND(), FIXED(), FORMAT(), LEFT(), LEN(), LOWER(), MID(), REPLACE(), REPT(), RIGHT(), SEARCH(), SUBSTITUTE(), TRIM(), UPPER(), VALUE()

CONCATENATE() 1/2

Often, your source data is heavily normalized and names and addresses are parsed into separate columns. This does not always make for easy viewing in a pivot table. Maybe you want to put columns back together again. You can use the CONCATENATE() function to reassemble text columns (it also works against numeric columns or a mix of text and numeric). Slicing or filtering is probably easier if you have the full name of each employee, rather than only the surname (you might have two or more employees sharing a surname). The examples are calculated columns on the Northwind Employees table.

Syntax

```
=CONCATENATE('Employees'[LastName],'Employees'[FirstName])
=CONCATENATE('Employees'[LastName],", ",'Employees'[FirstName])
=CONCATENATE('Employees'[LastName],
CONCATENATE(", ",'Employees'[FirstName]))
='Employees'[LastName] & ", " & 'Employees'[FirstName]
```

Result

LastName	City	Region	PostalCode	Country	HomePhone	Extension	Notes	ReportsTo	CalculatedColumn1
Davolio	Seattle	WA	98122	USA	(206) 555-9857	5467	Educatio...	2	Davolio, Nancy
Fuller	Tacoma	WA	98401	USA	(206) 555-9482	3457	Andrew ...		Fuller, Andrew
Leverling	Kirkland	WA	98033	USA	(206) 555-3412	3355	Janet ha...	2	Leverling, Janet
Peacock	Redm...	WA	98052	USA	(206) 555-8122	5176	Margare...	2	Peacock, Margaret
Buchanan	London		SW1 8JR	UK	(71) 555-4848	3453	Steven ...	2	Buchanan, Steven
Suyama	London		EC2 7JR	UK	(71) 555-7773	428	Michael ...	5	Suyama, Michael
King	London		RG1 9SP	UK	(71) 555-5598	465	Robert K...	5	King, Robert
Callahan	Seattle	WA	98105	USA	(206) 555-1189	2344	Laura re...	2	Callahan, Laura
Dodsworth	London		WG2 7LT	UK	(71) 555-4444	452	Anne ha...	5	Dodsworth, Anne

Analysis

The first example works, although the third example is easier to read with a comma and a space between the LastName and the FirstName. If you try them all, you'll find that the second example fails—CONCATENATE() accepts a maximum of two parameters. If you wish to join three strings, you'll have to use nested CONCATENATE() functions; the third formula shows how. Alternatively, you can use the ampersand (&) operator instead, as in the fourth formula. This method is not limited to two parameters, and is often preferred over CONCATENATE(). The result shown is that from the third or fourth formulas.

CONCATENATE() 2/2

The DAX text functions are often quite simple. Frequently, they are employed in conjunction with other functions to produce useful output. The formula here allows you to slice and filter your data in a pivot table on both customer country and region at the same time (or just country if there is no region). The examples are Northwind Customers table calculated columns.

Syntax

```
=CONCATENATE(CONCATENATE('Customers'[Country]," - "),
'Customers'[Region])
=IF(ISBLANK('Customers'[Region]),'Customers'[Country],
CONCATENATE(CONCATENATE('Customers'[Country]," - "),
'Customers'[Region]))
```

Result

CompanyName	ContactName	ContactTitle	Address	City	Region	PostalCode	Country	Phone	Fax	CalculatedColumn1
Alfred Futterkiste	Maria Anders	Sales Represe...	Obere Str. 57	Berlin		12209	Germany	030-0074...	030-0...	Germany
Ana Trujillo Empa...	Ana Trujillo	Owner	Avda. de l...	Mèxic...		05021	Mexico	(5) 555-4...	(5) 55...	Mexico
Antonio Moreno ...	Antonio Moreno	Owner	Mataderos...	Mèxic...		05023	Mexico	(5) 555-3...		Mexico
Around the Horn	Thomas Hardy	Sales Represe...	120 Hanov...	London		WA1 1DP	UK	(171) 555...	(171) ...	UK
Berglunds snabbk...	Christina Berglu...	Order Adminis...	Berguvsvä...	Luleå		S-958 22	Sweden	0921-12...	0921-...	Sweden
Blauer See Delika...	Hanna Moos	Sales Represe...	Forsterstr. ...	Mann...		68306	Germany	0621-08460	0621-...	Germany
Blondesddsl père ...	Frédérique Cite...	Marketing Ma...	24, place K...	Strasb...		67000	France	88.60.15.31	88.60...	France
Bólido Comidas p...	Martín Sommer	Owner	C/ Araquil,...	Madrid		28023	Spain	(91) 555 ...	(91) 5...	Spain
Bon app'	Laurence Lebihan	Owner	12, rue de...	Marse...		13008	France	91.24.45.40	91.24...	France
Bottom-Dollar Ma...	Elizabeth Lincoln	Accounting Ma...	23 Tsawass...	Tsawa...	BC	T2F 8M4	Canada	(604) 555...	(604) ...	Canada - BC
B's Beverages	Victoria Ashworth	Sales Represe...	Fauntlero...	London		EC2 5NT	UK	(171) 555...		UK

Analysis

The first formula works—only if there's no region, it looks a little strange (for example, UK-). Unlike SQL Server (unless the CONCAT_NULL_YIELDS_NULL database option is set to OFF), PowerPivot treats nulls as blanks, so adding a null region to a country does not return null. The second formula produces a more pleasing result and is the one shown in the preceding illustration. If the region is blank (probably because it's originally a null value in the source data), then the hyphen (-) is not appended to the country. The second example has a nested CONCATENATE(). The position of the nested CONCATENATE() is different from that in the previous set of examples, where it appears immediately after the outer CONCATENATE(). Both varieties work.

The second example here is a lengthy formula. As such, part of it may scroll out of view as you edit. There are two tricks that are quite handy in these situations. One, you can increase the height of the formula bar (for calculated columns) or the Formula text box (for measures) by dragging. Two, you can force your formula to word-wrap by pressing ALT-ENTER.

EXACT()

EXACT() compares two text values and returns either TRUE or FALSE. The first formula is an example. The second example shows an alternative approach (using an equality test) that produces the same result. More useful is the third formula, or its equivalent in the fourth formula. The examples are calculated columns in the Northwind Orders table.

Syntax

```
=EXACT('Orders'[CustomerID],"QUICK")
=IF('Orders'[CustomerID] = "QUICK", TRUE(), FALSE())
=IF(EXACT('Orders'[CustomerID],"QUICK"), "QUICK-Stop", "Others")
=IF('Orders'[CustomerID] = "QUICK", "QUICK-Stop", "Others")
```

Result

Ord...	ShipAddress	ShipCity	ShipRegion	ShipPostalCode	ShipCountry	Year	CalculatedColumn1
10249	Luisenstr. 48	Münster		44087	Germany	1996	Others
10260	Mehrheimerst...	Köln		50739	Germany	1996	Others
10267	Berliner Platz 43	München		80805	Germany	1996	Others
10273	Taucherstraße 10	Cunewalde		01307	Germany	1996	QUICK-Stop
10277	Heerstr. 22	Leipzig		04179	Germany	1996	Others
10279	Magazinweg 7	Frankfurt a...		60528	Germany	1996	Others
10284	Magazinweg 7	Frankfurt a...		60528	Germany	1996	Others
10285	Taucherstraße 10	Cunewalde		01307	Germany	1996	QUICK-Stop
10286	Taucherstraße 10	Cunewalde		01307	Germany	1996	QUICK-Stop
10301	Adenauerallee...	Stuttgart		70563	Germany	1996	Others
10312	Adenauerallee...	Stuttgart		70563	Germany	1996	Others

Analysis

The result is from the third formula. This enables you to slice to see values or measures associated with the customer "QUICK-Stop" and to compare with those from all other customers. A total of 830 orders from a maximum of 91 customers have been summarized into 830 orders from a maximum of two customers/customer groups. Instead of 91 choices in a slicer, you have only 2. EXACT() is case-sensitive as in the third example. The fourth example is not case-sensitive.

FIND()

FIND() and its related function, SEARCH(), are used to see if one text value occurs within another text value. The difference between the two functions is due to case sensitivity. The examples are calculated columns on any table.

Syntax

```
=FIND("e","bottles",1)
=FIND("E","bottles",1)
```

Result

Ord...	ShipAddress	ShipCity	ShipRegion	ShipPostalCode	ShipCountry	Year	CalculatedColumn1
10249	Luisenstr. 48	Münster		44087	Germany	1996	6
10260	Mehrheimerst...	Köln		50739	Germany	1996	6
10267	Berliner Platz 43	München		80805	Germany	1996	6
10273	Taucherstraße 10	Cunewalde		01307	Germany	1996	6
10277	Heerstr. 22	Leipzig		04179	Germany	1996	6
10279	Magazinweg 7	Frankfurt a...		60528	Germany	1996	6
10284	Magazinweg 7	Frankfurt a...		60528	Germany	1996	6
10285	Taucherstraße 10	Cunewalde		01307	Germany	1996	6
10286	Taucherstraße 10	Cunewalde		01307	Germany	1996	6
10301	Adenauerallee...	Stuttgart		70563	Germany	1996	6
10312	Adenauerallee...	Stuttgart		70563	Germany	1996	6

Analysis

FIND(), unlike SEARCH(), is case-sensitive. Unfortunately, it only accepts literal text values for its two parameters and can't work directly against table columns. The number returned is the start position of the text in the first parameter. The final parameter is the start position for the search. The result is from the first example. The second example returns an error, as the string is not found.

FIXED()

This time, we have a text function used in a measure rather than in a calculated column. FIXED() is handy for formatting numbers with a specified number of decimal places and with or without a thousands separator. The example is a calculated measure in a pivot table, although FIXED() can also be used in a calculated column.

Syntax

```
=FIXED(SUM('Order Details'[Sales Amount]),2,0)
```

Result

Row Labels	Beverages	Condiments	Confections	Dairy Products	Grains/Cereals	Meat/Poultry	Produce	Seafood	Grand Total
Argentina	1,798.00	907.00	2,135.10	1,143.50	390.00	0.00	1,139.00	606.50	8,119.10
Austria	26,452.05	16,802.40	14,653.35	30,342.90	14,854.25	12,001.48	13,755.95	10,634.25	139,496.63
Belgium	5,864.40	2,714.70	7,711.18	8,825.00	3,226.00	2,258.50	3,223.20	1,312.00	35,134.98
Brazil	40,400.50	12,139.00	12,164.73	16,894.50	6,638.00	8,008.12	5,385.15	13,338.48	114,968.48
Canada	13,829.70	5,010.60	9,302.40	10,102.00	5,765.10	4,266.00	2,112.00	4,946.30	55,334.10
Denmark	12,025.70	4,455.40	2,815.30	2,753.20	105.00	3,700.70	4,626.00	4,300.95	34,782.25
Finland	2,222.00	1,873.00	1,033.05	6,027.80	2,800.00	3,345.25	1,161.05	1,316.30	19,778.45
France	13,670.00	7,148.40	13,215.85	9,318.90	6,493.45	11,142.96	8,769.80	15,739.40	85,498.76
Germany	57,644.60	17,395.10	37,799.44	53,170.90	14,603.15	22,607.44	17,265.90	24,154.10	244,640.63
Ireland	3,339.40	3,898.50	1,739.20	11,093.40	1,442.40	24,040.90	3,821.70	7,941.89	57,317.39
Italy	1,155.00	1,448.25	2,787.70	4,376.80	1,794.00	1,167.00	2,216.80	1,759.60	16,705.15
Mexico	8,097.50	1,235.45	2,066.95	4,912.40	559.50	2,828.90	2,517.75	1,855.00	24,073.45
Norway	2,756.00	234.00	280.15	786.00	0.00	164.00	578.40	936.60	5,735.15
Poland	828.50	627.00	779.10	810.00	0.00	22.35	306.00	159.00	3,531.95
Portugal	1,190.40	3,869.45	1,122.50	1,008.00	2,415.20	1,355.90	763.20	744.00	12,468.65
Spain	1,363.20	1,789.45	1,809.05	646.00	1,843.00	7,919.10	2,120.00	1,942.09	19,431.89
Sweden	13,407.05	4,970.30	5,675.65	6,585.20	3,250.00	9,625.95	9,116.00	6,893.55	59,523.70
Switzerland	2,357.50	2,054.30	3,246.16	7,747.30	4,931.00	7,155.64	2,236.00	3,191.60	32,919.50
UK	7,596.20	4,576.05	9,223.26	14,553.70	5,195.20	6,445.15	8,142.80	4,884.15	60,616.51
USA	63,361.15	18,555.85	38,804.05	41,549.30	20,411.30	45,394.06	10,465.90	25,025.37	263,566.98
Venezuela	7,168.10	1,990.55	8,734.93	18,683.70	4,010.25	4,739.40	5,546.00	9,941.96	60,814.89
Grand Total	286,526.95	113,694.75	177,099.10	251,330.50	100,726.80	178,188.80	105,268.60	141,623.09	1,354,458.59

Analysis

The second parameter to the formula is the number of decimal places. The third parameter is for stipulating thousands separators (either 0 or 1). Counterintuitively, a value of 1 will suppress thousands separators. Although FIXED() is a text function, it accepts a number as the first parameter. It's a text function, as it returns a text value. However, it can still serve as an additive measure in the value section of a pivot table because PowerPivot will automatically convert it back into a number (unless it's passed as a parameter to a function expecting a numeric parameter), but keeping the formatting you specify. Unlike with a pure number, PowerPivot will left-align the result—you'll have to manually right-align it (right-click, Format Cells | Alignment | Text Alignment | Horizontal | Right (Indent)). You can achieve the same format result with the FORMAT() function, which is far more versatile. FORMAT() is covered next.

FORMAT()

There are five examples of the FORMAT() function here. Unlike FIXED(), it can format date/time values as well as numeric values. Here the FORMAT() function is part of a measure rather than a calculated column. The examples are calculated measures in a pivot table.

Syntax

```
=FORMAT('Order Details'[Sum of Sales Amount],"Currency")
=FORMAT(SUM('Order Details'[Sales Amount]),"Currency")
=FORMAT(SUM('Order Details'[Sales Amount]),"$#,###.00")
=FORMAT(SUM('Order Details'[Sales Amount]),"£#,###.00")
=FORMAT(SUM('Order Details'[Sales Amount]),"#,###.00 ")
```

Result

Year: 1996, 1997, 1998

Category: Beverages, Condiments, Confections, Dairy Products, Grains/Cereals, Meat/Poultry, Produce, Seafood

Measure 1

Row Labels	Beverages	Condiments	Confections	Dairy Products	Grains/Cereals	Meat/Poultry	Produce	Seafood	Grand Total
Argentina	1,798.00€	907.00€	2,135.10€	1,143.50€	390.00€		1,139.00€	606.50€	8,119.10€
Austria	26,452.05€	16,802.40€	14,653.35€	30,342.90€	14,854.25€	12,001.48€	13,755.95€	10,634.25€	139,496.63€
Belgium	5,864.40€	2,714.70€	7,711.18€	8,825.00€	3,226.00€	2,258.50€	3,223.20€	1,312.00€	35,134.98€
Brazil	40,400.50€	12,139.00€	12,164.73€	16,894.50€	6,638.00€	8,008.12€	5,385.15€	13,338.48€	114,968.48€
Canada	13,829.70€	5,010.60€	9,302.40€	10,102.00€	5,765.10€	4,266.00€	2,112.00€	4,946.30€	55,334.10€
Denmark	12,025.70€	4,455.40€	2,815.30€	2,753.20€	105.00€	3,700.70€	4,626.00€	4,300.95€	34,782.25€
Finland	2,222.00€	1,873.00€	1,033.05€	6,027.80€	2,800.00€	3,345.25€	1,161.05€	1,316.30€	19,778.45€
France	13,670.00€	7,148.40€	13,215.85€	9,318.90€	6,493.45€	11,142.96€	8,769.80€	15,739.40€	85,498.76€
Germany	57,644.60€	17,395.10€	37,799.44€	53,170.90€	14,603.15€	22,607.44€	17,265.90€	24,154.10€	244,640.63€
Ireland	3,339.40€	3,898.50€	1,739.20€	11,093.40€	1,442.40€	24,040.90€	3,821.70€	7,941.89€	57,317.39€
Italy	1,155.00€	1,448.25€	2,787.70€	4,376.80€	1,794.00€	1,167.00€	2,216.80€	1,759.60€	16,705.15€
Mexico	8,097.50€	1,235.45€	2,066.95€	4,912.40€	559.50€	2,828.90€	2,517.75€	1,855.00€	24,073.45€
Norway	2,756.00€	234.00€	280.15€	786.00€		164.00€	578.40€	936.60€	5,735.15€
Poland	828.50€	627.00€	779.10€	810.00€		22.35€	306.00€	159.00€	3,531.95€
Portugal	1,190.40€	3,869.45€	1,122.50€	1,008.00€	2,415.20€	1,355.90€	763.20€	744.00€	12,468.65€
Spain	1,363.20€	1,789.45€	1,809.05€	646.00€	1,843.00€	7,919.10€	2,120.00€	1,942.09€	19,431.89€
Sweden	13,407.05€	4,970.30€	5,675.65€	6,585.20€	3,250.00€	9,625.95€	9,116.00€	6,893.55€	59,523.70€
Switzerland	2,357.50€	2,054.30€	3,246.16€	7,747.30€	4,931.00€	7,155.64€	2,236.00€	3,191.60€	32,919.50€
UK	7,596.20€	4,576.05€	9,223.26€	14,553.70€	5,195.20€	6,445.15€	8,142.80€	4,884.15€	60,616.51€
USA	63,361.15€	18,555.85€	38,804.05€	41,549.30€	20,411.30€	45,394.06€	10,465.90€	25,025.37€	263,566.98€
Venezuela	7,168.10€	1,990.55€	8,734.93€	18,683.70€	4,010.25€	4,739.40€	5,546.00€	9,941.96€	60,814.89€
Grand Total	286,526.95€	113,694.75€	177,099.10€	251,330.50€	100,726.80€	178,188.80€	105,268.60€	141,623.09€	1,354,458.59€

Sheet1 Sheet2 Sheet3

Analysis

The result is from the last example. The first two formulas set the currency symbol implicitly; Currency is a predefined format, based on your Windows regional settings. The currency symbol is explicitly nominated in the third, fourth, and fifth examples. These last three are custom formats—a custom format gives you a lot of control and you are referred to your DAX help for a full list of all the possibilities for formatting numbers and dates.

The second parameter is the format string. In our case, there is only one entry in the format string. It will apply to positive and negative numbers and zero. If you have two entries in the format string (separated by semicolons [;]), the first applies to positive and zero values and the second to negative values. With three entries, the first is for positive numbers, the second for negative, and the third for zeros.

LEFT()

LEFT() is pretty straightforward and probably self-explanatory if you have used Excel, Visual Basic for Applications (VBA), or SQL before. Unlike the Excel version, it can operate against columns (as shown here) as well as against literal text or numeric values—as a reminder, the DAX functions don't operate on worksheet cells. The example is a calculated column in the Customers table.

Syntax

```
=LEFT('Customers'[Country],3) & "-" & 'Customers'[CustomerID]
```

Result

CompanyName	ContactTitle	Address	City	Region	PostalCode	Country	Phone	Fax	CalculatedColumn1
Alfred Futterkiste	Sales Represe...	Obere Str. 57	Berlin		12209	Germany	030-0074...	030-0...	Ger-ALFKI
Ana Trujillo Empa...	Owner	Avda. de l...	Méxic...		05021	Mexico	(5) 555-4...	(5) 55...	Mex-ANATR
Antonio Moreno ...	Owner	Mataderos...	Méxic...		05023	Mexico	(5) 555-3...		Mex-ANTON
Around the Horn	Sales Represe...	120 Hanov...	London		WA1 1DP	UK	(171) 555...	(171)...	UK-AROUT
Berglunds snabbk...	Order Adminis...	Berguvsvä...	Luleå		S-958 22	Sweden	0921-12...	0921-...	Swe-BERGS
Blauer See Delika...	Sales Represe...	Forsterstr. ...	Mann...		68306	Germany	0621-08460	0621-...	Ger-BLAUS
Blondesddsl père ...	Marketing Ma...	24, place K...	Strasb...		67000	France	88.60.15.31	88.60....	Fra-BLONP
Bólido Comidas p...	Owner	C/ Araquil,...	Madrid		28023	Spain	(91) 555...	(91) 5...	Spa-BOLID
Bon app'	Owner	12, rue de...	Marse...		13008	France	91.24.45.40	91.24...	Fra-BONAP
Bottom-Dollar Ma...	Accounting Ma...	23 Tsawass...	Tsawa...	BC	T2F 8M4	Canada	(604) 555...	(604)...	Can-BOTTM
B's Beverages	Sales Represe...	Fauntlero...	London		EC2 5NT	UK	(171) 555...		UK-BSBEV

Analysis

The formula is creating a new identifier for each customer. This new identifier is the old primary key prefixed by the first three letters of the country and a hyphen. If you add this to your pivot table rows, you can right-click to sort on country and old primary key. I've been a little lazy here—the concatenation is done with ampersands rather than a nested CONCATENATE().

LEN()

Again, the LEN() function is very similar to the old Excel equivalent, except it can accept a column as a parameter. The example is a Products table calculated column.

Syntax

```
=LEN('Products'[QuantityPerUnit])
```

Result

ProductName	UnitsInStock	UnitsOnOrder	ReorderLevel	Discontinued	Category	CalculatedColumn1
Chai	39	0	10	FALSE	Beverages	18
Chang	17	40	25	FALSE	Beverages	18
Aniseed Syrup	13	70	25	FALSE	Condiments	19
Chef Anton's Caj...	53	0	0	FALSE	Condiments	14
Chef Anton's Gu...	0	0	0	TRUE	Condiments	8
Grandma's Boys...	120	0	25	FALSE	Condiments	14
Uncle Bob's Org...	15	0	10	FALSE	Produce	15
Northwoods Cra...	6	0	0	FALSE	Condiments	15
Mishi Kobe Niku	29	0	0	TRUE	Meat/Poultry	16
Ikura	31	0	0	FALSE	Seafood	16
Queso Cabrales	22	30	30	FALSE	Dairy Products	9

Analysis

The returned length of the QuantityPerUnit column includes any embedded spaces. Each character counts as 1, even if your data is in 2-byte Unicode.

LOWER()

The LOWER() function simply converts a string or a column containing a text value into lowercase. The example is a Products table calculated column.

Syntax

```
=LOWER('Products'[ProductName])
```

Result

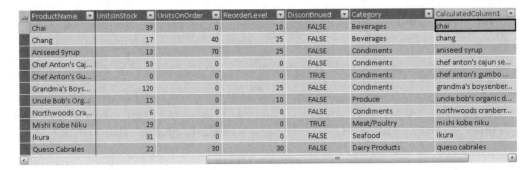

ProductName	UnitsInStock	UnitsOnOrder	ReorderLevel	Discontinued	Category	CalculatedColumn1
Chai	39	0	10	FALSE	Beverages	chai
Chang	17	40	25	FALSE	Beverages	chang
Aniseed Syrup	13	70	25	FALSE	Condiments	aniseed syrup
Chef Anton's Caj...	53	0	0	FALSE	Condiments	chef anton's cajun se...
Chef Anton's Gu...	0	0	0	TRUE	Condiments	chef anton's gumbo ...
Grandma's Boys...	120	0	25	FALSE	Condiments	grandma's boysenber...
Uncle Bob's Org...	15	0	10	FALSE	Produce	uncle bob's organic d...
Northwoods Cra...	6	0	0	FALSE	Condiments	northwoods cranberr...
Mishi Kobe Niku	29	0	0	TRUE	Meat/Poultry	mishi kobe niku
Ikura	31	0	0	FALSE	Seafood	ikura
Queso Cabrales	22	30	30	FALSE	Dairy Products	queso cabrales

Analysis

There's nothing very sophisticated here. Often, the text functions are used in combination to provide meaningful manipulation of data. Any good book on Excel functions and formulas will contain lots of interesting examples—but please remember that the DAX versions of the Excel functions can *usually* accept columns as input parameters.

MID()

The MID() function strips out a substring from a text column or text value (it also works on numeric columns and values). The example is a Products table calculated column.

Syntax

```
=MID('Products'[ProductName],2,3)
```

Result

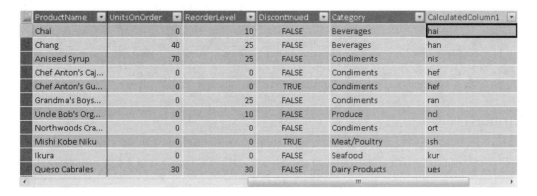

ProductName	UnitsOnOrder	ReorderLevel	Discontinued	Category	CalculatedColumn1
Chai	0	10	FALSE	Beverages	hai
Chang	40	25	FALSE	Beverages	han
Aniseed Syrup	70	25	FALSE	Condiments	nis
Chef Anton's Caj...	0	0	FALSE	Condiments	hef
Chef Anton's Gu...	0	0	TRUE	Condiments	hef
Grandma's Boys...	0	25	FALSE	Condiments	ran
Uncle Bob's Org...	0	10	FALSE	Produce	ncl
Northwoods Cra...	0	0	FALSE	Condiments	ort
Mishi Kobe Niku	0	0	TRUE	Meat/Poultry	ish
Ikura	0	0	FALSE	Seafood	kur
Queso Cabrales	30	30	FALSE	Dairy Products	ues

Analysis

The result is a three-character string starting at the second character of the ProductName column.

REPLACE()

The REPLACE() function is potentially more useful! I don't think you'll be too surprised if the REPLACE() function "replaces" some existing text. There is also a SUBSTITUTE() function that replaces text, but it does so in a different way. SUBSTITUTE() is covered shortly. The example is a Customers table calculated column.

Syntax

```
=REPLACE('Customers'[CustomerID],4,2,"XXX")
```

Result

CompanyName	City	Region	PostalCode	Country	Phone	Fax	CalculatedColumn1
Alfred Futterkiste	Berlin		12209	Germany	030-0074...	030-0...	ALFXXX
Ana Trujillo Empa...	Méxic...		05021	Mexico	(5) 555-4...	(5) 55...	ANAXXX
Antonio Moreno ...	Méxic...		05023	Mexico	(5) 555-3...		ANTXXX
Around the Horn	London		WA1 1DP	UK	(171) 555...	(171) ...	AROXXX
Berglunds snabbk...	Luleå		S-958 22	Sweden	0921-12...	0921-...	BERXXX
Blauer See Delika...	Mann...		68306	Germany	0621-08460	0621-...	BLAXXX
Blondesddsl père ...	Strasb...		67000	France	88.60.15.31	88.60...	BLOXXX
Bólido Comidas p...	Madrid		28023	Spain	(91) 555 ...	(91) 5...	BOLXXX
Bon app'	Marse...		13008	France	91.24.45.40	91.24...	BONXXX
Bottom-Dollar Ma...	Tsawa...	BC	T2F 8M4	Canada	(604) 555...	(604) ...	BOTXXX
B's Beverages	London		EC2 5NT	UK	(171) 555...		BSBXXX

Analysis

Here's an example of how to create a new identifier for each customer. The formula replaces two characters starting from position 4 with the characters XXX.

REPT()

The REPT() function repeats a nominated string a number of times. The examples are Customers table calculated columns.

Syntax

```
='Customers'[CustomerID] & REPT(".",3)
=LEFT('Customers'[CustomerID],3) & REPT("X",3)
```

Result

CompanyName	City	Region	PostalCode	Country	Phone	Fax	CalculatedColumn1
Alfred Futterkiste	Berlin		12209	Germany	030-0074...	030-0...	ALFKI...
Ana Trujillo Empa...	México...		05021	Mexico	(5) 555-4...	(5) 55...	ANATR...
Antonio Moreno ...	México...		05023	Mexico	(5) 555-3...		ANTON...
Around the Horn	London		WA1 1DP	UK	(171) 555...	(171) ...	AROUT...
Berglunds snabbk...	Luleå		S-958 22	Sweden	0921-12 ...	0921-...	BERGS...
Blauer See Delika...	Mann...		68306	Germany	0621-08460	0621-...	BLAUS...
Blondesddsl père ...	Strasb...		67000	France	88.60.15.31	88.60...	BLONP...
Bólido Comidas p...	Madrid		28023	Spain	(91) 555 ...	(91) 5...	BOLID...
Bon app'	Marse...		13008	France	91.24.45.40	91.24...	BONAP...
Bottom-Dollar Ma...	Tsawa...	BC	T2F 8M4	Canada	(604) 555...	(604) ...	BOTTM...
B's Beverages	London		EC2 5NT	UK	(171) 555...		BSBEV...

Analysis

The first example adds three trailing dots to the CustomerID column, the result shown. The second one has the same result as the previous example formula for REPLACE().

RIGHT()

The RIGHT() function returns a specified number of characters from the end of a text column or literal string value (trailing spaces count as characters). The example is a Customers table calculated column.

Syntax

```
=RIGHT('Customers'[CustomerID],3) & LEFT('Customers'[CustomerID],2)
```

Result

CompanyName	City	Region	PostalCode	Country	Phone	Fax	CalculatedColumn1
Alfred Futterkiste	Berlin		12209	Germany	030-0074...	030-0...	FKIAL
Ana Trujillo Empa...	México...		05021	Mexico	(5) 555-4...	(5) 55...	ATRAN
Antonio Moreno ...	México...		05023	Mexico	(5) 555-3...		TONAN
Around the Horn	London		WA1 1DP	UK	(171) 555...	(171) ...	OUTAR
Berglunds snabbk...	Luleå		S-958 22	Sweden	0921-12 ...	0921-...	RGSBE
Blauer See Delika...	Mann...		68306	Germany	0621-08460	0621-...	AUSBL
Blondesddsl père ...	Strasb...		67000	France	88.60.15.31	88.60...	ONPBL
Bólido Comidas p...	Madrid		28023	Spain	(91) 555 ...	(91) 5...	LIDBO
Bon app'	Marse...		13008	France	91.24.45.40	91.24...	NAPBO
Bottom-Dollar Ma...	Tsawa...	BC	T2F 8M4	Canada	(604) 555...	(604) ...	TTMBO
B's Beverages	London		EC2 5NT	UK	(171) 555...		BEVBS

Analysis

Here we are jiggling with the customer identifier.

SEARCH()

The SEARCH() function is the same as FIND() apart from case sensitivity. The examples are calculated columns on any table.

Syntax

```
=SEARCH("e","bottles",1)
=SEARCH("E","bottles",1)
```

Result

ProductName	ReorderLevel	Discontinued	Category	CalculatedColumn1
Chai	10	FALSE	Beverages	6
Chang	25	FALSE	Beverages	6
Aniseed Syrup	25	FALSE	Condiments	6
Chef Anton's Caj...	0	FALSE	Condiments	6
Chef Anton's Gu...	0	TRUE	Condiments	6
Grandma's Boys...	25	FALSE	Condiments	6
Uncle Bob's Org...	10	FALSE	Produce	6
Northwoods Cra...	0	FALSE	Condiments	6
Mishi Kobe Niku	0	TRUE	Meat/Poultry	6
Ikura	0	FALSE	Seafood	6
Queso Cabrales	30	FALSE	Dairy Products	6

Analysis

SEARCH(), just like FIND(), only works on literal values. It's not possible to search a column—if you try, you'll receive an error. The third parameter is the start position for the search. SEARCH() is not case-sensitive, so both examples work.

SUBSTITUTE()

The SUBSTITUTE() function is slightly different from the REPLACE() function. The example is a Products table calculated column.

Syntax

```
=SUBSTITUTE('Products'[QuantityPerUnit],"oz","ounce",1)
```

Result

ProductName	Produ...	SupplierID	Catego...	QuantityPerUnit	CalculatedColumn1
Chai	1	1	1	10 boxes x 20 bags	10 boxes x 20 bags
Chang	2	1	1	24 - 12 oz bottles	24 - 12 ounce bottles
Aniseed Syrup	3	1	2	12 - 550 ml bottles	12 - 550 ml bottles
Chef Anton's Caj...	4	2	2	48 - 6 oz jars	48 - 6 ounce jars
Chef Anton's Gu...	5	2	2	36 boxes	36 boxes
Grandma's Boys...	6	3	2	12 - 8 oz jars	12 - 8 ounce jars
Uncle Bob's Org...	7	3	7	12 - 1 lb pkgs.	12 - 1 lb pkgs.
Northwoods Cra...	8	3	2	12 - 12 oz jars	12 - 12 ounce jars
Mishi Kobe Niku	9	4	6	18 - 500 g pkgs.	18 - 500 g pkgs.
Ikura	10	4	8	12 - 200 ml jars	12 - 200 ml jars
Queso Cabrales	11	5	4	1 kg pkg.	1 kg pkg.

Analysis

Instead of a number of characters to replace (as in the REPLACE() function), you specify a replacement string. Here we are changing "oz" to "ounce." The third parameter is the number of the occurrence to replace (or all occurrences if omitted); SUBSTITUTE() is case-sensitive.

TRIM()

Use TRIM() to remove leading and trailing space characters. The example is a Customers table calculated column.

Syntax

```
=TRIM('Customers'[Country])
```

Result

CompanyName	City	Region	PostalCode	Country	Phone	Fax	CalculatedColumn1
Alfred Futterkiste	Berlin		12209	Germany	030-0074...	030-0...	Germany
Ana Trujillo Empa...	Méxic...		05021	Mexico	(5) 555-4...	(5) 55...	Mexico
Antonio Moreno ...	Méxic...		05023	Mexico	(5) 555-3...		Mexico
Around the Horn	London		WA1 1DP	UK	(171) 555...	(171) ...	UK
Berglunds snabbk...	Luleå		S-958 22	Sweden	0921-12 ...	0921-...	Sweden
Blauer See Delika...	Mann...		68306	Germany	0621-08460	0621-...	Germany
Blondesddsl père ...	Strasb...		67000	France	88.60.15.31	88.60....	France
Bólido Comidas p...	Madrid		28023	Spain	(91) 555 ...	(91) 5...	Spain
Bon app'	Marse...		13008	France	91.24.45.40	91.24...	France
Bottom-Dollar Ma...	Tsawa...	BC	T2F 8M4	Canada	(604) 555...	(604) ...	Canada
B's Beverages	London		EC2 5NT	UK	(171) 555...		UK

Analysis

Leading (and trailing) spaces can cause problems sorting in your pivot tables, so it's often a good idea to employ TRIM(). It does not remove embedded spaces, nor does it remove the special Unicode non-breaking-space character. The example here is somewhat artificial, as there are no leading or trailing spaces—it's for illustration purposes only.

UPPER()

This function converts a column or string literal into uppercase. The example is a Customers table calculated column.

Syntax

```
=UPPER('Customers'[Country])
```

Result

CompanyName	City	Region	PostalCode	Country	Phone	Fax	CalculatedColumn1
Alfred Futterkiste	Berlin		12209	Germany	030-0074...	030-0...	GERMANY
Ana Trujillo Empa...	Méxic...		05021	Mexico	(5) 555-4...	(5) 55...	MEXICO
Antonio Moreno ...	Méxic...		05023	Mexico	(5) 555-3...		MEXICO
Around the Horn	London		WA1 1DP	UK	(171) 555...	(171) ...	UK
Berglunds snabbk...	Luleå		S-958 22	Sweden	0921-12 ...	0921-...	SWEDEN
Blauer See Delika...	Mann...		68306	Germany	0621-08460	0621-...	GERMANY
Blondesddsl père ...	Strasb...		67000	France	88.60.15.31	88.60....	FRANCE
Bólido Comidas p...	Madrid		28023	Spain	(91) 555 ...	(91) 5...	SPAIN
Bon app'	Marse...		13008	France	91.24.45.40	91.24...	FRANCE
Bottom-Dollar Ma...	Tsawa...	BC	T2F 8M4	Canada	(604) 555...	(604) ...	CANADA
B's Beverages	London		EC2 5NT	UK	(171) 555...		UK

Analysis

This function might be quite handy for display purposes in your pivot tables and charts.

VALUE()

VALUE() is used to convert text into a number. It accepts both literals and column references. It also works against dates. The text, of course, must be a valid number—"123" will work while "x123" will not. The examples are Products table calculated columns.

Syntax

```
=VALUE(LEFT('Products'[QuantityPerUnit],1))
=VALUE(LEFT('Products'[QuantityPerUnit],2))
```

Result

ProductName	Produ...	SupplierID	Catego...	QuantityPerUnit	CalculatedColumn1
Chai	1	1	1	10 boxes x 20 bags	1
Chang	2	1	1	24 - 12 oz bottles	2
Aniseed Syrup	3	1	2	12 - 550 ml bottles	1
Chef Anton's Caj...	4	2	2	48 - 6 oz jars	4
Chef Anton's Gu...	5	2	2	36 boxes	3
Grandma's Boys...	6	3	2	12 - 8 oz jars	1
Uncle Bob's Org...	7	3	7	12 - 1 lb pkgs.	1
Northwoods Cra...	8	3	2	12 - 12 oz jars	1
Mishi Kobe Niku	9	4	6	18 - 500 g pkgs.	1
Ikura	10	4	8	12 - 200 ml jars	1
Queso Cabrales	11	5	4	1 kg pkg.	1

Analysis

The second formula will produce an error. That's because the second character for the QuantityPerUnit column for the product Queso Cabrales is a space character, which can't be cast as a number. It's quite likely you won't ever need the VALUE() function. By default, PowerPivot will attempt to convert text into numbers where appropriate. This is true in general. However, this is not always the case with measures imported from an SSAS cube. If a cube measure is used in a DAX function, it may well be converted. If a cube measure is added to the Values drop-zone in a pivot table, it may not be converted. Implicit data conversion on cube measures (from text to numeric) may not work as cube numeric measures can contain non-numeric values (as a result of a cube calculated measure or an MDX Scope statement in a cube script). The first example can probably be left as

```
=LEFT('Products'[QuantityPerUnit],1)
```

Chapter 11

Math & Trig Functions

This is the final chapter dealing with DAX functions and formulas. It deals with the Math & Trig functions. However, you won't find any trigonometric functions as such—expect these to appear in a later version of PowerPivot for Excel. Some of the functions, for example, EXP() and LN(), are probably for specialized use only. However, many of the others are going to be very popular—particularly, the eight functions devoted to rounding numbers. SUM() and SUMX() are Math & Trig functions, although they have much in common with the Statistical functions as well. They were both covered in an earlier chapter on aggregate functions (that is, Statistical functions with SUM() and SUMX()), but are mentioned here again for completeness. In any case, SUMX() is worth a second look, as it will be very useful in many BI situations.

► **Key concepts**   Arithmetic manipulation, exponents and logarithms, rounding up and/or down, summing data

► **Keywords**   ABS(), CEILING(), EXP(), FACT(), FLOOR(), INT(), ISO. CEILING(), LN(), LOG(), LOG10(), MOD(), MROUND(), PI(), POWER(), QUOTIENT(), RAND(), RANDBETWEEN(), ROUND(), ROUNDDOWN(), ROUNDUP(), SIGN(), SQRT(), SUM(), SUMX(), TRUNC()

ABS()

ABS() simply converts a negative number into a positive one, and leaves positive numbers unchanged. The example uses the Products table.

Syntax

=ABS(Products[UnitsInStock]-Products[ReorderLevel])

Result

ProductName	UnitPrice	UnitsInStock	ReorderLevel	CalculatedColumn1
Chai	£18	39	10	29
Chang	£19	17	25	8
Aniseed Syrup	£10	13	25	12
Chef Anton's Cajun Seasoning	£22	53	0	53
Chef Anton's Gumbo Mix	£21.35	0	0	0
Grandma's Boysenberry Spread	£25	120	25	95
Uncle Bob's Organic Dried Pears	£30	15	10	5
Northwoods Cranberry Sauce	£40	6	0	6
Mishi Kobe Niku	£97	29	0	29
Ikura	£31	31	0	31
Queso Cabrales	£21	22	30	8
Queso Manchego La Pastora	£38	86	0	86
Konbu	£6	24	5	19
Tofu	£23.25	35	0	35
Genen Shouyu	£15.5	39	5	34
Pavlova	£17.45	29	10	19

Analysis

The result of UnitsInStock minus ReorderLevel for the product Chang is negative. ABS() has converted this to a positive value.

CEILING()

The CEILING() function rounds a number up to the nearest multiple of significance. The second parameter is the unit of significance. If both parameters are negative, CEILING() will round down—this distinguishes CEILING() from ISO.CEILING(). The example uses the Products table.

Syntax

```
=CEILING(Products[UnitPrice],1)
=CEILING(Products[UnitPrice],.1)
```

Result

ProductName	UnitPrice	UnitsInStock	ReorderLevel	CalculatedColumn1
Chai	£18	39	10	£18
Chang	£19	17	25	£19
Aniseed Syrup	£10	13	25	£10
Chef Anton's Cajun Seasoning	£22	53	0	£22
Chef Anton's Gumbo Mix	£21.35	0	0	£21.4
Grandma's Boysenberry Spread	£25	120	25	£25
Uncle Bob's Organic Dried Pears	£30	15	10	£30
Northwoods Cranberry Sauce	£40	6	0	£40
Mishi Kobe Niku	£97	29	0	£97
Ikura	£31	31	0	£31
Queso Cabrales	£21	22	30	£21
Queso Manchego La Pastora	£38	86	0	£38
Konbu	£6	24	5	£6
Tofu	£23.25	35	0	£23.3
Genen Shouyu	£15.5	39	5	£15.5
Pavlova	£17.45	29	10	£17.5

Analysis

The result shown is from the second example. If you look at Chef Anton's Gumbo Mix, the price has been rounded up to the nearest tenth of a pound (or dollar or euro, depending upon your Control Panel regional settings)—here it's been changed from 21.35 to 21.4.

EXP()

EXP() takes just one parameter, which is the power to which to raise the exponent e (2.71828182845904). The example can be used in any table or as part of a measure.

Syntax

=EXP(2)

Result

ProductName	UnitPrice	UnitsInStock	ReorderLevel	CalculatedColumn1
Chai	£18	39	10	7.38905609893065
Chang	£19	17	25	7.38905609893065
Aniseed Syrup	£10	13	25	7.38905609893065
Chef Anton's Cajun Seasoning	£22	53	0	7.38905609893065
Chef Anton's Gumbo Mix	£21.35	0	0	7.38905609893065
Grandma's Boysenberry Spread	£25	120	25	7.38905609893065
Uncle Bob's Organic Dried Pears	£30	15	10	7.38905609893065
Northwoods Cranberry Sauce	£40	6	0	7.38905609893065
Mishi Kobe Niku	£97	29	0	7.38905609893065
Ikura	£31	31	0	7.38905609893065
Queso Cabrales	£21	22	30	7.38905609893065
Queso Manchego La Pastora	£38	86	0	7.38905609893065
Konbu	£6	24	5	7.38905609893065
Tofu	£23.25	35	0	7.38905609893065
Genen Shouyu	£15.5	39	5	7.38905609893065
Pavlova	£17.45	29	10	7.38905609893065

Analysis

The result (7.38905609893065) is e squared. This is a useful function if you are engaged in scientific or mathematical work. EXP() is the inverse of LN().

FACT()

If you want the factorial of a number, then use FACT(). The example can be used in any table or as part of a measure.

Syntax

=FACT(5)

Result

ProductName	UnitPrice	UnitsInStock	ReorderLevel	CalculatedColumn1
Chai	£18	39	10	120
Chang	£19	17	25	120
Aniseed Syrup	£10	13	25	120
Chef Anton's Cajun Seasoning	£22	53	0	120
Chef Anton's Gumbo Mix	£21.35	0	0	120
Grandma's Boysenberry Spread	£25	120	25	120
Uncle Bob's Organic Dried Pears	£30	15	10	120
Northwoods Cranberry Sauce	£40	6	0	120
Mishi Kobe Niku	£97	29	0	120
Ikura	£31	31	0	120
Queso Cabrales	£21	22	30	120
Queso Manchego La Pastora	£38	86	0	120
Konbu	£6	24	5	120
Tofu	£23.25	35	0	120
Genen Shouyu	£15.5	39	5	120
Pavlova	£17.45	29	10	120

Analysis

The answer, 120, is 5 multiplied by 4 multiplied by 3 multiplied by 2 multiplied by 1. FACT() has lots of applications, including in statistics.

FLOOR()

As you might expect, FLOOR() is the opposite of CEILING(). It rounds numbers down to the unit of significance, which is the second parameter. The example uses the Products table.

Syntax

```
=FLOOR(Products[UnitPrice],.1)
```

Result

ProductName	UnitPrice	UnitsInStock	ReorderLevel	CalculatedColumn1
Chai	£18	39	10	£18
Chang	£19	17	25	£19
Aniseed Syrup	£10	13	25	£10
Chef Anton's Cajun Seasoning	£22	53	0	£22
Chef Anton's Gumbo Mix	£21.35	0	0	£21.3
Grandma's Boysenberry Spread	£25	120	25	£25
Uncle Bob's Organic Dried Pears	£30	15	10	£30
Northwoods Cranberry Sauce	£40	6	0	£40
Mishi Kobe Niku	£97	29	0	£97
Ikura	£31	31	0	£31
Queso Cabrales	£21	22	30	£21
Queso Manchego La Pastora	£38	86	0	£38
Konbu	£6	24	5	£6
Tofu	£23.25	35	0	£23.2
Genen Shouyu	£15.5	39	5	£15.5
Pavlova	£17.45	29	10	£17.4

Analysis

This time, Chef Anton's Gumbo Mix has changed from 21.35 to 21.3.

INT()

INT() rounds a number down to an integer. The example uses the Products table.

Syntax

```
=INT(Products[UnitPrice])
```

Result

ProductName	UnitPrice	UnitsInStock	ReorderLevel	CalculatedColumn1
NuNuCa Nuß-Nougat-Creme	£14	76	30	£14
Gumbär Gummibärchen	£31.23	15	0	£31
Schoggi Schokolade	£43.9	49	30	£43
Rössle Sauerkraut	£45.6	26	0	£45
Thüringer Rostbratwurst	£123.79	0	0	£123
Nord-Ost Matjeshering	£25.89	10	15	£25
Gorgonzola Telino	£12.5	0	20	£12
Mascarpone Fabioli	£32	9	25	£32
Geitost	£2.5	112	20	£2
Sasquatch Ale	£14	111	15	£14
Steeleye Stout	£18	20	15	£18
Inlagd Sill	£19	112	20	£19
Gravad lax	£26	11	25	£26
Côte de Blaye	£263.5	17	15	£263
Chartreuse verte	£18	69	5	£18
Boston Crab Meat	£18.4	123	30	£18

Analysis

If you scroll down to the product Schoggi Schokolade, the price of 43.9 has been rounded down to 43. The same result could have been achieved by using the TRUNC() function. INT() and TRUNC() differ in how they operate on negative numbers. The following syntax, using FLOOR(), also produces the same result:

```
=FLOOR(Products[UnitPrice],1)
```

ISO.CEILING()

This function, ISO.CEILING(), is similar to CEILING(). The difference between the two functions lies in how they behave when both parameters are negative. In that situation, ISO.CEILING() will round up, while CEILING() will round down. The second parameter is the unit of significance. The example uses the Products table.

Syntax

```
=ISO.CEILING(Products[UnitPrice],.1)
```

Result

ProductName	UnitPrice	UnitsInStock	ReorderLevel	CalculatedColumn1
Chai	£18	39	10	£18
Chang	£19	17	25	£19
Aniseed Syrup	£10	13	25	£10
Chef Anton's Cajun Seasoning	£22	53	0	£22
Chef Anton's Gumbo Mix	£21.35	0	0	£21.4
Grandma's Boysenberry Spread	£25	120	25	£25
Uncle Bob's Organic Dried Pears	£30	15	10	£30
Northwoods Cranberry Sauce	£40	6	0	£40
Mishi Kobe Niku	£97	29	0	£97
Ikura	£31	31	0	£31
Queso Cabrales	£21	22	30	£21
Queso Manchego La Pastora	£38	86	0	£38
Konbu	£6	24	5	£6
Tofu	£23.25	35	0	£23.3
Genen Shouyu	£15.5	39	5	£15.5
Pavlova	£17.45	29	10	£17.5

Analysis

Chef Anton's Gumbo Mix is now 21.4 rather than 21.35.

LN()

LN() returns the natural logarithm of a number. The example can be used in any table or as part of a measure.

Syntax

=LN(5)

Result

ProductName	UnitPrice	UnitsInStock	ReorderLevel	CalculatedColumn1
Chai	£18	39	10	1.6094379124341
Chang	£19	17	25	1.6094379124341
Aniseed Syrup	£10	13	25	1.6094379124341
Chef Anton's Cajun Seasoning	£22	53	0	1.6094379124341
Chef Anton's Gumbo Mix	£21.35	0	0	1.6094379124341
Grandma's Boysenberry Spread	£25	120	25	1.6094379124341
Uncle Bob's Organic Dried Pears	£30	15	10	1.6094379124341
Northwoods Cranberry Sauce	£40	6	0	1.6094379124341
Mishi Kobe Niku	£97	29	0	1.6094379124341
Ikura	£31	31	0	1.6094379124341
Queso Cabrales	£21	22	30	1.6094379124341
Queso Manchego La Pastora	£38	86	0	1.6094379124341
Konbu	£6	24	5	1.6094379124341
Tofu	£23.25	35	0	1.6094379124341
Genen Shouyu	£15.5	39	5	1.6094379124341
Pavlova	£17.45	29	10	1.6094379124341

Analysis

There are two other logarithmic functions, LOG() and LOG10(). LN(), the natural logarithm, has a base of the constant e. It's the inverse of EXP().

LOG()

Here is the second of three logarithmic functions. LOG() accepts two parameters, a number and the base for the logarithm. The example can be used in any table or as part of a measure.

Syntax

=LOG(5,5)

Result

ProductName	UnitPrice	UnitsInStock	ReorderLevel	CalculatedColumn1
Chai	£18	39	10	1
Chang	£19	17	25	1
Aniseed Syrup	£10	13	25	1
Chef Anton's Cajun Seasoning	£22	53	0	1
Chef Anton's Gumbo Mix	£21.35	0	0	1
Grandma's Boysenberry Spread	£25	120	25	1
Uncle Bob's Organic Dried Pears	£30	15	10	1
Northwoods Cranberry Sauce	£40	6	0	1
Mishi Kobe Niku	£97	29	0	1
Ikura	£31	31	0	1
Queso Cabrales	£21	22	30	1
Queso Manchego La Pastora	£38	86	0	1
Konbu	£6	24	5	1
Tofu	£23.25	35	0	1
Genen Shouyu	£15.5	39	5	1
Pavlova	£17.45	29	10	1

Analysis

If you omit the second parameter, it is assumed you want the logarithm to the base of 10—it then returns an identical result to the function LOG10().

LOG10()

LOG10() is the third of our three logarithmic functions. The example can be used in any table or as part of a measure.

Syntax

=LOG10(100)

Result

ProductName	UnitPrice	UnitsInStock	ReorderLevel	CalculatedColumn1
Chai	£18	39	10	2
Chang	£19	17	25	2
Aniseed Syrup	£10	13	25	2
Chef Anton's Cajun Seasoning	£22	53	0	2
Chef Anton's Gumbo Mix	£21.35	0	0	2
Grandma's Boysenberry Spread	£25	120	25	2
Uncle Bob's Organic Dried Pears	£30	15	10	2
Northwoods Cranberry Sauce	£40	6	0	2
Mishi Kobe Niku	£97	29	0	2
Ikura	£31	31	0	2
Queso Cabrales	£21	22	30	2
Queso Manchego La Pastora	£38	86	0	2
Konbu	£6	24	5	2
Tofu	£23.25	35	0	2
Genen Shouyu	£15.5	39	5	2
Pavlova	£17.45	29	10	2

Analysis

LOG(100) would also return the same result as LOG10(100).

MOD()

MOD() is the modulo function. The second number is the divisor, the number you wish to divide by. The example uses the Products table.

Syntax

```
=MOD(Products[ReorderLevel],2)
```

Result

ProductName	UnitPrice	UnitsInStock	ReorderLevel	CalculatedColumn1
Chai	£18	39	10	0
Chang	£19	17	25	1
Aniseed Syrup	£10	13	25	1
Chef Anton's Cajun Seasoning	£22	53	0	0
Chef Anton's Gumbo Mix	£21.35	0	0	0
Grandma's Boysenberry Spread	£25	120	25	1
Uncle Bob's Organic Dried Pears	£30	15	10	0
Northwoods Cranberry Sauce	£40	6	0	0
Mishi Kobe Niku	£97	29	0	0
Ikura	£31	31	0	0
Queso Cabrales	£21	22	30	0
Queso Manchego La Pastora	£38	86	0	0
Konbu	£6	24	5	1
Tofu	£23.25	35	0	0
Genen Shouyu	£15.5	39	5	1
Pavlova	£17.45	29	10	0

Analysis

MOD() returns the remainder after the division. Here, the divisor is 2, and MOD() has identified odd and even values. The product Chang, for example, has an odd number (25) for its ReorderLevel.

MROUND()

There are quite a few rounding functions in DAX. MROUND() rounds up or down to the nearest unit (or multiple, hence the name MROUND()) of significance. The example uses the Products table.

Syntax

```
=MROUND(Products[UnitPrice],5)
```

Result

ProductName	UnitPrice	UnitsInStock	ReorderLevel	CalculatedColumn1
Chai	£18	39	10	£20
Chang	£19	17	25	£20
Aniseed Syrup	£10	13	25	£10
Chef Anton's Cajun Seasoning	£22	53	0	£20
Chef Anton's Gumbo Mix	£21.35	0	0	£20
Grandma's Boysenberry Spread	£25	120	25	£25
Uncle Bob's Organic Dried Pears	£30	15	10	£30
Northwoods Cranberry Sauce	£40	6	0	£40
Mishi Kobe Niku	£97	29	0	£95
Ikura	£31	31	0	£30
Queso Cabrales	£21	22	30	£20
Queso Manchego La Pastora	£38	86	0	£40
Konbu	£6	24	5	£5
Tofu	£23.25	35	0	£25
Genen Shouyu	£15.5	39	5	£15
Pavlova	£17.45	29	10	£15

Analysis

The price of the product, Mishi Kobe Niku, has been changed from 97 to 95. With
CEILING() the result would be 100. FLOOR() would have given the same result—but
FLOOR() and MROUND() would have returned different results for Tofu. MROUND()
can act as CEILING() or FLOOR(), depending on the number that is the first
parameter. There are even more rounding functions. INT() and TRUNC() always
round to an integer; their behavior is only different on negative numbers. ROUND(),
ROUNDDOWN(), and ROUNDUP() round to a given number of figures, rather than to a
multiple of significance like MROUND().

PI()

PI() returns the constant *pi*. It is accurate to 14 decimal places. The example can be
used in any table or as part of a measure.

Syntax

```
=PI()
```

Result

ProductName	UnitPrice	UnitsInStock	ReorderLevel	CalculatedColumn1
Chai	£18	39	10	3.14159265358979
Chang	£19	17	25	3.14159265358979
Aniseed Syrup	£10	13	25	3.14159265358979
Chef Anton's Cajun Seasoning	£22	53	0	3.14159265358979
Chef Anton's Gumbo Mix	£21.35	0	0	3.14159265358979
Grandma's Boysenberry Spread	£25	120	25	3.14159265358979
Uncle Bob's Organic Dried Pears	£30	15	10	3.14159265358979
Northwoods Cranberry Sauce	£40	6	0	3.14159265358979
Mishi Kobe Niku	£97	29	0	3.14159265358979
Ikura	£31	31	0	3.14159265358979
Queso Cabrales	£21	22	30	3.14159265358979
Queso Manchego La Pastora	£38	86	0	3.14159265358979
Konbu	£6	24	5	3.14159265358979
Tofu	£23.25	35	0	3.14159265358979
Genen Shouyu	£15.5	39	5	3.14159265358979
Pavlova	£17.45	29	10	3.14159265358979

Analysis

This might be useful if you have a column that records a radius and you also use it in conjunction with the POWER() function!

POWER()

The first parameter of POWER() is a number or a numeric column or an expression evaluating to a number. The second parameter is the power to which to raise the number. The example can be used in any table or as part of a measure.

Syntax

=POWER(4,3)

Result

ProductName	UnitPrice	UnitsInStock	ReorderLevel	CalculatedColumn1
Chai	£18	39	10	64
Chang	£19	17	25	64
Aniseed Syrup	£10	13	25	64
Chef Anton's Cajun Seasoning	£22	53	0	64
Chef Anton's Gumbo Mix	£21.35	0	0	64
Grandma's Boysenberry Spread	£25	120	25	64
Uncle Bob's Organic Dried Pears	£30	15	10	64
Northwoods Cranberry Sauce	£40	6	0	64
Mishi Kobe Niku	£97	29	0	64
Ikura	£31	31	0	64
Queso Cabrales	£21	22	30	64
Queso Manchego La Pastora	£38	86	0	64
Konbu	£6	24	5	64
Tofu	£23.25	35	0	64
Genen Shouyu	£15.5	39	5	64
Pavlova	£17.45	29	10	64

Analysis

If you did have a radius of a circle column, then that column could be the first parameter. The second parameter could be 2 and you might then multiply by PI(), to give you the area of a circle. Of course, POWER() and PI() have rather more uses than that!

QUOTIENT()

QUOTIENT() divides the first numeric parameter by the second one and returns the integer part of the result. The example uses the Products table.

Syntax

`=QUOTIENT(Products[ReorderLevel],2)`

Result

ProductName	UnitPrice	UnitsInStock	ReorderLevel	CalculatedColumn1
Chai	£18	39	10	5
Chang	£19	17	25	12
Aniseed Syrup	£10	13	25	12
Chef Anton's Cajun Seasoning	£22	53	0	0
Chef Anton's Gumbo Mix	£21.35	0	0	0
Grandma's Boysenberry Spread	£25	120	25	12
Uncle Bob's Organic Dried Pears	£30	15	10	5
Northwoods Cranberry Sauce	£40	6	0	0
Mishi Kobe Niku	£97	29	0	0
Ikura	£31	31	0	0
Queso Cabrales	£21	22	30	15
Queso Manchego La Pastora	£38	86	0	0
Konbu	£6	24	5	2
Tofu	£23.25	35	0	0
Genen Shouyu	£15.5	39	5	2
Pavlova	£17.45	29	10	5

Analysis

You can achieve the same result by using this alternative syntax:

```
=INT(Products[ReorderLevel]/2)
```

RAND()

There are two functions for generating random numbers, RAND() and RANDBETWEEN(). RAND() accepts no parameters and returns a random number between 0 and 1. The examples can be used in any table or as part of a measure.

Syntax

```
=RAND()
=RAND()*(10-1)+1
```

Result

ProductName	UnitPrice	UnitsInStock	ReorderLevel	CalculatedColumn1
Chai	£18	39	10	4.67745125170834
Chang	£19	17	25	2.31677301908855
Aniseed Syrup	£10	13	25	8.24154012476279
Chef Anton's Cajun Seasoning	£22	53	0	6.76901275075456
Chef Anton's Gumbo Mix	£21.35	0	0	9.30037043426134
Grandma's Boysenberry Spread	£25	120	25	7.49511311603688
Uncle Bob's Organic Dried Pears	£30	15	10	7.227845229455
Northwoods Cranberry Sauce	£40	6	0	3.05447348364864
Mishi Kobe Niku	£97	29	0	3.78330313858864
Ikura	£31	31	0	5.9585454242837
Queso Cabrales	£21	22	30	8.87087169923035
Queso Manchego La Pastora	£38	86	0	8.99872703949261
Konbu	£6	24	5	4.61329989119943
Tofu	£23.25	35	0	9.81557202310163
Genen Shouyu	£15.5	39	5	2.92946042618202
Pavlova	£17.45	29	10	9.65233782323393

Analysis

The result shown is from the second example. It demonstrates how to generate a random number between 1 and 10. Your results will differ. Also, the result is different for every row. If you refresh the table, or force a manual recalculation, the results will change.

RANDBETWEEN()

RANDBETWEEN() takes two parameters, a bottom boundary number and a top boundary number. It returns random integers between those two numbers, inclusive. The example can be used in any table or as part of a measure.

Syntax

=RANDBETWEEN(1,10)

Result

ProductName	UnitPrice	UnitsInStock	ReorderLevel	CalculatedColumn1
Chai	£18	39	10	9
Chang	£19	17	25	10
Aniseed Syrup	£10	13	25	2
Chef Anton's Cajun Seasoning	£22	53	0	7
Chef Anton's Gumbo Mix	£21.35	0	0	6
Grandma's Boysenberry Spread	£25	120	25	8
Uncle Bob's Organic Dried Pears	£30	15	10	3
Northwoods Cranberry Sauce	£40	6	0	3
Mishi Kobe Niku	£97	29	0	7
Ikura	£31	31	0	1
Queso Cabrales	£21	22	30	9
Queso Manchego La Pastora	£38	86	0	7
Konbu	£6	24	5	5
Tofu	£23.25	35	0	2
Genen Shouyu	£15.5	39	5	5
Pavlova	£17.45	29	10	8

Analysis

If you recalculate your DAX functions, or refresh the source data, which forces recalculation, then both RAND() and RANDBETWEEN() as calculated columns will return different results. In the example, RANDBETWEEN returns whole numbers. Your results will differ. This is different from the second example in the previous query:

```
=RAND()*(10-1)+1
```

ROUND()

Coming up are three more rounding functions for you to try. ROUND() is the first one. ROUND() will round up or round down. It differs from MROUND() in that the second parameter is the number of significant figures rather than a unit or multiple of significance. The example uses the Products table.

Syntax

```
=ROUND(Products[UnitPrice],-1)
```

Result

ProductName	UnitPrice	UnitsInStock	ReorderLevel	CalculatedColumn1
Chai	£18	39	10	£20
Chang	£19	17	25	£20
Aniseed Syrup	£10	13	25	£10
Chef Anton's Cajun Seasoning	£22	53	0	£20
Chef Anton's Gumbo Mix	£21.35	0	0	£20
Grandma's Boysenberry Spread	£25	120	25	£30
Uncle Bob's Organic Dried Pears	£30	15	10	£30
Northwoods Cranberry Sauce	£40	6	0	£40
Mishi Kobe Niku	£97	29	0	£100
Ikura	£31	31	0	£30
Queso Cabrales	£21	22	30	£20
Queso Manchego La Pastora	£38	86	0	£40
Konbu	£6	24	5	£10
Tofu	£23.25	35	0	£20
Genen Shouyu	£15.5	39	5	£20
Pavlova	£17.45	29	10	£20

Analysis

ROUND() can round down (like ROUNDDOWN()) or round up (like ROUNDUP()). The second parameter in this example is negative: -1 means "round to an integer value." If you wish to round to a number of decimal places, then make the second parameter positive. Negative values for the second parameter round to the left of the decimal point. It may be useful to compare the products Chang and Chef Anton's Cajun Seasoning. The first is rounded up, and the second is rounded down.

ROUNDDOWN()

ROUNDDOWN(), unlike ROUND(), always rounds down. If the second argument is negative, it rounds down to the left of the decimal point. The example uses the Products table.

Syntax

```
=ROUNDDOWN(Products[UnitPrice],-1)
```

Result

ProductName	UnitPrice	UnitsInStock	ReorderLevel	CalculatedColumn1
Chai	£18	39	10	£10
Chang	£19	17	25	£10
Aniseed Syrup	£10	13	25	£10
Chef Anton's Cajun Seasoning	£22	53	0	£20
Chef Anton's Gumbo Mix	£21.35	0	0	£20
Grandma's Boysenberry Spread	£25	120	25	£20
Uncle Bob's Organic Dried Pears	£30	15	10	£30
Northwoods Cranberry Sauce	£40	6	0	£40
Mishi Kobe Niku	£97	29	0	£90
Ikura	£31	31	0	£30
Queso Cabrales	£21	22	30	£20
Queso Manchego La Pastora	£38	86	0	£30
Konbu	£6	24	5	£0
Tofu	£23.25	35	0	£20
Genen Shouyu	£15.5	39	5	£10
Pavlova	£17.45	29	10	£10

Analysis

It might be instructive to look at Chang and Chef Anton's Cajun Seasoning again.

ROUNDUP()

As you probably expect, ROUNDUP() always rounds up. A negative second parameter rounds up to the left of the decimal point. The example uses the Products table.

Syntax

```
=ROUNDUP(Products[UnitPrice],-1)
```

Result

ProductName	UnitPrice	UnitsInStock	ReorderLevel	CalculatedColumn1
Chai	£18	39	10	£20
Chang	£19	17	25	£20
Aniseed Syrup	£10	13	25	£10
Chef Anton's Cajun Seasoning	£22	53	0	£30
Chef Anton's Gumbo Mix	£21.35	0	0	£30
Grandma's Boysenberry Spread	£25	120	25	£30
Uncle Bob's Organic Dried Pears	£30	15	10	£30
Northwoods Cranberry Sauce	£40	6	0	£40
Mishi Kobe Niku	£97	29	0	£100
Ikura	£31	31	0	£40
Queso Cabrales	£21	22	30	£30
Queso Manchego La Pastora	£38	86	0	£40
Konbu	£6	24	5	£10
Tofu	£23.25	35	0	£30
Genen Shouyu	£15.5	39	5	£20
Pavlova	£17.45	29	10	£20

Analysis

Once more, please take a look at both Chang and Chef Anton's Cajun Seasoning. Hopefully, you can see the difference between ROUND(), ROUNDDOWN(), and ROUNDUP(). If you would like to experiment further, you may like to try the following example, which has a positive second parameter, and look at Chef Anton's Gumbo Mix:

```
=ROUNDUP(Products[UnitPrice],1)
```

SIGN()

You might use SIGN() to help you identify positive and negative numbers in a pivot table. The function returns a zero for zero values. The example uses the Products table.

Syntax

```
=SIGN(Products[UnitsInStock]-Products[ReorderLevel])
```

Result

ProductName	UnitPrice	UnitsInStock	ReorderLevel	CalculatedColumn1
Gumbär Gummibärchen	£31.23	15	0	1
Schoggi Schokolade	£43.9	49	30	1
Rössle Sauerkraut	£45.6	26	0	1
Thüringer Rostbratwurst	£123.79	0	0	0
Nord-Ost Matjeshering	£25.89	10	15	-1
Gorgonzola Telino	£12.5	0	20	-1
Mascarpone Fabioli	£32	9	25	-1
Geitost	£2.5	112	20	1
Sasquatch Ale	£14	111	15	1
Steeleye Stout	£18	20	15	1
Inlagd Sill	£19	112	20	1
Gravad lax	£26	11	25	-1
Côte de Blaye	£263.5	17	15	1
Chartreuse verte	£18	69	5	1
Boston Crab Meat	£18.4	123	30	1
Jack's New England Clam Chowder	£9.65	85	10	1

Analysis

If you scroll down to Nord-Ost Matjeshering, it looks as if we forgot to place an order with our supplier!

SQRT()

SQRT() simply returns the square root of a number or a numeric column or numeric expression. If the expression used as the only parameter evaluates to a negative number, SQRT() returns an error. The example uses the Products table.

Syntax

```
=SQRT(Products[ReorderLevel])
```

Result

ProductName	UnitPrice	UnitsInStock	ReorderLevel	CalculatedColumn1
Chai	£18	39	10	3.16227766016838
Chang	£19	17	25	5
Aniseed Syrup	£10	13	25	5
Chef Anton's Cajun Seasoning	£22	53	0	0
Chef Anton's Gumbo Mix	£21.35	0	0	0
Grandma's Boysenberry Spread	£25	120	25	5
Uncle Bob's Organic Dried Pears	£30	15	10	3.16227766016838
Northwoods Cranberry Sauce	£40	6	0	0
Mishi Kobe Niku	£97	29	0	0
Ikura	£31	31	0	0
Queso Cabrales	£21	22	30	5.47722557505166
Queso Manchego La Pastora	£38	86	0	0
Konbu	£6	24	5	2.23606797749979
Tofu	£23.25	35	0	0
Genen Shouyu	£15.5	39	5	2.23606797749979
Pavlova	£17.45	29	10	3.16227766016838

Analysis

Maybe we ought to use one of the rounding functions with the result for Chai.

SUM()

Although we are using SUM() in a calculated column, it's a very common function to use in a measure as well. SUM() is officially a Math & Trig function; that's why it's included here. However, it has a lot in common with the Statistical functions, which is why it was also covered in the earlier chapter on aggregate (that is, Statistical with SUM() and SUMX()) functions. The example uses the Products table.

Syntax

```
=SUM(Products[UnitsInStock])
```

Result

ProductName	UnitPrice	UnitsInStock	ReorderLevel	CalculatedColumn1
Chai	£18	39	10	3119
Chang	£19	17	25	3119
Aniseed Syrup	£10	13	25	3119
Chef Anton's Cajun Seasoning	£22	53	0	3119
Chef Anton's Gumbo Mix	£21.35	0	0	3119
Grandma's Boysenberry Spread	£25	120	25	3119
Uncle Bob's Organic Dried Pears	£30	15	10	3119
Northwoods Cranberry Sauce	£40	6	0	3119
Mishi Kobe Niku	£97	29	0	3119
Ikura	£31	31	0	3119
Queso Cabrales	£21	22	30	3119
Queso Manchego La Pastora	£38	86	0	3119
Konbu	£6	24	5	3119
Tofu	£23.25	35	0	3119
Genen Shouyu	£15.5	39	5	3119
Pavlova	£17.45	29	10	3119

Analysis

The formula returns the total number of all products in stock. This may or may not be a valid aggregation; that's a business decision. The result could be divided into UnitsInStock for each product to calculate the percentage contribution to total stock.

SUMX()

Like SUM(), SUMX() is also a Math & Trig function. It too was covered earlier when we looked at aggregate functions. SUMX() is one of the X-functions, which means it requires a table (and not a numeric value) as its first parameter. The example uses the Categories table.

Syntax

```
=SUMX(RELATEDTABLE(Products),Products[UnitsInStock])
```

Result

Catego...	CategoryName	Description	CalculatedColumn1
1	Beverages	Soft drinks, co...	559
2	Condiments	Sweet and sa...	507
3	Confections	Desserts, can...	386
4	Dairy Products	Cheeses	393
5	Grains/Cereals	Breads, crack...	308
6	Meat/Poultry	Prepared meats	165
7	Produce	Dried fruit an...	100
8	Seafood	Seaweed and ...	701

Analysis

Here RELATEDTABLE() is being used to return a table as the first parameter for SUMX(). The second parameter is a numeric column in the referenced table. The result indicates that, for example, we have 559 beverage products in stock. If you add the figures for each row, the answer is 3119, the result of our total stock from the previous query.

TRUNC()

This is our final Math & Trig function. TRUNC() strips away decimals to leave a whole number. The example uses the Products table.

Syntax

```
=TRUNC(Products[UnitPrice])
```

Result

ProductName	UnitPrice	UnitsInStock	ReorderLevel	CalculatedColumn1
Chai	£18	39	10	£18
Chang	£19	17	25	£19
Aniseed Syrup	£10	13	25	£10
Chef Anton's Cajun Seasoning	£22	53	0	£22
Chef Anton's Gumbo Mix	£21.35	0	0	£21
Grandma's Boysenberry Spread	£25	120	25	£25
Uncle Bob's Organic Dried Pears	£30	15	10	£30
Northwoods Cranberry Sauce	£40	6	0	£40
Mishi Kobe Niku	£97	29	0	£97
Ikura	£31	31	0	£31
Queso Cabrales	£21	22	30	£21
Queso Manchego La Pastora	£38	86	0	£38
Konbu	£6	24	5	£6
Tofu	£23.25	35	0	£23

Analysis

You can return the same result by using INT(). However, to illustrate the difference between INT() and TRUNC(), you may want to try the following two examples:

```
=INT(-7.2)
=TRUNC(-7.2)
```

INT() and TRUNC() are the same when applied to positive values—they behave differently on negative values. The results are -8 and -7, respectively.

Part III

PowerPivot and DAX Applied

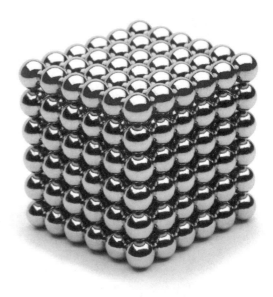

Chapter 12

A Few Ideas: PowerPivot and DAX Solutions

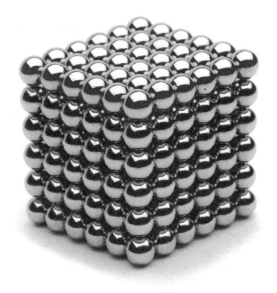

The real world is the real world. Software, and books about software, can only give you "out-of-the-box" solutions. Real-world solutions require a bit more work. This chapter presents a few ideas for moving beyond "out-of-the-box" answers. It is all about implementing PowerPivot and DAX to deal with common business problems. The three appendixes that follow this chapter have a narrower focus, of how to write SQL, MDX, and DMX queries for assembling data in your PowerPivot model. In contrast, this chapter is more concerned with using DAX and the PowerPivot GUI to provide solutions, once you already have the data in place. That said, there is a little on importing data to address the problem of working effectively with dates and dealing with self-joins.

Working with dates can lead to a number of problems—some of these are addressed here. There are also a few "classic" BI solutions in this chapter: percentage of total and subtotal, running totals, changes over time, moving averages, suppressing totals for non-additive numbers, dealing with semi-additive numbers, customizing DAX formulas for individual rows or columns, predefining filters, predefining Column Labels and Row Labels with named sets, working without pivot tables, sharing your pivot reports with others through SharePoint, and a few other things.

- ▶ **Key concepts** Date and time solutions, totals and subtotals, contributions to totals and subtotals, changes over time, non-additive and semi-additive numbers, moving averages, predefining filters and sets, self-joins, working without pivot tables, PowerPivot for SharePoint

- ▶ **Preparation** Many of the examples in this chapter use a Northwind PowerPivot model. Instructions on how to create this model from a SQL Server Northwind source are in Chapter 1. Instructions on how to do so from an Access, Excel, or data feed Northwind are in Chapter 2. One or two examples will use another data source, namely the SQL Server sample database, ContosoRetailDW.

Do You Have a Problem on Dates?

Maybe you don't always get the results you would like on dates—I often don't! Most PowerPivot models will include a date somewhere. Users often want to see the data by year or quarter or month. Frequently, they will want to drill down or drill up on dates. Dates are notoriously difficult to handle. This section includes a number of suggestions.

Parsing Dates

The Northwind sample has an OrderDate column in the Orders table. This has a data type of date and is simply a date. Users like to slice, filter, and view years and quarters, but these are not present as separate columns. Splitting a date into constituent parts is called *parsing* a date. There are a number of ways of doing this. One, you can do it in PowerPivot using DAX. Two, you can parse the date by writing a query for data import into your model. Three, you can create the columns in the source data. Neither of these is that difficult, but establishing fiscal years and quarters is more of a challenge. If you do have fiscal periods, it might also be a good idea to concatenate FY, and also CY to calendar periods, so dates in a pivot table are unambiguous. Let's consider calendar years and calendar quarters first—month names are the same for calendar and fiscal, but month numbers may or may not be, depending upon your accounting conventions.

If you want to parse dates within the PowerPivot model, use DAX formulas. Here are a few formulas to get you started. The first one is a calculated column to return the calendar year—it's called Year in some of the examples in this chapter. The second one returns the month as a number—this column is called Month and is used by the next three formulas, as well as later in the chapter. The month name (called MonthName later in the chapter) is the result of the third example—it's also easy to return the full name, rather than an abbreviation. Formulas four and five are two alternative methods of returning the calendar quarter (called Quarter).

```
=YEAR(Orders[OrderDate])

=MONTH(Orders[OrderDate])

=IF(Orders[Month]=1,"Jan",
IF(Orders[Month]=2,"Feb",
IF(Orders[Month]=3,"Mar",
IF(Orders[Month]=4,"Apr",
IF(Orders[Month]=5,"May",
IF(Orders[Month]=6,"Jun",
IF(Orders[Month]=7,"Jul",
IF(Orders[Month]=8,"Aug",
IF(Orders[Month]=9,"Sep",
IF(Orders[Month]=10,"Oct",
IF(Orders[Month]=11,"Nov",
"Dec")))))))))))

=IF(Orders[Month]<4,"Q1",
IF(Orders[Month]<7,"Q2",
IF(Orders[Month]<10,"Q3","Q4")))

=CONCATENATE("Q",ROUNDUP(Orders[Month]/3,0))
```

Another way of extracting date parts is to write a query to import the table containing the date. Here is the SQL to do so, against the SQL Server Northwind database. It returns the date column itself, followed by the calendar year, the calendar quarter, the month number, and the month name. Of course, you would want further columns, such as OrderID and Freight. If you return both the month number and the month name, it's going to help you sort by, and show, month name in a slicer—more on this shortly.

```
select OrderDate, 'CY ' + cast(DATEPART (yy,OrderDate) as char(4))
as [Calendar Year], 'Q' + cast(datepart(qq,OrderDate) as char(1))
as [Calendar Quarter], datepart(mm,OrderDate) as [Month Number],
datename(mm,OrderDate) as [Month Name]
from
Orders
```

It's reasonably trivial to concatenate the year to the quarter—this is helpful if the user only has quarters in Column Labels or Row Labels; it shows the year for each quarter. You could also do the same for month number. However, if you add the year to the month name, you may experience problems sorting by name in the pivot table.

You might want to experiment with the DAX and/or the SQL approach on the Orders table. There is a third way of parsing dates. It's even easier. However, it requires that you have SSAS and BIDS. In an Analysis Services project, the dimension wizard can generate all of this data (and more) for you. In addition, it can create fiscal as well as calendar periods. There is more on this wizard in the next section on having a separate table for dates.

Separate and Contiguous Date Table

It's generally recommended that you create a separate table, just for holding dates. You can then relate your other tables (such as Orders) to this separate table. When you create a separate table, it's usually called a date dimension or a time dimension. Having such a table is standard practice in "traditional" BI. It confers a number of benefits. One, it centralizes your dates and date manipulation—you don't have to perform date parsing across multiple tables containing dates. Two, it makes it easy to have contiguous dates. If you look at the OrderDate column, some dates are missing. Having contiguous dates helps the DAX time intelligence functions to return intuitive results—it doesn't matter that some of the dates are missing from the many-side table (in this case, that would be Orders). This is particularly true when navigating dates and comparing dates across time. Creating contiguous dates is fairly straightforward; you can use Excel or BIDS. There is one drawback to having a separate time dimension. This occurs when you have more than one date column in a table. You can only relate *one* of those columns back to the one-side time dimension. The Orders table has OrderDate, RequiredDate, and ShippedDate. If you went for the separate time dimension approach, you would need three time dimensions. In this release, PowerPivot does not support multiple relationships between tables. You can verify this (if you have SQL Server AdventureWorksDW2008) by importing the DimDate and FactInternetSales tables—two of the three relationships between those two tables are dropped during the import. However, it's simple to create two more time dimensions—select and copy all of DimDate (press CTRL-A, and click Copy on the Home ribbon), and paste (click the Paste button on the Home ribbon) into the PowerPivot model.

You can use Excel to create a separate time dimension from your dates. It's recommended that you make the dates contiguous. But where do you start and where do you finish? A good place to start is January 1 of the first year for which you have dates, and finish with December 31 of the last year for which you have dates. You might choose Sort Oldest to Newest, then Sort Newest to Oldest, on the OrderDate column to do this—or you could try MAX() and MIN(). To create a time dimension in Excel:

1. Enter a start date in a cell of an empty worksheet. With focus on that cell, click the Fill button in the Editing group of the Excel Home ribbon. This opens a drop-down menu, which is shown in Figure 12-1.

2. In the drop-down choose Series, which opens the Series dialog, shown in Figure 12-2. In this dialog, turn on the option button for Columns and enter a finish date (for instance, **12/31/2020**, or **31/12/2020**, depending upon your regional settings) for the Stop value, before clicking OK.

3. Import this worksheet (or use a linked table) into your PowerPivot model.

4. Relate a date column in an existing PowerPivot table to the single date column in this new table.

Figure 12-1 *Fill drop-down menu*

Figure 12-2   *Series dialog*

If you have BIDS, there's even more you can accomplish easily, including generating fiscal time periods. To create a time dimension using BIDS (BIDS is beyond the scope of this book—only an outline is given here, rather than detailed steps):

1. In BIDS, create a new SSAS project. Right-click Data Sources, in Solution Explorer, in order to create a new data source. Point this to a relational database, for example, SQL Server Northwind.

2. Right-click Dimensions and launch the Dimension Wizard. In the Select Creation Method dialog, turn on the option button for Generate a Time Table in the Data Source. The Select Creation Method dialog is shown in Figure 12-3.

3. In the Define Time Periods dialog, shown in Figure 12-4, specify the start and finish dates, the first day of the week, and the time periods you require. Please note, if you turn on Month, it will generate both month number and month name.

4. The next dialog, shown in Figure 12-5, is the Select Calendars dialog. In addition to Regular Calendar, which means calendar dates, you might want Fiscal Calendar and others.

5. When you are finished in the wizard, you should be looking at the dimension designer for your new dimension. At the right-hand side, click on the link to generate a data source view. This starts the Schema Generation Wizard. Step through this wizard, and check that the table has been generated in the Schema Generation Progress dialog, shown in Figure 12-6, before clicking Close. That's all! You can now import this new table into PowerPivot and relate your existing date columns, in your existing tables, to the date column in the new table (it's called PK_Date by default and has a `date` data type). A sample generated table is shown in Figure 12-7.

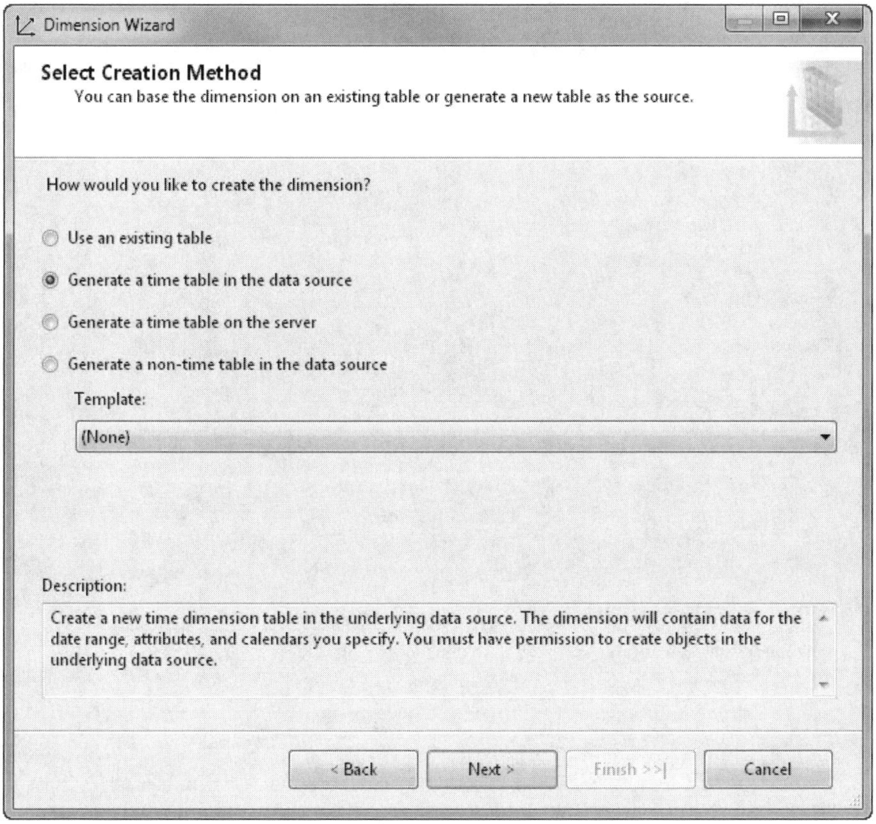

Figure 12-3   *Select Creation Method dialog*

Perhaps a word of caution is necessary for those readers who have a BI background. In "traditional" BI solutions, the time dimension often has an integer (Whole Number) surrogate dimension key. The foreign keys that relate to this from fact tables are also integers. The SQL Server sample database, AdventureWorksDW2008, uses an intelligent key (for example, 20030701) rather than a surrogate key, but it's still an integer. DAX time intelligence functions require a date that's a date data type. You have to convert the primary and foreign keys to dates. Once that's done, remove the integer key relationship and relate the two tables on date. The DAX to convert an intelligent integer key (in the form of 20030701) to a date is as follows:

```
=DATE(LEFT(DimDate[DateKey],4),MID(DimDate[DateKey],5,2),
RIGHT(DimDate[DateKey],2))
```

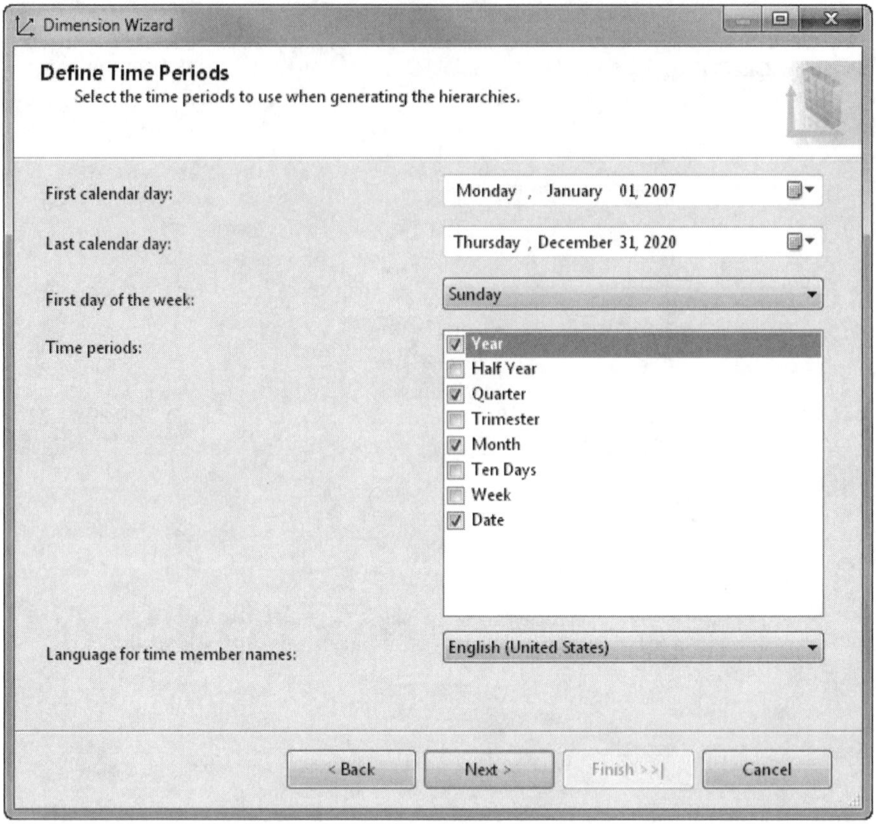

Figure 12-4 *Define Time Periods dialog*

If you have the ContosoRetailDW SQL Server sample database, you don't have to do this—the primary and foreign keys are already dates.

Sorting on Dates

Sorting on dates, especially months, is not always an out-of-the-box solution. If you add month numbers to Column Labels or Row Labels or to a slicer, they should sort correctly. However, your users will likely prefer to see month names. Naturally enough, these are going to sort alphabetically—which is not what you want. The problem is illustrated in Figure 12-8 for Row Labels, and in Figure 12-9 for a slicer.

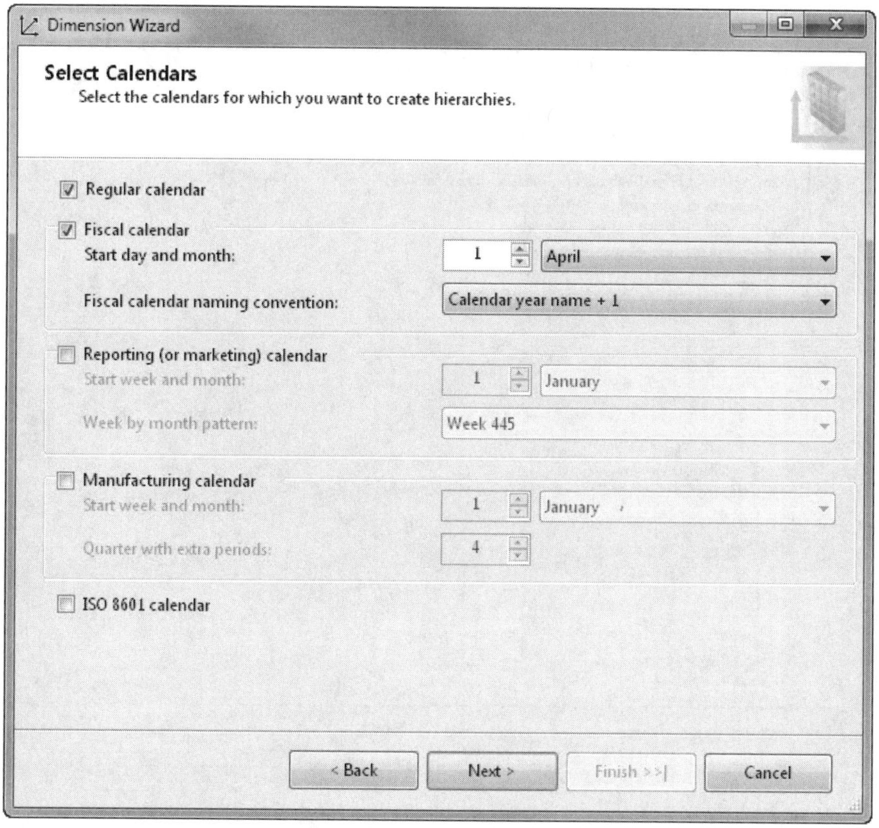

Figure 12-5   *Select Calendars dialog*

Neither looks that good. The solution to the problem depends on whether it's Column Labels/Row Labels or a slicer. Here are some simple steps to sort month names correctly in either Column Labels or Row Labels:

1. Add Sales Amount to Values, and Year, Quarter, and MonthName (the formulas for these date parts are at the start of this chapter) to Row Labels.

2. Right-click on any month name. Choose Sort followed by Sort A to Z. This does not sort alphabetically! When you choose this option, Excel's own intelligent sorting algorithm takes over. For this to work you must use standard names for the months, for example, Jan or January—FirstMonth as a name would not work. The pivot table, shown in Figure 12-10 now has the month names sorting correctly.

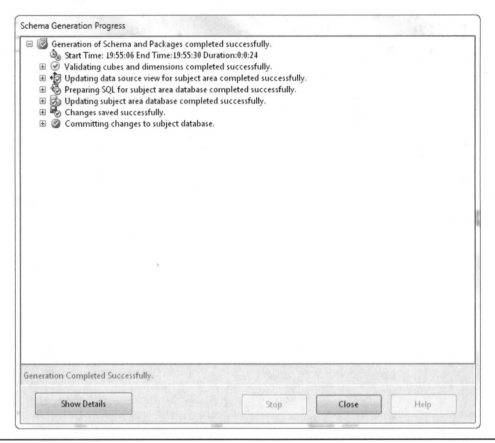

Figure 12-6 *Schema Generation Progress dialog*

PK_Date	Date_Name	Year	Year_Name	Quarter	Quarter_Name
Jan 01, 07	Monday, January 01 2007	Jan 01, 07	Calendar 2007	Jan 01, 07	Quarter 1, 2007
Jan 02, 07	Tuesday, January 02 2007	Jan 01, 07	Calendar 2007	Jan 01, 07	Quarter 1, 2007
Jan 03, 07	Wednesday, January 03 2007	Jan 01, 07	Calendar 2007	Jan 01, 07	Quarter 1, 2007
Jan 04, 07	Thursday, January 04 2007	Jan 01, 07	Calendar 2007	Jan 01, 07	Quarter 1, 2007
Jan 05, 07	Friday, January 05 2007	Jan 01, 07	Calendar 2007	Jan 01, 07	Quarter 1, 2007
Jan 06, 07	Saturday, January 06 2007	Jan 01, 07	Calendar 2007	Jan 01, 07	Quarter 1, 2007
Jan 07, 07	Sunday, January 07 2007	Jan 01, 07	Calendar 2007	Jan 01, 07	Quarter 1, 2007
Jan 08, 07	Monday, January 08 2007	Jan 01, 07	Calendar 2007	Jan 01, 07	Quarter 1, 2007
Jan 09, 07	Tuesday, January 09 2007	Jan 01, 07	Calendar 2007	Jan 01, 07	Quarter 1, 2007
Jan 10, 07	Wednesday, January 10 2007	Jan 01, 07	Calendar 2007	Jan 01, 07	Quarter 1, 2007

Figure 12-7 *Generated time dimension in PowerPivot*

Figure 12-8   *Month names in Row Labels*

Unfortunately, the previous steps do not apply to slicers. For a slicer, you have to prepend the month name with the month number. This is not perfect, and will not be necessary in the next release of PowerPivot. But for now, here are the steps to sort on month name correctly in a slicer:

1. Add a calculated column to the Orders table and enter the following DAX formula:

    ```
    =IF(LEN([Month]) = 1,"0" & [Month] & " - " & [MonthName],
    [Month] & " - " & [MonthName])
    ```

2. Use this calculated column in the slicer. The result is shown in Figure 12-11. Please note that the zero in front of single-digit month numbers is necessary for a correct sort.

Figure 12-9   *Month names in a slicer*

	A	B	C
1	Row Labels	Sum of Sales Amount	
2	1996	226298.5	
3	Q3	84437.5	
4	Jul	30192.1	
5	Aug	26609.4	
6	Sep	27636	
7	Q4	141861	
8	Oct	41203.6	
9	Nov	49704	
10	Dec	50953.4	
11	1997	658388.75	
12	1998	469771.34	
13	Grand Total	1354458.59	

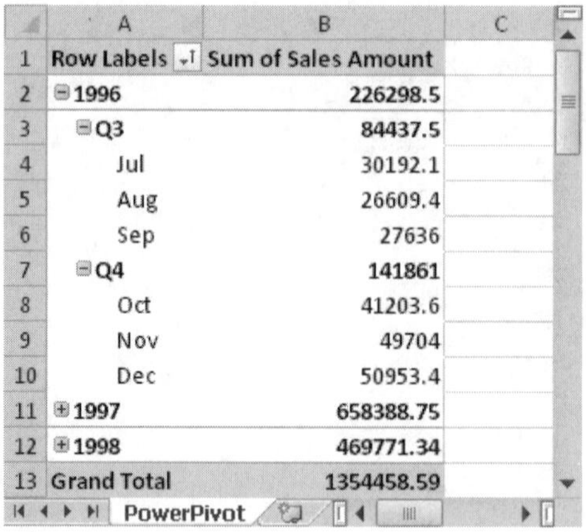

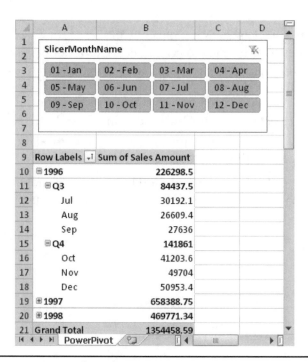

Figure 12-10 *Month names sorting correctly in Row Labels*

	A	B	C	D
9	Row Labels	Sum of Sales Amount		
10	1996	226298.5		
11	Q3	84437.5		
12	Jul	30192.1		
13	Aug	26609.4		
14	Sep	27636		
15	Q4	141861		
16	Oct	41203.6		
17	Nov	49704		
18	Dec	50953.4		
19	1997	658388.75		
20	1998	469771.34		
21	Grand Total	1354458.59		

Figure 12-11 *Month names sorting correctly in a slicer*

Numbers That Don't Add Up

Many numbers (whether from calculated columns or calculated measures) can be aggregated in all situations. In our Northwind PowerPivot model, such numbers are Quantity and Sales Amount from the Order Details table. It makes sense to see subtotals and totals for these numbers, whether by product or employee or customer or date. Such numbers are full-additive numbers. Some numbers, however, can never be usefully aggregated or only aggregated in certain circumstances. The former are called *non-additive numbers* and the latter, *semi-additive numbers*. A semi-additive number might be a bank balance. If you have two bank accounts, you can add them together to give you your total balance. Unfortunately, you can't add them together solely by time! If you had $100 in your account last week and $200 this week, sadly, you don't necessarily have $300. Bank balances are only additive in certain circumstances. A non-additive number might be an inventory figure. If you have 10 of the product Chai in stock and 20 of the product Chang, it might not be meaningful to say you had 30 in stock. That is a business decision; you *could* argue that to say you had 30 products in stock was sensible. To take another example, if you had 10 Chai last week and 5 Chai this week, the answer is probably not 15. Maybe the answer is 5, the last non-blank value (there is a DAX function called LASTNONBLANK(), which is very useful when looking at totals across time). This section deals with non-additive and semi-additive numbers in a pivot table.

Take a look at Figure 12-12. The pivot table is filtered to show only a few products. You might conclude that the grand total for UnitsInStock (from the Products table) is not a valid total. What if you would prefer to hide this total?

You can easily hide the grand total for UnitsInStock by going through the Grand Totals button in the Layout group of the PivotTable Tools/Design ribbon. However, that is also going to hide the total for Sales Amount, which is perfectly valid and may be required by end users. Here's an approach that can be used to selectively hide totals. Add a new measure to the pivot table with the following formula:

```
=IF(COUNTROWS(VALUES(Products[ProductName]))=1,SUM(Products[UnitsInStock])))
```

	A	B	C	D
1	Row Labels	Sum of Sales Amount	Sum of UnitsInStock	
2	Alice Mutton	35482.2	0	
3	Aniseed Syrup	3080	13	
4	Boston Crab Meat	19048.3	123	
5	Camembert Pierrot	50286	19	
6	Carnarvon Tigers	31987.5	42	
7	Grand Total	139884	197	

Figure 12-12   *Incorrect total for inventory?*

	A	B	C	D	E
1	Row Labels	Sum of Sales Amount	Sum of UnitsInStock	Stock	
2	Alice Mutton	35482.2	0	0	
3	Aniseed Syrup	3080	13	13	
4	Boston Crab Meat	19048.3	123	123	
5	Camembert Pierrot	50286	19	19	
6	Carnarvon Tigers	31987.5	42	42	
7	Grand Total	139884	197		

PowerPivot

Figure 12-13 *Correct total for inventory?*

The formula is counting the number of rows in the current filter context for the product name. If the number of rows is 1, then the current context is at the individual product level. The third parameter for the `IF()` function is missing. That's the false result, and if it's missing, it returns a blank—or you could explicitly use `BLANK()`. The result is shown in Figure 12-13.

An interesting problem arises when you aggregate UnitsInStock across time. Here, you may want to see a total. The most meaningful total for a product would be equal to the last stock-take figure for that product. In SSAS, there are two useful aggregations called LastChild and LastNonEmpty for working with inventory figures. Fortunately, there is a DAX equivalent of LastNonEmpty, the DAX function `LASTNONBLANK()`. In order to demonstrate this, we need inventory figures across time. The Northwind UnitsInStock column is a static picture, and the stock-take is not dated. However, if you have the SQL Server sample database, ContosoRetailDW (you can download it from www.microsoft.com—search on ContosoRetailDW), you can look at inventory figures across time—you'll need the DimDate and FactInventory tables. The practical shows how to handle numbers that do not add up over time. Here are the step-by-step instructions:

1. Add the DimDate, DimProduct, and FactInventory tables from ContosoRetailDW to a PowerPivot model. DimDate contains dates, and FactInventory includes stock-take figures for different dates and products. DimProduct is added so you can see the product name, rather than a product key. You may need to verify the relationships between these tables. FactInventory should be related to DimDate through the DateKey column. It should also be related to DimProduct through the ProductKey column. When you add tables separately, the relationships in the source data are not discovered by PowerPivot.
2. Insert a pivot table and add CalendarYear (from DimDate) to Column Labels, ProductName (from DimProduct) to Row Labels, and OnHandQuantity (from FactInventory) to Values. Set a label filter on the rows to **adventure works laptop12**, using Label Filters, Begins With (and I thought Adventure Works only made bikes!)—the result is shown in Figure 12-14.

	A	B	C	D	E	F
1	Sum of OnHandQuantity	Column Labels				
2	Row Labels	2007	2008	2009	Grand Total	
3	Adventure Works Laptop12 M1200 Black	10455	851		11306	
4	Adventure Works Laptop12 M1201 Blue	10881	17984	38045	66910	
5	Adventure Works Laptop12 M1201 Red	10467	17968	36197	64632	
6	Adventure Works Laptop12 M1201 Silver	11039	17409	18194	46642	
7	Adventure Works Laptop12 M1201 White	9619	16484	36525	62628	
8	Grand Total	52461	70696	128961	252118	

Figure 12-14 *An incorrect inventory pivot table*

3. The Grand Total for each row is incorrect. It should be equal to the last annual stock-take figure, and not a summation. To start fixing the problem, replace the entry for OnHandQuantity in Values with a new measure called BadInventory. You may want to add this to the FactInventory table. The formula follows:

```
=SUM(FactInventory[OnHandQuantity])
```

4. The totals are still incorrect, and there is no figure for M1200 Black for 2009. Remove BadInventory from the Values drop-zone (but not from the field list), and add another measure, called Inventory. The formula is:

```
=SUMX(VALUES(DimProduct[ProductKey]),CALCULATE([BadInventory],
LASTNONBLANK(DimDate[Datekey],[BadInventory])))
```

This is a reasonably complex piece of DAX. It means "sum all the values in the DimProduct table, but only using the last inventory figure found for each date." The result is shown in Figure 12-15. The Grand Total for each row is now correct. The inventory figures for each year also look better—they are now using the last stock-take figure in each year, rather than a sum.

	A	B	C	D	E	F
1	Inventory	Column Labels				
2	Row Labels	2007	2008	2009	Grand Total	
3	Adventure Works Laptop12 M1200 Black	243	13		13	
4	Adventure Works Laptop12 M1201 Blue	239	359	518	518	
5	Adventure Works Laptop12 M1201 Red	233	309	874	874	
6	Adventure Works Laptop12 M1201 Silver	188	348	560	560	
7	Adventure Works Laptop12 M1201 White	217	510	851	851	
8	Grand Total	1120	1539	2803	2816	

Figure 12-15 *A better inventory pivot table*

Figure 12-16 *A correct inventory pivot table*

5.   However, there is still a problem. The figure for M1200 Black is missing for 2009. If this entire product had been sold in 2009, the figure would presumably be zero. A blank, on the other hand, means that no stock-take was performed in 2009. In that case, it might be reasonable to assume that the 2009 figure should be the same as the 2008 figure (implying that there were no sales from stocks in 2009). Change the DAX formula to this:

```
=SUMX(VALUES(DimProduct[ProductKey]),CALCULATE([BadInventory],
LASTNONBLANK(DATESBETWEEN(DimDate[Datekey],BLANK(),
LASTDATE(DimDate[Datekey])),[BadInventory])))
```

The final result is shown in Figure 12-16. There is now an entry for M1200 Black for 2009. In addition, we now have the stock figures for 2010 and 2011. The correct answers are being returned. The DATESBETWEEN() function looks at all dates up to the last, or current context, date from the beginning of time. The last date is given by LASTDATE(). LASTNONBLANK() then finds the last stock-take figure within the date range returned by DATESBETWEEN().

Classic BI Solutions

This section considers some classic BI solutions. The ones examined are percentage of all, percentage of a row or column total, percentage of parent, a measure customized for a row or column context, changes over time, a moving average, and two forms of a running total. You can build a lot of these by using the pivot table GUI, but a DAX solution gives you a lot more control over the filter context.

Percentage of All

Our starting point is shown in Figure 12-17. It's using the Northwind PowerPivot model (Category, ProductName, Year, and Quantity).

Sum of Quantity	Column Labels				
Row Labels	1996	1997	1998	Grand Total	
⊟ Beverages	1842	3996	3694	9532	
Chai	125	304	399	828	
Chang	226	435	396	1057	
Chartreuse verte	266	283	244	793	
Côte de Blaye	140	223	260	623	
Guaraná Fantástica	158	421	546	1125	
Ipoh Coffee	136	258	186	580	
Lakkalikööri	146	447	388	981	
Laughing Lumberjack Lager	5	65	114	184	
Outback Lager	156	413	248	817	
Rhönbräu Klosterbier	120	630	405	1155	
Sasquatch Ale	90	171	245	506	
Steeleye Stout	274	346	263	883	
⊞ Condiments	962	2895	1441	5298	
⊞ Confections	1357	4137	2412	7906	
⊞ Dairy Products	2086	4374	2689	9149	
⊞ Grains/Cereals	549	2636	1377	4562	
⊞ Meat/Poultry	950	2189	1060	4199	
⊞ Produce	549	1583	858	2990	
⊞ Seafood	1286	3679	2716	7681	
Grand Total	9581	25489	16247	51317	

Figure 12-17 *A Northwind pivot table*

To work out the percentage of all, add a new measure to the Order Details table. The formula is:

```
=SUM('Order Details'[Quantity])/
CALCULATE(SUM('Order Details'[Quantity]),ALL('Order Details'))
```

This returns the percentage of all because the filter context for the denominator is always the *total* quantity—ALL('Order Details'). The result is shown in Figure 12-18; the figures are formatted as percentages (right-click, Number Format).

Percentage of Column or Row Total

Figure 12-19 shows the addition of a percentage of column total measure. The DAX formula for this is:

```
=SUM('Order Details'[Quantity])/
CALCULATE(SUM('Order Details'[Quantity]),ALL(Products))
```

This uses ALL(Products) rather than ALL('Order Details').

	A	B	C	D	E	F	G	H	I
1		1996		1997		1998		Total Quantity	Total All
2		Quantity	All	Quantity	All	Quantity	All		
3	⊟Beverages	1842	3.59%	3996	7.79%	3694	7.20%	9532	18.57%
4	Chai	125	0.24%	304	0.59%	399	0.78%	828	1.61%
5	Chang	226	0.44%	435	0.85%	396	0.77%	1057	2.06%
6	Chartreuse verte	266	0.52%	283	0.55%	244	0.48%	793	1.55%
7	Côte de Blaye	140	0.27%	223	0.43%	260	0.51%	623	1.21%
8	Guaraná Fantástica	158	0.31%	421	0.82%	546	1.06%	1125	2.19%
9	Ipoh Coffee	136	0.27%	258	0.50%	186	0.36%	580	1.13%
10	Lakkalikööri	146	0.28%	447	0.87%	388	0.76%	981	1.91%
11	Laughing Lumberjack Lager	5	0.01%	65	0.13%	114	0.22%	184	0.36%
12	Outback Lager	156	0.30%	413	0.80%	248	0.48%	817	1.59%
13	Rhönbräu Klosterbier	120	0.23%	630	1.23%	405	0.79%	1155	2.25%
14	Sasquatch Ale	90	0.18%	171	0.33%	245	0.48%	506	0.99%
15	Steeleye Stout	274	0.53%	346	0.67%	263	0.51%	883	1.72%
16	⊞Condiments	962	1.87%	2895	5.64%	1441	2.81%	5298	10.32%
17	⊞Confections	1357	2.64%	4137	8.06%	2412	4.70%	7906	15.41%
18	⊞Dairy Products	2086	4.06%	4374	8.52%	2689	5.24%	9149	17.83%
19	⊞Grains/Cereals	549	1.07%	2636	5.14%	1377	2.68%	4562	8.89%
20	⊞Meat/Poultry	950	1.85%	2189	4.27%	1060	2.07%	4199	8.18%
21	⊞Produce	549	1.07%	1583	3.08%	858	1.67%	2990	5.83%
22	⊞Seafood	1286	2.51%	3679	7.17%	2716	5.29%	7681	14.97%
23	Grand Total	9581	18.67%	25489	49.67%	16247	31.66%	51317	100.00%

Figure 12-18   *Percentage of all*

	A	B	C	D	E	F	G	H	I	J
1		1996			1997			1998		
2		Quantity	All	Column	Quantity	All	Column	Quantity	All	Column
3	⊟Beverages	1842	3.59%	19.23%	3996	7.79%	15.68%	3694	7.20%	22.74%
4	Chai	125	0.24%	1.30%	304	0.59%	1.19%	399	0.78%	2.46%
5	Chang	226	0.44%	2.36%	435	0.85%	1.71%	396	0.77%	2.44%
6	Chartreuse verte	266	0.52%	2.78%	283	0.55%	1.11%	244	0.48%	1.50%
7	Côte de Blaye	140	0.27%	1.46%	223	0.43%	0.87%	260	0.51%	1.60%
8	Guaraná Fantástica	158	0.31%	1.65%	421	0.82%	1.65%	546	1.06%	3.36%
9	Ipoh Coffee	136	0.27%	1.42%	258	0.50%	1.01%	186	0.36%	1.14%
10	Lakkalikööri	146	0.28%	1.52%	447	0.87%	1.75%	388	0.76%	2.39%
11	Laughing Lumberjack Lager	5	0.01%	0.05%	65	0.13%	0.26%	114	0.22%	0.70%
12	Outback Lager	156	0.30%	1.63%	413	0.80%	1.62%	248	0.48%	1.53%
13	Rhönbräu Klosterbier	120	0.23%	1.25%	630	1.23%	2.47%	405	0.79%	2.49%
14	Sasquatch Ale	90	0.18%	0.94%	171	0.33%	0.67%	245	0.48%	1.51%
15	Steeleye Stout	274	0.53%	2.86%	346	0.67%	1.36%	263	0.51%	1.62%
16	⊞Condiments	962	1.87%	10.04%	2895	5.64%	11.36%	1441	2.81%	8.87%
17	⊞Confections	1357	2.64%	14.16%	4137	8.06%	16.23%	2412	4.70%	14.85%
18	⊞Dairy Products	2086	4.06%	21.77%	4374	8.52%	17.16%	2689	5.24%	16.55%
19	⊞Grains/Cereals	549	1.07%	5.73%	2636	5.14%	10.34%	1377	2.68%	8.48%
20	⊞Meat/Poultry	950	1.85%	9.92%	2189	4.27%	8.59%	1060	2.07%	6.52%
21	⊞Produce	549	1.07%	5.73%	1583	3.08%	6.21%	858	1.67%	5.28%
22	⊞Seafood	1286	2.51%	13.42%	3679	7.17%	14.43%	2716	5.29%	16.72%
23	Grand Total	9581	18.67%	100.00%	25489	49.67%	100.00%	16247	31.66%	100.00%

Figure 12-19   *Percentage of column*

Percentage of Parent

This time, a new measure has been added with the following formula:

```
=SUM('Order Details'[Quantity])/
CALCULATE(SUM('Order Details'[Quantity]),
ALLEXCEPT(Products,Products[Category]))
```

Figure 12-20 shows this new measure. The filter context for the denominator is now the product category.

Customizing Measures for Each Row or Column

Often, you will want a value in the data area to behave differently depending upon the current row or column filter context. Suppose, for example, that all sales are recorded in U.S. dollars—apart from the U.K., where sales are recorded in pounds sterling. You may

	A	B	C	D	E	F	G	H	I
1		1996				1997			
2		Quantity	All	Column	Parent	Quantity	All	Column	Parent
3	⊟ Beverages	1842	3.59%	19.23%	100.00%	3996	7.79%	15.68%	100.00%
4	Chai	125	0.24%	1.30%	6.79%	304	0.59%	1.19%	7.61%
5	Chang	226	0.44%	2.36%	12.27%	435	0.85%	1.71%	10.89%
6	Chartreuse verte	266	0.52%	2.78%	14.44%	283	0.55%	1.11%	7.08%
7	Côte de Blaye	140	0.27%	1.46%	7.60%	223	0.43%	0.87%	5.58%
8	Guaraná Fantástica	158	0.31%	1.65%	8.58%	421	0.82%	1.65%	10.54%
9	Ipoh Coffee	136	0.27%	1.42%	7.38%	258	0.50%	1.01%	6.46%
10	Lakkalikööri	146	0.28%	1.52%	7.93%	447	0.87%	1.75%	11.19%
11	Laughing Lumberjack Lager	5	0.01%	0.05%	0.27%	65	0.13%	0.26%	1.63%
12	Outback Lager	156	0.30%	1.63%	8.47%	413	0.80%	1.62%	10.34%
13	Rhönbräu Klosterbier	120	0.23%	1.25%	6.51%	630	1.23%	2.47%	15.77%
14	Sasquatch Ale	90	0.18%	0.94%	4.89%	171	0.33%	0.67%	4.28%
15	Steeleye Stout	274	0.53%	2.86%	14.88%	346	0.67%	1.36%	8.66%
16	⊞ Condiments	962	1.87%	10.04%	100.00%	2895	5.64%	11.36%	100.00%
17	⊞ Confections	1357	2.64%	14.16%	100.00%	4137	8.06%	16.23%	100.00%
18	⊞ Dairy Products	2086	4.06%	21.77%	100.00%	4374	8.52%	17.16%	100.00%
19	⊞ Grains/Cereals	549	1.07%	5.73%	100.00%	2636	5.14%	10.34%	100.00%
20	⊞ Meat/Poultry	950	1.85%	9.92%	100.00%	2189	4.27%	8.59%	100.00%
21	⊞ Produce	549	1.07%	5.73%	100.00%	1583	3.08%	6.21%	100.00%
22	⊞ Seafood	1286	2.51%	13.42%	100.00%	3679	7.17%	14.43%	100.00%
23	Grand Total	9581	18.67%	100.00%	100.00%	25489	49.67%	100.00%	100.00%
	◄ ► ►│ PowerPivot								

Figure 12-20 *Percentage of parent*

▲	A	B	C	D
3	Austria	139496.63	139496.63	
4	Belgium	35134.98	35134.98	
5	Brazil	114968.48	114968.48	
6	Canada	55334.1	55334.1	
7	Denmark	34782.25	34782.25	
8	Finland	19778.45	19778.45	
9	France	85498.76	85498.76	
10	Germany	244640.63	244640.63	
11	Ireland	57317.39	57317.39	
12	Italy	16705.15	16705.15	
13	Mexico	24073.45	24073.45	
14	Norway	5735.15	5735.15	
15	Poland	3531.95	3531.95	
16	Portugal	12468.65	12468.65	
17	Spain	19431.89	19431.89	
18	Sweden	59523.7	59523.7	
19	Switzerland	32919.5	32919.5	
20	UK	60616.51	90924.765	
21	USA	263566.98	263566.98	
22	Venezuela	60814.89	60814.89	
23	**Grand Total**	1354458.59	1354458.59	

PowerPivot

Figure 12-21 *A measure customized for rows*

want to see the dollar value of U.K. sales. Figure 12-21 shows the result of adding the following measure to the Order Details table, called DollarSales, with Country from the Customers table on the rows:

```
=IF(COUNTROWS(VALUES(Customers[Country]))=1,
IF(VALUES(Customers[Country])="UK",
SUM('Order Details'[Sales Amount]) * 1.5,
SUM('Order Details'[Sales Amount])),
SUM('Order Details'[Sales Amount]))
```

Please note that DollarSales is different from Sales (=SUM('Order Details' [Sales Amount])) for the U.K., and uses an exchange rate of 1.5 U.K. pounds for one U.S. dollar. The IF(COUNTROWS(VALUES())) construct is necessary; otherwise, the Grand Total row would throw an error. This is because VALUES() returns a table of more than one row for Grand Total, and the IF() test requires a single row.

Changes over Time

Another classic BI requirement is to show changes over time. For example, you may wish to see increases and decreases in sales from one year to the next. The DAX Date and Time functions are particularly useful in order to achieve such results. Some of these functions require contiguous dates. Without contiguous dates, functions, such as DATEADD() and SAMEPERIODLASTYEAR(), will either result in an error or produce nonintuitive results. The example here uses ContosoRetailDW, as Northwind lacks contiguous dates. You will need the DimDate, DimProduct, and FactSales tables. Make sure that FactSales is related to both DimDate (on DateKey) and DimProduct (on ProductKey). Add SalesAmount from FactSales to the Values drop-zone. Add CalendarYear from DimDate to Column Labels and BrandName from DimProduct to Row Labels. Interestingly, you will see that Adventure Works and Northwind supply products to Contoso! The example that follows uses DATEADD() to retrieve sales from the previous year and then compares the value to the current year to ascertain the change in sales over time. You could also try PARALLELPERIOD(), if you wish. Here is the DAX to work out a change in sales:

```
=SUM(FactSales[SalesAmount])-
CALCULATE(SUM(FactSales[SalesAmount]),DATEADD(DimDate[DateKey],-1,YEAR))
```

Moving Average

This example also uses ContosoRetailDW. The rows are from the DateKey in the DimDate table, and the first column of values is the SalesAmount column from the FactSales table. Figure 12-22 shows the result of a moving average measure. The formula for the measure is:

```
=CALCULATE(SUM(FactSales[SalesAmount]),DATESBETWEEN(DimDate[Datekey],
FIRSTDATE(DATEADD(DimDate[Datekey],-2,DAY)),
LASTDATE(DimDate[Datekey]))))/3
```

This is a three-day moving average. The divisor is 3, yet DATEADD() uses -2—that's going to return three dates including the current date. You can get rid of the first two entries by testing for blanks. Northwind is not really suitable here as it lacks contiguous dates.

◢	A	B	C	D
1		Sum of SalesAmount	MA	
2	Jan 01, 07	8310498.09	2770166.03	
3	Jan 02, 07	8326142.865	5545546.985	
4	Jan 03, 07	8409918.573	8348853.176	
5	Jan 04, 07	8231879.686	8322647.041	
6	Jan 05, 07	8089676.271	8243824.843	
7	Jan 06, 07	8656979.943	8326178.633	
8	Jan 07, 07	8964768.286	8570474.833	
9	Jan 08, 07	8277674.516	8633140.915	
10	Jan 09, 07	8400906.664	8547783.155	
11	Jan 10, 07	9060159.027	8579580.069	
12	Jan 11, 07	8921267.515	8794111.069	
13	Jan 12, 07	8504087.018	8828504.52	
14	Jan 13, 07	9203971.095	8876441.876	
15	Jan 14, 07	8544951.168	8751003.094	
16	Jan 15, 07	8877679.217	8875533.827	
17	Jan 16, 07	8754514.383	8725714.923	
18	Jan 17, 07	8922924.515	8851706.038	
19	Jan 18, 07	8671215.242	8782884.713	
20	Jan 19, 07	8727181.107	8773773.621	
21	Jan 20, 07	8668711.77	8689036.039	

I◀ ◀ ▶ ▶I   PowerPivot

Figure 12-22 *Moving average*

Running Total—Breaking

This example takes us back to the Northwind PowerPivot model. This is a Year-To-Date example on the Sales Amount. The result is shown in Figure 12-23 and the formula is:

```
=TOTALYTD(SUM('Order Details'[Sales Amount]),Orders[OrderDate])
```

This is a breaking (or resetting) total as it starts again for August 1996.

Running Total—Non-Breaking

This running total has a different DAX formula:

```
=TOTALYTD(SUM('Order Details'[Sales Amount]),
Orders[OrderDate],ALL(Orders))
```

⊿	A	B	C	D
1		Sum of Sales Amount	Running 1	
2	⊟ 1996	226298.5	226298.5	
3	⊟ Q3	84437.5	84437.5	
4	⊟ 7	30192.1	30192.1	
5	Jul 04, 96	440	440	
6	Jul 05, 96	1863.4	2303.4	
7	Jul 08, 96	2483.8	4787.2	
8	Jul 09, 96	3730	8517.2	
9	Jul 10, 96	1444.8	9962	
10	Jul 11, 96	625.2	10587.2	
11	Jul 12, 96	2490.5	13077.7	
12	Jul 15, 96	517.8	13595.5	
13	Jul 16, 96	1119.9	14715.4	
14	Jul 17, 96	2018.6	16734	
15	Jul 18, 96	100.8	16834.8	
16	Jul 19, 96	2194.2	19029	
17	Jul 22, 96	624.8	19653.8	
18	Jul 23, 96	2464.8	22118.6	
19	Jul 24, 96	724.5	22843.1	
20	Jul 25, 96	1176	24019.1	
21	Jul 26, 96	364.8	24383.9	
22	Jul 29, 96	4031	28414.9	
23	Jul 30, 96	1101.2	29516.1	
24	Jul 31, 96	676	30192.1	
25	⊞ 8	26609.4	26609.4	
26	⊞ 9	27636	27636	
27	⊞ Q4	141861	141861	
28	⊞ 1997	658388.75	658388.75	
	◄ ◄ ► ►│ PowerPivot			

Figure 12-23 *Running total—breaking*

The result in the last column in Figure 12-24 is different from the previous example. This time, the total does not start again for August 1996. Also, some of the quarterly and monthly totals are different. You should find that the yearly totals are identical to the previous example (it's using TOTALYTD()).

▲	A	B	C	D	E
1		Sum of Sales Amount	Running 1	Running 2	
2	⊟1996	226298.5	226298.5	226298.5	
3	⊟Q3	84437.5	84437.5	84437.5	
4	⊞7	30192.1	30192.1	30192.1	
5	⊟8	26609.4	26609.4	56801.5	
6	Aug 01, 96	1424	1424	31616.1	
7	Aug 02, 96	1456	2880	33072.1	
8	Aug 05, 96	2142.4	5022.4	35214.5	
9	Aug 06, 96	538.6	5561	35753.1	
10	Aug 07, 96	307.2	5868.2	36060.3	
11	Aug 08, 96	420	6288.2	36480.3	
12	Aug 09, 96	1200.8	7489	37681.1	
13	Aug 12, 96	1488.8	8977.8	39169.9	
14	Aug 13, 96	468	9445.8	39637.9	
15	Aug 14, 96	699.7	10145.5	40337.6	
16	Aug 15, 96	155.4	10300.9	40493	
17	Aug 16, 96	1414.8	11715.7	41907.8	
18	Aug 19, 96	1452	13167.7	43359.8	
19	Aug 20, 96	2179.2	15346.9	45539	
20	Aug 21, 96	3016	18362.9	48555	
21	Aug 22, 96	924	19286.9	49479	
22	Aug 23, 96	89	19375.9	49568	
23	Aug 26, 96	479.4	19855.3	50047.4	
24	Aug 27, 96	2721.8	22577.1	52769.2	
25	Aug 28, 96	1296	23873.1	54065.2	
26	Aug 29, 96	848.7	24721.8	54913.9	
27	Aug 30, 96	1887.6	26609.4	56801.5	
28	⊞9	27636	27636	84437.5	
29	⊞Q4	141861	141861	226298.5	
30	⊞1997	658388.75	658388.75	658388.75	

⊪ ◂ ▸ ▹| PowerPivot ▓

Figure 12-24   *Running total—non-breaking*

Predefining Filters and Sets

One way to improve the end-user experience is to create filters and sets for them. A set
is an MDX term. A *set* is a defined list of values that you want to appear on Column
Labels and Row Labels. If you predefine filters and sets, the end user doesn't have to use
Report Filter or slicers or other methods to see the required results.

	A	B	C	D
1		Sum of Sales Amount	Davolio	
2	Beverages	286526.95	48832	
3	Condiments	113694.75	14033.85	
4	Confections	177099.1	30343.54	
5	Dairy Products	251330.5	38012.8	
6	Grains/Cereals	100726.8	9173.95	
7	Meat/Poultry	178188.8	16346.07	
8	Produce	105268.6	20454.45	
9	Seafood	141623.09	24947.05	
10	Grand Total	1354458.59	202143.71	

PowerPivot

Figure 12-25 *A predefined filter*

Predefined Filter

This predefined filter in this example is a measure. It's been added alongside Sales Amount. The predefined filter is showing the sales for Davolio. Its formula is:

```
=CALCULATE(SUM('Order Details'[Sales Amount]),
Employees[LastName]="Davolio")
```

You can see the results in Figure 12-25. Please note that there is no Report Filter nor slicer needed to set the filter context for the Employees table to Davolio.

Predefined Set

A predefined set functions pretty much like a table. It allows you to control which elements are visible to the end user in a pivot table. Some people simply call them sets or named sets. This is a new topic, so here are the step-by-step instructions:

1. Create a pivot table like the one in Figure 12-26. It's using Category from the Products table and Sales Amount from the Order Details table.
2. With the focus in the pivot table, click Fields, Items, & Sets in the Calculations group of the PivotTable Tools/Options ribbon. This opens the drop-down menu shown in Figure 12-27.
3. From this drop-down menu, choose Create Set Based on Row Items to open the New Set dialog. This dialog is shown in Figure 12-28. In this dialog, you can specify a name for your set and, optionally, a display folder. Without a display folder, the set will appear under Sets in the PowerPivot Field List—it looks like a regular table. With a display folder, the set will appear under a "table" with the folder name. You can accomplish quite a lot in the New Set dialog. For example, you can delete rows from the set. But here, we're going to edit the MDX behind the set.

Figure 12-26 *Simple pivot table*

4. Click Edit MDX, and click OK to see the MDX behind the rows in the pivot table. It's reproduced here for clarity, as well as being shown in Figure 12-29.

```
{
([Products].[Category].&[Beverages]),
([Products].[Category].&[Condiments]),
([Products].[Category].&[Confections]),
([Products].[Category].&[Dairy Products]),
([Products].[Category].&[Grains/Cereals]),
([Products].[Category].&[Meat/Poultry]),
([Products].[Category].&[Produce]),
([Products].[Category].&[Seafood]),
([Products].[Category].[All])
}
```

	Calculated Field...
	Calculated Item...
	Solve Order...
	List Formulas
	Create Set Based on Row Items...
	Create Set Based on Column Items...
	Manage Sets...

Figure 12-27 *Fields, Items, & Sets drop-down menu*

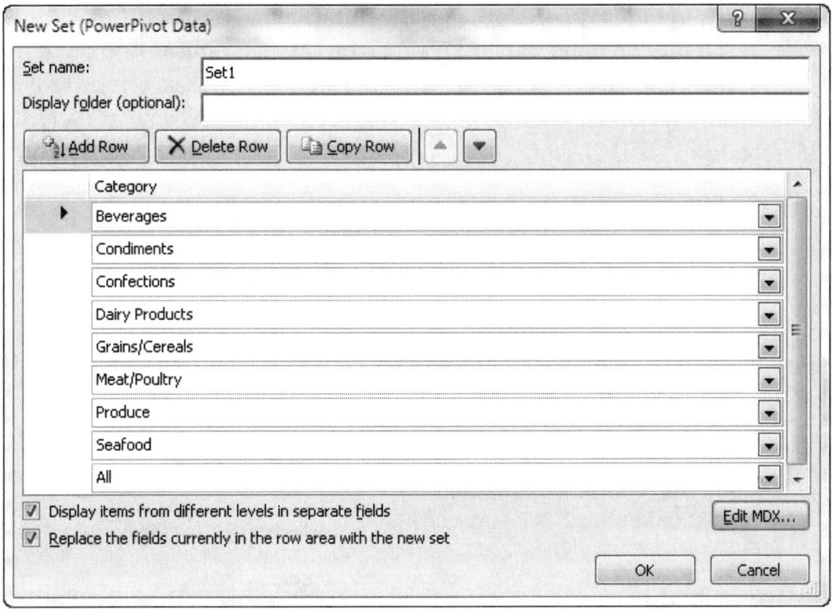

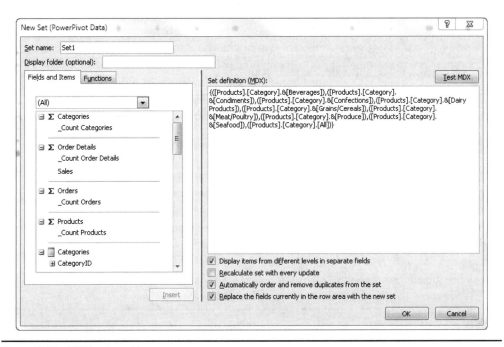

Figure 12-28 *New Set dialog*

Figure 12-29 *MDX for pivot table rows*

This is MDX, not DAX! MDX is a query language for SSAS cubes—it's talking directly to the hidden cube, called PowerPivot Data, behind PowerPivot. MDX is beyond the scope of this book—if you are interested, please refer to my book, *Practical MDX Queries for Microsoft SQL Server Analysis Services 2008* (McGraw-Hill/Professional, 2010).

5. Edit the MDX so it looks like the following:

```
Topcount
(
{
([Products].[Category].&[Beverages]),
([Products].[Category].&[Condiments]),
([Products].[Category].&[Confections]),
([Products].[Category].&[Dairy Products]),
([Products].[Category].&[Grains/Cereals]),
([Products].[Category].&[Meat/Poultry]),
([Products].[Category].&[Produce]),
([Products].[Category].&[Seafood])
},
3,
[Measures].[Sales]
)
```

There are a few changes in this MDX. ([Products].[Category].[All]) has been removed—this is going to remove Grand Total from the column in the pivot table. Before the first curly bracket, Topcount (has been added. After the last curly bracket, , 3, [Measures].[Sales]) has been added. This is assuming you have a measure called Sales (=SUM('Order Details'[Sales Amount])) that sums up Sales Amount.

6. You may want to click Test MDX before clicking OK. Your set is visible in the PowerPivot Field List, under Sets. Your pivot table should look like Figure 12-30.

The rows are showing the top three categories for sales. The third one, in my example, is Meat/Poultry.

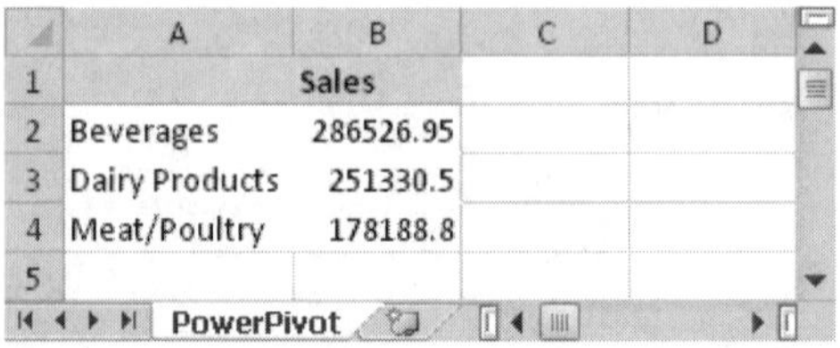

Figure 12-30 *A predefined set*

7. Remove Sales from Values and add Quantity from Order Details. You should still see the same three categories. However, these are the top three by sales, not by quantity. In fact, Meat/Poultry is only number seven by quantity. You can prove this by replacing the set in Row Labels with Category from Products again and sorting largest to smallest on quantity. This is really quite powerful stuff! You can display rows (or columns) with a particular measure, but with the criteria determined by a non-visible measure. A little MDX gives you lots of control. You *could* do this through the GUI (Row Labels, Value Filters, Top 10… and choose a different measure from the current measure)—however, it involves a bit of work every time. A set can simply be reused as and when required. The following example would be a little bit more difficult through the GUI—it shows the second and third top categories by sales, no matter which measure is being displayed:

```
Except
(
topcount
(
{
([Products].[Category].&[Beverages]),
([Products].[Category].&[Condiments]),
([Products].[Category].&[Confections]),
([Products].[Category].&[Dairy Products]),
([Products].[Category].&[Grains/Cereals]),
([Products].[Category].&[Meat/Poultry]),
([Products].[Category].&[Produce]),
([Products].[Category].&[Seafood])
},
3,
[Measures].[Sales]),
topcount
(
{
([Products].[Category].&[Beverages]),
([Products].[Category].&[Condiments]),
([Products].[Category].&[Confections]),
([Products].[Category].&[Dairy Products]),
([Products].[Category].&[Grains/Cereals]),
([Products].[Category].&[Meat/Poultry]),
([Products].[Category].&[Produce]),
([Products].[Category].&[Seafood])},
1,
[Measures].[Sales]
)
)
```

8. If you want to change a set, click Fields, Items, & Sets again. This time, choose Manage Sets from the drop-down menu. This opens the Set Manager dialog, as shown in Figure 12-31. Select your set and click Edit to see the Modify Set dialog. This dialog is the same as the New Set dialog shown earlier in Figure 12-28.

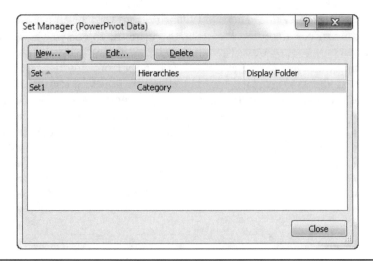

Figure 12-31 *Set Manager dialog*

PowerPivot Without Pivot Table Data

So far, this book has used pivot tables (and occasionally pivot charts) to display data from the PowerPivot model. However, you don't *have* to use pivot reports to display data. This section shows how to visualize PowerPivot model data without doing so in a pivot table. There are a couple of reasons why you might want to do this. One, you want to create your own custom front end in an Excel worksheet. Two, you might want to manipulate the data further with functions from Excel's formidable arsenal of functions. There are many ways to access PowerPivot data without a pivot table. You could use VBA in Excel, or, perhaps, create an SSRS report on a PowerPivot model published to SharePoint. In this section, two alternative approaches are considered. One exploits the Excel GETPIVOTDATA() function, and the other uses the Excel CUBE() family of functions.

GETPIVOTDATA()

Maybe this one is cheating slightly. There is still a pivot table, except it might be on a separate worksheet—which, optionally, you can hide. There is an Excel function called GETPIVOTDATA(). This function extracts data from a pivot table. You place the function in a cell that is away from the pivot table, or, better, on a separate worksheet. Fortunately, this function is self-generating. From a cell, type = in the Excel formula bar, then click on a value in the data area of a pivot table, then press ENTER. The GETPIVOTDATA() syntax to reference the data in the pivot table is generated. Here's an example:

```
=GETPIVOTDATA("[Measures].[Sum of Quantity]",$A$1,
"[Products].[Category]","[Products].[Category].&[Beverages]")
```

The first parameter is a reference to the measure you wish to return. The second parameter locates the pivot table you wish to reference. Then you can have any number of parameters that provide the coordinates for the data. Here, it's going to show the sales for Beverages.

If you want to write this function by hand, the syntax to reference a pivot table on a different worksheet is slightly different. Following is the same example, but it's referencing a pivot table in Sheet2 (please note the addition of `Sheet2!`):

```
=GETPIVOTDATA("[Measures].[Sum of Quantity]",Sheet2!$A$1,
"[Products].[Category]","[Products].[Category].&[Beverages]")
```

You can use `GETPIVOTDATA()` to calculate BI answers that are not so easy through the pivot table GUI or DAX. For example, you might want to show the sales of two products from two separate product categories as a percentage of the two product categories combined.

Should `GETPIVOTDATA()` not self-generate, it may be turned off. To check this, click File | Options | Formulas and look at the setting for Use GetPivotData functions for PivotTable references. Alternatively, check the setting for Generate GetPivotData in the Options drop-down menu in the PivotTable group of the PivotTable Tools/Options ribbon.

CUBE() Functions

This time, the example uses the Excel `CUBE()` functions. If these are new to you, here are the step-by-step instructions:

1. Add a new pivot table to an existing worksheet and position it at $A$1. If you add it to a new worksheet it will be positioned at cell $B$3. Should you do the latter, *please adjust all cell references in these step-by-step instructions*—you will need to move every reference across by one column and down by two rows. Click in the empty pivot table to activate the PowerPivot Field List. Add Year to the Slicers Horizontal drop-zone, and Year again to the Report Filter drop-zone. Verify the Report Filter position as A9:B9—if not, change the reference to $B$9 that appears in step 6.

2. Click in cell C9 and enter the following formula:

    ```
    =CUBEMEMBER("PowerPivot Data","[Measures].[Sales]","Sales")
    ```

    This assumes you have a measure called Sales that sums the Sales Amount (`=SUM('Order Details'[Sales Amount])`). The first parameter is the connection to PowerPivot—you can check this name by going through PivotTable Tools/Options | Data | Change Data Source | Connection Properties. This opens the Connection Properties dialog. The connection name is at the top of this dialog. The full connection string is on the Definition tab. The second parameter of our formula is the measure to show, and the third parameter is a caption.

3. Click in cell A10. Enter the following formula:

    ```
    =CUBESET("PowerPivot Data","[Products].[Category].[All].Children",
    "Category")
    ```

    This is using MDX to create the children of the All member of Category (for example, Beverages). The third parameter is a caption. Further parameters, not shown here, allow you to specify a sort order and a measure to sort on. For a full discussion of the CUBE() functions, you are referred to Excel Help. To understand the CUBE() functions, it helps to have a little knowledge of MDX.

4. Click in cell A11 and enter the following formula:

    ```
    =IFERROR(CUBERANKEDMEMBER("PowerPivot Data",$A$10,ROW(A1)),"")
    ```

    This formula is going to retrieve the first product category, Beverages, from the set defined in cell A10. ROW(A1) returns 1, but you can't use 1, as this cell is going to be copied down and we want it to return the second category, then the third, and so on. Hard-coded numerals are, well, hard-coded. The IFERROR() function is to suppress nonexistent categories, if we copy too far down.

5. Copy cell A11 from A12 to about A20. You should see a total of eight categories (including Beverages). You may want to widen column A, to display the complete names of the categories.

6. Click in cell B11 and enter this formula:

    ```
    =IFERROR(CUBEVALUE("PowerPivot Data",$A11,$B$9,$C$9),"")
    ```

    This function is referencing Beverages (A11) and the report filter on Year (B9) and the Sales measure (C9). In other words, it's returning the Sales for Beverages for the current filter on Year. You may have to widen the column for the number to display in non-scientific format.

7. Copy B11 from B12 to about B20. Hopefully, you can see the sales for each category. Experiment with the Year filter. My result is shown in Figure 12-32.

8. Instead of a Report Filter on Year, you may prefer to use the Year slicer. It's also probably overkill to have Year in both a Report Filter and a slicer, as here. If you do reference the slicer, the formula for B11 might look like this:

    ```
    =IFERROR(CUBEVALUE("PowerPivot Data",$A11,Slicer_Year,$C$9),"")
    ```

    Please note the third parameter of CUBEVALUE() now references the slicer. To verify the name of a slicer, open the Slicer Settings dialog and check the Name to use in formulas entry. The slicer name is not enclosed in quotes. In addition, this example formula assumes that Excel column and row references are still valid. If you want to use a slicer, it's probably a good idea to add the slicer before

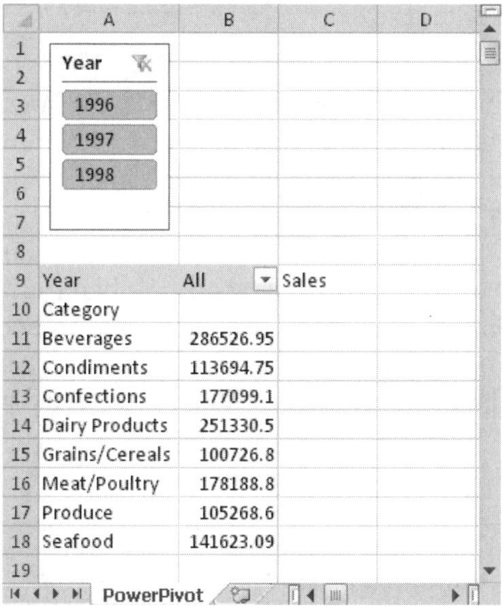

Figure 12-32   *PowerPivot data not in pivot table*

you start using cell references. Please note that adding or removing entries in the PowerPivot Field List drop-zones may invalidate any cell references you may have—or lose your CUBE() function formulas altogether. If you are interested, you can view the MDX behind CUBERANKEDMEMBER() and CUBEMEMBER(). To do so, view the Immediate Window in VBA (press ALT-FII), type the following command, and press ENTER:

```
? ActiveCell.MDX
```

Self-Joins

Self-joins are not supported in PowerPivot. Here is the SQL to denormalize the Northwind Employees table:

```
select E.EmployeeID, E.LastName, E.FirstName,
M.LastName + ', ' + M.FirstName as Manager from employees as E
left outer join employees as M
on E.ReportsTo = M.EmployeeID
```

Now you can analyze sales by employee by manager. This example is also in Appendix A about SQL queries for PowerPivot, but included here in case you miss it in Appendix A.

Data Mining

Appendix C is an introduction to writing DMX queries for PowerPivot. A DMX query allows you to return data from an SSAS data mining model or mining structure. There is another way to use data mining data without having to write DMX. If you download the Data Mining Add-in for Excel, you can generate data mining data in a worksheet with no writing of DMX yourself required. You can then import or link the worksheet into PowerPivot. You have to use the Table Tools/Analyze ribbon and not the Data Mining ribbon—the latter ribbon uses SSAS graphical interfaces and does not create data in a worksheet. The add-in is downloadable from www.sqlserverdatamining.com. As of this writing, only the Excel 2007 version was available, but it should work with Excel 2010 (32-bit only).

SSRS

Very early in this book, there was a discussion of importing data from an SSRS report into a PowerPivot model. You can also export from an SSRS report into a PowerPivot model—use the Export to Data Feed button, while viewing a report in Report Manager, to do so. You can even reverse the whole process and base an SSRS report on a PowerPivot model. To do this, you must first have published your PowerPivot for Excel model to PowerPivot for SharePoint.

SharePoint

If you want to share your PowerPivot for Excel models and pivot reports, you can publish from Excel to SharePoint. Go through File | Save & Send | Save to SharePoint to accomplish this. Naturally, for this to work you have to have SharePoint (2010 not 2007), and that means a 64-bit SharePoint server. In addition, you will need SQL Server 2008 R2 and SSAS installed in SharePoint-integrated mode. Further steps involve enabling PowerPivot for SharePoint and Excel Services within SharePoint administration. PowerPivot for SharePoint uses SSAS 2008 R2 in integrated mode to look after the data. Excel Services is responsible for rendering the workbook containing the PowerPivot pivot reports for thin clients, such as Internet Explorer.

Is It Really a Cube?

I hesitated before adding this topic—how to see PowerPivot as a cube. Please do not try this on an *important* PowerPivot model—if you change the cube design, you can easily invalidate the model! Copy an Excel workbook containing a PowerPivot model. Change the file extension from .xlsx to .zip. Unzip the zip file. In the folder called xl, open the folder called customData. In this last folder is a file called item1.data—this is the cube data behind PowerPivot. Copy item1.data to your SSAS backup directory and change the file extension from .data to .abf (Analysis Services backup file). You can now restore the backup to an SSAS database and cube—this only works with SSAS 2008 R2 in SharePoint-integrated mode (or in-memory VertiPaq mode).

How Old Is Nancy?

Many years ago, when people learned SQL for SQL Server with the Northwind database, there was a classic query. It was called "Nancy married the CEO." The idea was to practice the SQL Update statement and change Nancy's Title from Ms. to Mrs. and her LastName from Davolio to Fuller. If you look at the self-join on the Employees just above, Andrew Fuller has no manager—he's the boss!

This, possibly, will be the DAX equivalent of that SQL classic. It's called "How old is Nancy." Here's the DAX formula to work out age (on the Northwind Employees table):

```
=YEAR(TODAY())-YEAR(Employees[BirthDate])
```

It seems a shame to end a book on something that doesn't always give the correct result—that is, if you try it any time of the year apart from later on in December. Here's the one that does work (both results are shown in Figure 12-33):

```
=IF(MONTH(TODAY())>MONTH(Employees[BirthDate]),
YEAR(TODAY())-YEAR(Employees[BirthDate]),
IF(AND(MONTH(TODAY())=MONTH(Employees[BirthDate]),
DAY(TODAY())>=DAY(Employees[BirthDate])),
YEAR(TODAY())-YEAR(Employees[BirthDate]),
(YEAR(TODAY())-YEAR(Employees[BirthDate]))-1))
```

Can you find a more elegant way of calculating Nancy's age?

That's it, some nice DAX to finish. Well done if you got this far! Finito (oh, maybe apart from just three appendixes).

LastName	BirthDate	Age 1	Age 2
Davolio	Dec 08, 48	62	61
Fuller	Feb 19, 52	58	58
Leverling	Aug 30, 63	47	46
Peacock	Sep 19, 37	73	72
Buchanan	Mar 04, 55	55	55
Suyama	Jul 02, 63	47	46
King	May 29, 60	50	49
Callahan	Jan 09, 58	52	52
Dodsworth	Jan 27, 66	44	44

Figure 12-33 *How old is Nancy?*

Part IV

Appendixes: Queries for PowerPivot

Appendix A

SQL Queries
for PowerPivot

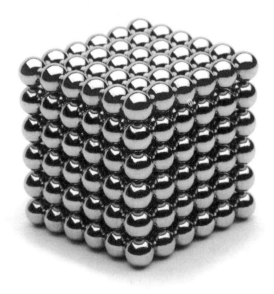

This is a short appendix. It's aimed at those readers who need a brief introduction to SQL, with some basic syntax examples. We also discuss the reasons for writing your own queries to import data into PowerPivot, rather than simply importing complete tables. A few query fundamentals are covered: filtering, sorting, grouping, and denormalizing data with joins and self-joins. There are also examples of using a stored procedure and writing SQL queries against Excel.

▶   **Key concepts**   SQL, selecting columns, calculated columns, filtering data, sorting data, grouping data, denormalizing data with joins and self-joins, stored procedures, querying Excel

Why Write SQL Queries?

Structured Query Language (SQL) is a standard language for extracting data from a relational database. When you connect to many of the relational data sources in PowerPivot, you have the option to write your own queries, rather than simply choosing table names. Among other sources, this would apply to SQL Server, Access, Oracle, and IBM DB2. All of these products support the SQL language in queries. The SQL language is generic and widely popular—and there is an agreed standard called ANSI SQL. Most vendors adhere very closely to this standard, although each dialect of SQL (for example, T-SQL in SQL Server or PL/SQL in Oracle) may depart slightly from that standard and incorporate many proprietary extensions. This appendix concentrates on writing SQL queries for SQL Server (that is, in T-SQL or Transact-SQL dialect). However, most of the syntax is generic and also relevant for other software, and you should be able to adapt the queries for your own database vendor (of course, you will have to change database, table, and column names!).

If you decide to write your own queries, you can reduce the amount of work you have to do in the PowerPivot window. This has a number of potential benefits. One, for calculated columns, you may be more familiar with doing this in SQL, rather than in DAX, and hence, find it easier. Two, you can use stored procedures to import the data. Three, you can handle self-joins, which are not supported in this release of PowerPivot. Four, the evaluation and recalculation of some calculated columns may be faster, if done in SQL rather than DAX. Five, you may be able to prepare data in a way that is not possible in PowerPivot (for example, outer joins or complex filters). Six, you may be able to access other external data sources from your queries that are not options in PowerPivot (for example, you can use DMX inside a T-SQL linked server query to extract data from a data mining model).

If you are interested in learning a bit more about SQL (in particular, T-SQL for SQL Server), refer to my book *Practical SQL Queries for Microsoft SQL Server 2008* published by McGraw-Hill (although nearly all of the SQL in the book is generic). Almost all of the examples here are taken from that book.

Where to Create and Test SQL Queries

You could enter the SQL directly in the PowerPivot Table Import Wizard. However, many software vendors provide elegant and powerful query editors. These often provide substantial benefits in entering, testing, and debugging your queries. This appendix concentrates on SQL Server, which has a client tool called SQL Server Management Studio (SSMS). This tool has color-coding, line numbering, word wrap, IntelliSense, context-sensitive help, debugging aids, drag-and-drop of object names, drag-and-drop of functions, metadata view of a database and its objects, and easy visualization of query results. So, maybe it's better to prepare your query in SSMS (or the query editor applicable to your database vendor) first. Once you are happy with the results, then it's a simple copy-and-paste into PowerPivot.

Where to Use SQL Queries in PowerPivot

If you are importing from SQL Server or Access, click From Database in the Get External Data group of the Home ribbon. You then choose either From SQL Server or From Access in the drop-down menu. If you wish to import from another relational source, click From Other Sources in the Get External Data group and choose the relevant source. All of these are entry points into the Table Import Wizard. After you set up connection information, you will see the Choose How to Import the Data dialog. The dialog is shown in Figure A-1. In this dialog, choose Write a Query That Will Specify the Data to Import and click Next. The next dialog is Specify a SQL Query. This dialog is shown in Figure A-2. In this dialog, type or copy and paste your SQL into the SQL Statement text box. There is also a Design button that will take you into a graphical query designer (SQL Server import only) that can generate some of the SQL for you to get you started. When your query is finished, click Validate to check the syntax, and then click Finish. The data retrieved by your query will be displayed in a new PowerPivot table.

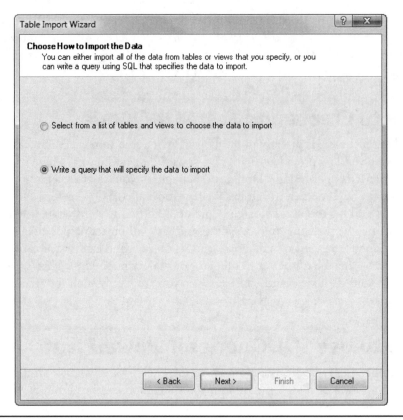

Figure A-1   *Choose How to Import the Data dialog*

If you get it wrong, you can alter the SQL retrospectively. You do so by clicking the Table Properties button in the Properties group of the Design ribbon. This opens the Edit Table Properties dialog, where you can amend your SQL statement.

Figure A-2   *Specify a SQL Query dialog*

SQL Examples

If you want to try these examples, you will need SQL Server 2008 or 2008 R2, and the AdventureWorksDW2008 relational database (available from www.codeplex.com). You should also be able to adapt many of the queries to work with SQL Server 2005 and the AdventureWorksDW relational database (also available from www.codeplex.com), or the new SQL Server 2008 R2 ContosoRetailDW sample database. One example (on self-joins) uses Northwind, so if you followed the practicals in Chapters 1 and 2, you can amend your PowerPivot model.

Figure A-3   *Specific columns*

Selecting Specific Columns

This is a simple column list (PowerPivot table result shown in Figure A-3):

```
select FirstName, LastName from DimCustomer
```

Using a T-SQL Function

Here, a simple function is used to manipulate data (PowerPivot table result shown in Figure A-4):

```
select Birthdate, datediff(yy,birthdate,GETDATE()) as Age
from DimCustomer
```

Unless you use an asterisk for all columns, every column must have a name. For example, the second column here would result in an error without the alias, Age. The appearance of the Birthdate column is governed by the setting in the Format drop-down on the Home ribbon.

Birthdate	Age	Add Column
15 February, 1968	42	
8 August, 1968	42	
18 January, 1968	42	
6 August, 1968	42	
9 May, 1968	42	
15 May, 1968	42	
22 June, 1968	42	
5 February, 1968	42	
25 January, 1968	42	

Figure A-4   *A SQL calculated column*

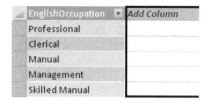

Figure A-5   *Distinct values*

Suppressing Duplicates

This query eliminates duplicate values (PowerPivot table result shown in Figure A-5):

```
select distinct EnglishOccupation from DimCustomer
```

Creating Buckets

This technique is very useful when you want to reduce a large range of values into a small range of bucket values. Some people call this discretization, or even bucketization! The PowerPivot table result is shown in Figure A-6.

```
select
LastName,
case
when yearlyincome <= 30000 then 'Low'
when yearlyincome <= 70000 then 'Medium'
else 'High'
end
as [Income Group]
from DimCustomer
```

LastName	Income Group	Add Column
Diaz	Medium	
Diaz	Medium	
Diaz	Medium	
Hernandez	Medium	
Hernandez	Medium	

Figure A-6   *Buckets of data*

LastName	▾	FirstName	▾	EnglishEducation	▾	EnglishOccupation
Yang		Jon		Bachelors		Professional
Huang		Eugene		Bachelors		Professional
Torres		Ruben		Bachelors		Professional
Zhu		Christy		Bachelors		Professional
Johnson		Elizabeth		Bachelors		Professional

Figure A-7   *Filtering data*

Implementing a Filter

This is an example of using the classic SQL Where clause to filter data (PowerPivot table result shown in Figure A-7):

```
select FirstName, LastName, EnglishEducation, EnglishOccupation
from DimCustomer
where englisheducation not in
('partial college','high school','graduate degree')
```

A More Complex Filter

Here is another filtering query (PowerPivot table result shown in Figure A-8):

```
select FirstName, LastName, EnglishEducation, EnglishOccupation
from DimCustomer
where (englisheducation = 'Partial College' and
englishoccupation = 'Clerical') or englishoccupation = 'Manual'
```

LastName	▾	FirstName	▾	EnglishEducation	▾	EnglishOccupation
Rai		Clarence		Partial College		Clerical
Sai		Harold		Partial College		Clerical
Zhao		Jessie		Partial College		Clerical
Jimenez		Jill		Partial College		Clerical
Moreno		Jimmy		Partial College		Clerical

Figure A-8   *Another filtering example*

LastName	FirstName	Add Column
Li	Tiffany	
Li	Todd	
Li	Jose	
Li	Jamie	
Li	Amy	
Li	Marshall	

Figure A-9 *Wildcard search*

Using Wildcards

In this query, a wildcard has been used to filter the data (PowerPivot table result shown in Figure A-9):

```
select FirstName, LastName from DimCustomer
where LastName like 'Li%'
```

Sorting Records

Here, you are retrieving the top ten percent by income (PowerPivot table result shown in Figure A-10):

```
select top 10 percent LastName, FirstName, YearlyIncome from DimCustomer
order by YearlyIncome desc
```

LastName	FirstName	YearlyIncome	Add Column
Liang	Randy	130000	
Ashe	Jimmy	130000	
Ramos	Lance	130000	
Blanco	Gina	130000	
Luo	Kara	130000	
Smith	Jasmine	130000	

Figure A-10 *Top 10 percent earners*

EnglishProductName ▼	EnglishProductSubcategoryName ▼	Add Column
HL Road Frame - Black, 58	Road Frames	
HL Road Frame - Red, 58	Road Frames	
HL Road Frame - Red, 62	Road Frames	
HL Road Frame - Red, 62	Road Frames	
HL Road Frame - Red, 62	Road Frames	
HL Road Frame - Red, 44	Road Frames	
HL Road Frame - Red, 44	Road Frames	

Figure A-11 *Denormalized data*

Denormalizing Data

As an alternative to the DAX RELATED() function, you can denormalize your data before it reaches PowerPivot with a SQL Inner Join (PowerPivot table result shown in Figure A-11):

```
select EnglishProductName, EnglishProductSubcategoryName
from DimProduct inner join DimProductSubcategory
on DimProduct.ProductSubcategoryKey =
DimProductSubcategory.ProductSubcategoryKey
```

Self-Join

The Northwind Employees table is joined to itself. This is called a *self-join*, and this type of join is not supported in PowerPivot. If you wanted to browse employee sales by manager in a pivot table, you have to join the table to itself in a SQL query. Here's the syntax for joining the Employees table to itself (PowerPivot table result shown in Figure A-12):

```
select E.EmployeeID, E.LastName, E.FirstName,
M.LastName + ', ' + M.FirstName as Manager from employees as E
left outer join employees as M
on E.ReportsTo = M.EmployeeID
```

Please note this is a left outer join, not an inner join. An inner join would not return Andrew Fuller as an employee—because he is the CEO of Northwind and has no manager! You may want to include him, as he has sales in the Orders table. This query is against the Northwind and not the AdventureWorksDW2008 database.

EmployeeID	LastName	FirstName	Manager	Add Column
1	Davolio	Nancy	Fuller, Andrew	
2	Fuller	Andrew		
3	Leverling	Janet	Fuller, Andrew	
4	Peacock	Margaret	Fuller, Andrew	
5	Buchanan	Steven	Fuller, Andrew	
6	Suyama	Michael	Buchanan, Steven	
7	King	Robert	Buchanan, Steven	
8	Callahan	Laura	Fuller, Andrew	
9	Dodsworth	Anne	Buchanan, Steven	

Figure A-12 *Self-join data*

Grouping Data

You may want to group imported data, and perhaps use SQL aggregate functions, such as `SUM()`, rather than the DAX equivalents. Following is an example using the Group By clause (PowerPivot table result shown in Figure A-13):

```
select ProductKey, OrderDateKey, sum(OrderQuantity) As SumOrderQuantity
from FactInternetSales group by ProductKey, OrderDateKey
```

Stored Procedure

Often, you may not have permissions to query tables directly. Perhaps your SQL Server DBA only allows access to data through stored procedures—if that is so, you can't write queries against the tables, nor can you import the tables directly. Here's some sample

ProductKey	OrderDateKey	SumOrderQuantity	Add Column
477	20030814	12	
477	20031212	16	
477	20040515	14	
477	20040406	13	
477	20040329	9	
477	20040120	15	
477	20030917	13	
477	20031026	12	

Figure A-13 *Grouping data*

Firstname	Lastname	EnglishEducation	EnglishOccupation
Grace	Butler	Partial College	Professional
Caleb	Carter	Partial College	Professional
Ryan	Brown	Partial College	Professional
Tamara	Liang	Partial College	Professional
Trevor	Bryant	Partial College	Professional
Dalton	Perez	Partial College	Professional
Blake	Flores	Partial College	Professional
Danielle	Cox	Partial College	Professional

Figure A-14 *Stored procedure result data*

code to create a parameterized stored procedure (sometimes stored procedures can return data faster than a normal Select statement):

```
create procedure spGetCustomersByEducation
@education nvarchar(40)
as
begin
set nocount on
select Firstname, Lastname, EnglishEducation, EnglishOccupation
from DimCustomer
where englisheducation = @education
end
```

Whether you create your own stored procedures, or use those created by others, you need to call the stored procedure to return the data. Here's an example that returns data from the stored procedure created in the preceding code (PowerPivot table result shown in Figure A-14):

```
exec spGetCustomersByEducation @Education = 'Partial College'
```

SQL Queries for Excel

You may be surprised to learn that you can write SQL queries against Excel worksheets! You might also ask why anyone should want to do so, when PowerPivot supports imports from Excel worksheets directly. The answer may be that you want to include complex filters and/or join the Excel data to a table from another source. T-SQL supports the concept of a linked server—the linked server does not have to be SQL Server, yet you can query it from T-SQL. Here is some sample code to set up Excel as a linked server using T-SQL (please note, this is no longer generic SQL and may not work in other SQL dialects):

```
exec sp_addLinkedServer @server='MyExcel',
@srvproduct='ACE 12.0',
@provider='Microsoft.ACE.OLEDB.12.0',
-- this is a comment
-- in the next line, specify a valid path to an Excel workbook
@datasrc='C:\users\art\documents\book1.xlsx',
@provstr='Excel 12.0;HDR=No'
```

There are three occurrences of "12.0" in the code. The number you specify may be different. You can establish the correct number (it's actually the Office version number) by looking at linked server providers in Object Explorer. After setting up the linked server, you can then query the Excel workbook using SQL:

```
select * from myexcel...sheet1$
```

If you are tempted to try this, there are a few things to consider. First, your SQL Server DBA may disapprove of permanent linked servers (there are alternatives, such as Openrowset). Second, you'll need some sensible data in the workbook—it's helpful to have column headers in the first row (if you do, replace HDR=No with HDR=Yes in the above syntax). Third, there are three dots between the linked server name and the worksheet name in the preceding syntax (for SQL Server users, Excel does not have a concept of a database name, nor a schema name—the dots are placeholders). Fourth, instead of the worksheet name (sheet1$), you can use the name of an Excel named range—it's also possible to query cells and unnamed ranges.

Of course, there is rather more to SQL than this! This appendix is designed to help readers who are not familiar with SQL get started with writing their own SQL queries for PowerPivot.

Appendix B

MDX Queries for PowerPivot

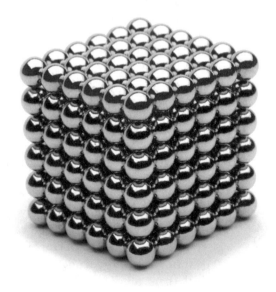

MultiDimensional eXpressions (MDX) is a very powerful query language for extracting data from cubes. While PowerPivot can generate sophisticated MDX for you, you may want the total control that writing your own MDX gives you. You can use MDX to import from either an SSAS cube or a PowerPivot model that has been published to PowerPivot for SharePoint. This appendix demonstrates some of the fundamentals of MDX. It also shows how best to adapt your MDX for PowerPivot.

▶ **Key concepts**   Cube dimensions and measures, `Crossjoin()` function, navigating hierarchies, ranges, sorting, filtering, calculated measures, key performance indicators (KPIs), natural user hierarchies, attribute hierarchies

Why Write MDX Queries?

MDX is a standard language for extracting data from a multidimensional database. Specifically, it is the language used to query cubes in an SSAS database or to extract data from a PowerPivot model that has been published to PowerPivot for SharePoint. Both are supported from PowerPivot for Excel. Hyperion Essbase and SAP BW cubes also use MDX, but these are not directly supported by PowerPivot.

Writing your own MDX gives you more power and flexibility. There is a graphical query designer for MDX in PowerPivot—it's very good, but sometimes you need just that little extra control. In addition, you can avail yourself of the extra power of the SSMS MDX query editor. There is one small proviso—sometimes, the MDX you write in SSMS is better expressed in a slightly different way for PowerPivot. This appendix contains a couple of examples that show this.

If you are interested in learning a bit more about MDX (in particular, MDX for SQL Server Analysis Services), you are referred to my book *Practical MDX Queries for Microsoft SQL Server Analysis Services 2008* (McGraw-Hill/Professional, 2010). Most of the examples in this appendix are adapted from that book—the rewritten examples (rewritten to provide better data specifically for PowerPivot) are new. All of the examples are against an SSAS cube, not a PowerPivot model published to SharePoint, although the principles are the same.

Where to Create and Test MDX Queries

MDX is a standard language for querying cubes. The MDX discussed here is for SSAS. The MDX used by other vendors of multidimensional databases may differ in minor ways. In PowerPivot, you can only use MDX directly against SSAS cubes or PowerPivot models on SharePoint.

It's probably a good idea to write and test your MDX queries in SSMS. If they don't work there, they are not going to work in PowerPivot.

Where to Use MDX Queries in PowerPivot

You start from the Home ribbon in PowerPivot. Click From Database in the Get External Data group on the ribbon. In the resulting drop-down, choose From Analysis Services or PowerPivot. You'll need to set up the connection to an SSAS server and a database (although you could alternatively provide the URL to a PowerPivot workbook in SharePoint) before clicking Next. The next dialog is entitled Specify a MDX Query. This dialog is shown in Figure B-1. Within this dialog, type or paste your MDX (it's a good idea to copy it from SSMS) into the MDX Statement text box. Click Validate, and then click Finish.

Figure B-1   *Specify a MDX Query dialog*

MDX Examples

If you want to try these examples, you will need SQL Server Analysis Services 2008 or 2008 R2, and the Adventure Works DW 2008 multidimensional database (available from www.codeplex.com), which contains the Adventure Works cube used in the following queries. You should also be able to adapt many of the queries to work with SQL Server Analysis Services 2005 and the Adventure Works DW multidimensional database (also available from www.codeplex.com). The MDX syntax is simply given, with nothing much by way of explanation. A full analysis of MDX is beyond the scope of this book.

A Basic MDX Query

```
select [Date].[Calendar].[Calendar Year] on columns
from [Adventure Works]
select {[Date].[Calendar].[Calendar Year].members} on columns
from [Adventure Works]
```

In this example, you have two versions of the same query. The first is informal syntax, and the second is more formal, which many consider to be better practice. There is no measure in this query. Therefore, it uses the default measure for the cube, Reseller Sales Amount. The resulting cellset looks great in SSMS, but not in PowerPivot. The years are returned as column headers, not as part of the data in the PowerPivot table. It would be nice to see the years in the rows, not as column headers. Column headers are metadata, and rows are data. This is a common problem when importing via an MDX query. The solution is not to place non-measure dimension members on the Columns axis of the MDX query (see the next query). The resulting table is shown in Figure B-2.

Having non-measure dimensions on the Columns axis is not allowed in the MDX graphical query designer in PowerPivot. There is a Design button in the Specify a MDX Query dialog. This opens the graphical designer, where you can click on the last button on the toolbar (Design Mode) to switch to text mode. If you paste in this query, and try to execute the query, you receive an error message indicating that the designer

DateCalendarCalendar Year2001	DateCalendarCalendar Year2002	DateCalendarCalendar Year2003
8065435.3053	24144429.654	32202669.4252

Figure B-2 *PowerPivot table*

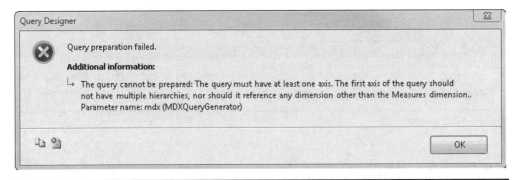

Figure B-3   *Error message*

only supports measures on columns. The error message is shown in Figure B-3. It's probably better not to do this, unless you decide not to use the graphical query designer! But the error is a sensible one—non-measure dimensions on columns don't look good in PowerPivot, and they are of limited use in a pivot table. The next query is much better.

A Basic MDX Query Rewritten to Give Better Results

```
select {[Measures].[Reseller Sales Amount]} on columns,
{[Date].[Calendar].[Calendar Year].members} on rows
from [Adventure Works]
```

This is a far nicer query. It looks better as a PowerPivot table and will make a subsequent pivot table more meaningful. The non-measure dimension (Date) has been placed on the Rows axis. The default measure is made explicit and placed on the Columns axis. The resulting table is shown in Figure B-4.

DateCalendarCalendar Year	MeasuresReseller Sales Amount	Add Column
CY 2001	8065435.3053	
CY 2002	24144429.654	
CY 2003	32202669.4252	
CY 2004	16038062.5978	
CY 2006		

Figure B-4   *PowerPivot table*

ProductProduct CategoriesCategory	DateCalendarCalendar Year2001	DateCalendarCalendar Year2002
Accessories	20235.3646	92735.3534
Bikes	7395348.6266	19956014.6741
Clothing	34376.3353	485587.1546
Components	615474.9788	3610092.4719

Figure B-5   *PowerPivot table*

Adding Another Dimension

```
select { [Date].[Calendar].[Calendar Year].members} on columns,
{[Product].[Product Categories].[Category].members} on rows
from [Adventure Works]
```

This query sees the addition of a second non-measure dimension (Product). Once again, it doesn't look satisfactory as a PowerPivot table. The resulting table is shown in Figure B-5.

Adding Another Dimension Rewritten to Give Better Results

```
select {[Measures].[Reseller Sales Amount]} on columns,
{crossjoin( {[Date].[Calendar].[Calendar Year].members},
{[Product].[Product Categories].[Category].members} )} on rows
from [Adventure Works]
```

Here we have the same query but rewritten to produce sensible results for PowerPivot. When you have more than one non-measure dimension, it's a good idea to place them both on the Rows axis and only have a measure or measures on the Columns axis. To place two dimensions on the same axis, you can use the MDX Crossjoin() function as here. The resulting table is shown in Figure B-6. You may see an alternative syntax that uses the asterisk (*) or multiplication symbol, instead of explicitly using the Crossjoin() function. Indeed, this is the syntax generated by the graphical query designer.

Crossjoin() Query

```
Select {[Measures].[Internet Sales Amount],
[Measures].[Reseller Sales Amount]} on columns,
{crossjoin( {[Date].[Calendar].[Calendar Year].members},
{[Date].[Month of Year].[Month of Year].members} )} on rows
from [Adventure Works]
```

DateCalendarCalendar Year	ProductProduct CategoriesCategory	MeasuresReseller Sales Amount
CY 2001	Accessories	20235.3646
CY 2001	Bikes	7395348.6266
CY 2001	Clothing	34376.3353
CY 2001	Components	615474.9788
CY 2002	Accessories	92735.3534
CY 2002	Bikes	19956014.6741
CY 2002	Clothing	485587.1546
CY 2002	Components	3610092.4719

Figure B-6   *PowerPivot table*

You can even have different attributes from the same dimension in a Crossjoin(). There is one proviso; they must be from different hierarchies in the dimension—here the Calendar (for SSAS veterans, it's a user hierarchy) and the Month of Year (this is an attribute hierarchy) hierarchies are used. The resulting table is shown in Figure B-7.

More Complex Crossjoin() Query

```
select
{crossjoin( {[Sales Territory].[Sales Territory].[Country].members},
{crossjoin( {[Product].[Product Categories].[Category].members},
{[Measures].[Internet Order Count],[Measures].[Reseller Order Count]} )} )}
on columns,
{crossjoin( {[Date].[Calendar].[Calendar Year].members},
{[Date].[Month of Year].[Month of Year].members} )} on rows
from [Adventure Works]
```

DateCalendarCalendar Year	DateMonth of YearMonth of Year	MeasuresInternet Sales Amount	MeasuresReseller Sales Amount
CY 2001	July	473388.163	489328.5787
CY 2001	August	506191.6912	1538408.3122
CY 2001	September	473943.0312	1165897.0778
CY 2001	October	513329.474	844720.9963
CY 2001	November	543993.4058	2324135.7975
CY 2001	December	755527.8914	1702944.5428
CY 2002	January	596746.5568	713116.6943
CY 2002	February	550816.694	1900788.9304

Figure B-7   *PowerPivot table*

DateCalendarCalendar Year	DateMonth of YearMonth of Year	Sales TerritorySales TerritoryCountryFranceProductProduct CategoriesCategory4Measures:Internet Order	Sale
CY 2004	February	155	3
CY 2004	March	162	3
CY 2004	April	163	2
CY 2004	May	156	7
CY 2004	June	161	3
CY 2004	July	68	
CY 2004	August		
CY 2006	November		

Figure B-8 *PowerPivot table*

This example is getting more sophisticated (and complex). It involves three dimensions, four dimension hierarchies, and two measures. The resulting table is shown in Figure B-8.

More Complex Crossjoin() Query Rewritten to Give Better Results

```
Select {[Measures].[Internet Order Count],
[Measures].[Reseller Order Count]}
on columns,
{crossjoin({[Sales Territory].[Sales Territory].[Country].members},
{crossjoin({[Product].[Product Categories].[Category].members},
{crossjoin({[Date].[Calendar].[Calendar Year].members},
{[Date].[Month of Year].[Month of Year].members})} )} )}
on rows
from [Adventure Works]
```

Hopefully, this is a big improvement. You may have to scroll to see measures with values. Please note that only measures appear on the Columns axis. The Rows axis has a `Crossjoin()` within a `Crossjoin()` within a `Crossjoin()`. The resulting table is shown in Figure B-9.

Sales TerritorySales TerritoryGroup	Sales TerritorySales TerritoryCountry	ProductProduct CategoriesCategory
Europe	United Kingdom	Bikes
Europe	United Kingdom	Bikes
Europe	United Kingdom	Bikes
Europe	United Kingdom	Bikes
Europe	United Kingdom	Clothing
Europe	United Kingdom	Clothing
Europe	United Kingdom	Clothing
Europe	United Kingdom	Clothing

Figure B-9 *PowerPivot table*

CustomerCustomer GeographyCountry	CustomerCustomer GeographyState-Province	CustomerCustomer Geogra
France	Charente-Maritime	Saint Ouen
France	Essonne	Les Ulis
France	Essonne	Morangis
France	Essonne	Verrieres Le Buisson
France	Garonne (Haute)	Colomiers
France	Gers	Aujan Mournede
France	Hauts de Seine	Boulogne-Billancourt
France	Hauts de Seine	Colombes

Figure B-10 *PowerPivot table*

A Navigation Query

```
select {[Measures].[Internet Sales Amount]} on columns,
{descendants([Customer].[Customer Geography].[Country].[France],
[Customer].[Customer Geography].[City])}
on rows
from [Adventure Works]
```

The navigation functions within MDX are very useful. PowerPivot has converted a `Descendants() self` to a `Descendants() self_and_before` when flattening the result set. Here's an example using `Descendants()`. The resulting table is shown in Figure B-10.

A Range Query

```
select {[Date].[Calendar].[Calendar Quarter].[Q1 CY 2003]:
[Date].[Calendar].[Calendar Quarter].[Q3 CY 2003]} on columns,
{[Measures].[Reseller Sales Amount]} on rows
from [Adventure Works]
```

This time, it's a range query with the colon (:) operator. The results may not be to your liking. The resulting table is shown in Figure B-11. Please note that the range operator requires that both members belong to the same attribute hierarchy or to the same level of a user hierarchy.

MeasuresMeasuresLevel	DateCalendarCalendar Quarter20031	DateCalendarCalendar Quarter20032
Reseller Sales Amount	5266343.505	6733903.8214

Figure B-11 *PowerPivot table*

DateCalendarCalendar Year	DateCalendarCalendar Semester	DateCalendarCalendar Quarter	MeasuresReseller Sales Amount
CY 2003	H1 CY 2003	Q1 CY 2003	5266343.505
CY 2003	H1 CY 2003	Q2 CY 2003	6733903.8214
CY 2003	H2 CY 2003	Q3 CY 2003	10926196.0872

Figure B-12 *PowerPivot table*

A Range Query Rewritten to Give Better Results

```
select {[Measures].[Reseller Sales Amount]} on columns,
{[Date].[Calendar].[Calendar Quarter].[Q1 CY 2003]:
[Date].[Calendar].[Calendar Quarter].[Q3 CY 2003]} on rows
from [Adventure Works]
```

Let's have another go at the range query. This should look nicer. If you are familiar with MDX, PowerPivot adds a lovely twist. It also brings back the user hierarchy above the quarters as it flattens the result set—you won't see this in SSMS. The resulting table is shown in Figure B-12.

Attribute or User Hierarchies?

```
select {[Measures].[Reseller Sales Amount]} on columns,
{[Date].[Calendar Quarter].[Calendar Quarter].[Q1 CY 2003]:
[Date].[Calendar Quarter].[Calendar Quarter].[Q3 CY 2003]} on rows
from [Adventure Works]
```

The previous query returned the user hierarchy above the quarter. If you don't want the hierarchy, then you can use an attribute hierarchy, as here. The resulting table is shown in Figure B-13.

DateCalendar QuarterCalendar Quarter	MeasuresReseller Sales Amount	Add Column
Q1 CY 2003	5266343.505	
Q2 CY 2003	6733903.8214	
Q3 CY 2003	10926196.0872	

Figure B-13 *PowerPivot table*

ProductProduct CategoriesCategory	ProductProduct CategoriesSubcategory	MeasuresInternet Sales Amount
Bikes	Road Bikes	14520584.0363
Bikes	Mountain Bikes	9952759.5644
Bikes	Touring Bikes	3844801.05

Figure B-14 *PowerPivot table*

Sorting Results on a User Hierarchy

```
Select {[Measures].[Internet Sales Amount]} on columns,
{order({[Product].[Product Categories].[Subcategory].members},
[Measures].[Internet Sales Amount],bdesc)} on rows
from [Adventure Works]
```

This is a classic sort that breaks the Product Categories hierarchy—the subcategories are sorted regardless of the category to which they belong. Note that it returns the hierarchy above the subcategory. The resulting table is shown in Figure B-14.

Sorting Results on an Attribute Hierarchy

```
select {[Measures].[Internet Sales Amount]} on columns,
{order( {[Product].[Subcategory].[Subcategory].members},
[Measures].[Internet Sales Amount],bdesc)} on rows
from [Adventure Works]
```

If you don't want to return the hierarchy above the subcategory, use an attribute hierarchy, rather than a user hierarchy, as there's no user hierarchy to break, then you can use `desc` rather than `bdesc` for the `Order()` function. The resulting table is shown in Figure B-15.

ProductSubcategorySubcategory	MeasuresInternet Sales Amount	*Add Column*
Road Bikes	14520584.0363	
Mountain Bikes	9952759.5644	
Touring Bikes	3844801.05	
Tires and Tubes	245529.32	
Helmets	225335.6	
Jerseys	172950.68	
Shorts	71319.81	
Bottles and Cages	56798.19	

Figure B-15 *PowerPivot table*

ProductProduct CategoriesCategory	MeasuresInternet Sales Amount	MeasuresReseller Sales Amount
Bikes	28318144.6507	66302381.557
Clothing	339772.61	1777840.8391
Components		11799076.6584

Figure B-16 *PowerPivot table*

Filtering Results

```
select {[Measures].[Internet Sales Amount],
[Measures].[Reseller Sales Amount]} on columns,
{filter({[Product].[Product Categories].[Category].members},
[Measures].[Internet Sales Amount] > 750000 or
[Measures].[Internet Sales Amount] < 500000)} on rows
from [Adventure Works]
```

The `Filter()` function in MDX operates like a Where clause in SQL. The resulting table is shown in Figure B-16.

A Calculated Measure

```
with member [Measures].[Customer Sales] as
[Measures].[Internet Sales Amount]
member [Measures].[Retailer Sales] as
[Measures].[Reseller Sales Amount]
member [Measures].[Total Sales] as
[Measures].[Internet Sales Amount] + [Measures].[Reseller Sales Amount]
select {[Measures].[Customer Sales],[Measures].[Retailer Sales],
[Measures].[Total Sales]} on columns,
{[Date].[Calendar].[Calendar Year].members} on rows
from [Adventure Works]
```

Here you are extending the cube by adding an ad-hoc measure on the fly. Please remember that a lot of this work can be done graphically—do you recall the Calculated Member Builder dialog from much earlier in the book? The resulting table is shown in Figure B-17.

DateCalendarCalendar Year	MeasuresCustomer Sales	MeasuresRetailer Sales	MeasuresTotal Sales
CY 2001	3266373.6566	8065435.3053	11331808.9619
CY 2002	6530343.5264	24144429.654	30674773.1804
CY 2003	9791060.2977	32202669.4252	41993729.7229

Figure B-17 *PowerPivot table*

KPI Query

```
with member [Measures].[Actual] as
KPIValue("Product Gross Profit Margin"),format_string = "Percent"
member [Measures].[Target] as
KPIGoal("Product Gross Profit Margin"),format_string="Percent"
member [Measures].[Status] as
KPIStatus("Product Gross Profit Margin")
member [Measures].[Trend] as
KPITrend("Product Gross Profit Margin")
select {crossjoin({[Date].[Fiscal].[Fiscal Year].[FY 2003],
[Date].[Fiscal].[Fiscal Year].[FY 2004]},{[Measures].[Actual],
[Measures].[Target],[Measures].[Status],[Measures].[Trend]})}
on columns,
{[Product].[Product Categories].[Category].members} on rows
from [Adventure Works]
```

This is how you pull key performance indicators (KPIs) out of the SSAS cube. It's valid MDX but doesn't look that good in a PowerPivot table. It's the same problem as before, with the non-measure dimensions on the Columns axis. The resulting table is shown in Figure B-18.

KPI Query Rewritten to Give Better Results

```
with member [Measures].[Actual] as
KPIValue("Product Gross Profit Margin"),format_string = "Percent"
member [Measures].[Target] as
KPIGoal("Product Gross Profit Margin"),format_string="Percent"
member [Measures].[Status] as
KPIStatus("Product Gross Profit Margin")
member [Measures].[Trend] as
KPITrend("Product Gross Profit Margin")
select {[Measures].[Actual],
[Measures].[Target],[Measures].[Status],[Measures].[Trend]}
```

ProductProduct CategoriesCategory	DateFiscalFiscal Year2003MeasuresActual	DateFiscalFiscal Year2003MeasuresTarget
Accessories	0.292292296163294	0.40000000000000002
Bikes	0.097994400280492	0.12
Clothing	0.2346210797159653	0.20000000000000001

Figure B-18 *PowerPivot table*

DateFiscalFiscal Year ▼	ProductProduct CategoriesCategory ▼	MeasuresActual ▼	MeasuresTarget ▼	MeasuresStatus ▼
FY 2003	Accessories	0.292292296163294	0.40000000000000...	-1
FY 2003	Bikes	0.097994400280492	0.12	0
FY 2003	Clothing	0.2346210797159653	0.20000000000000...	1
FY 2003	Components	0.12398838919714...	0.10000000000000...	1
FY 2004	Accessories	0.52188867561894...	0.40000000000000...	1
FY 2004	Bikes	0.11353395802735...	0.12	1

Figure B-19   *PowerPivot table*

```
on columns,
{crossjoin({[Date].[Fiscal].[Fiscal Year].[FY 2003],
[Date].[Fiscal].[Fiscal Year].[FY 2004]},
{[Product].[Product Categories].[Category].members})}
on rows
from [Adventure Works]
```

This is our last query in this appendix. It fixes the previous query. The resulting table is shown in Figure B-19.

MDX is quite a powerful language! We have seen only a few queries in this appendix. However, there may be just enough to get you started writing your own MDX queries.

Appendix C

DMX Queries for PowerPivot

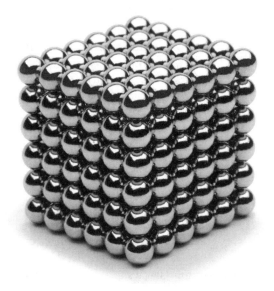

Y ou may have SSAS data mining structures and data mining models. You normally query these objects using Data Mining eXtensions (DMX), perhaps from SQL Server Management Studio (SSMS) or from SQL Server Reporting Services (SSRS). Although this release of PowerPivot supports the graphical design of SQL and MDX queries, it does not support the graphical design of DMX queries. You can, however, write your own DMX. You do so by connecting to an SSAS source and entering the DMX into the MDX Statement area of the Specify a MDX Query dialog, in the Table Import Wizard. Another way is to embed your DMX query within a SQL query and import the data returned from the outer SQL query. To do that, you connect to a SQL Server source and enter the SQL/DMX into the SQL Statement area of the Specify a SQL Query dialog of the Table Import Wizard. Alternatively, you can query *some* data mining data from Excel itself—for this you will need to download the data mining add-in for Excel (the data mining results are shown in an Excel worksheet when you use the Table Tools/Analyze ribbon, rather than the Data Mining ribbon), you can then import or link into the PowerPivot window from the Excel worksheet). Stand-alone DMX, or DMX embedded in SQL, works for DMX Cases, Content, Prediction, and other queries. This chapter includes sample code for a few Cases, Content, and Prediction queries.

▶ **Key concepts** DMX, linked servers, Cases queries, Content queries, Prediction queries

Why Write DMX Queries?

DMX, or Data Mining eXtensions, is a standard language for extracting data from data mining models. Specifically, it is the language used to query data mining structures and data mining models in an SSAS database. By using DMX, you are no longer confined to SSAS imports from cubes only—you can also import data from mining models. You can write your own stand-alone DMX queries during data import. One other way to get DMX imports working is to set up a SQL Server linked server to SSAS, and embed the DMX within a SQL query. This appendix shows both approaches.

If you are interested in learning a bit more about DMX (in particular, DMX for SQL Server Analysis Services), refer to my book, *Practical DMX Queries for Microsoft SQL Server Analysis Services 2008* (McGraw-Hill/Professional, 2010). Most of the examples here are taken from that book.

Where to Create and Test DMX Queries

DMX is a standard language for querying data mining models. The DMX discussed here is for SSAS. The DMX used by other vendors of data mining software may differ in minor ways.

You need to create and then test your DMX queries—first, as pure DMX, and, second, as DMX embedded inside SQL (specifically, T-SQL for SQL Server), if you opt to use a linked server. The best place to do both is within SSMS. From the SSMS Object Explorer, right-click on your SSAS database and choose New Query | DMX. Write and validate your DMX and copy it to the Clipboard. If you prefer to embed the DMX within SQL, then right-click on a SQL Server database (any one will do, unless you need to reference a SQL Server table or view from the DMX) and choose New Query. This will open the SQL query editor. Write a SQL wrapper and paste in your DMX. Test and validate the SQL containing the DMX, before copying to the Clipboard.

The examples here use both stand-alone DMX and a SQL Server SSAS linked server. If you want to experiment with the latter, you will need to set up an SSAS linked server to SQL Server. You can do this from the GUI or from a SQL query. From the GUI, expand your SQL Server in the SSMS Object Explorer. Expand Server Objects, right-click on Linked Servers, and choose New Linked Server. Make sure the Provider is set to Microsoft OL DB Provider for Analysis Services 10.0. From a SQL query, enter code similar to the following (your may need to change the `@datasrc` and `@catalog` properties to point to your SSAS server and database, respectively):

```
exec sp_addlinkedserver
@server='MySSAS',
@srvproduct='',
@provider='MSOLAP',
-- change server as necessary
@datasrc='localhost',
-- change database as necessary
@catalog='Adventure Works DW 2008'
```

The `@server` property can be anything reasonable—it is *not* the name of your SSAS server (that is the `@datasrc` property). Here, `@server` is MySSAS. This is the name by which you reference the linked server. There may be one step involved—you must allow SSAS to run in-process with SQL Server. To check or set this, follow these steps:

1. In the SSMS Object Explorer, expand your SQL Server, then Server Objects, followed by Linked Servers and Providers.
2. Right-click on the MSOLAP provider and choose Properties. This opens the Provider Options dialog shown in Figure C-1.
3. If necessary, turn on the Allow Inprocess check box, and click OK.

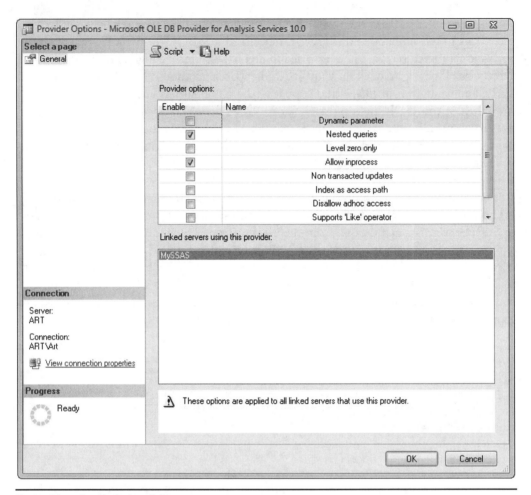

Figure C-1   *Provider Options dialog*

Where to Use DMX Queries in PowerPivot

For stand-alone DMX, you go through From Analysis Services or PowerPivot by clicking From Database in the Get External Data group of the PowerPivot Home ribbon. The steps are identical to those for writing MDX queries, which is documented in Appendix B. For DMX embedded within SQL, you begin by clicking From Database in the Get External Data group of the PowerPivot Home ribbon. In the drop-down menu, choose From SQL Server (neither From Access nor From Analysis Services nor PowerPivot is going to work). Connect to your SQL Server and any database (one example requires the AdventureWorksDW2008 or the AdventureWorksDW database, so you could connect appropriately if you are able to). The next dialog in the Table Import Wizard is the Choose How to Import the Data dialog. This is shown in Figure C-2.

In this dialog you have to select the Write a Query That Will Specify the Data to Import radio button. When you click Next, the Specify a SQL Query dialog appears. The dialog is shown in Figure C-3.

Paste your code (copied from SSMS) into the SQL Statement box and then click Validate, followed by Finish. Your data mining data is imported into a PowerPivot table.

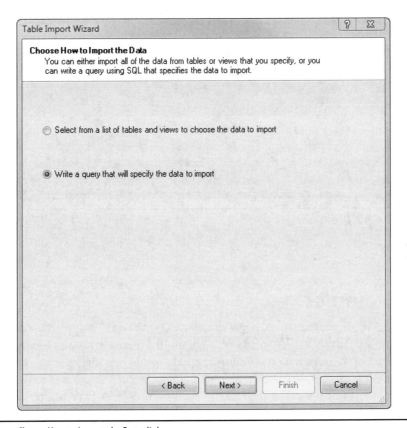

Figure C-2   *Choose How to Import the Data dialog*

Figure C-3   *Specify a SQL Query dialog*

DMX Examples

If you want to try these examples, you will need SQL Server Analysis Services 2008 or 2008 R2, and the Adventure Works DW 2008 multidimensional database (available from www.codeplex.com), which contains the data mining models used in the following queries. You should also be able to adapt many of the queries to work with SQL Server Analysis Services 2005 and the Adventure Works DW multidimensional database (also available from www.codeplex.com). You will also need SQL Server itself, if you opt for the linked server approach, in order to run the SQL that contains the DMX. One of the examples references a SQL Server view (vTargetMail)—for that example to work, whether as stand-alone or embedded DMX, you will need either the AdventureWorksDW2008 or the AdventureWorksDW sample SQL Server database).

All of the embedded examples use a linked server called MySSAS—this name was defined in the SQL to add a linked server, shown immediately above.

You may discover that not all of your DMX works during a PowerPivot import. There are a couple of provisos. One, if the DMX returns a nested table, this will fail if the DMX is embedded within SQL—you have to flatten nested tables using the DMX keyword Flattened. Two, for embedded DMX only, if your DMX contains single quotes, you must add another single quote to each single quote. Here is the generic SQL wrapper syntax for embedded DMX:

```
select * from openquery(MySSAS,'')
```

Here, the name of the linked server is MySSAS—this does not have to match your actual SSAS server name. You paste your DMX (presumably, tested as a stand-alone DMX query first) between the single quotes. For each example, the pure stand-alone DMX is shown first, followed by the DMX inside the SQL. For all of the examples (apart from the first one, which fails), there is a screenshot of the resulting data in a PowerPivot table.

NOTE

It is quite possible that your data may be different—the results of DMX queries can be affected by which data SSAS chose to train the mining models.

Cases Query: Nested Table Failure

Many DMX queries return nested tables. If the DMX is embedded within SQL, the outer SQL query will fail.

DMX: Stand-Alone

```
select * from mining structure [customer mining].cases
```

DMX: Embedded in SQL

```
select * from openquery(MySSAS,'select * from
mining structure [customer mining].cases')
```

The second query will fail within a PowerPivot import, as the DMX returns a nested table that the outer SQL doesn't like. There are no results for the second example, so it can't be used to import into a PowerPivot table—it will not validate during the Table Import Wizard.

Cases Query: Flattened Table Success

In the two examples here, the nested table is flattened.

DMX: Stand-Alone

```
select flattened * from mining structure [customer mining].cases
```

DMX: Embedded in SQL

```
select * from openquery(MySSAS,'select flattened * from
mining structure [customer mining].cases')
```

This is similar to the previous query—except that, this time, both examples work! Please note the introduction of the DMX keyword Flattened. This is a simple Cases query. The resulting PowerPivot table is shown in Figure C-4.

Cases Query on Specific Columns

Instead of returning all columns, you can ask for specific columns.

DMX: Stand-Alone

```
select flattened [customer counts] as Customer, (select [Subcategory],
  [internet sales amount] as Sales from [subcategories])
from mining structure [customer mining].cases
```

SubcategoriesInternet Sales Amount	SubcategoriesSubcategory	Customer Counts	Commute Distance
233.82	Tires and Tubes	Luke L. Lal	5-10 Miles
43.57	Tires and Tubes	Jasmine A. Taylor	5-10 Miles
48.56	Tires and Tubes	Jonathan M. Hende...	5-10 Miles
46.27	Tires and Tubes	Angela R. James	5-10 Miles
41.28	Tires and Tubes	Hannah E. Long	5-10 Miles
37.29	Tires and Tubes	Jose Wright	5-10 Miles
39.99	Tires and Tubes	Samuel Edwards	5-10 Miles
37.29	Tires and Tubes	Logan A. Diaz	5-10 Miles
39.99	Tires and Tubes	Seth Martin	5-10 Miles

Figure C-4   *PowerPivot table*

DMX: Embedded in SQL

```
select * from openquery(MySSAS,'select flattened [customer counts]
as Customer, (select [Subcategory], [internet sales amount] as Sales
from [subcategories]) from mining structure [customer mining].cases')
```

This is a Cases query returning specific columns. The resulting PowerPivot table is shown in Figure C-5.

Content Query with DMX Subquery

This example, like the last one, is DMX within DMX (a DMX subquery).

DMX: Stand-Alone

```
select flattened node_caption as [Cluster], node_description as
Demographics,(select [attribute_name], [attribute_value], [Support],
[Probability] * 100 as [Probability] from node_distribution)
from [TM Clustering].content where node_type = 5
```

DMX: Embedded in SQL

```
select * from openquery(MySSAS,'select flattened node_caption as [Cluster],
node_description as Demographics,(select [attribute_name],
[attribute_value], [Support], [Probability] * 100 as [Probability]
 from node_distribution) from [TM Clustering].content
where node_type = 5')
```

This is a Content query. The resulting PowerPivot table is shown in Figure C-6.

Customer	ExpressionSubcategory	ExpressionSales	Add Column
Jon V. Yang	Helmets	34.99	
Eugene L. H...	Helmets	34.99	
Ruben Torres	Helmets	34.99	
Rob Verhoff	Helmets	34.99	
Shannon C. ...	Helmets	34.99	
Lauren M. ...	Helmets	34.99	
Clarence D. ...	Helmets	34.99	
Jimmy L. M...	Helmets	34.99	
Jaime Nath	Helmets	34.99	
Jennifer C. ...	Helmets	34.99	

Figure C-5   *PowerPivot table*

Figure C-6 *PowerPivot table*

Content Query with Embedded Single Quotes

Single quotes within DMX queries require special treatment when the DMX is embedded within SQL.

DMX: Stand-Alone

```
select flattened node_description as Demographics, (select [attribute_name],
[attribute_value], [Support], [Probability] * 100 as [Probability]
from node_distribution where [attribute_value] = '1')
from [TM Decision Tree].content
where node_type = 3 or node_type = 4
```

DMX: Embedded in SQL

```
select * from openquery(MySSAS,'select flattened node_description
as Demographics, (select [attribute_name], [attribute_value], [Support],
[Probability] * 100 as [Probability] from node_distribution
where [attribute_value] = ''1'') from [TM Decision Tree].content
where node_type = 3 or node_type = 4')
```

This is another Content query—note that embedded single quotes have been doubled-up with an extra single quote in the second example. The resulting PowerPivot table is shown in Figure C-7.

Demographics	Expressionattribute_name	Expressionattribute_value
Number Cars Owned = 0	Bike Buyer	1
Number Cars Owned = 3	Bike Buyer	1
Number Cars Owned = 1	Bike Buyer	1
Number Cars Owned = 4	Bike Buyer	1
Number Cars Owned = 2	Bike Buyer	1
Number Cars Owned = 2 and Yea...	Bike Buyer	1
Number Cars Owned = 2 and Yea...	Bike Buyer	1
Number Cars Owned = 2 and Yea...	Bike Buyer	1
Number Cars Owned = 2 and Yea...	Bike Buyer	1

Figure C-7   *PowerPivot table*

Prediction Query with Embedded Single Quotes

This one needs a SQL Server view, vTargetMail, which is part of the
AdventureWorksDW2008 or the AdventureWorksDW database.

DMX: Stand-Alone

```
select TM.* , Predict([Bike Buyer]) as [Bike Buyer],
vba!format(PredictProbability([Bike Buyer]),'Percent') as [Probability]
from [TM Decision Tree] prediction join openquery ([Adventure Works DW],
'select Age, Gender, Region, NumberCarsOwned from vTargetMail') as TM
on [TM Decision Tree].[Age] = TM.[Age] and [TM Decision Tree].[Gender] =
TM.[Gender] and [TM Decision Tree].[Region] = TM.[Region]
and [TM Decision Tree].[Number Cars Owned] = TM.[NumberCarsOwned]
```

DMX: Embedded in SQL

```
select * from openquery(MySSAS,'select TM.* , Predict([Bike Buyer]) as
[Bike Buyer], vba!format(PredictProbability([Bike Buyer]),''Percent'') as
[Probability] from [TM Decision Tree] prediction join
openquery([Adventure Works DW],''select Age, Gender, Region,
NumberCarsOwned from vTargetMail'') as TM
on [TM Decision Tree].[Age] = TM.[Age] and [TM Decision Tree].[Gender] =
TM.[Gender] and [TM Decision Tree].[Region] = TM.[Region]
and [TM Decision Tree].[Number Cars Owned] = TM.[NumberCarsOwned]')
```

Age	Gender	Region	NumberCarsOwned	Bike Buyer	Probability
53	M	North America	2	0	59.90%
53	M	North America	2	0	59.90%
53	M	North America	2	0	59.90%
53	M	North America	2	0	59.90%
53	M	North America	2	0	59.90%
53	M	North America	2	0	59.90%
53	M	North America	2	0	59.90%
53	M	North America	2	0	59.90%
53	M	North America	2	0	59.90%

Figure C-8   *PowerPivot table*

This is a Prediction query from a decision tree model. The single quotes have been doubled up in the second example. The reference Adventure Works DW is to a SQL Server data source within the SSAS database. The code is getting quite complex, especially in the second example. The SQL has a reference to an SSAS linked server, which, in turn, has a reference to a SQL Server database! The resulting PowerPivot table is shown in Figure C-8.

Prediction Forecast Query with Embedded Single Quotes

These two examples show how to forecast quantity sold in the future.

DMX: Stand-Alone

```
select flattened [Model Region], (select $Time as [Year Month], Quantity
from PredictTimeSeries([Quantity],3)) as [Future] from [Forecasting]
where [Model Region] = 'T1000 North America'
or [Model Region] = 'T1000 Europe'
```

DMX: Embedded in SQL

```
select * from openquery(MySSAS,'select flattened [Model Region],
(select $Time as [Year Month], Quantity
from PredictTimeSeries([Quantity],3))
as [Future] from [Forecasting]
where [Model Region] = ''T1000 North America''
or [Model Region] = ''T1000 Europe''')
```

Model Region ▼	FutureYear Month ▼	FutureQuantity ▼	Add Column
T1000 Europe	200407	42	
T1000 Europe	200408	41	
T1000 Europe	200409	43	
T1000 North Am...	200407	82	
T1000 North Am...	200408	78	
T1000 North Am...	200409	78	

Figure C-9   *PowerPivot table*

This is a Prediction query on a time series model. Please note the doubling of single quotes in the embedded example. The resulting PowerPivot table is shown in Figure C-9.

SQL Used to Format and Manipulate the DMX Result Set

The second example demonstrates the benefit of embedding DMX within SQL.

DMX: Stand-Alone

```
select flattened node_description , (select [attribute_value],
[probability] * 100,[support] from node_distribution)
from [TM Decision Tree].content
```

DMX: Embedded in SQL

```
select node_description as Demographics,
left([expression.expression],5) +
'%' as Probability,[expression.support] as Support from
openquery(MySSAS,'select flattened node_description ,
(select [attribute_value],[probability] * 100,[support]
from node_distribution) from [TM Decision Tree].content') where
[expression.support] > 100 and [expression.attribute_value]=
CONVERT(nvarchar(10),1) order by [expression.expression] desc
```

The second example includes rather more in the SQL wrapper. The SQL has been used to further manipulate the DMX result set. The resulting PowerPivot table is shown in Figure C-10.

Demographics	Probability	Support	Add Column
Number Cars Owned = 0 and Region = 'Europe' and Ye...	98.21%	330	
Number Cars Owned = 0 and Region = 'Pacific' and Tot...	94.37%	340	
Number Cars Owned = 0 and Region = 'Europe' and Ye...	94.10%	463	
Number Cars Owned = 2 and Yearly Income >= 58000 a...	93.28%	292	
Number Cars Owned = 3 and Yearly Income >= 122000 ...	92.48%	148	
Number Cars Owned = 0 and Region = 'Europe' and Ye...	92.01%	127	
Number Cars Owned = 0 and Region = 'Pacific'	91.68%	356	
Number Cars Owned = 0 and Region = 'North America...	89.75%	298	
Number Cars Owned = 0 and Region = 'Europe' and Ye...	85.24%	133	
Number Cars Owned = 0 and Region = 'North America...	84.81%	324	

Figure C-10   *PowerPivot table*

Hopefully, this short appendix is enough to get you started in importing data mining data into PowerPivot. Two methods have been demonstrated: first, DMX queries as stand-alone queries that you write as MDX statements, and second, DMX queries as embedded queries that you write as SQL statements. There is a third alternative. This involves using the data mining add-in in Excel (Table Tools/Analyze ribbon) and importing, or linking, the resulting Excel worksheet data into PowerPivot.

Index